Potter's Raid

The Union Cavalry's Boldest Expedition in Eastern North Carolina

by
David A. Norris

Copyright © 2007 by David A. Norris

All rights reserved. No part of this book may be reproduced in any form or by any electronic or mechanical means, including information storage and retrieval systems, without written permission from the publisher, except by a reviewer who may quote brief passages in a review.

First Edition 2008
Published in the United States of America by Dram Tree Books.

Publisher's Cataloging-in-Publication Data
(Provided by DRT Press)

Norris, David A.
   Potter's raid / David A. Norris.
   p. cm.
   Includes bibliographical references and index.
   ISBN 978-0-9814603-2-1
1. Potter's Raid, N.C., 1863. 2. North Carolina —History —Civil War, 1861-1865. 3. United States —History —Civil War, 1861-1865. 4. United States. Army. Cavalry —History —Civil War, 1861-1865. 5. New Bern (N.C.)—History. 6. Greenville (N.C.)—History. 7. Tarboro (N.C.)—History. 8. Rocky Mount (N.C.)—History. 9. Kinston (N.C.)—History. I. Title.

E477.7 N67 2008
973.7/378 20—dc22

Volume discounts available.
Call or e-mail for terms.

10 9 8 7 6 5 4 3 2 1

Dram Tree Books
P.O. Box 7183
Wilmington, N.C. 28406
(910) 538-4076
www.dramtreebooks.com
Potential authors: visit our website or email us for submission guidelines

For Carol

Acknowledgements

Most of all, I owe this book to the people who wrote down their invaluable eyewitness accounts of Potter's Raid. Some of these contemporary writings were, of course, somewhat less than strictly impartial. I tried to balance accounts and opinions from both sides in such a way as to come as close as I can to a truthful picture of Potter's Raid.

This book would also not have been possible without the hard work and cooperation of libraries that have saved manuscripts, photographs, and other historical materials, and made them available to researchers. First among them is the Joyner Library at East Carolina University in Greenville. Much of this book was drawn from their extensive materials, particularly from the North Carolina Collection. Maury York, who was in charge of the North Carolina Collection at that time, was ever-helpful in providing me with source material.

Other major institutions that I could not have done without include the National Archives in Washington, D.C.; the North Carolina State Archives in Raleigh; the Southern Historical Collection at the University of North Carolina at Chapel Hill; and the United States Army Military History Institute at Carlisle Barracks, Pennsylvania.

Just as they say "all politics is local", "they" might say that "all history is local". I've been lucky to have help and encouragement from several historians with great knowledge and affection for eastern North Carolina. Mike Edge has contributed many useful tips about Pitt, Greene, and Edgecombe County history and local stories about Potter's Raid, and he kindly provided several of his photographs. Monika S. Fleming read portions of the manuscript, and contributed useful suggestions and information on Tarboro and Edgecombe County.

For advice and useful historical information I also thank Watson Brown, Jo Webb, Mickey Harris, and Timothy Copeland. Amos L. "Bucky" Moore, Jr. contributed some information and rare photographs related to the skirmish at Otter Creek. Pam Edmondson and the Edgecombe County Memorial Library found some fine old photographs of Tarboro. Chris Fonvielle has been helpful and encouraging to me in the writing of this book, as well as several of my other projects.

Terry Prior and the Oswego County Historical Society in Oswego, New York, kindly granted permission to quote from letters in their collection, written by William Davies and Gleason Wellington of the 12th New York Cavalry. I also thank the Colorado Historical Society for permission to quote from their 1901 manuscript, *A True Narrative of the Incidents Which Happened in the Life of W. H. Graves.*

I appreciate the patience of my friends Joe and Peg Argent, and Paula Harrell, who endured hearing more than they would ever want to know about Potter's Raid over the years. The same goes for my parents, Barbara A. and the late Charles A. Norris, and my in-laws, James and the late Grace Busam.

Lastly, I dedicate this book to my wife, Carol.

David A. Norris
Wilmington, N.C.
July 2008

Contents

Introduction...i
Chapter 1.....1
Chapter 2.....13
Chapter 3.....23
Chapter 4.....39
Chapter 5.....47
Chapter 6.....51
Chapter 7.....57
Chapter 8.....69
Chapter 9.....87
Chapter 10.....103
Chapter 11.....115
Chapter 12.....129
Chapter 13.....139
Chapter 14.....147
Chapter 15.....159
Chapter 16.....165
Chapter 17.....175
Chapter 18.....183
Chapter 19.....187

Appendices

- Units Involved in Potter's Raid.....203
- Casualties and Prisoners from Potter's Raid.....204
- Casualties on the Kenansville-Warsaw Raid.....222
- Additional Regional Actions...225

Notes.....232
Bibliography...273
Index...281

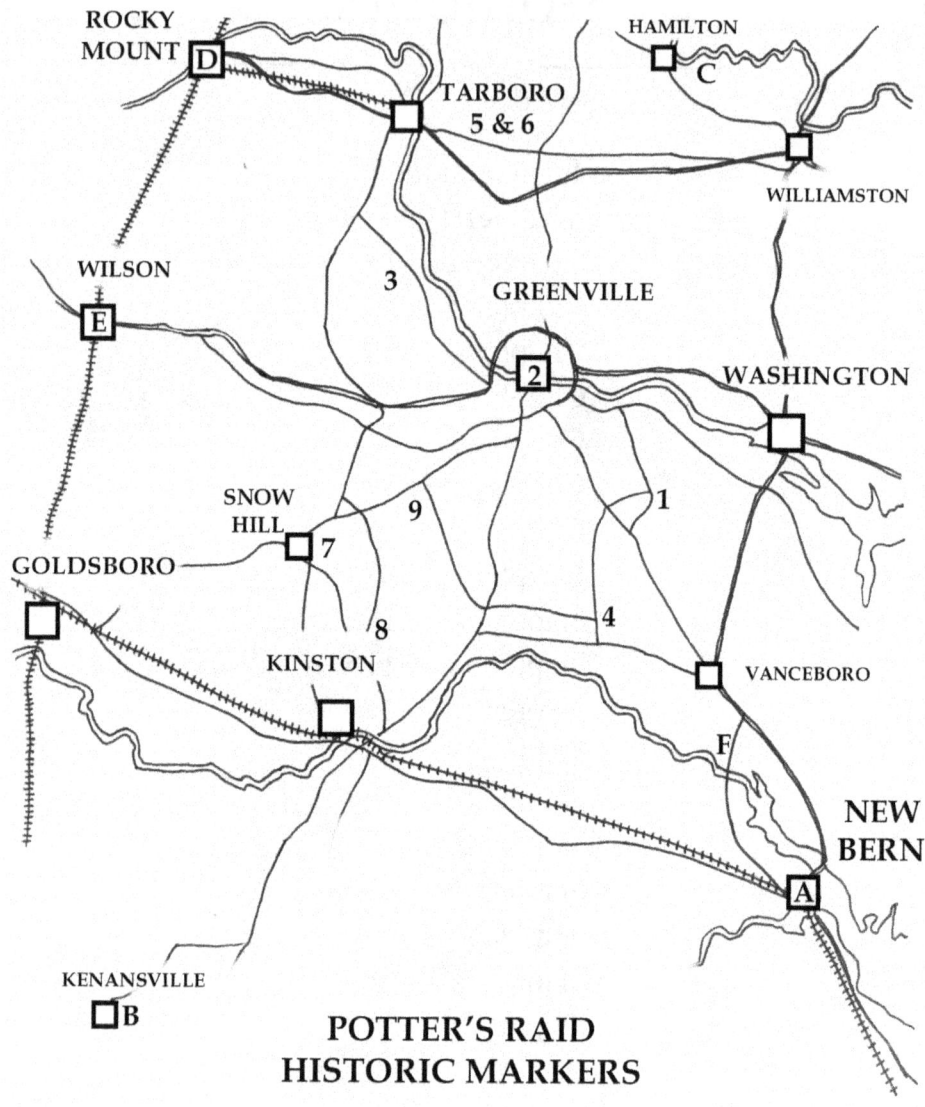

**POTTER'S RAID
HISTORIC MARKERS**

(Map by the author)

Pitt County
1. Black Jack: Parking lot of the Black Jack Free Will Baptist Church Activity Building off Black Jack-Simpson Road, 1/2 mile south of its intersection with Mills Road
2. Greenville: Town Common Park off First Street, at the Boat Ramp Access entrance
3. Falkland (Otter Creek Bridge Skirmish): Town Hall building, Route 43
4. St. John's Episcopal Church (Burney Place): 5 miles east of Route 11, at the end of Hanarahan Road

Edgecombe County

5. Occupation of Tarboro: Town Common, intersection of Main and Wilson streets
6. Occupation of Tarboro (Daniel's Schoolhouse Engagement): 130 Bridgers St., Tarboro

Greene County

7. Grimsley Church: Intersection of Routes 903 and 13
8. Hookerton: Center of town on Main Street, Route 123
9. Scuffleton Bridge: Church parking lot on Route 903, at the border of Greene and Pitt counties

North Carolina Highway Historical Markers Related to Sites Mentioned in this Book

A. **Fort Totten**, Trent Boulevard at Second Street, New Bern.
B. **Confederate Arms Factory**, NC 11/24/50/905 (South Main Street, Kenansville); there is also a Civil War Trails marker here.
C. **Fort Branch**, NC 125, northeast of Williamston.
D. **Rocky Mount Mills**, NC 43/48 near Tar River Bridge.
E. **Military Hospital**, Herring Avenue at Gold Street, Wilson
F. **Streets Ferry**, NC 43 at Neuse River Bridge.

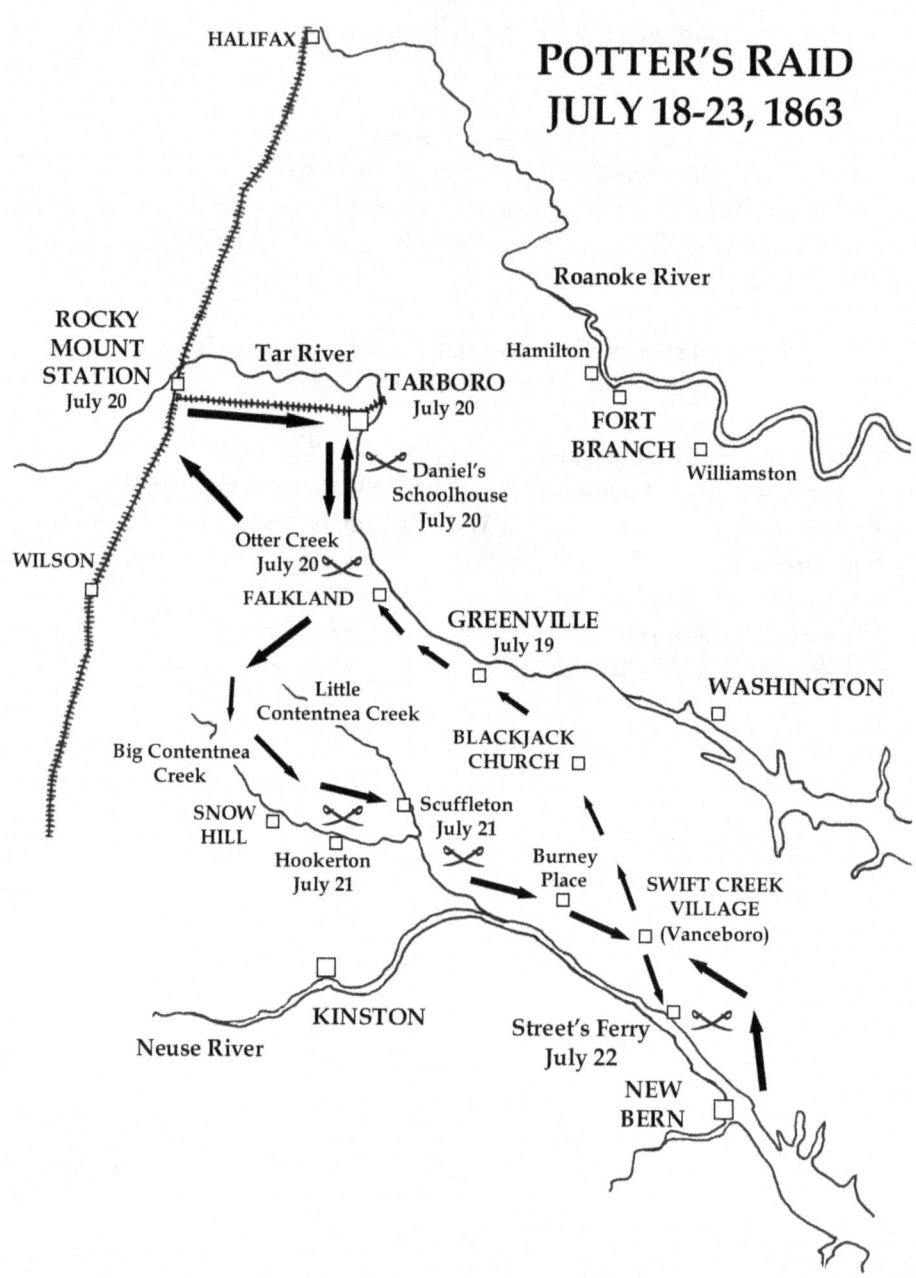

(Map by the author)

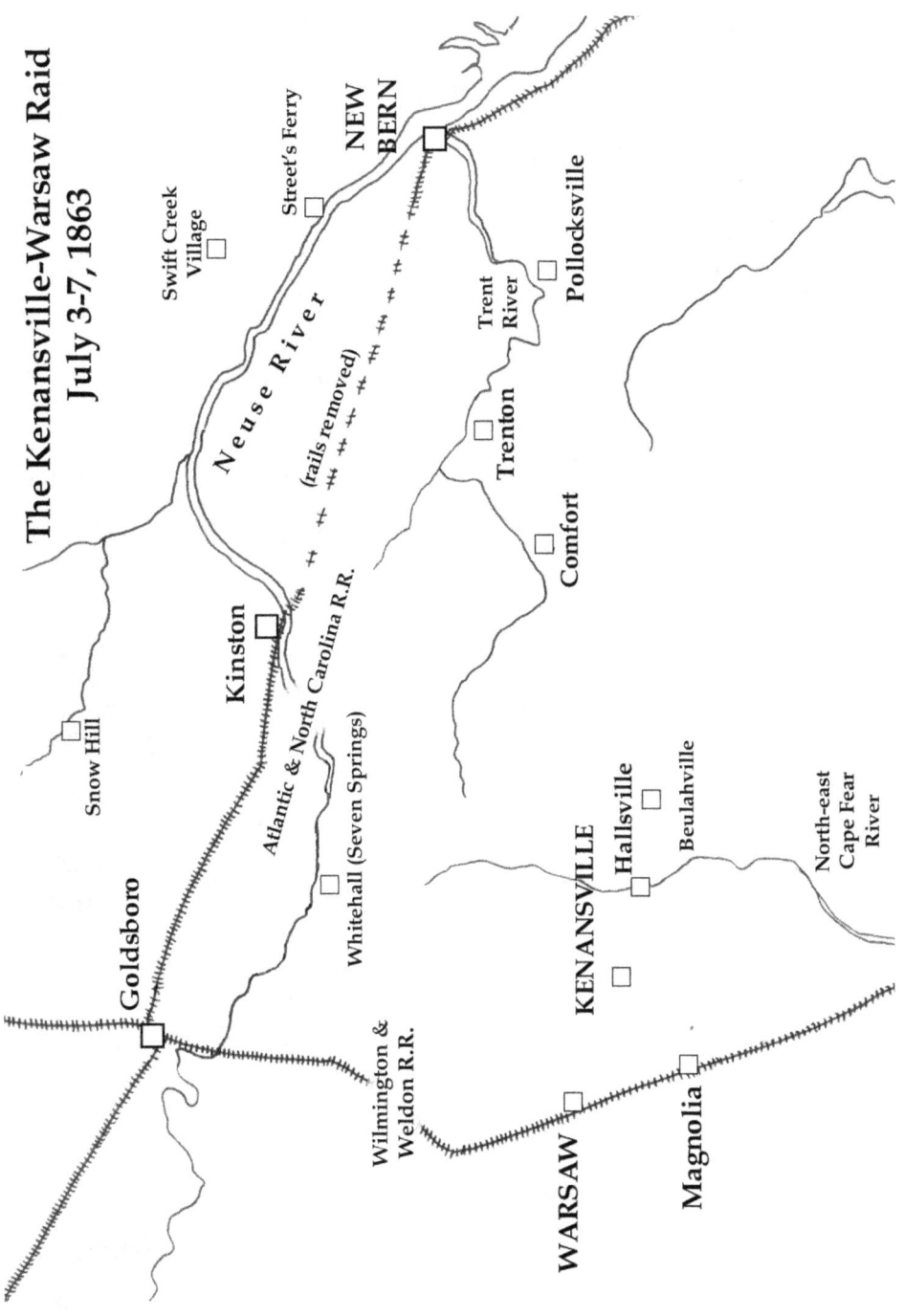

(Map by the author)

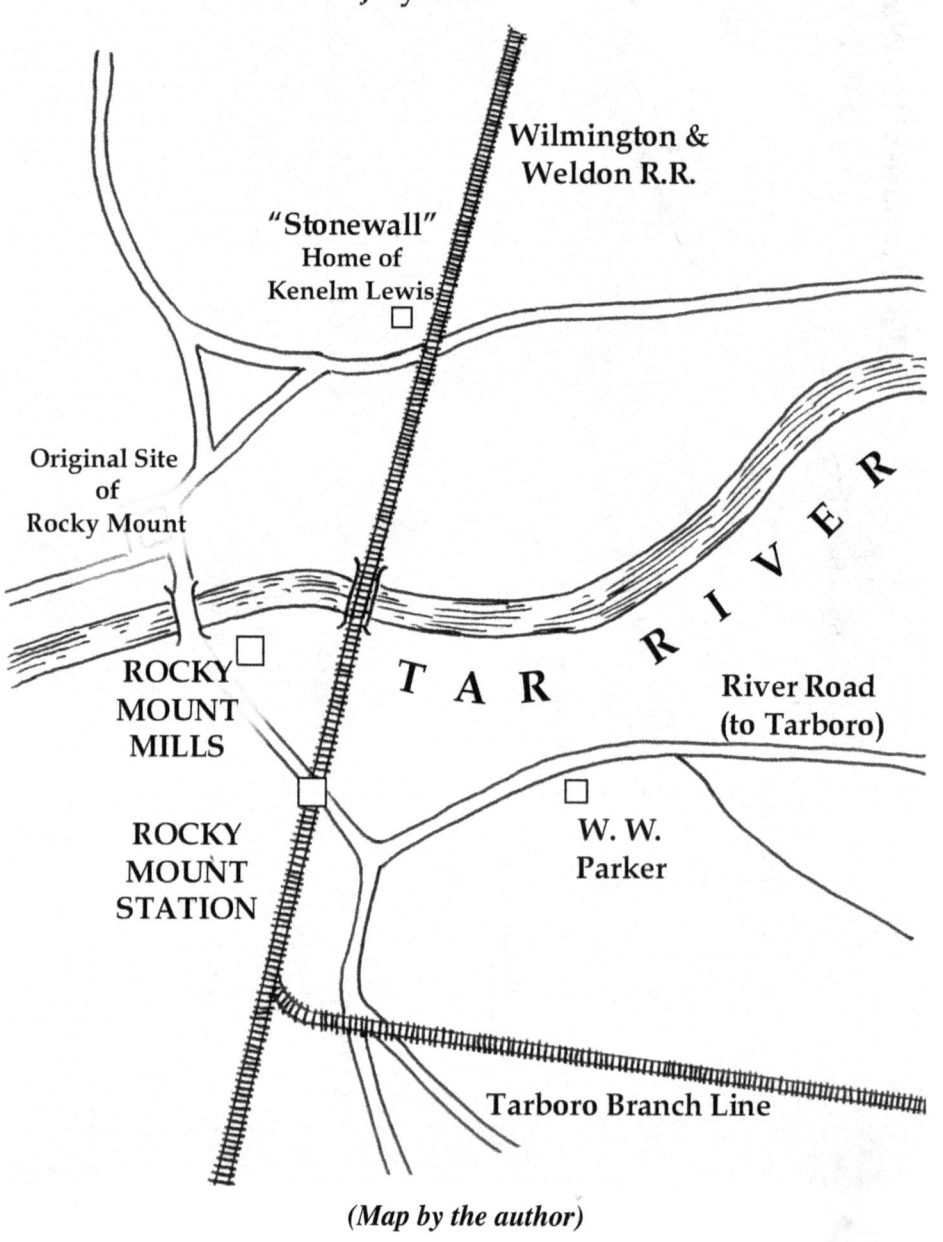

(Map by the author)

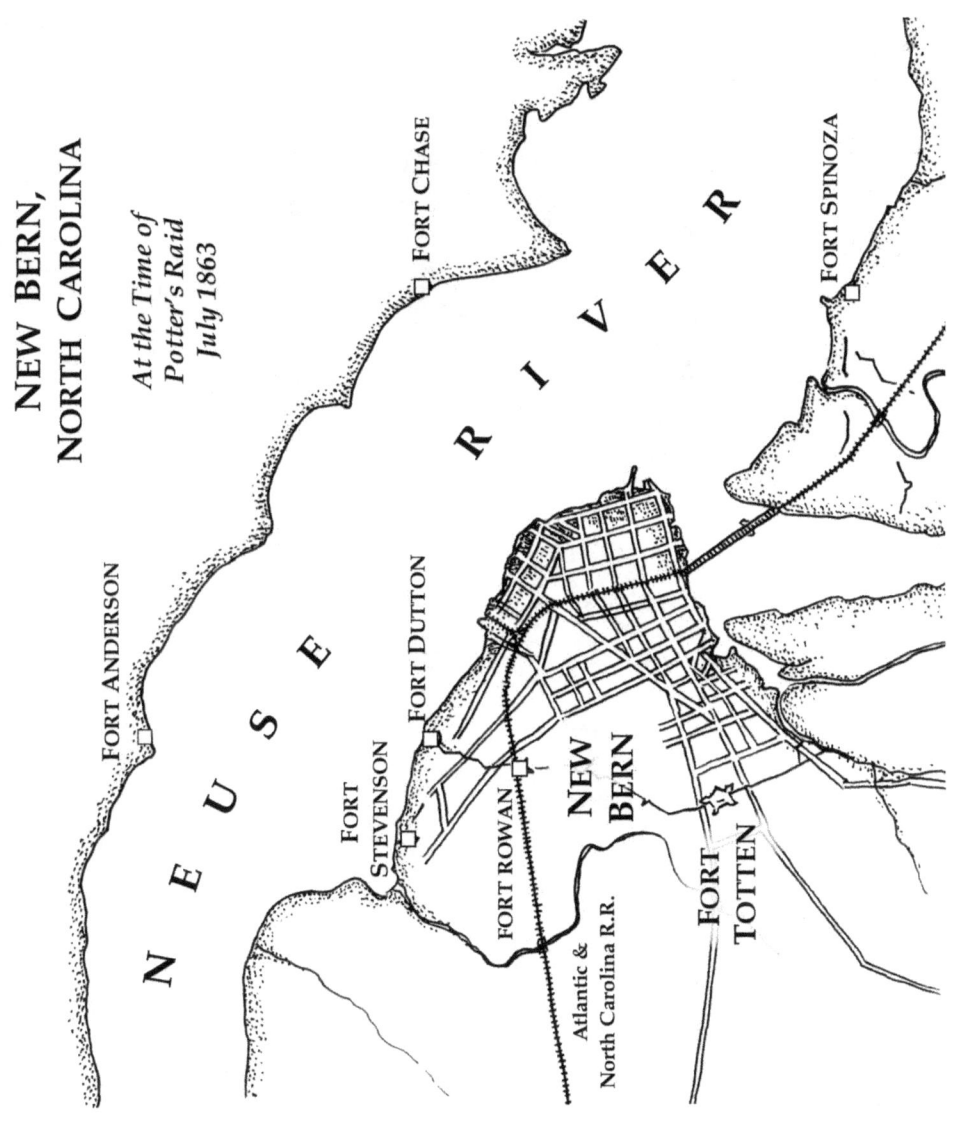

(Map by the author)

Introduction

My fascination with the Civil War goes back to when I was in the second grade. One of my pals at school had a collection of minie balls and other Civil War artifacts that he'd found near his hometown of Richmond, Virginia. Most impressive of all, though, was his Civil War soldier play set. Hundreds of blue and gray plastic soldiers, horses, and cannons were scattered across a landscape of plastic fences, trees, and buildings. The centerpiece was a replica of "Burnside's Bridge", from the Battle of Antietam. The bridge had a clockwork spring that could be wound up with a key to "explode" the bridge.

I remained interested in the Civil War. When I moved to Greenville, North Carolina to attend East Carolina University, I began to wonder what had happened there during the war. Several people who I asked about the war simply said, "nothing!" The slightest bit of research showed that this was wrong, and that the region was intertwined with quite a bit of Civil War history. For starters, the Union Navy raided Greenville on November 9, 1862, and there was a small cavalry raid there on February 18, 1865.

But, the biggest action of the Civil War in the Tar River Valley was Potter's Raid. Over 800 men led by Brig. Gen. Edward E. Potter struck Greenville on July 19, 1863, before making simultaneous strikes on Rocky Mount and Tarboro on July 20. Confederate troops chasing Potter fought sharp clashes at Daniel's Schoolhouse near Tarboro; at Otter Creek Bridge near Falkland in Pitt County; near Hookerton, at Scuffleton, and other places in

Greene County; and at Street's Ferry, on the Neuse River in Craven County. On July 27, 1863, Potter's Raid was front page news in the *New York Times*.

In a way, Potter's Raid could be considered the central event of a mini-campaign aimed at cutting the Wilmington & Weldon Railroad. In mid-1863, that line was one of the most important railroads in the South, linking General Robert E. Lee's Army of Northern Virginia with food supplies drawn from North Carolina's farmlands, the blockade-running port of Wilmington and the rest of the eastern seaboard of the Confederacy. Union Maj. Gen. John Gray Foster sent a small raid against the railroad depot of Warsaw in Duplin County from July 3-7. He followed with Potter's Raid from July 18-23, which caused major damage to the railroad at Rocky Mount. His third and potentially most dangerous raid, from July 25 to August 3, 1863, failed before reaching the Wilmington & Weldon.

If Potter's Raid had happened in a "slow news" month, or in a more famous theatre of the war, it would be better known today. But, newspapers in July 1863 were packed with news of the Battle of Gettysburg, the fall of Vicksburg, the New York City Draft Riots, and the attack on Fort Wagner near Charleston. Most of the major Union newspapers had pulled their correspondents out of North Carolina by that time. Even so, news of Potter's Raid was carried in newspapers throughout the Confederacy and the North, and it was eventually picked up by newspapers in London, England and Melbourne, Australia.

A close look at Potter's Raid enriches our understanding of the Civil War. It details the lives of soldiers and civilians who experienced the war in the regions around New Bern and Greenville, Tarboro, and Rocky Mount. Further, it illuminates what the Civil War was like for millions of Americans whose wartime experiences were in "quiet" regions that were for the most part overlooked by history.

An early version of this book appeared as an article called "'The Yankees Have Been Here!': The Story of Brig. Gen. Edward E. Potter's Raid on Greenville, Tarboro and Rocky Mount, July 19-23, 1863", in the *North Carolina Historical Review* LXXIII (January 1996).

David A. Norris
Wilmington, N.C.
June 2008

Chapter 1

"I Am In a Peck of Trouble"
The Anxious Days Before the Raid
July 1863

Henry T. Clark was almost plucked from retirement and hurled into a Union prison on July 20, 1863. Clark, an Edgecombe County planter, went into politics and rose to the post of speaker of the North Carolina senate. Because North Carolina then did not have a lieutenant governor, Clark stepped into the governorship when Gov. John Ellis died in 1861. Clark found himself caught between attacking Union forces in eastern North Carolina, angry citizens clamoring for better military protection, and the Confederate administration in Richmond, which drained the state of manpower and money without providing for its defense. Clark was not nominated to run for another term in 1862. Returning to his home just outside Tarboro, Clark retired to a quieter life away from the political turmoil of Raleigh.

Clark always took a horseback ride every day. It was about nine o'clock on that warm summer morning. His horse, saddled and ready, stood by his front porch. Then, glancing to his right up the Wilson Road, he saw a thundering pack of Yankee cavalrymen riding toward him. Clark climbed into the saddle, spurred his horse, and tore away from his house. If the Yankees wanted this ex-governor, they'd have to catch him first.

Former Gov. Henry T. Clark
N.C. State Archives

Rumors Along the Tar River

Two days before the unwelcome visitors galloped onto the Clark plantation, Brig. Gen. Edward E. Potter led a large Federal cavalry force from New Bern for a raid into Confederate territory. The appearance of the Yankees in Tarboro was not really a surprise, but merely a confirmation of the rumors that had tormented the area during the summer of 1863. The *Daily Dispatch* in Richmond printed two wildly contradictory rumors on July 16. One report claimed that the enemy was "organizing a force of mounted infantry, 3,000 strong ... to advance simultaneously on both sides of the Neuse River." Another report, though, which was from "a most reliable gentleman", had it that the Yankees "are moving most of their valuables from Newbern to Morehead City, as if they intend to evacuate ... very soon ..." When two such reports were in the same newspaper, it was hard to know what to expect next.[1]

George Howard, Jr. was a judge of the Superior Court and a prominent citizen of Tarboro. A few days before Clark's desperate ride, he wrote, "I am as busy as a bee preparing for the coming of the Yankees. I believe they will certainly be here this Fall, probably this summer ... And I am attempting to so arrange matters that the family can all leave in case of an emergency. Mother is very nervous about affairs and Alice is terribly frightened — all her boasted courage has oozed out of her fingers' ends ..." The failure of Maj. Gen. John Gray Foster's "Mud March", a failed Union expedition against Tarboro in November 1862, brought a brief period of safety to the town. The feeling of relief was entirely gone by the next summer.[2]

George Howard, Jr.

Union gunboats and troops appeared on the Roanoke River early in July. With these Union forces within one or two day's march of Tarboro, Judge Howard was "up all night on the look-out for Yankee raiders." Most of North Carolina's Confederate troops were serving in Virginia or South Carolina. Tarboro was defended only by the local militia, which was made up mostly of men whose age, poor health (or government jobs, such as Howard's position as a judge) kept them out of the regular army.[3]

A heavy succession of stormy days pounded and soaked Tarboro and the surrounding area in July 1863. "... the people are very despondent. It has rained — rained — rained until the freshets have swept the low grounds & the abundance of water ruined or nearly so the upland crops," as Judge Howard explained in one of several letters he wrote to his wife as he attended to their property in Tarboro.[4]

In the summer of 1863, most space on the South's railroads was tied up with military traffic. Mail and newspapers arrived sporadically in Tarboro, which had no telegraph. Most of the news that reached town was bad, and with the depressing weather, it added a heavy burden to Confederate morale. Union forces hammered at the important Southern strongholds of Vicksburg and Charleston. Rumors drifted down from the north, about General Lee's army fighting a great battle on Northern soil. The first reports of the Battle of Gettysburg that reached Tarboro were "glorious news". The Union Army had been shattered at Gettysburg, according to the rumors, with thousands of prisoners taken. Howard wrote on July 9, " ... we were elevated to a real glorificatious state. A band of music discoursed most eloquently of joy & hope and 'all went merry as a marriage bell'".[5]

The feeling of joy and hope did not last long. Howard wrote on July 9 that "... last night the news came a little muddy and we are nothing like so much elated." When accurate news finally arrived, it was of disasters falling like pounding rain. Vicksburg, the last major Confederate town on the Mississippi, was lost on July 4 and left the Confederacy cut in two. The dreams of victory in Pennsylvania were dashed when Lee's army returned to Virginia after withdrawing from Gettysburg.[6]

On July 8, the 1st North Carolina Artillery was rushed to Tarboro by train from Goldsboro, in case the Union forces moved south of the Roanoke River. After an anxious wait, news arrived that the Yankee boats had steamed back downriver. The regiment boarded a train to return to Goldsboro.[7]

The Tarboro Train Wreck

When the train was halfway to Rocky Mount, an axle on the tender snapped. Soldiers were thrown from their perches as their flatcars flew off the tracks. James Knight, "one of the oldest and most experienced engineers of the Wilmington & Weldon Railroad", averted an even worse disaster by "promptly reversing his engine". As it was, a veteran remembered, "more than half the flatcars were dashed to pieces; men, guns, ambulances and ammunition were piled in heaps on both sides of the track ... the sight and sounds were piteous – wounded men lay everywhere, bleeding and moaning."[8]

Some time later, the mail train from Tarboro halted behind the shattered cars. The officers were still directing the care of the injured men. More concerned with the railroad schedule than patriotism, the conductor of the mail train refused to take the injured soldiers back to the army hospital at Tarboro. The conductor yielded only when the soldiers threatened to seize his train. Engineer James Knight also pointed out to the conductor that the tracks would be blocked for several hours by the wreckage.[9]

Lt.Col. Stephen D. Pool obtained a handcar and pressed on to Rocky Mount to send a telegram regarding the accident. The wounded men, with Lt. James H. Pool in charge, were taken back to Tarboro in the mail train. Judge Howard heard that "13 were injured – three badly. A capt. is now seriously ill from internal injury & one of the soldiers will have his leg amputated today..." A member of the unit wrote many years later that "The number wounded exceeded twenty, and two were disabled for life."[10]

Even after the Yankee steamers withdrew from the Roanoke, Howard prepared for the worst. His family's real property, which included a hotel in Tarboro, could not be kept out of danger. But, Howard wanted to put his cotton and as much of his moveable property as possible out of the path of a Union raiding party. On July 15, he worried, "I am in a peck of trouble about affairs down here. I think a raid is threatening either through or near here." Howard purchased a wagon to carry his family's provisions to William Norfleet's plantation, which was 12 miles outside of town. Howard also wanted to buy some larger and stronger mules than ones he owned, but he couldn't find any likely mules for sale.[11]

Howard's slaves apparently gave him considerable concern. To keep them out of range of the Union Army, the judge decided to send slaves "up the country and hire them out." (Hiring slaves to work inland, further away from the Union lines, was a common practice.) Jane, another of the Howards' slaves, posed more of a problem. "Tired of being troubled with her", he was going to sell Jane, if he could find someone who would take her and both of her children together. Even with these preparations, Howard was positive that he would lose at least half a dozen slaves if the Yankees came to Tarboro.[12]

The Confederate Military Outlook In Eastern North Carolina

Union forces captured Plymouth, Washington, and New Bern in the spring of 1862, blocking the mouths of the Roanoke, Tar, and Neuse Rivers. The Federals periodically launched raids from these strong points deep into the interior of the coastal plain. Zebulon Vance, the governor of North Carolina, warned Secretary of War James Seddon in 1863 that "the Roanoke, the Tar, and the Neuse, embracing the richest corn growing regions of the state, upon which the army of General Lee has been subsisting for months, have no heavy artillery for their defense."[13]

Maj. Gen. D. H. Hill was placed in charge of the Confederate troops in North Carolina on February 7, 1863. On April 1, his command was designated the Department of North Carolina. Hill warned Richmond that because of the fear of Union raids, "the planters on the Neuse, Tar, and Roanoke" were sending their slaves inland out of reach of potential Yankee raids. They "are now at a loss to know what to do and will not pitch another crop until the presence of a competent force in North Carolina will guarantee protection ..." Hill also believed that the four Confederate cavalry regiments stationed in the state were all together "not worth four companies of inferior infantry." He would have preferred to get rid of them entirely, if he "did not need a large number of couriers" in his vast district.[14]

MajGen. Daniel Harvey Hill, CSA
Library of Congress

The area around Wilmington, designated the District of the Cape Fear, was commanded by Maj. Gen. William Henry Chase Whiting. Whiting was obsessed with the security of Wilmington, which was to become the South's most important port after the Union Navy tightened its blockade of Charleston and the Confederacy's other ports. The general strongly fortified the mouth of the Cape Fear. Its crowning strong point was Fort Fisher, a massive earthwork fortification bristling with a formidable array of heavy artillery that kept the Union navy far out to sea.[15]

Hill led Confederate operations against New Bern and Washington. First, he moved on New Bern. An attack by Junius Daniel's brigade captured Union works at Deep Gully outside the town on March 13. But, other moves to tighten the hold on New Bern failed, and Hill turned to Washington.

MajGen. W.H.C. Whiting, CSA
Library of Congress

From March 30 to April 15, Hill laid siege to Washington. However, Generals Lee and Longstreet had both advised Hill that an all-out attack would cost more casualties than they thought Washington was worth. The attack was seen by the high command as a diversion to allow the Confederates to gather food for the army from eastern counties, without the interference of the Yankees. Hill broke off operations when Union gunboats reinforced the garrison, and most of his troops were wanted for fighting in Virginia. Although Hill's management of the campaign failed to dislodge the Union from eastern North Carolina, it did allow substantial amounts of supplies to be gathered for the army.[16]

On July 14, Hill was transferred to duty in Mississippi, and Whiting was placed in command of the Department of North Carolina. Whiting's attention still centered on the defense of Wilmington, and he divided his new command into two sections. Whiting remained in Wilmington and kept the District of the Cape Fear directly under his eye. The rest of the state was designated the District of North Carolina, and was assigned to the command of Brig. Gen. James G. Martin.[17]

Martin was born in Elizabeth City, North Carolina, in 1819. He graduated from the U.S. Military Academy at West Point in 1840, and entered the United States Army as a second lieutenant in the artillery. During the War with Mexico, he lost his right arm to a blast of grapeshot at the Battle of Churubusco on August 20, 1847. Thereafter, his nickname in the antebellum U.S. army was "Old One Wing". He finished the war with a brevet rank of major, and remained in the army until he resigned after the outbreak of the Civil War in 1861. Soon after his resignation, Martin was appointed Adjutant General of North Carolina by Gov. John Ellis. Martin performed a superb job in directing the recruitment, training, and organization of the state's regiments, which were widely regarded as the best equipped in the Confederacy.[18]

Brig. Gen. James G. Martin, CSA
N.C. State Archives

As commander of the District of North Carolina, among Martin's chief responsibilities was the protection of the Wilmington & Weldon Railroad. The food from North Carolina's farms, and the weapons, ammunition, and medicines brought through the blockade from Europe into Wilmington, all had to pass over that one railroad to get to Virginia. Cutting that railroad was a major objective of the Union army in North Carolina. It was an attack on that railroad that brought Potter's cavalrymen to ex-governor Clark's doorstep in Tarboro.[19]

Martin made his headquarters at Kinston. A Neuse River port town that was also on the Atlantic & North Carolina Railroad, Kinston was a good place to keep watch on the Yankees in New Bern, who were about 35 miles away. In July 1863, Martin's "effective total present" (men actually on duty, not counting the sick, deserters, or soldiers under arrest or on special assignments) was 4,288 men and 26 pieces of artillery. It was a small force to cover the District of North Carolina, a domain that stretched from the Albemarle Sound to the Appalachian Mountains, and covered an area not much smaller than England. [20]

In Martin's district, the threat of Union spies worried Rebel soldiers and civilians alike. Lt. John G. Smith of the 62nd Georgia Cavalry wrote that there were a surprising "number of Judases we had to contend with ... hence it was necessary for us to watch them as well as the Yankees ... The *Petersburg Express,* writing about eastern North Carolina raids later that summer, complained about the local guides who showed Union expeditions short cuts and little-known roads. "Wherever there is a cow path or hog track" said the newspaper, "through the treachery of Tories, or the willingness of negroes to lend their aid, our enemies will be sure to find them out."[21]

Griffin's Regiment

In late July 1863, Martin's only available cavalry was a handful of companies from two regiments, the 62nd Georgia Cavalry and the 7th Confederate Cavalry Regiments. Some of the 7th Confederate Cavalry was on duty at Kenansville and other points, which were technically part of Whiting's District of the Cape Fear, and some of the Georgia regiment was in Virginia.[22]

The 62nd Georgia Cavalry was commanded by Col. Joel R. Griffin, who before the war was an attorney in Fort Valley, Georgia. His regiment had seven companies from Georgia and North Carolina. Griffin and his second-in-command, Lt.-col. Randolph Towns, were Georgians. "As an acknowledgement" to the...North Carolina companies in the 62nd, John T. Kennedy of Wayne County was promoted to major. Recruiting ads in a Georgia newspaper promised that men joining Griffin's regiment would be "furnished with the most effective gun in the service, the Richmond rifle", a fifty dollar bonus, and "full valuation of all property taken from the enemy." [23]

In mid-1863, Griffin and most of his regiment were on duty in southeastern Virginia. Only companies C, E, G, and I, under Major Kennedy, were left north of the Tar River to cover the Yankees in Washington and Plymouth. Kennedy made his headquarters between Greenville and Washington, at the plantation of William Grimes. (The planter's brother, Bryan Grimes, served with Lee's Army of Northern Virginia and rose to the rank of major general by the end of the war.) Kennedy's men guarded roads and river landings, and kept an eye on movements of the Union Army. His four companies were considered a battalion.[24]

In May, some of Kennedy's men were encamped at "the Clark place", a plantation then owned by Virginia Streeter Atkinson. At the Clark place, which was on the north side of the Tar River across from Falkland, "it was easier to get supplies", and Mrs. Atkinson allowed them pasturage. Company G, under Capt. Patrick Gray, remained on duty closer to Washington. A detachment of Gray's company was posted near Williamston on the Roanoke River.[25]

Like Major Kennedy, most of the men from the 62nd Georgia's Company E, (commanded by Capt. W. A. Thompson), and Company I (under Capt. James B. Edgerton), were from Wayne County. Company C, under Capt. William L. A. Ellis, was made up of men from Macon and Spalding Counties in Georgia. Before returning to his native Georgia, Ellis was in Texas and commanded a company of Texas Rangers in April 1861. Ellis's company was sent to Greenville in May. Edgerton was ordered from Grimes' Farm to a camp that was closer to Greenville on July 9, followed by Thompson three days later. It's tempting to wonder whether Kennedy was ordered to consolidate his companies near Greenville because the Confederates had some warning of a possible Union raid.[26]

On July 15, shortly before Potter left New Bern, General Martin ordered Kennedy to bring all of his men to Fort Branch, a Confederate post on the Roanoke River near Hamilton in Martin County. Gray's company was still camped "twelve miles below Greenville." Apparently Gray was too far away to get orders in time for his company to join the others. Kennedy's three available companies were at Fort Branch by the time that Potter swept through Greenville. It was lucky for them; their small force could have done little to block Potter in Pitt County, but they would soon be in a better position to confront the raiders.[27]

Claiborne's Regiment

Like the 62nd Georgia Cavalry, the companies of the 7th Confederate Cavalry were deployed separately across a wide area and rarely operated as a single unit. This regiment was also made up of North Carolina and Georgia soldiers. A recruiting ad for the regiment in 1862 specified that prospective enlistees had to provide their own horses. The regiment was commanded by Col. William C. Claiborne. In 1860, he was a 40-year-old farmer of Pittsylvania County, Virginia. Claiborne's real and personal property were valued at $63,000, a substantial amount for that time.[28]

Sending an officer from one state to command a regiment from another was often a source of resentment during the Civil War. Discontent and political wrangling seethed among the officers of the 7th Confederate Cavalry, who seemed to have been split into pro- and anti-Claibourne factions. While one soldier wrote that Colonel Claiborne was "a perfect gentleman and very indulgent to his men", Capt. J. J. Lawrence of the regiment freely vented several of his grievances with Claiborne in a letter to the *Tarboro Southerner*. [29]

Claiborne, Lawrence claimed, broke a promise to appoint him as a major in the regiment. The colonel had also promised Lawrence that his men would be stationed to defend their homes in eastern North Carolina, but soon after consenting to join Claiborne's regiment, they were sent to southeastern Virginia. Lawrence stated, "All of the North Carolina, and I believe all the other companies have been making strenuous efforts to get out of the unfortunate box they are in." Lawrence had another grievance as well. When he was at Tarboro preparing to take his company to join Claiborne, an administrative mistake led to an order that placed Lawrence under arrest for being absent without leave. [30]

The 62nd Georgia Cavalry and the 7th Confederate Cavalry were drilled by Brig. Gen. Beverly Robertson. The Virginia-born Robertson, who graduated from West Point in 1849, served before the Civil War in the 2nd U. S. Dragoons on the frontier. During the war, his superior Maj. Gen. J. E. B. Stuart found him "troublesome." Stuart got rid of Robertson by having him assigned away from Virginia. Maj. Gen. D. H. Hill, who ended up with Robertson, liked the "troublesome" general no more than Stuart did. The regiments of Griffin and Claiborne were among those four that Hill believed were "not worth four inferior companies of infantry".[31]

The companies of the 62nd Georgia Cavalry and 7th Confederate Cavalry serving in North Carolina drilled and worked together. One of Griffin's men remembered that they considered the companies of Captains Franklin Pitt and Lycurgus Barrett "ours", even though they were from Claiborne's regiment. Both Griffin and Claiborne were ordered to return a number of horses that their men had seized from Confederate citizens around Greenville in May 1863.[32]

The Troops at Fort Branch and Kinston

At Fort Branch, a post near Hamilton on the Roanoke River, Martin had the 17th North Carolina Infantry and the only heavy guns in his district. Martin's field artillery included the Petersburg Artillery of Virginia, at Fort Branch. At Kinston, there was also a battalion of artillery under Maj. William Saunders, consisting of the Montgomery True Blues of Alabama, and three North Carolina units: Dickson's Battery (2nd Company G, 3rd North Carolina Artillery), Bunting's Battery (the Wilmington Horse Artillery; at that time, the 1st Company

A of the 2nd North Carolina Artillery) and Cummings' Battery (the Cape Fear Light Artillery; at that time, 1st Company C, 2nd North Carolina Artillery).[33]

Most of the 17th North Carolina came from the eastern part of the state. Six of the original companies were captured at the fall of the forts as Hatteras Inlet on August 29, 1861. Two more companies were captured at the Battle of Roanoke Island on February 8, 1862. The 17th was disbanded on March 10, and re-organized under its old commander, Col. William F. Martin, in May 1862. Remaining in North Carolina, the 17th fought at Washington on September 6, and Plymouth on December 10, 1862. In May 1863, the regiment was transferred to Fort Branch.[34]

The Petersburg Artillery was commanded by Capt. Edward Graham. Born in Ireland, Graham was the son of a British army officer. He emigrated to Virginia and became a dry goods merchant in Petersburg. Graham was an officer in the Petersburg Artillery before the war, when they were a militia company. During the tense aftermath of John Brown's raid on Harper's Ferry, the Petersburg Artillery was one of the Virginia militia units that were called up to guard the town. Also known as Graham's Virginia Battery, the company spent much of the war in eastern North Carolina. The battery had an unusually high number of German immigrants, but also had recruited a number of North Carolinians during their time in that state. One of the Virginians, Theophilus Rainey, had been a member of the crew of the *CSS Virginia (Merrimac)*; he was remembered by his comrades for carrying his naval cutlass with him into action.[35]

Martin's forces at Kinston included Lt.-col Pool's four companies of the 1st North Carolina Artillery. Instead of handling guns, though, these men were often deployed as infantry, or as engineer troops specializing in pontoon bridges. Also available to Martin at Kinston was the 42nd North Carolina, as well as Col. James Washington's 50th North Carolina.[36]

Whitford's and Nethercutt's Partisan Rangers

Outside of the Union lines around New Bern, and scattered through Pitt, Greene, and Edgecombe Counties were two battalions of "local defense troops", commanded by Majors John N. Whitford and John H. Nethercutt. Technically, these local defense troops were "partisan rangers". Authorized by an act of the Confederate Congress, partisan rangers were a special category of troops that included the legendary guerillas of Col. John Singleton Mosby, who ran rings around the Yankees in Northern Virginia and in Maryland during the war. Local defense troops were permitted to live in their homes, providing that they turned out whenever they were called up by their officers to deal with a raid or perform scouting duty.

Whitford was previously the captain of Company I, 1st North Carolina Artillery. That company was transferred out of the regiment and divided into two new companies during March and April 1863. Both companies were stationed at Swift Creek in Craven County at the time of the reorganization. Whitford was promoted to major on May 14, and was assigned to command a battalion formed out of his old companies and several new ones that were recruited from the Confederate-held areas around New Bern. By late May, Whitford's Battalion (officially designated the 1st Battalion, North Carolina Local Defense Troops) numbered about 400 men.[37]

Nethercutt, who was from Jones County, was remembered as "a blunt, but brave and enterprising officer." Nethercutt's men were originally intended as a cavalry battalion. Because of the difficulty of finding enough horses for the entire unit, the battalion was reassigned as infantry by August 1863.[38]

Whitford's men, according to a veteran of the unit, "were paid, fed and clothed entirely by the State of North Carolina, were subject to the orders of the Governor of the State and could not be removed beyond the limits of the State without his consent and order." Whitford, Nethercutt, and some of their men were useful scouts, feeding intelligence about Yankee army and naval movements to Martin. They fought many skirmishes and pulled off some daring guerilla raids during the war.[39]

Maj. John H. Nethercutt, CSA
N.C. State Archives

The usefulness of partisan rangers as scouts and spies, though, was diminished by their lack of discipline and training. This was perhaps to be expected, because the men spent so little time in camp and so much at home. Despite the capability of some of Whitford's officers and men, several careless detachments of the same unit were overrun and captured by Yankee raiding parties between 1863 and 1864.[40]

Union soldiers in New Bern were scornful of these home troops. They called them "Nethercutt's gang", or just "bushwhackers", and respected them much less than they did the Confederate regulars.[41]

In September 1863, a party of Union soldiers visited Whitford's camp under a flag of truce. They met Whitford, who was "dressed in a neat suit of gray, with a gilt star upon his collar and embroidered knots upon his arms indicating his rank." The Federals were less impressed with Whitford's men, who they found "armed with various kinds of fire-arms, and clothed with every style of garments. They were ignorant in the extreme, morose and revengeful in appearance, evidently fair exponents of the poor whites and their squalid poverty."[42]

Major Whitford worked closely with General Hill. Among Whitford's activities was sending spies into the Union lines. These spies pretended to be Confederate deserters, and when debriefed fed false information to the Yankees. Hill learned that two of these "deserters" were found out and put in chains. The general suggested that the next time Whitford sent out such spies, he arrange a show of firing at the men to make their "escape" look real. [43]

The July 8 train wreck outside Tarboro also highlighted the slow speed of General Martin's communications. Telegraph lines followed the Wilmington & Weldon Railroad, and another line ran from Goldsboro east along the Atlantic & North Carolina tracks as far as Kinston. To send orders and receive reports from Tarboro, Greenville, and elsewhere, Martin relied on mounted couriers. Lt. John G. Smith of the 7th Confederate Cavalry commanded a small detachment of couriers that linked the Wilmington & Weldon Railroad at Rocky Mount with much of eastern North Carolina.[44]

Even having a telegraph line available was no guarantee of speedy delivery of a message. After the train wreck near Tarboro in July 1863, Lt.-col. Stephen D. Pool sent a telegram from Rocky Mount to headquarters about the accident. After the damage to the track was repaired, the regiment overtook the message on their way home. They were back in camp at Goldsboro for one hour before the telegram about their accident arrived![45]

Back in Tarboro, Judge Howard began to relax as the end of July drew near. Not a single Yankee soldier had shown up yet. Howard wrote on July 19, 1863, "Everything is more quiet here now than we have been for the past two weeks — less apprehension felt of a Yankee raid. We all feel relieved." On the same day he penned that letter to his wife, a Union brigadier general, 800 cavalrymen, and four cannons were already in neighboring Pitt County and were drawing a bead on Tarboro.[46]

Chapter 2

"Foster's Mud March"
*The Union War Effort in Eastern North Carolina,
And the First Attempt to Strike Tarboro
Summer 1862 - Summer 1863*

About one year before Potter's Raid, Maj. Gen. John Gray Foster replaced Maj. Gen. Ambrose Burnside as the commander of the Union Army's Department of North Carolina in July 1862. Foster was born in New Hampshire in 1823. He graduated from West Point in 1846, with the class that produced 20 future Union and Confederate generals, including George B. McClellan and Thomas J. "Stonewall" Jackson. Foster distinguished himself several times, including at the Battle of Churubusco, where his future adversary General Martin was wounded and promoted. After the Mexican War, Foster remained in the sleepy antebellum army as an engineer. Foster was a captain in 1860 when he was sent to Charleston, South Carolina as the chief engineer in charge of the fortifications in the harbor. He was

MajGen. John Gray Foster
Library of Congress

A bird's-eye view of New Bern, the main Union stronghold in eastern North Carolina, in 1864. Library of Congress

part of the garrison during the bombardment that began the Civil War on April 12, 1861. Like several of the other officers of Fort Sumter, Foster rose quickly in rank. He became a brigadier general in October 1861.[47]

The Union's Department of North Carolina operated from their main garrison at New Bern, where the Neuse and Trent Rivers met. Other detachments held Beaufort, Morehead City and Fort Macon; Washington, to bottle up the Tar-Pamlico River; Plymouth, to block the Roanoke River; Roanoke Island; and a few smaller scattered outposts. Every strong point was also under the protection of the Union Navy. The Navy could repel Confederate forces from any spot with enough water to float a heavily armed gunboat.

To prepare for Confederate attacks, Foster took "measures to be fully informed through deserters, spies, &c. of the enemy's strength, preparations for defense, and movements in the department." When Foster took command, there was already an intelligence service that employed former slaves from eastern North Carolina. These spies were first organized by Vincent Colyer, who was appointed Superintendent of the Poor during Burnside's tenure. Besides arranging education, church services, and jobs, Colyer also recruited "upwards of fifty" former slaves into a spy service for the Union. His spies went as far inland as Goldsboro and Tarboro. They visited the Confederates' "principal camps and most important posts", and brought "back important and reliable information". Colyer's scouts passed for ordinary slaves without arousing Confederate suspicions, and so they could move unchallenged deep into enemy territory. The scouts also eluded the Union pickets as well. Colyer noted that because "either of the extreme sagacity and ability of some of these scouts, or the carelessness of our picket guards … I have known these spies on their return from their journeys, to arrive at my head quarters at different hours of the day and night, without having encountered one of our guards on the way".[48]

Foster strengthened his fortifications around New Bern and Washington. With his main bases secure, in November 1862 he asked the War Department for reinforcements to achieve more ambitious goals: "the cutting of the railroad (Weldon and Wilmington) and the taking of Wilmington and the works at New Inlet [that is, Fort Fisher] and the mouth of the Cape Fear River."[49]

If Foster's planned operations against the railroad succeeded, they would be of tremendous value to the Union. He understood the importance of the Wilmington & Weldon Railroad in supplying the Confederate troops in Virginia, and rushing reinforcements south or north when needed to counter Union moves.

Col. Edward E. Potter and the Fight at Washington

Early in Foster's period of command, one of the sharpest clashes in eastern North Carolina was a Confederate attack against Washington on September 6, 1862. Col. Stephen D. Pool, with detachments from the 8th, 17th, and 55th North Carolina, and his 1st North Carolina Artillery (fighting as infantry), approached the Beaufort County town before dawn. Also with Pool was Capt. R. S. Tucker's Company I of the 3rd North Carolina Cavalry. Hidden by fog, the Confederates slipped past the Union pickets. Rebel yells and gunshots awoke the Federal troops as Pool's men poured into Washington. The Confederates overran a company of artillery in their quarters in the Washington Academy building on Second and Bridge Streets. Four brass 6-pounder guns, taken by the Federals at the Battle of New Bern, were again in Confederate hands.[50]

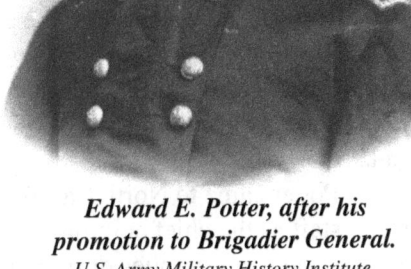

Edward E. Potter, after his promotion to Brigadier General.
U.S. Army Military History Institute

In the Pamlico River, just off Washington's waterfront, the crews of the *USS Louisiana* and of the little army gunboat *Picket* rushed to their battle stations. While the gunners aboard the *Picket* aimed their cannon muzzles at the enemy, other hands scrambled to bring them ammunition. According to one report, the gunboat's magazine was only a large chest in the captain's cabin. Observers on the shore were shocked to see the *Pickett* disappear in a swirl of smoke and flames. According to Union sources, the explosion was "undoubtedly from carelessness and accident," rather than Confederate fire. The blast ripped the steamer to pieces. Capt. Sylvester D. Nicholl of the 1st New York Marine Artillery, the commander of the boat, was killed along with 19 of his men. After the explosions, the Confederates cheered, "Little Washington is ours!"[51]

The shouts of victory were premature. The Union force at Washington was under the command of Col. Edward E. Potter. Under orders from Foster, Potter was on his way from Washington to Plymouth when Pool attacked. With Potter were Lt.Col. John H. Mix, four companies of the 3rd New York Cavalry, and Battery H of the 3rd New York Artillery. [52]

Potter's force was just at the edge of town when they heard the firing. They rushed back to find Confederate infantry trying to push between the Union land forces and the gunboats in the river. For two and half hours, the fighting continued "without cessation". Twice, Potter's gun crews were shot down and replaced, and the colonel's horse was shot from under him during the fighting. Pool and the Confederates withdrew with the captured guns, leaving Washington in Union hands.[53]

Potter's Background

The man who would command "Potter's Raid", Edward Elmer Potter, was born in New York City in 1823. He delivered the valedictorian address at Columbia College (now Columbia University) in 1842. Potter's address was titled, "The Character of a People as Displayed by Their Amusements." He studied law before heading out for California during the Gold Rush. The dates he was in the Gold Rush are not known, but possibly, a journey across Central America to reach California was the reason that Potter applied for a U.S. passport in January 1849.[54]

By 1860, he was back in the eastern U.S., living in the home of his brother Ellis Potter in Chatham Township, Morris County, New Jersey. The census of that year listed Potter's occupation as "gentleman". He enlisted as a captain in the army commissary service a few months after the Civil War began.[55]

Potter came to North Carolina with the Burnside Expedition. He joined Foster's staff as the chief commissary officer for his brigade, helping to unload and move food and supplies during the battle of Roanoke Island on February 8, 1862. Potter also accompanied Foster during the Battle of New Bern on March 14, 1862.[56]

As the Federals consolidated their hold on eastern North Carolina after the fall of New Bern and of Fort Macon, they were pleasantly surprised to find that there were substantial numbers of Southerners who wanted to fight for the Union. In May 1862, General Burnside authorized a loyalist regiment, the 1st North Carolina Union Volunteers. Captain Potter had by then impressed Foster well enough that the general made him the acting colonel of the new regiment. Potter went to Washington to organize his new his regiment. The cool, competent handling of the surprise attack on Washington undoubtedly showed Foster that his confidence in Potter was well placed. Foster wrote that Potter's North Carolinians "fought well and held their position."[57]

Foster's men marched overland from the Roanoke River towards Tarboro in November 1862. The failed expedition was known as "Foster's Mud March" by the Union troops.

The "Mud March": the First Tarboro Expedition

After the attack on Washington, Foster took back the initiative with a large-scale expedition. Intelligence reports from the Union Navy warned that three Confederate regiments were gathering supplies in Washington and Hyde Counties. Foster planned to capture these regiments, and then move up the Roanoke River to destroy two Confederate ironclads that the Navy believed were under construction at the river town of Hamilton. With a little luck, he might be able to push further inland and strike a blow against the Wilmington & Weldon. General Foster led the expedition himself. On November 2, they left Washington, North Carolina with around five thousand troops and 21 pieces of artillery. Their plans had already changed. "Owing to the condition of the roads", the Confederate regiments they had hoped to capture were left alone.[58]

Late on the same day they left Washington, they fought a skirmish at Rawle's Mill, on Little Creek in Martin County. Two days later, they reached Hamilton, only to learn that the naval intelligence was wrong and the gunboats were not being built there. They turned west to follow Confederate troops retreating toward Tarboro.[59]

On November 6, they were only a few miles from Tarboro when they heard a noisy commotion coming from the town. The engineer of the Tarboro Branch Railroad train sped the engine up to the depot, wildly ringing the bell and blowing the whistle. The handful of Confederate soldiers on the scene got all the townspeople they could find to cheer as loudly as they could. Then, the engineer backed the train a short distance down the line, and then rushed it up to the depot again. To Foster's men, the noise sounded like train after train of Confederate troops pouring into Tarboro. This noisy charade seemed to confirm intelligence reaching Foster about Confederate reinforcements. Foster abandoned his goal of attacking Tarboro.[60]

Foster's men returned to New Bern, by way of Plymouth. They had destroyed a great deal of Confederate and private property, but brought back only five prisoners. The grumbling soldiers called the expedition "the Tarboro Mud March". Potter earned Foster's praise for his "efficient conduct" during the operation.[61]

The Goldsboro Expedition

Foster got another chance to attack the Wilmington & Weldon in December. By cutting the line at Goldsboro, Foster would also divert Confederate troops from Virginia and relieve pressure on Maj. Gen. Ambrose Burnside, who was leading the Army of the Potomac in what would become the Battle of Fredericksburg. Cutting the railroad would also prevent Confederate reinforcements from Virginia from interfering with the second phase of the plan: an overland attack on Wilmington.

In one of the war's largest operations in North Carolina, Foster's 11,000 men and 40 guns left New Bern on December 11, 1862. Their line of march was roughly parallel to the Neuse River, where a force of five gunboats shadowed them. The Federals took Kinston after a battle on December 14. In another battle at Whitehall, on December 15 and 16, they damaged the Confederate gunboat *Neuse*, which was under construction.[62]

On December 17, Foster neared the Wilmington & Weldon Railroad's Neuse River bridge near Goldsboro. The Federals pushed the defending

Confederate troops north of the river, but the Rebels clung to their new position and returned a heavy fire.

After several men were shot down trying to reach the railroad bridge across the Neuse River, Lt. George W. Graham of the 24th New York Battery volunteered for another try. Graham, Lt. Barnabas N. Mann of the 17th Massachusetts, and two privates of the 9th New Jersey rushed toward the bridge bearing portfires. (Portfires were tubes of stiff paper filled with explosive material, and were rather similar to flares.) Mann was shot and wounded, but Graham made it to the bridge and set it ablaze. He avoided capture by jumping into the river and swimming back toward the Union troops.[63]

Foster's main objective, the destruction of the railroad bridge, was accomplished. But, after this success, Foster learned that Burnside had been defeated at Fredericksburg, and Confederate reinforcements were heading south to North Carolina. He turned back and reached New Bern on December 20. Plans for the attack on Wilmington were called off. Despite three victories on the battlefield, Foster's Expedition yielded little for its 600 casualties. It took little time to repair the railroad bridge, and the Confederates resumed work on the gunboat *Neuse*.[64]

During the Goldsboro Expedition, Potter served on Foster's staff. The general praised Potter for being "of the greatest aid and assistance to me by his coolness and observation." Like several other officers who were under Foster's eye, Potter was promoted to brigadier general on December 24, 1862. On January 12, 1863, Foster appointed Potter as his chief of staff.[65]

Also on December 24, Foster was promoted to command the 18th Army Corps, which included all of the Union army in North Carolina. Late in January 1863, 12,000 Federal troops were assembled in Beaufort for a planned land and sea attack on Wilmington, but plans for that attack were dropped in favor of an

Union officers pose in front of their New Bern headquarters at the Slover House. Gen. Foster is fifth from the left; Gen. Potter is fifth from left. U.S. Army Military History Institute

Rear Adm. S. P. Lee, USN

attack on Charleston. 10,000 of Foster's 24,000 men in North Carolina were ordered to Port Royal, South Carolina for the move against Charleston. Foster went with his men, who were to fight under the command of Maj. Gen. David Hunter. The two commanders quarreled, and Foster returned to North Carolina – minus his 10,000 troops. [66]

It was a bad time to weaken the Union defenses in North Carolina. Reports of Confederate gunboats under construction on the Tar and the Roanoke continued to worry the Union Navy. Admiral S. P. Lee, in charge of the North Atlantic blockading Squadron, proposed a combined army and navy operation to destroy the ironclads before they were finished. On February 19, 1863, Foster even requested the transfer of the 9th Army Corps to assist in the attack on the Confederate gunboats. [67]

Foster soon had more to worry about than the gunboats. The Confederates took advantage of the winter slowdown, when fighting eased in Virginia. Lee felt that he could spare a few regiments for campaigning in North Carolina and southeastern Virginia. While Maj. Gen. James Longstreet moved against Norfolk, Virginia, Maj. Gen. Daniel Harvey Hill menaced the Union garrisons of New Bern and Washington. Neither Longstreet nor Hill pushed hard enough to capture the Union-held towns. But both operations pinned down Union forces behind their fortifications for weeks, while Confederate troops protected commissary officers who gathered tons of food from farms in eastern North Carolina and southeastern Virginia.

After some unsuccessful moves against New Bern that began on March 13, Hill moved toward Washington, where he began a siege on March 30. A Federal relief column under Brig. Gen. Francis Barretto Spinola left New Bern to end the siege. On April 9, Spinola collided with part of Brig. Gen. James Johnston Pettigrew's brigade at Blount's Creek. After a skirmish, Spinola scurried back to New Bern. [68]

Disgusted at Spinola's failure, Foster himself boarded the steamer *Escort,* to run past the Confederate batteries that ringed Washington along the Pamlico River. Distrusting "Captain Pedrick", his loyalist North Carolinian pilot, Foster stayed in the pilothouse with a drawn revolver. Pedrick had just steered past the last Confederate obstruction in the river when he was struck down. His last words were "I'm killed, General, but by God, I'll get you through!" With the escape of the *Escort* on April 13, it was clear that Federal reinforcements would soon be on the way. Hill broke off the attack. A great deal of food from eastern North Carolina farms was already safely on its way to the Confederate Army, which was his main concern. Hill's troops would be sorely needed in Virginia when the spring campaigns began.[69]

When the fighting resumed in Virginia, all available Rebel troops were pulled out of North Carolina. On June 8, General-in-Chief Henry W. Halleck notified Foster that information received by the Union Army indicated that most of the Confederate troops "in Georgia and South Carolina have been sent west, to raise the siege of Vicksburg, and that those in North Carolina have been brought north to re-enforce General Lee. If such is the case, it is suggested that your army corps could resume offensive operations, destroy railroads, etc." Foster had already sent a force of five regiments against a Confederate outpost at Gum Swamp, eight miles below Kinston, in May. In a skirmish there on May 22, they captured 165 men of the 56th North Carolina before they withdrew to New Bern as Confederate reinforcements reached the field. [70]

Foster continued gathering intelligence about the Confederate territory beyond New Bern. By June 15, it was common knowledge in New Bern that "strong entrenchments" had been built around Greenville. Brig. Gen. Henry Wessells, who commanded the Federal garrison at Plymouth, told Foster in early July that according to his latest intelligence reports (which were two weeks old), there were no Confederate troops at Tarboro. As he sorted the incoming information on the enemy, Foster prepared another major raid.[71]

Laborers demostrate how to use levers and special tools to pull up rails. Notice the ties are laid in the soil without gravel ballast. The 1st North Carolina Colored Volunteers would have used such tools on the Wilmington & Weldon Railroad tracks in Warsaw.
Library of Congress

Chapter 3

"A Grand Jubilation on the 'Glorious Fourth'"
The 3rd New York Cavalry Raids Kenansville and Warsaw
July 3-7, 1863

Early in July 1863, an anonymous New York soldier wrote that the troops at New Bern "were preparing here for a grand jubilation on the 'Glorious Fourth', and all hands calculated on having an extra good time. Alas! However, for our bright hopes and anticipated joys, an order was received ... to prepare for a movement at daylight on the morning of the 4th."[72] Foster was ready to resume his attacks against the Wilmington & Weldon Railroad. This time, he aimed for a more remote point along the railroad, the depot at Warsaw, which was about 35 miles south of Goldsboro. For this raid, he would throw in almost all of the cavalrymen that he had available in New Bern.

Foster placed Lt.-col. George W. Lewis of the 3rd New York Cavalry in command of the expedition. The 1850 Census of Rochester, New York listed Lewis as a 24-year-old physician in the household of physician George Lewis. The

Lt.Col. George W. Lewis
U.S. Army Military History Institute

younger Lewis seemed to have given up medicine, though. Although an 1851 city directory listed him as a medical student, the 1853 directory listed him as "weigh master at weight lock" In 1855, he was a forwarding and commission merchant and by 1859, he was also a city alderman. After the war began, Lewis left his business and joined the army as captain of Company G, 13 New York Infantry on May 14, 1861. Lewis' company was transferred to the 3rd New York Cavalry and designated Company K in the new regiment. He was promoted to major in September 1861.[73]

Besides his regiment, Lewis also was given two companies of the 23rd New York Cavalry, Company L of the 1st North Carolina Union Volunteers, a 2-gun section of the Battery H, 3rd New York Artillery, under Lt. John D. Clark, and the "flying battery" of the 3rd New York Cavalry, under Lt. James A. Allis. "All told", wrote Lewis, it was "650 men." The companies of a new regiment, the 12th New York Cavalry, were just beginning to trickle into New Bern. However, this new regiment would wait just a bit longer for its baptism of fire.[74]

"They Are Bound To Win": The Third New York Cavalry

The 3rd New York Cavalry was also called the Van Alen Cavalry, after its first colonel, businessman and socialite James H. Van Alen. The companies, mustered in at Syracuse, Rochester, Albany, Elmira, and Boonville, New York were sent to Washington, D. C. where the regiment was organized in September 1861. The army bureaucracy also assigned the 6th Independent Ohio Cavalry, which had been recruited in Cincinnati and Xenia, Ohio, as Company L of the regiment. [75]

The regiment's early service along the Potomac included reconnaissance work before the Battle of Ball's Bluff, on October 21, 1861. In April, 1862, they were reviewed in Washington, D. C., by President Lincoln, who "stood uncovered upon the sidewalk in front of the White House, until the entire regiment passed." The 3rd's military appearance was impressive, and, unusually for a Civil War regiment, "not a man was on the sick list" that day. Lincoln "complimented" the regiment "in the highest terms." [76]

Shortly after their review by Lincoln, they were transferred to strengthen the Union forces in North Carolina under Brig. Gen. Ambrose Burnside. Burnside had no horse soldiers at all until the arrival of the 3rd New York Cavalry, and for a year they were the only cavalry that the Union had in North Carolina. [77]

Van Alen resigned on April 8, 1862, and the regiment's lieutenant-colonel, Simon Hoosick Mix, took his place. Born in 1825, Mix was the son of a newspaper editor. The younger Mix followed his father in the newspaper business. Both father and son were among the "earliest and firmest Republicans". In 1860, Simon Mix narrowly lost election to Congress.[78]

Capt. Rowland M. Hall took over Company E of the 3rd New York Cavalry when its previous commander, Capt. Ferris Jacobs, Jr., was promoted to major in the regiment on June 12, 1863. Hall, a graduate of the Harvard Class of 1856, was a lawyer when the war began. The letters that Hall wrote to his family were spiced with barbed comments on everything from the tedium of life in "this earthly hell, in North Carolina" to the annoyances of putting up with the rest of the officers in his regiment. [79]

After Hall took over his new company, he wrote home to say that Company E was "largely composed of the *sons of Scotchmen*. They are a turbulent set of fellows but ... the company has always had the reputation of being one of the best in the regiment."[80]

Capt. Gustavus Jocknick of Company I, a Swedish immigrant, was an accountant in New Jersey in 1860. As a veteran of the War with Mexico, he was also one of the few officers on the expedition who had military experience before the Civil War.[81]

Private John Harris of Company F had three brothers in the Confederate army. This was natural enough, since Harris was a native of North Carolina. He enlisted in the regiment at Fairfield, in Hyde County, North Carolina, on March 12, 1863. Company F of the 3rd New York Cavalry was part of a Union raid on Hyde County from March 1-6, 1863, and another on March 7-14, 1863. [82]

Private George W. Merry of Company G had lived in North Carolina before the war. He later told a newspaper that in 1860, he was a resident of New Bern, but he returned home to New York in the fall so that he could safely vote for Abraham Lincoln.[83]

By the time that the 3rd New York Cavalry was saddling up for the expedition to Warsaw, they had fought in over 75 skirmishes and battles in North Carolina, besides their five earlier actions in Virginia. "The Rebbles are a fraid of the third", wrote an admiring soldier from the newly arrived 12th New York Cavalry, William Davies. "When they meet the Rebels they go in on a Charge and Cut them Down Like grass they are a hard lot of men to fight Jeff Davis has offered thirty dollars for Every one they Can take of them when they go in they are Bound to win." [84]

"Mix's New Cavalry"

The 23rd New York Cavalry was organized in October 1862. Its commander was Lt.Col. John H. Mix, the brother of Simon Mix. In 1860, John Mix was a sergeant in the 2nd United States Dragoons, and he was stationed at Fort Laramie in what is now Wyoming. In August 1861, he resigned from the regular army with the rank of second lieutenant to join the 3rd New York Cavalry as a major. John Mix rose to the rank of lieutenant-colonel, and "drilled and disciplined" the regiment before was transferred to command the new 23rd, which was sometimes called "Mix's New Cavalry".[85]

Three of the original six officers of the 23rd were also transferred from his old regiment. Recruiting for the 23rd did not go well; the unit never got more than two companies, compared with the normal 12-company allotment for a cavalry regiment. John Mix was transferred to another post. By August 1863, the "regiment" was a two-company unit that was sometimes still called "Mix's Cavalry Battalion", even though it was commanded by Capt. Emory Cummings.[86]

The North Carolina Loyalists

Rounding out Lewis' forces was one unit of local Union "loyalists", Company L of the 1st North Carolina Union Volunteers. They were part of the regiment that was begun under the command of Col. Edward E. Potter in 1862. The regiment was made up of men of eastern North Carolina. Its recruits were drawn from areas of Union control, from Confederate territory, and from the unsettled regions that neither side held firmly.

Col. Simon H. Mix, USA
Library of Congress

Company L was commanded by a New Yorker, Lt. George W. Graham. He was the same officer who made a name for himself by setting fire to the railroad bridge at the Battle of Goldsboro on December 17, 1862. Graham was transferred to the 3rd New York Cavalry, and then placed in command of Company L of 1st North Carolina Union Volunteers on May 1, 1863. A. W. Hahn, an officer of the 3rd New York Cavalry, later recalled that Graham was given permission to "go outside the federal lines for the purpose of raising loyal soldiers. Graham worked quickly, stated Hahn, "not being twenty days in recruiting and mounting nearly 100 loyal North Carolinians."[87]

Graham's Company L usually served as mounted infantry. Because they spent so much time in the saddle, they were sometimes unofficially called the "North Carolina Union Cavalry". Most soldiers of the company had enlisted at Plymouth, North Carolina. They often served as scouts and were valued for their knowledge of the eastern North Carolina countryside. Graham and his company earned a fine reputation. "A more gallant officer and braver man never sat a saddle. I could narrate many hair-breadth escapes and daring acts", wrote Hahn.[88]

The Pioneer Detail

In addition to the white cavalry troopers, there was a detail of 21 men and two sergeants of the 1st North Carolina Colored Infantry, under the command of Capt. Henry W. Wilson. Sgt. William Jackson and Private Manuel Butler of Company B, with 13 privates; seven privates from Company E, and Sgt. Edmund Williams of Company D were ordered to assemble "in front of Head Qtrs." at 4:15 "precisely this PM". Their orders stated that "the men will go so far as they can provided in Citizens clothes taking with them only canteens and blankets."[89]

Wilson was listed as a "civil engineer" attached to Foster's 18th Army Corps. His men were assigned as pioneers, a military term for laborers who worked at engineering projects such as building and repairing roads and bridges. This was one of the first times that the newly organized black soldiers from North Carolina were ordered into the field.[90]

At the time of Potter's Raid, three black North Carolina regiments were planned, which were to be part of an all-black infantry brigade commanded by Brig. Gen. Edward A. Wild. Furthest along in its organization in July 1863 was the 1st North Carolina Union Troops, commanded by Col. James C. Beecher (half-brother of Harriet Beecher Stowe, the author of the famous abolitionist novel *Uncle Tom's Cabin*).

It was early summer 1863 before the Union began to organize regiments of black soldiers in eastern North Carolina. After Union forces arrived with the Burnside Expedition in 1862, the Union authorities hired many former slaves as teamsters, laborers, laundresses, cooks, and servants. Some men were employed by the army to chop wood, build and repair fortifications, and perform other heavy work.

Captain Wilson led a detachment of black pioneers, all of whom were civilians, during Foster's Raid back in December 1862. Late in the day on December 11, the Federal troops were about fifteen miles west of New Bern, when they found "the road densely blockaded by felled trees; this blockade extended for several hundred yards, being situated in the midst of a swamp possessing an abundance of creeks." Foster's army halted for the night, while parties of soldiers worked with "a strong force of 'pioneer contrabands'" under Wilson's command to clear the way.[91]

An expedition of the 3rd New York Cavalry into Jones and Onslow Counties in January 1863 also included a detachment of black civilian pioneers. Col. Simon H. Mix, in charge of the expedition, does not mention the pioneers in his report, although a correspondent for the *Herald* of New York did.[92]

Finding a bridge at Pollocksville had been destroyed, the "native pioneers" went to work on a replacement. According to the reporter, the task took "six hours' hard labor, a good deal of sweating and considerable swearing."

Grove Camp, near New Bern, was home of the 3rd New York Cavalry and the 25th Massachusetts Infantry at the time of Potter's Raid. U.S. Army Military History Institute

Later, their road was blocked "with felled timber for as far as they could observe, extending over a mile." Mix ordered "the auxiliary corps of contrabands" to work clearing the road. Until nightfall, the pioneers worked, the woods resounding with "the music of axes", interrupted by the "quaint sayings" of the workmen and their bosses' orders.[93]

Evidently, many men stepped from civilian labor crews into the US Colored Troops. A recruiting agent from Massachusetts stopped at a logging camp of contrabands outside New Bern early in 1863. He wrote that after giving a recruiting speech at the camp, one hundred men swamped an enlistment office in New Bern the day before the office was scheduled to open. A newspaper reported that some of the new black recruits in North Carolina were already owed one year or more in pay for civilian labor for the Federal government.[94]

The Expedition Begins

Lewis left New Bern for the Wilmington & Weldon Railroad on the morning of July 3. When they were about five miles from Trenton, in Jones County, Lewis' advance captured three enemy videttes (cavalry pickets). They pushed on to Trenton, but their attack on the town was delayed by "a wide and very deep ford" that gave time for the enemy troops that were "stationed in the town to give the alarm". Lewis' advance chased a few Confederates about two miles beyond Trenton. They captured "one or two prisoners" before giving up, "owing to the extreme heat, and my horses suffering from the effects of a charge of seven miles." The Yankee expedition covered about 25 miles before they halted for the night at Trenton.[95]

As the Yankee cavalrymen rousted themselves from their bedrolls the next morning, Brig. Gen. Charles A. Heckman left New Bern with a large infantry force. Following Lewis' trail, Heckman took the 9th New Jersey, parts of the 17th and the 23rd Massachusetts, the 81st New York, and Belger's Battery, from Rhode Island. At Pollocksville, they met the infantry brigade of Col. James Jourdan. Together, Heckman and Jourdan would divert Confederate attention from the cavalry, as well as shorten the distance for Lewis' return to the Union lines.[96]

Lewis captured a Rebel courier and some mail bags at Comfort, which was about twelve miles past Trenton. On the way to Hallsville, they captured two more pickets. The Federal troopers crossed a ford that was so deep that all of the "ammunition had to be carried across on the wagons to avoid the water."[97]

Lewis moved as rapidly as possible toward Hallsville, where he would have to cross a "very long bridge" over the Northeast Cape Fear River. The Federals were concerned that the Confederates might learn of the expedition's plans and burn the bridge. About one mile from Hallsville, Lewis sent his "advance platoon" to charge a Confederate picket station. Although the pickets got away, the Yankees captured their horses and weapons, and seized the bridge.[98]

The Confederate prisoners informed the Yankees that there was a company of Rebel cavalry at Kenansville. Lewis decided to divide his force. Although it was already dark, and they'd ridden over 35 miles, he sent the battalion of Maj. Ferris Jacobs, Jr. on to Kenansville. Jacobs had orders to swoop down upon the town and capture the enemy troops. The rest of the detachment would follow behind them.[99]

A Moonlit Dash into Kenansville

Kenansville was 75 miles from New Bern and about seven miles from Magnolia, the nearest station on the Wilmington & Weldon Railroad. The county seat of Duplin County, Kenansville grew and prospered in the years after the railroad reached the county in 1839. The town supported several stores, a Masonic lodge, and a number of churches, and was "especially noted for her fine schools". After the war, a resident remembered that during antebellum times it was "one of the most dashing and flourishing little towns in North Carolina." Several beautiful Greek Revival homes survive today to show something of the pleasant pre-war elegance of the town.[100]

The waning moon was still nearly full and lit the way for Captain Hall. He wrote that his men "approached the town at a fast walk in the bright beautiful moonlight [and] charged into Duplin Court House" (as he called the town of Kenansville). They found that the town, "shaded by oaks & cypress … was in profound silence."[101]

The Duplin County Courthouse was built in 1785. It was a brick building, forty feet square, and two stories high. "We rode up to the Court House, where we expected to find the enemy quartered, pistol in hand, but the silence continued …" [102]

The silence was broken soon enough. Private Joseph E. Williams of the 1st North Carolina Colored Volunteers described the raid to the *Christian Recorder* of Philadelphia. Upon hearing that thirty escaped slaves were being held in the county jail, Williams wrote that the soldiers "worked for about an hour" to "break down the door with axes". The door, though, seemed to be "as hard as any iron safe". At length, the county sheriff was brought to the scene and persuaded to give up the key with the threat of "a can of tar and feathers". The rumored thirty prisoners turned out to be merely three men. Interestingly, Williams wrote that only two of them opted to return to New Bern with them, where they enlisted in one of the new regiments of Wild's Brigade.[103]

The Confederates that Hall was looking for were Capt. William K. Lane's Company F of the 7th Confederate Cavalry. Hall learned that that the enemy troopers were camped at the county fairgrounds, and he gathered a detachment to capture them. The Federals were delayed because "a well dressed negro (the only one I never knew to deceive us) & probably an officer's servant" supplied them with misleading directions. When Hall finally reached the Confederate camp, he found that "they had escaped into the woods". [104]

The old Duplin County Courthouse in Kenansville.
N.C. State Archives

The 30 men of Lane's company left "nearly all of their horses and equipments and arms", which Hall thought "the best I have ever seen in their service". The Yankees captured several soldiers near the camp, along with "a large Confederate flag and some cavalry guidons." (At the end of Appendix II will be found the names of seven men of the 7th Confederate Cavalry, and three other soldiers, who were captured at Kenansville.) Perhaps forgetting that the raiders struck at midnight, the *North Carolina Standard* in Raleigh charged that Captain Lane was asleep when the raiders struck.[105]

Hall was amused to see his men "loaded down with every kind of plunder, the handsome grey uniforms of the officers made in England like Genl. Washington's & covered with gold lace, under clothing, &c." At the Confederate camp, he picked up some war trophies for his younger brother

David, including a "horse pistol", "a lancer's pike, of Southern manufacture", and a "sabre with the letters C. S. A. in the hilt."[106]

The Kenansville Arms Factory

The "sabre" that Hall grabbed for his brother came from the raiders' main target in Kenansville. The little town was the site of a Confederate arms factory that was owned by a German immigrant named Louis Froelich. Back in April 1861, Froelich and his partner, Bela Estvan (sometimes spelled "Eastvan", opened an arms factory in Wilmington. Estvan impressed the Confederate authorities with his military bearing and his claims of serving as a colonel in the Hungarian army.[107]

"Colonel" Estvan's sophisticated façade helped win arms contracts, but soon, complaints about the swords and bayonets made at the Wilmington factory poured in from the army. Of a shipment of sabers to the 2nd North Carolina Cavalry, for which the government "paid high prices ... three-fourths of the swords proved worthless." Eventually, Estvan slipped out of North Carolina. After getting to New York, Estvan wrote a book about the

The marker at the site of Froelich's armory.
Photo by the Author

Confederacy. He spun some tall tales about seeing famous battles, and having spoken with "Stonewall" Jackson and other Southern luminaries. He didn't discuss the sword factory in Wilmington.[108]

Later in 1862, Froelich opened another arms factory in Kenansville, which was about sixty miles north of Wilmington. It may have been easier for him to run a factory there, without competing for workers and materials with the other wartime industries in Wilmington. Early in 1863, a fire destroyed Froelich's Wilmington factory, and he shifted his entire operation to Kenansville. "Kenansville swords", noted for a distinctive hand guard made of brass formed with the letters "CSA", are highly sought after by collectors today. The Froelich company also made military buttons, knapsacks, naval cutlasses, pikes, belts and other accoutrements, and even sets of surgical instruments.[109]

In the Froelich armory, Lewis' men found "2,500 sabers and large quantities of saber bayonets, bowie knives, and other small arms, a steam engine and implements for the manufactory of knapsacks, and some large commissary store-houses …" The armory building, with its "large and splendid engine and boiler" was burned. Oddly, although Lewis burned the "tools, saddles, and all the stock" of an adjacent saddle factory, but didn't set fire to the building itself, "there being no machinery in it." The *Richmond Dispatch* reported that the raiders took $35,000 in cash from Froelich.[110]

Froelich's armory stood by modern-day NC Highway 11, about one quarter of a mile south of the Duplin County courthouse. A Dollar General store and its parking lot occupy the armory site today. The spot is commemorated with historic markers.

A Nervous Visit to Warsaw Station

The Yankees stayed the night at Kenansville, then broke camp at 4 a.m. Lewis reported that Magnolia was the closest station on the railroad, but according to information they had, it was held by a "part or the whole of a brigade and four pieces of artillery". General Whiting had in fact ordered four companies of infantry and a section of artillery from Wilmington to Magnolia in June "to protect the road from a cavalry raid by that fellow Mix". So, instead of hitting the railroad at Magnolia, Lewis ordered the column to ride to Warsaw, which was about ten miles northwest of Kenansville.[111]

Lewis' men swept into Warsaw at 8 a.m. Apparently, there was some warning of the impending raid. The *North Carolina Standard* reported that "the people of Warsaw had time to secure their horses." As soon as the raiders reached the town, they cut the telegraph wires. Lewis put a few of the men to work tearing up the railroad tracks, but kept most of the troopers on horseback in case any Rebels showed up. The Warsaw depot, with "30,000 pounds of bacon", was burned, along with two railroad cars, the water tank, "about 1,000 or more barrels of tar and turpentine", and a warehouse filled with flour, bacon, and corn.[112]

15,000 pounds of the bacon at Warsaw was earmarked for the Confederate Army. J. D. Southerland, the commissary agent who had purchased the bacon for the army, had been trying to get it shipped to Richmond. But, for two months, the Wilmington & Weldon Railroad brushed off Southerland's pleas to find space on their crowded freight cars for the bacon. Blaming the Wilmington & Weldon's neglect, Southerland urged the army to make the railroad pay for the supply of bacon.[113]

The fire at the Warsaw depot also destroyed "the scales, weights, safe, &c." that belonged to the railroad, as well as "two large pianos". The Fayetteville stagecoach was captured at Warsaw, with the horses and mail, although the passengers escaped. "The post office was sacked", said the *North Carolina Standard,* "and the Express messenger shot at". Altogether, the cavalry captured "three or four bags of mail."[114]

The captured mail was examined later, but it "contained scarcely a single letter concerning valuable information. Many of the private letters speak of being tired of the war, and praying for peace."[115]

Southern newspapers recorded in detail some of the losses suffered by citizens of Duplin County during the raid. Some of the raiders stole a watch from a "Mr. Roals", and burned a buggy belonging to a Mr. Bell, "together with the sheds of Mr. Southerland." Stores owned by "E. F. Matix", "Morton & Zaery", "Bell & Blackman", and a "Mr. Rivenbark", were looted. Large amounts of cash were taken from "Isaac Kelly and Mr. McCarthy". Troopers took horses, mules, bacon, and other provisions from several farmers, and the raiders also "destroyed growing fields of corn". At first, the raiders "carried off several gentlemen prisoners", but they "finally detained only James Love, a wagoner from Virginia." The secessionist townspeople noted with some alarm that the black troops accompanying the expedition were armed.[116]

"Amid the scoundrelism" of the raiders, one Southerner noted "a tinge of remaining humanity." The Yankees reached one home near Kenansville, where a man was worried about his daughter, who "was very ill. He met them in the yard and asked them not to go in on that account and they respected his request."[117]

The Raiders Leave Warsaw

While they were in Warsaw, Lewis heard that a Confederate force was expected to get there by train within "one and a half hours". He later reported that "my pickets fired on guerillas repeatedly while at this point." By 2 p.m., Lewis decided that it was too risky to linger any longer so deep in enemy territory, and ordered a return to New Bern. Captain Hall vented his frustration with Lewis in a letter to his father, "no enemy opposed us, yet out *incompetent Lieut. Col.* hurried us along as though he expected to find a rebel regiment in every bush and *hardly waited long enough* in Warsaw ... *to destroy, or injure ... half a mile of the track."* [118]

Lewis was worried about the Confederates, but that was nothing compared to how much the Confederates were worried about him. A report that reached Raleigh by telegraph inflated Lewis' force to 2,000 men (which was about three times what he really had), with "six pieces of artillery". On Monday, July 6, Governor Zebulon B. Vance notified the Secretary of War in Richmond, "A heavy cavalry force is threatening us ... I am getting the citizens and militia under arms, but have no artillery." He asked for some artillery and for a brigade of infantry to be sent to Raleigh. On the same day, Vance and Maj. Gen. Braxton Bragg addressed a large crowd in Raleigh, and urged them "to volunteer in defense of their homes". The 39th North Carolina Militia (one of Wake County's militia units), as well as the conscripts at a training camp near Raleigh, were called out. They would defend Raleigh if Lewis pushed on to the state capital.[119]

Maj. Gen. D. H. Hill, upon learning the raid, worried that the enemy cavalry had "broken through" the Confederates at Magnolia, and that their next target was the arsenal at Fayetteville.[120]

Maj. George Jackson, who was at the railroad town of Magnolia, commanded the Confederate forces that were closest to Warsaw. At the end of July 1863, Major Jackson's command included three companies of the 7th Confederate Cavalry, three of the 61st North Carolina, and two companies of the 5th South Carolina Cavalry. Jackson was a West Point graduate and a former US dragoon officer. His brother, William Lowther Jackson, became a brigadier general in 1864. These two Jackson brothers were second cousins of "Stonewall" Jackson. (William's troops gave him the unfortunate nickname of "Mudwall Jackson.")[121]

After the Yankee cavalry left Warsaw, Major Jackson "marched down to Hallsville, eight miles below Kenansville". Jackson then sent a rider to check on the damage done to the railroad. Jackson's courier "looked so suspicious" to the people of Warsaw that "he was arrested and sent back under guard." Explaining part of the "suspicious" appearance of Jackson's courier, a newspaper added, "He was a Marylander." Because the border state of Maryland stayed with the Union, secessionists from that state had to leave and come to the South to fight for the Confederacy. Many Southerners suspected Marylanders of being Union spies, or regarded than as grafters angling for army commissions or government jobs. [122]

One of Lewis' men wrote that while the Union horsemen were at Warsaw, "Some of the boys who are over fond of the 'critter' came out very 'blue' having discovered a large quantity of what we call apple-jack ..."[123]

When Jackson's troops at last reached Warsaw, the enemy was long gone. But, they did find one Yankee cavalryman who was so drunk that he had been left behind. "This fellow", said one newspaper, "had $150 in Confederate money". The prisoner told his captors that some of his comrades had taken over $1,000 each in Confederate currency on the raid.[124]

After leaving Warsaw, the Union cavalry again rode through Kenansville. By this time, the town had been reinforced. Pickets opened fire, killing a horse and wounding one of the North Carolina Union soldiers. The Confederates fell back from Kenansville toward Magnolia, which Lewis believed to be full of Rebel troops. "I pushed my advance on rapidly", wrote Lewis, "seeing indications of the enemy all along the lines, and the citizens boasting that I would never get back again..." When they got back to Hallsville, they scattered the Confederate pickets there and halted for a brief rest. [125]

At 1 a.m. on July 6, the bluecoats were on the move again. Lewis had word that twelve miles ahead, Major Nethercutt's rangers held a crossroads that they needed to pass. When they reached the crossroads, however, they found only one courier and a few "guerillas", which they captured. Again, the Confederate prisoners told them that the Federals were being chased by a column of infantry. [126]

Lewis sent a platoon under Lt. Sherman Grieg to press on ahead to Comfort and hold it until he got there. Grieg reached Comfort, but a messenger he sent to Lewis was blocked by "guerillas" and had to return. The lieutenant then sent a squad of four volunteers, who got through to Lewis. With "the woods in my rear being full of infantry", and the sound of firing from the direction of Trenton reaching them, Lewis pushed on as quickly as possible. At Comfort, he found not only Grieg but part of Heckman's infantry. After an anxious day, the worries of the Union horsemen were over.[127]

During that day, Heckman skirmished with Confederate cavalry and artillery along the Comfort and Free Bridge Roads. Lt.-col. John G. Chambers of the 23rd Massachusetts was wounded in the shoulder, and Bugler John Albert of the 9th New Jersey was "seriously wounded in the face". Heckman and Lewis both hoped to catch the elusive Confederate force between them, but the enemy force got away. The cavalry moved to "within 4 miles of Pollocksville" in Jones County to camp on the night of July 6. They left early the next morning and were back at camp in New Bern by noon on July 7. [128]

Lieutenant-colonel Lewis wrote that his force had "marched 170 miles in five days, and during that time [had] been out of the saddle less than twenty hours." He claimed that they destroyed "nearly a million dollars' worth of property and captured between 40 and 50 prisoners and over 100 horses and mules." He added, "Nearly 500 contrabands (men, women, and children) were brought in." Among them were nine slaves belonging to "Col. C. D. Hill". The raid was accomplished with little loss to the Union. News of the expedition hit Southern and Northern newspapers in the next few days, and even appeared in the *San Francisco Evening Bulletin* on July 11, by way of the transcontinental telegraph.[129]

Col. Charles Edmonston Thorburn, a Virginian who commanded the City and River Defenses of Wilmington, captured "two or three" Yankees on July 6. Thorburn "pursued them ... as far as Sandy Foundation, Lenoir County", and also retrieved a few of the stolen horses. Thorburn's later career included an assignment in London and Paris. He accompanied Jefferson Davis for part of his final flight after the fall of Richmond in April 1865.[130]

Five of Lewis' men were listed as missing or prisoners, one from the 3rd New York Cavalry and four from the 23rd New York Cavalry. One of missing men, Private John F. Baker of the 3rd, was listed as a deserter while "on march from Warsaw" on July 6. The company muster roll duly noted that Baker owed the U.S. Ordnance department for his "Colt's revolver", holster, saber, cartridge box, and percussion cap pouch. [131]

After the raiders returned to New Bern, Lewis was not completely out of trouble. A quarrel arose over the amount of track that was actually destroyed. Lewis claimed that "I tore up all of the track, and totally destroyed the rails for between 3 and 4 miles in both directions". Foster reduced that amount to two miles in his report to Washington, adding that the rails were twisted after they were pulled up. (Bent rails could be straightened and reused, but the South had no machinery that could restore a twisted rail.) Two miles of the telegraph line that followed the tracks were also said to have been destroyed, with "the poles cut down, wire removed, &c." Lewis asserted that they also burned all of the culverts for five miles along the tracks. [132]

Captain Hall was not the only officer who was angry with Lewis for causing so little damage to the railroad. Capt. Henry W. Wilson went over Lewis' head and filed a report that contradicted his glowing claims. At Warsaw, Wilson's "pioneers unloaded the implements for railroad destruction, and cut a number of levers". But, despite Wilson's repeated requests, Lewis detailed "only four gangs" to tear up the tracks. They succeeded, according to Wilson, in only "twisting less than 50 rails and turning over about as many". This meant only about "one-quarter of a mile of track" was wrecked. Wilson also claimed that "no ties were burned". [133]

Foster called upon Lewis for an explanation for Wilson's accusations, and asked why Lewis had not divided his men "one-half in gangs for work, and one-half for defense". Lewis protested that he had "no doubt as to the truth of my report of having destroyed 2 miles of track. There were at least twelve gangs at work." He went on to "respectfully protest against Mr. Wilson making his report other than through the commandant of the expedition". [134]

Anger simmered in North Carolina after the raid. Confederates grumbled that "the vandals have made their escape entirely" and that "our noble old state is overrun by a *few hundred thieving Yankees ...*" Raleigh newspapers blamed Major Jackson for letting the Yankees escape. A letter sent from a "Camp near Kinston" pointed the blame higher. Without naming Martin or Whiting, the writer complained of "a want of efficiency ... or ... of that untiring and unceasing activity, which marked the course of Gen. D. H. Hill while in command here." He claimed that a large force was sent from Kinston to intercept the Yankee cavalry, but was called back after they had gone seven miles. [135]

At any rate, the Confederates easily repaired the damage to the railroad. Wilson's claim that only one quarter of a mile of track was torn up was in line with a Confederate estimate. Col. Sewall S. Fremont, the superintendent of the Wilmington & Weldon, reported on July 6 that the track was already being repaired, and that it would be ready for train traffic the next morning. [136]

Despite the damage that was done to his factory, Froelich resumed operations after the raid. Froelich stayed on in Kenansville for some time after the war ended. His house became a memorable local landmark. In the late 1800s, it was distinguished by an unusual picket fence made of dozens of Froelich's old Confederate sabers, stuck into the ground.[137]

One Southern newspaper stated that 24 horses belonging to the 7th Confederate Cavalry were captured at Kenansville. Some of Lane's men filed reimbursement claims for their lost horses, with values running as high as $500. Captain Lane himself lost two horses in the raid. Lt. William F. Parker, also of Lane's company, wrote to an auditor at the Confederate treasury at Richmond in December 1863. The soldiers had filed claims, which were backed by General Whiting, but they still had heard nothing about reimbursement by that time. "Several of the men are poor", wrote Parker, "and unable to remount themselves without assistance."[138]

Chapter 4

"We May Have Some Fun Before a Great Many Days"

*The 12th New York Cavalry in New Bern
And the Preparations for Potter's Raid
June-July, 1863*

General Foster's new mounted regiment, the 12th New York Cavalry, was still very "green" in contrast with the 3rd New York Cavalry. Although the regiment's beginnings dated back to October 1862, mistakes and inefficiency marred its recruiting and organization. It was May 1863 before the first men left their training camp for North Carolina.[139]

William H. Graves suffered through the confusion of the early days of the regiment. Graves was in his hometown of Oswego, New York when he saw recruiting posters that called for volunteers to join an "independent command" of cavalry. The new outfit would have a "roving commission". Adding to the prospect of excitement was the promise of "$15 per month in gold". Graves signed up in November 1862.[140]

Because the recruits were informed that they must provide their own horses, Graves bought a "very fine" and very spirited black horse. The new horse was five years old, but had never been broken to harness or saddle, so Graves sent him to a horse trainer. After what was certainly a great outlay of money, orders came to the new soldiers that they were not going to be allowed to take their horses. Most men had to sell their mounts quickly, and lost considerable money in the process.[141]

Camp Washington, on Staten Island, where the 12th New York Cavalry trained.
Library of Congress

The men who signed up with Graves became Companies A and B of the new 12th New York Cavalry. Later in 1862, both companies were sent to New York City. To their simultaneous amazement and delight, Graves and his comrades were quartered in a restaurant on Grand Street in lower Manhattan for six weeks. The recruits were "allowed to order for our meals anything we might fancy." Graves remarked, "I never heard of any other troops being so fortunate." They stayed in these luxurious conditions for so long that finally, "the boys were getting very uneasy". After all, the "boys" had signed up to fight in the war instead of being left in New York City. And, the contradictory orders to buy their own horses, and then to get rid of them, still rankled.[142]

Weeks of easy living came to an end when the regiment was sent to Camp Washington, near New Dorp on Staten Island. At first, the men were glad of it, even though they "were deprived of waiters to supply our wants". Their joy was short-lived, and gave way to boredom and resentment as the regiment stagnated in camp. No training was accomplished, no arms were issued to the men, and supplies were scarce. It looked like the War Department had forgotten them. One trooper complained to his home town newspaper, "… we have been deceived and disappointed in every promise made. *We have not* received the whole of our bounty, nor the whole of our clothing; no arms; no horses; not much meat, and extremely nasty at that; no place to sleep half the time but the soft sides of bare boards with a suspicion of vermin, and today with the thermometer below zero and a *severe snow storm,* we are in barracks which we have built ourselves out of materials which we found (or stole), 125 feet long by 20 feet wide – one old stove which we found on the camp ground, and such fuel which we can pick up when the storm lulls." The writer said he would go on longer with his accusations, but his lament was ended by his "intensely cold fingers".[143]

Discipline crumbled as the morale of the recruits sank. Men smuggled in liquor, and officers had difficulty enforcing their orders. To stabilize the regiment, enough revolvers and sabers were scraped up to outfit Companies A and B as *de facto* military police. Loud disturbances and displays of insubordination and drunkenness were stamped out. Peace was restored, although the two armed "police" companies were unpopular with the rest of the regiment for some time. Graves was promoted to corporal, and for a few weeks was sent back to New York City with a detail "to guard the ferry landing" and watch for deserters.[144]

Despite the efforts of Graves' detachment, many men deserted from the regiment. In fact, so many of the men of the 12th New York Cavalry deserted that eight companies had to be disbanded and reorganized into only four new companies. Officers in the disbanded companies had the choice of returning to New York and finding enough men to refill their companies, or losing their commissions. Graves believed that "no doubt many" of the deserters "accepted bounties and joined other regiments."[145]

The arrival of spring found the regiment still languishing on Staten Island. Sgt. Gleason Wellington of Company A wrote, "I my self am getting tired of this kind of life and want to get away from here; if I am going to be a soldier I want to smell powder, I want to get into the field and not … moping away our time, doing nothing …" He would get his wish soon enough.[146]

On To New Bern

Companies A and B of the 12th left Staten Island for North Carolina at the end of May 1863. While they crowded aboard a transport ship, a paymaster arrived with six months' pay for the men. Most men of the Companies A and B were from Oswego or other nearby towns in Oswego County, New York. Lt. Alonzo Cooper, another man from Oswego who had many friends in the company, had worked his way up from private to officer's rank. Now, he was one of the officers in the disbanded companies and in danger of losing his commission. Cooper would miss Potter's Raid while trying to recruit more men back home.[147]

Capt. J. Ward Gasper of Company A was promoted to major in February. Capt. George H. Nichols of Company B was discharged in July and apparently did not take part in Potter's Raid. To replace these two company commanders, two brothers from Oswego County, Cyrus Church of Company A and Simeon Church of Company B, were both promoted from lieutenant to captain on the same day, April 23, 1863. Friends of the two brothers called them Cy and Sim. They looked so much alike that they were often mistaken for twins, although the 34-year-old Cyrus Church was two years younger than his brother.[148]

Many years later, an old acquaintance remembered the grocery store that the Church brothers ran in Oswego before the war. Like several of the other grocery stores in town, the Church's place always "had a game of faro or poker going continuously in the back room. ... Cy Church offered to let any man nail thirteen cards to the grocery counter and he would play 'bank' for any amount." Besides the store, Cyrus Church also owned a canal boat named the *H. Fayette*, which in 1856 set a record for the largest load of wheat that had ever been brought to Oswego by canal.[149]

One of "Cy" Church's men was William Cromack. Known as "Billy", Cromack was born in Leeds, England in 1838. He came to the Lake Ontario port of Oswego for the first time at the age of 15, as a sailor on a canal schooner. Two days after he married Ellen Amelia Calkins in Oswego on August 12, 1862, Cromack enlisted in Cyrus Church's company. In the army, the former sailor also worked as a servant for Captain Church.[150]

Company A had two men with the same name, designated on the rolls as "William Thompson 1st", aged 22, and "William Thompson 2nd", aged 45. The younger William Thompson enlisted at Fulton, New York on August 15, 1863. He was first enrolled as a wagoner, and was promoted to corporal before being reduced to the ranks on May 20, 1863. "William Thompson 2nd" enlisted two days earlier, also at Fulton. It is not certain if the two William Thompsons were related. The elder William Thompson appears on the Oswego County Census of 1860, with his family, including a 22-year-old farm laborer named William J. Thompson. However, a Civil War pension document for the elder Thompson makes no mention of a son serving in the 12th New York Cavalry. And, just to add to the confusion, the 12th New York Cavalry had two more men who were also named William Thompson, who served in different companies. Odder still, on Potter's Raid, the William Thompsons of Company A would fight a skirmish with Confederate forces including a Georgia company commanded by ... Capt. William A. Thompson![151]

Free of the aggravations of the desolate camp on Staten Island, the New Yorkers of the 12th were at last really part of the war. They struggled to adapt to life in exotic but dangerous Dixie. Sent to a spot about six miles outside of New Bern, according to Graves, they set up "a fine camp and put up shelter for the horses which we expected very soon."[152]

Replacing a Deserter

The commissions of several of the officers of the regiment were hanging on their ability to recruit enough men to fill up their companies. Helping these officers attain their goal was a recruiting agent named Daniel Mulligan. Mulligan arrived in Fort Covington, New York, a town that was only a short hop from the Canadian border, in the spring of 1863. It took him only two days to persuade fourteen men from the town to sign up. The nation was weary of the war, and recruiting had fallen off drastically since the early outburst of patriotism in 1861. Mulligan was lucky to find that Fort Covington contained "a lot of youngsters whose parents had succeeded in keeping them at home during the first enlistments, but whose ardor burst all bounds."[153]

While his recruits waited for a stagecoach, Mulligan gave them a stirring speech. The boys would "ride to eternal fame" in the "strange and beautiful sunny south". He assured them that a glorious victory was only six months away, and then they "would ride home again through lines of cheering countrymen with chevrons on their shoulders and medals on their breasts." Mulligan told them that he would be joining them in the ranks of Company F of the 12th New York Cavalry just as soon as he finished up some government business. Then, right after the stage left town with the recruits, Mulligan picked up his baggage at the hotel. He had already been paid $8 apiece for signing up the new recruits. With the money in hand, he skipped over the border into Canada.[154]

Among Mulligan's recruits was 20-year-old William "Bill" Brown. When the fourteen men from Fort Covington arrived at the 12th New York Cavalry camp in Staten Island, an army surgeon refused to allow him into the service. Brown had a scar on his leg, which the surgeon was sure would burst open during active service.[155]

The rejected recruit was waiting for arrangements to send him home when orders came for Company F to move out for North Carolina. Capt. John W. Flinn called the roll and found that Private Daniel Mulligan was not present. When the men told him that Mulligan had slipped into Canada, he exploded. Flinn "damned his luck, his subordinate officers, and recruiting system, and the world in general. But principally, he damned Mulligan". The last thing that Flinn needed was another deserter on his company's record, especially one who apparently had never even bothered to show up in camp.[156]

Bill Brown, a.k.a. Daniel Mulligan

After Flinn calmed down, Brown saw his chance and offered a solution. He would take Mulligan's place. Captain Flinn agreed and sent Brown to get a uniform. The captain told Brown that he would call the roll again, and that he would answer it as Mulligan. The surgeon would pose no problem, because the real Mulligan had already passed his medical examination. And so it was that Brown rode off to war under the name of the deserter, Daniel Mulligan.[157]

A cabin used by the 12th New York Cavalry at Camp Palmer, outside New Bern.
U.S. Army Military History Institute

Their Horses Arrive at Last

At last, the happy news arrived that a boat load of horses had arrived in New Bern for the regiment. The officers were allowed first choice of the horses, and then the men were allowed to make their selections. Naturally, "there was considerable hustling to do this", said William Graves. While his comrades were picking "the fastest and best looking horses they could find", Graves had his eye on what looked like an unprepossessing nag, an animal that looked "poor and seemed to be all run down". His friends teased him, "the crows have got a mortgage on your horse sure…" Looking closely at his choice, Graves felt that this horse's "eyes were bright and his limbs were clean, and … very good care would make him as fine a horse as would be found in the regiment." [158]

Hard work with a curry comb and brush, and a steady diet of "good hay and oats" turned Graves' worn-down horse into a splendid cavalry mount. The only trouble was his horse's unusually keen intelligence. Graves found that his horse "learned the bugle calls so that he knew them as well as I did." When "charge" was sounded during their training exercises, "I could no more hold him than I could hold a lion", and Graves found himself leading the charge. The rider worried that in real combat, "he might take me into the business a little sooner than … was quite necessary." [159]

Graves was very fond of his new horse by the time they were sent out on a training exercise outside of New Bern. They charged across a stretch of ground where a ditch lurked under the cover of some thick weeds and brush. His horse stumbled when they crashed into the four-foot-deep ditch, and Graves saw he was bleeding freely from a sharp cut in his mouth. Graves feared that his horse might bleed to death. The corporal and the regimental veterinarian stayed up all night trying to stop the flow of blood from the horse's mouth. By the next morning, they had stopped the bleeding. His horse looked as bad, or even worse, than he had on the first time Graves saw him. But, in a few weeks, "my horse was looking better than ever ... and he had life enough to suit me or any one else."[160]

Sgt. John Miller, who also served with Graves in Company A, was the 19-year-old son of an Oswego alderman. Miller, like Graves, also ended up with a high-spirited horse that was hard to control.[161]

In the same company as Graves and Miller was Private William Davies, a 35 year old coach maker from Oswego. Davies (the soldier who had written so admiringly of the 3rd New York Cavalry), explained his first experiences of picket duty outside New Bern in a letter to his wife. "I can tell you it is not very pleasant to be too ours on a horse and Cant See yor nose on yor face in the night and lisen and Don't know but a Reb is Crawling up in the Bushes to you owr Orders to Shoot the first man that Comes to wards us we Sit on the horse with Cock Revolvers and keep verry Still ..."[162]

Davies made light of the dangers and trials of his new life in the army when he told his wife, "i have Cut Off my hair Clost to my head and Shave Clean i think it is more ... [comfortable?] here if i was home you Could not get hold of My hair pull it for going off to war and Leaving [you] and the Childern's ..."[163]

Sergeant Wellington, writing home on June 28, assured his mother that "Jonny" Miller and Billy Cromack were "quite well". Some of the other men were sick with dysentery or fever. The weather was hot, and their drinking water was "not the best".[164]

The hot weather in June seemed to affect the regiment's horses as well. "We have lost some horses since we came here", wrote Davies. "The men seem to stand it better than the northern horses here."[165]

But, Wellington felt like he was in the war at last. He couldn't complain about his own accommodations: "I am living very well. I mess with the Commissary Sergeant and so have the best ..." Wellington had also hired a black servant to cook for him. By mid-July, he had "a splendid French pony, swift as a fox". Riding through the country on foraging jaunts, he found "plenty of apples, peaches (not quite ripe), figs, watermelons, and ... potatoes.[166]

William Graves was proud of his company. Years later, he recalled that at their camp in New Bern, "each man's horse was always hitched in front of his tent; his arms, carbine, sabre, and revolver were always placed in his tent just where he could get them at once the darkest night there should be. Our saddles were always directly behind our horses."[167]

Despite Graves' pride in his unit, the long, wasted winter months at Staten Island meant that the 12th New York Cavalry had far to go to match the 3rd New York Cavalry's efficiency. An inspection of Companies A, B, and F of the

12th for July and August 1863 rated each company "not good" for discipline, training, and military appearance. Their arms, accoutrements, and clothing were, at least, rated "good". Their time for training was fast running out, as the date for Foster's planned raids on the Wilmington & Weldon Railroad drew near.[168]

Company A of the 12th New York Cavalry got its first close-up look at the war during the raid on July 5. They were ordered from camp as an escort for General Edward E. Potter, and they rode 35 miles into the interior, as far as Trenton. Their part of the expedition was quiet, and they returned to New Bern on July 6.[169]

Chapter 5

"A Circuit of 200 Miles"
Foster Prepares to Launch Potter's Raid
Early-mid July 1863

The damage done to the Wilmington & Weldon Railroad at Warsaw on July 5 was repaired so quickly that the whole four-day expedition was really little more than a nuisance to the Confederates. Just the same, Lewis's successful return encouraged a much a more ambitious raid. Foster planned that his next expedition into Rebel territory would "... traverse a circuit of 200 miles, and will, I hope, do much damage."[170]

Foster's next raid would strike a much sharper blow against the Confederacy. This time, the major objectives were Tarboro and Rocky Mount, where the cavalry could destroy considerable amounts of Confederate supplies, and do much more damage to the Wilmington & Weldon Railroad.

Tarboro was an important regional river port and railroad town. Confederate Army warehouses were filled with food and supplies. Although it was a small town, Tarboro was the home of a number of wealthy and influential North Carolinians, notably former governor Henry T. Clark.

Tarboro's most important target, though, was in a shipyard across the river from the town. There, navy carpenters labored on the hull of an ironclad gunboat that was similar to the famous C.S.S. *Virginia* (also called the *Merrimac*). Newspaper reports in the North labeled the vessel as "quite a formidable affair – some two hundred feet in length." [171]

The Union Navy was very worried about the armored gunboat at Tarboro, as well as another that was under construction on the Roanoke River near Edwards' Ferry in Halifax County. On November 9, 1862, a small Union naval expedition that steamed up the Tar River hoped to burn the gunboat. Because of low water, they could get no further than Greenville. (See page 225 for a brief account of this raid.) General Foster had even considered swinging toward Tarboro to burn the gunboat after cutting the Wilmington & Weldon at Goldsboro in his December 1862 expedition.[172]

Rocky Mount was the location of the largest cotton mill in North Carolina, and of a long bridge that carried the Wilmington & Weldon Railroad over the Tar River. The destruction of this bridge would shake the South's overburdened rail system. On the way to Tarboro and Rocky Mount, they would also hit the Tar River town of Greenville, and numerous farms and plantations in the region that supplied the South with food and cotton.

Foster used the Warsaw Raid as a model for planning this new, more extensive expedition. Although it is always risky to divide one's forces while in enemy territory, Lewis had decided to detach Jacobs' battalion to make a quick strike on Kenansville before they moved on to Warsaw. Lewis' move had led to no harm, and even bagged a few prisoners. This time, Foster planned to divide his cavalry force in two, and send the segments to strike Rocky Mount and Tarboro simultaneously before reuniting to fight their way back to New Bern.

The heavy rains that oppressed the spirits of the people of Tarboro during early and mid-July also protected them from Foster's cavalry for several days. The skies evidently cleared in the middle of July, because on July 16, Foster set a date to send out the cavalry again. Although the streams they had to cross might still be running high, the sandy roads of the upland areas would dry quickly. And, any lingering moisture would help damp down the telltale clouds of dust that would spread warning of approaching cavalry raiders. The new moon rose on July 15. With the moon in its first quarter, it would be of minimal help in navigating at night during this raid – or helping the Confederates find them in the dark.[173]

The First Stage of Potter's Raid

General Foster's plans for the raid opened with sending a brigade of infantry from New Bern one day ahead of the cavalry. The foot soldiers would "clear the road" for the cavalry. Later, they would draw Confederate attention away from Potter's expedition until the cavalry had a good start. The infantry would march as far as Swift Creek Village (modern-day Vanceboro, in Craven County), which was about 17 miles distant from New Bern.

To secure Swift Creek Village, Foster sent the brigade of Col. James Jourdan, which consisted of the 25th and 27th Massachusetts, and the 158th New

York. Jourdan, who was born in Ireland, entered the Union Army as a major on May 23, 1861. He rose to the rank of colonel in the 158th New York on September 5, 1862. Although later given command of a brigade, Jourdan was not promoted to brigadier general until 1864.[174]

Jourdan's Brigade started across the Neuse River about 2 p.m. on Friday, July 17. The 27th Massachusetts and a two-gun section of Angel's Battery (Battery K, 3rd New York Artillery) crossed the Neuse on the steamer *Bombshell*. Before the war, the 90-foot long *Bombshell* was an Erie Canal boat. The 25th Massachusetts traveled aboard a larger steamer, the 209-foot-long *Port Royal*. They landed at Fort Anderson, a Union post on the north bank of the Neuse that was within sight of New Bern. Jourdan's men camped that night "in a swamp" near the fort.[175]

The infantrymen were on the march again at sunrise. Newton Wallace recorded in his diary that his outfit marched until 11, captured a small picket post, and moved on until they reached Swift Creek Village. On the way, Jourdan divided his force. He sent the 158th New York and the 25th Massachusetts to approach Swift Creek Village from different directions, to close off escape routes for any Confederate soldiers who were trapped there. Lieutenant-Colonel McNary, who commanded the 158th New York now that Jourdan was handling the brigade, arrested seven local citizens. McNary apparently wanted the locals as hostages.[176]

Col. James Jourdan, USA
Library of Congress

Jourdan then pushed on to the village with the 27th Massachusetts. Private Newton Wallace of the 27th Massachusetts wrote that when they got to Swift Creek, their advance troops "received a volley from a force of the enemy, who were stationed on the other side of Swift Creek, near the ruins of the burnt bridge. Our boys returned the fire with interest ..." Jourdan's Brigade "entered the village on the double quick", as the small Confederate force scattered. [177]

Swift Creek Village

At Swift Creek Village, a drawbridge crossed the creek, which permitted the passage of small craft that carried passengers, lumber, and barrels of naval stores down the creek toward the Neuse. Confederate troops burned the bridge early in April 1863, before the approach of a Union force under Brig. Gen. Francis Barreto Spinola, during his unsuccessful attempt to relieve Washington from a Confederate siege. The bridge had not been repaired by the time the Massachusetts troops occupied the village.

In the months after the fall of New Bern, Union cavalry patrols often rode through Swift Creek Village. A reporter for a New York paper, who accompanied an earlier Union expedition to the area, wrote, "Swift Creek is a poor, little, straggling village, with its few dwellings and brace of stores, its dilapidated fences, [and its] weedy lawns ..." The creek itself, he wrote, "is deep — some say more than 40 feet deep — and its dark waters are made darker yet by the shade of the high steep banks, and the dense overhanging woods..." A New York soldier wrote that "the village was entirely surrounded by breast-works and rifle pits ..." [178]

The 25th Massachusetts captured Private Furnifold Powell of Company A, Whitford's Battalion. Powell was turned over to the provost-marshal. For some reason, Powell was not quickly exchanged (as were most of the Confederate enlisted men who were captured later during Potter's Raid). He was sent to the prison at Point Lookout, Maryland, and was later was transferred to Elmira, New York prison. Powell was not released until February 1865. [179]

After securing the village, Jourdan sent two companies of the 158th New York across Swift Creek to see if they could bring in some more prisoners. They did not catch any soldiers, but Jourdan reported, "We seized five head of cattle and one ox-cart, the property of a rebel; also one double-barreled shotgun, loaded with large size buckshot, and one brace of old flint-lock pistols. We found abandoned on the road one horse and cart, and in the cart one Colt's revolver (navy size)." (The "Navy Colt" was the .36 caliber Colt revolver, so-called because the original models had an engraving of a naval battle on the cylinder. The "Army Colt" was the .45 caliber gun. Cavalrymen usually carried the lighter, .36 caliber model.) Colonel Jourdan observed that had he been assigned some cavalry, they would have captured several more Confederate soldiers. [180]

Potter's Raid   51

Chapter 6

"The Old Bugle Sounded 'To Horse'"
The Cavalry Leaves New Bern
Thursday, July 16 - Saturday, July 18, 1863

Perhaps Foster was disappointed with Lewis' performance on the previous raid, because so little damage was done to the tracks at Warsaw. To command the next raid, General Foster turned to his trusted chief of staff, Brig. Gen. Edward E. Potter. Potter had proven himself to Foster by repulsing the attack on Washington during the previous September, and as an aide during the Goldsboro Expedition in December. Also, Potter was well acquainted with the Unionist North Carolina soldiers from his old regiment, who would be needed as guides for the raid.

Potter also took three staff officers. Capt. George Gouraud was plucked from the 3rd New York Cavalry to serve as Potter's *aide de camp*. Indiana-born Lt. Jasper Myers, of the U. S. Army Ordnance Corps, graduated from West Point just the year before the raid. [181]

Lt. Francis U. Farquahar accompanied Potter as a topographic engineer. Farquahar graduated from West Point in 1861; he was second in the same class in which a cadet named George Armstrong Custer graduated last. Farquahar's drawings of fortifications and his battle maps are valuable records of North Carolina history today, although any maps that he may have made of Potter's Raid have not been located. There is an editor's note in the *"Official Records"*

Potter's force assembled in front of Fort Totten on July 18 to begin the expedition.
U.S. Army Military History Institute

about a sketch map Farquhar made during an expedition from New Bern to Trenton and Swansborough in March 1863: "omitted as unimportant".[182]

On July 16, orders went out to the cavalry officers in New Bern to prepare their men for another raid. Company A of the 12th New York Cavalry officially learned of the raid with this order:

Lt. Francis U. Farquhar, USA
U.S. Army Military History Institute

*Special Order No. 5 from HQ
12th New York Cavalry
July 16, 1863*

Capt. Cyrus S. Church of Co. A will comply with the enclosed circular promptly – Holding the cooked rations until he receives orders to move – He will take the number of men named in the list by Major Clarkson Yesterday, and as many men as you can mount on a war footing – He will draw in his pickets in the morning, July 17, and have your entire Command get themselves in perfect order.

*By command of
Lt. Col. P. G. Vought*[183]

Although the soldiers knew that a raid was in the works, they didn't know where they were going. Sgt. Gleason Wellington, of Cyrus Church's company, wrote home that, " ... we are expecting marching orders every hour to go off on a rade ... " He said that orders were issued two days before for "us to get redy with fifty men and six days rations to march at any time and I think we will get our orders tonight they seldom get ready unless they go in this department; our destination I have not yet learned but I don't think we will be gone more than six days and we may not that; there are but few reb[s] in this state ..." [184]

Captain Rowland M. Hall of Company E, 3rd New York Cavalry, wrote to his father on July 17, "Tomorrow we sail on board transports, destination unknown ..." He added, "I am a little cheered by the prospect of seeing something new ..."[185]

For this new raid, Foster gave Potter eighteen companies of cavalry – which were just about all of the Union horsemen in North Carolina. All twelve companies of the veteran 3rd New York Cavalry would go. Maj. Floyd Clarkson led three companies of the 12th New York Cavalry, which was still being transferred to North Carolina. The two companies of the 23rd New York Cavalry, and the mounted infantrymen of Company L of the 1st North Carolina Volunteers, under Lt. George W. Graham, rounded out the cavalry. The 3rd New York Cavalry was divided into two battalions commanded by Majors George W. Cole and Ferris Jacobs, Jr.; the remaining companies formed a battalion under Major Clarkson.[186]

Foster, Potter, and the other Union officers made no mention of a detachment of the 1st North Carolina Colored Volunteers who accompanied them on this raid. However, "Special Orders No. 200" in the regimental order book of the 1st North Carolina Colored Troops, dated July 15, records an order sent to Brig. Gen. Edward A. Wild, commander of the all-black infantry brigade that was being formed in North Carolina. The order, sent by General Foster, required Wild to "detail Forty four (44) enlisted men" to report to Captain Wilson Civil Engineer." At least one Northern newspaper wrote that this expedition included "Captain Wilson, of the Pioneer Corps, with some fifty colored soldiers armed with axes, spades, and irons, prepared for destroying railroad track." Several Southern witnesses also mention black troops with Potter.[187]

All three of Potter's battalion commanders were seasoned officers. Maj. Floyd Clarkson was born into a prominent family of New York City in 1831. His great-grandfather William Floyd was a signer of the Declaration of Independence. Clarkson was a merchant in the city when the Civil War broke out. His military experience began when he joined the 7th New York Militia in 1856. He enlisted in the 6th New York Cavalry with the first wave of men who responded to Lincoln's call for troops in April, 1861, after the attack on Fort Sumter. He became a major of the 12th New York Cavalry in April, 1863. Sergeant Wellington approved of Clarkson, saying of the major, "... he is a well-drilled and very gentlemanly man. He is kind and agreeable and always reddy (sic) to give any advice we shall ask of him on the whole he is one of the best of officers and we like him very much."[188]

George W. Cole was promoted from captain to major on December 31, 1862, after his service on Foster's Goldsboro Expedition. Born in Lodi, New

York in 1828, Cole was trained as a physician, but was in business as a lumber dealer when the war started. Cole's older brother Cornelius was a Republican congressman from California. The major's reputation inspired a reporter to claim that Potter's "success was doubly sure" because "he is accompanied by Major Cole, the cavalry hero of this department …"[189]

Maj. Ferris Jacobs, Jr., a native of Delhi, New York, was 27 years old. He graduated from Williams College in Williamstown, Massachusetts, in 1856. His graduating class included his friend, future US president James A. Garfield. After graduation, Jacobs practiced law until he joined the Union Army. He was captain of Company E of the regiment until his promotion to major on June 29, 1863. Jacobs' competent handing of his battalion's descent upon Kenansville gave him a chance for a more important independent role during Potter's Raid.[190]

Potter's Artillery

Four mountain howitzers similar to these went with Potter.

The artillery assigned for the expedition was a two-gun section of the 3rd New York Cavalry's "Flying Battery", under Lt. James Allis, and another two guns from Battery H of the 3rd New York Light Artillery, under Lt. John D. Clark.[191]

The "Flying Battery" of the 3rd New York Cavalry was a separate company of the regiment. It was created by taking two or three men out of each of the regiment's original twelve companies. "Flying artillery", batteries of light guns pulled by swift horses to wherever they were needed on the battlefield, was a highly successful innovation that the US Army used to great advantage during the Mexican War. Each man had a horse to ride, in contrast to other batteries in which the men walked or rode on the caissons.[192]

Lieutenant Allis was one of the publishers of *The New Era*, a Unionist journal in occupied Washington, North Carolina in the summer of 1862. Allis found a newspaper office that had been abandoned by its secessionist owner. With his partner Private Allen W. Hahn, Allis set up *The New Era* using the old newspaper's press and type. The exploits of the 3rd New York Cavalry naturally filled many of its columns.[193]

The 3rd New York Artillery did not serve together as a single unit. In July 1863, the various batteries (as the companies of an artillery regiment were called) were scattered across eastern North Carolina, coastal South Carolina, and Virginia. Newspaper advertisements seeking recruits for the regiment offered some temptations in the summer of 1863. New recruits were offered a Federal enlistment bounty of $102, plus a state bounty of $75. The ads also promised an ideal life for a soldier: "no picket duty, no long marches on foot with a knapsack on your back. Do not wait to be drafted, and lose your bounty."[194]

All four of Potter's guns were 12-pounder mountain howitzers. Mountain howitzers were small guns that were designed to be taken apart and carried by pack animals, usually mules. The shiny brass smoothbore barrel, just over three feet long, was light enough for one mule to carry. A second pack animal carried the wheels and carriage, and a third hauled two ammunition chests. For emergency repairs to the guns, there were small portable forges that could be carried on another mule.[195]

A mountain howitzer weighed just over 500 pounds. This was about a quarter of the weight of a standard Civil War 12-pounder gun, which required four horses to pull it. Despite their small size, these little mountain guns fired the same standard ammunition as the larger 12-pounder field pieces. Mountain howitzers were originally developed for the US Army for use in the rugged terrain of the western frontier. But, because pack mules could also maneuver through the streams and swamps of eastern North Carolina, mountain howitzers turned out to be very useful there as well. In fact, Potter would find out that the Confederates also used the mountain howitzer in eastern North Carolina.[196]

The expedition's medical contingent included Surgeon William H. Palmer of the 3rd New York Cavalry. At least one other doctor, Asst. Surgeon Albert Potter of the 5th Rhode Island Artillery, accompanied Palmer. With the doctors were several ambulances.[197]

Among the swarms of last-minute details, Potter's officers had to find boats to get the men and horses across the Neuse River. Evidently this took longer than expected. Sgt. Herbert A. Cooley of the 3rd New York Cavalry wrote that on "... Friday [July 17] the old bugle sounded 'To Horse' and in due time you might have found us ready for a march with six days' rations going to some cause unknown to us. We were delayed until the next morning when bright and early we found ourselves in New Bern waiting for the flatboats to ferry us across the river." Perhaps the delay was caused by tying up the available river transports to get Jourdan's infantry brigade across the river first, so they could establish a base at Swift Creek Village.[198]

One cavalryman wrote that the troopers were issued "six days' cooked rations—three of them on our saddles, and the other three carried upon pack horses and mules fitted for the purpose." At 6 am on Saturday, July 18, they "formed in battalion line, in front of Fort Totten" (a major stronghold of the New Bern fortifications) before marching to board their boats. "The sun was shining hot", continued the soldier, "but before we were all embarked across the river … which took the whole forenoon, we got a good, thorough sprinkling, which wet to the hide." Another trooper noted that each man left New Bern with "twelve quarts of oats for his horse". [199]

Sergeant Wellington spent a very uncomfortable voyage aboard the flatboat that carried him across the Neuse River on Saturday, July 18. His comrades loaded their horses onto the flats at six a.m., but it was four hours later when they stepped off onto the opposite bank. Wellington had been afflicted with an unspecified malady for some time before the raid. He had been dosing himself with bottles of Harlem Oil, a patent medicine used for kidney, liver, and bladder trouble. The concoction apparently wasn't working. He was terribly sick before the flatboat "had got halfway acrost" the river. But, he told Capt. Cyrus Church that he would "stick it out as long as I could walk". [200]

Potter's men landed near Fort Anderson, a Union outpost on the north bank of the Neuse across from New Bern. By 11:30, they were ready to ride and "moved forward in splendid order" toward Swift Creek Village. They reached that place about six p.m., and joined the infantry brigade of Col. James Jourdan, which had been waiting for them for several hours. The cavalry found a handful of Confederate soldiers who were at a small outpost near the creek, possibly keeping an eye on Jourdan's Brigade. The Rebels fired a few shots at them before they escaped across the creek in small boats. The bluecoats posted guards, and bedded down for the night inside some abandoned breastworks.[201]

Night fell, and it became, according to a correspondent to a New York newspaper, "so dark that all the fiends of the Southern Confederacy could not have found us, even if they had tried." Potter's men built numerous fires while "each man made his own coffee" and ate their rations "with a relish." At last, each trooper stretched on the ground "and got a few hours of sleep which was sweet to be remembered."[202]

Chapter 7

"A Quiet Sabbath"
The Ride to Greenville and Sparta
Sunday, July 19, 1863

Before dawn on Sunday, July 19, Potter's men "were up, horses saddled and fed, as well as ourselves, and all ready for a start." When they rode out from their camp at Swift Creek Village, their destination was "a mistery to all." It soon was common knowledge that they were heading for Greenville, which was about 25 miles to the north.[203]

A Federal soldier who was on the raid later wrote that they "arrested every man we met and put him in the rear, so that the Rebels would not learn of our coming." About 10 a.m., the cavalry arrested a North Carolina state official named George Greene. A resident of New Bern before the war, Greene served as a delegate to the special convention of 1861, which officially pulled North Carolina out of the Union. Greene left Union-occupied New Bern, and was appointed as an agent in charge of distributing state relief funds to the needy families of North Carolina soldiers. When Potter's men captured Greene, he was carrying $6300 worth of North Carolina treasury notes that were intended for Craven County families. Besides taking the state relief funds, Potter's men also "*relieved* him of his horse, bridle and saddle, and even of his pocket knife."[204]

Greene's story later appeared in North Carolina newspapers. He overestimated Potter's strength, putting his force at 1500 men, which was almost twice what it really was. But, he correctly named the 3rd and 12th New York Cavalry, and reported the fact that Potter had "4 pieces of field artillery".[205]

Greene also said that the Union expedition included "50 mounted negroes", which were the pioneer troops commanded by Capt. Henry W. Wilson.[206]

The Surprise at "Four Corners"

Federal military and newspaper reports were vague about the exact route that they took to Greenville. Southern sources place them at Black Jack Church, on what was then known as the Lower New Bern Road, about 8 a.m. From there, Potter could have followed the Lower New Bern to its intersection with the Greenville-Washington Road, or River Road (today's NC 33), near present-day Simpson, about seven miles from Greenville. On the other hand, Pitt County historian John G. Duncan said they rode into Greenville on the old County Home Road (County Road 1725), which led to the Upper New Bern Road, which is today's Highway 43 and Charles Boulevard. Potter could have moved west from Black Jack on other local roads to reach the Upper New Bern Road.[207]

A trooper of the 3rd New York Cavalry in 1863.
U.S. Army Military History Institute

Along Potter's route through Pitt County was a Confederate picket station at a place that the Federals called "Four Corners" or "The Chapel". The exact location of this post is uncertain, but some evidence points to it being the Black Jack Church. The community of Black Jack reportedly got its name around 1831 when the Free Will Baptist church was being built there. The building site was surrounded by blackjack oak trees. A man working on the roof threw a hatchet that plunked squarely into one of the oaks. Bystanders accepted the hatchet thrower's suggestion that they name the place Black Jack. During the Civil War, the Black Jack Church's position on the Lower New Bern Road, and its location near the division between the Union-controlled area around Washington and the Confederate-held region of Pitt County meant that Confederate soldiers camped there regularly. Often, they were soldiers of Whitford's command. At last on March 26, 1864, a Federal raiding party from Washington surprised the troops at Black Jack and burned the church. (See page 228, "More Union Raids on Pitt County").[208]

On the day of Potter's approach, part of Company E of Whitford's Battalion, under Capt. Charles A. White, manned the "Four Corners" picket station. Most of White's men were from Pitt County, and they had been in the army for only a few weeks or months. Company G of the 3rd New York Cavalry, apparently the same company that captured George Greene, was in the advance of the expedition and charged the picket post.[209]

The New York *Herald* described the scene as Potter surprised the small outpost at "the Chapel": "On the approach of our men, the Rebels stood gaping with wonder, apparently not knowing whether we were friends or enemies, but a peremptory demand to 'surrender' brought them to their senses, and off they attempted to scamper. About fifteen were captured, and one who was making hasty tracks through the woods, refusing to obey the command to halt and surrender, was brought down by one of our carbineers, with a bullet through his thigh". One of Potter's men was probably referring to this incident when he later wrote, "we dashed down upon a Rebel camp, captured every man there, dumped their ammunition into a well, [and] cut their tents to pieces with our sabers ..."[210]

The prisoners taken at the picket post were paroled; that is, they were released upon giving their word that they would not bear arms again until they were officially exchanged. Presumably, Potter did not want to burden himself with prisoners at this early stage of the raid. The practice of granting parole to prisoners of war was common until later in the war. The Union cavalry then rode toward Greenville, leaving Captain White's men among the smoldering ruins of their tents and captured equipment. The available records of Whitford's Battalion do not include the name of the man who was wounded, nor indeed, of the fifteen men who were paroled.[211]

Pitt County historian Henry King reported that "there were other Confederates of the Sixty-seventh [Whitford's Battalion later became the 67th North Carolina Regiment] in Black Jack vicinity when those of Captain White's Company were captured, but they left in a hurry. It was said that Colonel Whitford ordered a retreat to Contentnea bridge, and that a regular, go-as-you-please race ensued, every man looking out for self. It is not known what became of some of them, as many never reached the bridge ...".[212]

The rest of the ride to Greenville was apparently not worthy of comment to the Union soldiers. George Greene, whom Potter had not yet released, noted only that "the Yankees plundered the country fore and aft as they went."[213]

The "Pretty Village of Greenville" in 1863

Around 2 p.m., Potter rode into sight of what he called "the pretty village" of Greenville. Out of Pitt County's 1860 population of 16,440, 828 people lived in Greenville: 304 whites, 14 free blacks, and 510 slaves. Greenville nestled atop a sandy hill overlooking the Tar River, more or less confined to what is considered the downtown area today. Creeks surrounded most of the high ground upon which the town was built. The Pitt County Court House, in the center of town, was a large, unfinished brick building. In 1858, the previous courthouse, and most of Pitt County's records, was burned down by an arsonist who was trying to destroy a will.[214]

There are no known photographs of Greenville from the Civil War years, but pictures from the following decades show an attractive town of wooden homes with yards comfortably shaded by large trees. Baptist, Methodist, and Episcopal churches; a handful of stores, several blocks of houses and yards, and, it seems, a number of saloons, made up the town. The business district was then just a short section of Evans Street and the surrounding side streets.[215]

Several months after Potter raided Greenville, a Confederate soldier who passed through town wrote, "the appearance of this place…has been greatly defaced and disfigured by desolating war. Upon her once beautiful lawns which are now bereft of all their loveliness, where the merry throngs of pleasure were wont to repair at eventide, solitude reigns triumphant. There are many of its loveliest mansions which are now disinhabited that are being greatly dismantled and going fast to decay."[216]

Greenville was strategically important to the Confederates because its bridge was one of the few convenient places to cross the Tar River. The only bridge downstream from Greenville, at Washington, was in Federal hands. Between Greenville and Tarboro were only two more bridges, at Falkland and Sparta. Greenville was not reached by a railroad until 1890, but it was the terminus of the Greenville and Raleigh Plank Road, chartered in 1850. Dickenson Avenue was the beginning of the Plank Road, and it followed the later path of old US 264 as far as Wilson, where the planks stopped.[217]

Greenville's Previous Invasion Scares

Twice before, Greenville was shaken by reports of Union invaders. One night in 1862, Confederate pickets awoke the town with alarming news. A large force of Yankees was approaching through a field at the edge of town. The officer in command allegedly panicked and ordered his soldiers to retreat upriver to Falkland. A handful of cavalrymen remained behind, determined to slow the enemy advance with a volley or two from their double-barrel shotguns. As they crept into the night to get a closer look at the invaders, they saw that the menacing "Yankees" were just a herd of cattle grazing in a field.[218]

The second alarm was real. A Union naval expedition from Washington captured Greenville for a couple of hours on November 9, 1862. (The naval raid and Potter's Raid both happened in Greenville on a Sunday.) After holding the town for a couple of hours, the Federals seized ten hostages, some horses, mules, and supplies, and then headed back downriver. (See page 225 for more details on this raid.)

The naval raid was a wake-up call to the Confederate authorities about the vulnerability of Greenville. In the spring of 1863, an extensive ring of earthworks was dug to surround the town. Confederate army engineer Capt. Thaddeus Coleman of Asheville designed the works, which were described as a series of "rifle pits and breastworks".[219]

Capt. Thaddeus Coleman, CSA

Coleman later helped survey and build railroads in western North Carolina before his death in 1895. In 1907, his daughter Sarah married the famous North Carolina writer William Sidney Porter, better known as O. Henry.[220]

General Martin was unhappy with Coleman's defenses, but he conceded that they were the best that he could have done, given the terrain that he had to work with. "26 free negroes" were at work on the Greenville entrenchments on June 16. The 50th North Carolina Regiment labored on the works as well, until they were ordered from Greenville to a new camp near Kinston on July 3.[221]

"I Hope the Yanks Don't Get This ..."

After Coleman's project, Greenville was "completely surrounded by a strong line of entrenchments" when Potter rode in. The Yankee commander found, however, that "there were no troops, excepting a few convalescents and sick in hospital." The Confederate hospital at Greenville was a small post hospital, and was not documented as well as the larger army hospitals at Tarboro and Wilson. One of the raiders later remembered that they had expected to capture a Confederate regiment that was stationed at Greenville. Perhaps they depended on outdated intelligence reports, and were unaware that the 50th North Carolina had been transferred out of Greenville.[222]

Sgt. Harold A. Cooley of the 3rd New York Cavalry was impressed with Greenville. He wrote to his father, rather exaggerating the town's size, "the breastworks that surround this place are worthy of passing notice. They were outside of the city on a high hill and commanded its approach for miles in every direction. They encircled the town and were nearly five miles in length, and were capable of holding fifty thousand men with cannon enough to take the whole of the Union Army with. This village contained eight thousand inhabitants and by the way it looks more like a city than any other with the exceptions of Tarboro, Kenansville, and one or two other little places than I have seen in the so called Southern Confederacy."[223]

Some of the raiders seized the post office and the courthouse, looking for official orders, newspapers, soldiers' letters, or any other written material that might give information on Southern troop movements. Not all of the papers seized were of military importance. One Union soldier wrote that "we captured a lot of love letters from the post office" in Greenville. Among the captured letters was one that was enclosed in its envelope with a braid of dark hair. "The letter," said the Yankee officer who still had it over 30 years later, "was written by a Greenville girl to her lover, who was fighting with Lee far up to the north. The girl had written: 'I hope the Yanks don't get this braid, as they did that last one.'" [224]

Another Union soldier found that "Greenville is a very nice looking and pleasantly situated little village. Its chief and about the only productions are some very pretty ladies, who were much admired by us all ... but secession was stamped on every feature of the birds, especially when we demanded the keys to the smokehouses and took out the many nice hams, honey, &c. ..."[225]

Other cavalrymen broke into the county jail (which was behind the courthouse) and released, according to the *New York Times*, "25 negroes ... who had been imprisoned in attempting to get inside our lines, in order to join the colored regiment at Newbern". The 25 men would "soon be clad in the military blue of our army." One cavalryman wrote that some of the men had been imprisoned for the "crime of aiding some slaves to obtain their liberty and freedom." [226]

Like the prisoners taken at "the Chapel", the few Confederates captured at Greenville were paroled. No one seems to have recorded their names. One of the captured officers was said to have been a "Rebel paymaster, with about $10,000 of North Carolina money in his possession".[227]

A soldier of Company G, 3rd New York Cavalry, wrote, "We bivouacked two or three hours at the corners of the streets, in the yards and vacant places in town and fed our hungry and jaded horses, from the barns and granaries of the place. The authorities ... gave us ... the freedom of the town, which we freely used, making ourselves intimate with the interior arrangements of stores, public buildings, dwelling houses, iron safes, money drawers and every other place where a single article contraband of war could possibly be secreted." Searches of Greenville homes yielded firearms, and a mixture of Confederate currency, old US silver and gold coins, and some new US greenbacks.[228]

Such large sums of money, and the watches, jewelry, and other valuable loot found during the raid were a great temptation to the Union cavalrymen. Official Union accounts are generally silent on this aspect of raiding, but Confederate accounts detail extensive lists of private property that was stolen during Potter's Raid. At least two of Potter's own men were troubled by the looting done by their comrades. Capt. Rowland M. Hall, of the 3rd New York Cavalry, wrote to his father, "I wish I could make some money on these raids consistently with honor and duty, but I cannot …"[229]

Sgt. Gleason Wellington, of the 12th New York Cavalry, thought that plundering by the Union troops helped turn many loyal or neutral North Carolinians against the Federal government. Many a Rebel guerilla, Wellington believed, was "made by our own soldiers' carelessness. … When our army passes through the country, they go into a farmer's premises and just take what they want and destroy the rest. Now this man may be a Union man or on the fence. He may be poor and they take all of his hard earnings. That gets him mad; he wants satisfaction in some shape, so he takes to bushwhacking. I suppose there are a great many of this kind of rebs …"[230]

U.S. Army Military History Institute

Capt. Newton Hall (above) and Capt. Maurice Leyden (below) of the 3rd New York Cavalry.

Photo courtesy of Scott Hahn

Some of the few Confederate troops in Greenville were on duty with the army's commissary department. Back on April 13, 1863, Maj. William Demill was appointed as the acting post commissary officer at Greenville. At this time, Demill would have been very busy handling food shipments for D. H. Hill's troops as they besieged Washington. After Hill's men were transferred out of North Carolina, Demill remained in Greenville as a commissary officer for Brig. Gen. James Martin's brigade. There are no records of Demill or any of his men being captured. But, Demill later noted in a letter, "…my papers were very much scattered in the raid on Greenville."[231]

Demill, whom the Federals considered to be "an ultra secesh", was a former mayor of Washington. After his hometown fell to the Union, his family fled to Greenville, where they remained during the war with other refugees from behind the Federal lines. After the war, Demill's family changed the spelling of their surname. The major's grandson, who was born in 1881, was motion picture director Cecil B. DeMille.[232]

A Confederate artilleryman wrote to the *Wilmington Journal* that while in Greenville, the "enemy ... gutted the place, taking twenty-eight hundred ($2,800) from Dr. Blow, and fifty-five hundred ($5,500) in banknotes from Alfred Forbes – destroyed the Commissary and Quartermaster stores, took the earrings and breast pins off the persons of ladies and the watches off of the gentlemen." Forbes was among the Greenville men who were captured during the Federal navy raid in November 1862. During the naval raid, Dr. William Blow had been pointed out as one of the "head men" of the town; he was interviewed but was not taken prisoner. After Potter left Greenville, Blow took off after the raiders and tried to lead pursuing Confederate troops after them.[233]

The Confederate artilleryman who wrote to the *Wilmington Journal* also described the near capture of a black Confederate soldier who served in his company. Potter's men "found out that a free negro named Jackson, very well known in Wilmington, and an enlisted bugler in Cummings' Battery, was detailed and acting in the Commissary department, and offered five hundred dollars for his head, and to vent their vengeance destroyed all of his clothing, but did not succeed in capturing him." James H. Jackson served in Company C of the 2nd North Carolina Artillery (also known as Cummings' Battery).[234]

Before the war, James H. Jackson was a mason in Wilmington. He enlisted as a "colored bugler" at Zeke's Island (near Fort Fisher, and the mouth of the Cape Fear River in North Carolina) on August 18, 1861. At the time of Potter's Raid, he was "detailed in Comsy Dept Martin's Brigade". Jackson, who reportedly of mixed black and Spanish ancestry, returned to Greenville after the war. The 1880 Census found him living in Greenville, with the occupation of "book keeper". According to that census, Jackson was born in England in 1833. His father was born in England, and his mother was from the West Indies. Jackson served as the assistant postmaster of Greenville before his death in 1891.[235]

Mrs. Peyton Atkinson lived near Greenville on a plantation at Bensboro across the Tar River from Falkland. (She also owned "the Clark Place", which had until recently been the camp of the 62nd Georgia Cavalry.) She wrote to Governor Vance, telling him that during the raid the "... Yankee wretches ... destroyed, it is thought, three hundred thousand dollars' worth of property, robbed citizens of every thing Valuable, such as watches, jewelry, silver, & money; they had large iron hooks, with which 2 men could throw a iron safe easily down & which they did, bursting out the back and taking its contents." Mrs. Atkinson continued, "Some persons were robbed of every cent & all of their notes, [and had their] valuable papers destroyed."[236]

Private Oren T. Wooster of Company B, 12th New York Cavalry, wrote that "I might have had a hundred dollars worth of stuff if I had any place to carry it some of the boys that went into the towns first got...considerable money and jewelry there were some of the 3rd boys broke open a safe and found about two thousand dollars in silver and gold that is what pays ..."[237]

There was no violent resistance to the raiders in Greenville. The New York *Herald* reported that "the day being a quiet Sabbath, and the rebel troops having all been withdrawn, the amazement of the inhabitants of this pretty village at the sudden advent of so formidable a cavalry host may be imagined. They threw no obstructions in the way of the officers executing the orders of General Potter; on the contrary, they either pretended to lend assistance or acted as if stupefied." The *Herald* continued, "some large guns, intended for the defenses of the place, were spiked, a number of small arms thrown into the river, and some damage done to the enemy's works."[238]

There is disagreement in the first-hand accounts of Potter's Raid about the fate of the Tar River bridge. Potter claimed that it was destroyed, as did Mrs. Atkinson and some Union newspaper accounts. Local historian Henry King, who certainly knew many people who could remember the raid, said that the Yankees "attempted" to destroy the bridge. A Confederate cavalryman who was stationed nearby wrote later that the Potter's men set fire to the bridge but "they were too hard pressed for time to see that their work of destruction was carried out." The long wooden bridge spanned not only the river but a long stretch of low ground on the north bank; perhaps the fire didn't destroy the entire length of the bridge.[239]

King also pointed out that Potter's men did not spare Greenville's saloons; they "raided bar-rooms, many got drunk ... and had a good time." Private Wooster noted that on the raid, "... the boys got all the tobacco they could carry and lots of wine most all the places keep lots of it and lots of corn whiskey."[240]

About 5 p.m., Potter's troops left of Greenville. They rode out along the Tar River Road, which ran west and north to lead through the villages of Falkland and Sparta. This part of the old road corresponds with modern NC Highway 43. The Tar River Road was lined with numerous farms, some of which were large and prosperous plantations. Occasional side roads ran to other farms, or led to landings along the river, which was a few hundred yards away to their right. Several homes along the River Road that were raided by Potter's men still stand today.[241]

At a point "four miles above Greenville", the prisoner George Greene was released. Greene said that they made him "double-quick it for the first mile". He estimated that they had taken him thirty miles from the place where he was captured near Swift Creek.²⁴²

The Raiders Hit Falkland

About 9 p.m., Potter descended upon "Green Wreath", the plantation of William Foreman, which was south of Falkland. In 1860, Foreman was 22 years old. He held 40 slaves, and his real and personal property was valued at $100,000. A letter written by one of Foreman's relatives passed along a glimpse of the raid: "Wm. Foreman says they reached his house at 9 o'clock that night and immediately out a guard at each window. Genl. Potter then came to the porch and asked him various Questions – 1ˢᵗ whether he owned that plantation or not – 2ⁿᵈ What was the news from Charleston – 3. Where was Genl. Lee's army – the Genl. Then asked if he had a cigar, and rode off – In the mean time his soldiers were plundering his wardrobe." Foreman lost "all his clothes, 2 negroes and his pony" in the raid. ²⁴³

The River Road crossed Tyson's Creek a short distance beyond Green Wreath. As soon as Potter's men started crossing the creek, a burst of gunfire halted the column. It was quickly apparent that it was not a major enemy attack, but only a small ambush. After a few shots had been fired, some of Potter's men rode away from the road after the attackers. It was dark by this time, and the cavalrymen were unable to find anyone. To this day, it's not certain who fired at the Yankees at Tyson's Creek. They were probably militiamen or armed civilians, as no regular Confederate troops were reported close enough to interfere with Potter. At any rate, their shots went astray and the unharmed Yankees resumed their march.²⁴⁴

The village of Falkland, ten miles from Greenville, was about one mile northwest of the River Road's bridge across Tyson's Creek. The Stantonsburg and Falkland Road (corresponding with modern NC Highway 222) ran into the River Road there, forming a "Y". ²⁴⁵

A traditional story that has been handed down in Falkland claims that on this raid, a Yankee cavalryman rode his horse into one home. Once inside, he spurred his horse all the way up the stairs to the second floor.²⁴⁶

Mrs. Peyton Atkinson informed Governor Vance that on this stage of the raid, Potter's men "stole all the horses they could get, robbed persons of all their money, watches, brandy, silver [and] arms [and] rushed into houses at midnight, bursting open doors, into Ladies' bedrooms, whilst they were in bed, tied citizens & locked them up in Gin houses ... Many a lady and her helpless little children slept in the woods with the Green grass for their beds & the Canopy of Heaven for their shelter, during this raid."²⁴⁷

Around midnight, Potter reached Sparta, which was just across the Pitt-Edgecombe County line. Sparta, near the intersection of modern-day NC 42 and NC 33, was a farming community and river landing. The town changed its name to "Old Sparta" after 1879, because a rival town also named Sparta, the county seat of Alleghany County, made a successful claim to the name. Here, too, the raiders "broke in the private houses and stores." At Sparta, Potter ordered a halt and the weary men set up camp. Captain Hall of the 3rd New York Cavalry noted that he and his men had been in the saddle for eighteen hours. They had covered about forty miles since breaking camp at Swift Creek Village that morning. [248]

There was no rest for Company M of the 3rd New York Cavalry; the company was ordered to do picket duty. Sergeant Cooley's platoon was sent to guard a bridge on the River Road (evidently the one that crossed Town Creek). They just missed a chance to take a couple of prisoners. Cooley wrote, "Arriving within pistol shot of the bridge we came upon two Rebel pickets but supposing them to be the advance videttes of our own column we did not charge upon them. They turned their horses' heads in the opposite direction and put off on a double quick." It's not known what unit these Confederates belonged to. [249]

The Yankees lucky enough to escape picket duty settled down to get what sleep they could. Before daylight, they would be rousted out of their bedrolls to mount up for another long ride.

A bird's-eye view of the Rocky Mount Mills and the county bridge in 1907. The mill was rebuilt after Potter's Raid and another fire in 1869. Library of Congress

Chapter 8

"Nothing Seems to Escape Them"
The Raiders in Rocky Mount
Morning, Monday, July 20, 1863

Early on Monday morning, July 20, a telegraph receiver in Wilmington clicked and clattered with the first news of the raid. Col. Sewall S. Fremont, the chief engineer and superintendent of the Wilmington & Weldon Railroad, received the first installment of bad news: " ... a force of the enemy's cavalry, numbering 300 or 400 men and four mountain howitzers, were moving in the direction of Greenville, evidently with the intention of striking" the railroad. Fremont's immediate worry was for Tarboro. He feared that the town's fate was "destruction, since there was nothing to attack but women and children."[250]

At 7:30 a.m., Fremont read an even more alarming telegram. About 10 p.m. on Sunday, news reached Tarboro that Potter's cavalry was heading that way. The Tarboro Branch Line train left Tarboro at 3 a.m. on Monday morning, which was much earlier than usually scheduled. The train was loaded with supplies that the army wanted to save from the Yankees. Conductor Robert A. Watson wired Fremont that "at daylight the cavalry (Third New York) had occupied the town." Watson was a little premature about the seizure of Tarboro; Potter's Tarboro strike force was still near Sparta at dawn. But, trouble was surely heading for Tarboro and Rocky Mount.[251]

Maj. Ferris Jacobs, Jr., USA
U.S. Army Military History Institute

Potter's weary troopers got little sleep at Sparta. It was here that Potter divided his force to make two simultaneous raids. Major Ferris Jacobs, Jr. volunteered to lead one part of Potter's cavalry to Rocky Mount. Once they had done as much damage as they could, they would then ride to Tarboro and rejoin the main force.[252]

Jacobs took his battalion, which was made up of Companies A, D, E, G, I, and L of the 3rd New York Cavalry. For artillery support, he had one of the mountain howitzers from the regiment's "flying battery", commanded by Lt. James Allis. Possibly, the detachment had two black scouts as guides; a witness in Rocky Mount later that day noted, "Two negroes were with the Yankees, their pilots we presume." Jacobs did not mention whether any of the troops of the 1st North Carolina Colored Volunteers detachment accompanied him. It seems logical that they would have been part of Jacobs' raiding party. The black North Carolina regiment had already furnished work crews for pulling up tracks at Warsaw on the raid in early July, and the destruction of the tracks at Rocky Mount was one of Jacob's main objectives.[253]

Jacobs left Sparta about 4 a.m. Potter waited about an hour before heading to Tarboro, with the battalions of Cole and Clarkson. The ride to Tarboro was shorter; perhaps Potter wanted his forces to strike Rocky Mount and

These rocks near the Tar River and Rocky Mount Mill give Rocky Mount its name.
Photo by the Author

Tarboro simultaneously, to reduce the chances of one place getting a warning to the other. The sun didn't rise for them that morning until 5:08 a.m. (remember that there was of course no Daylight Savings Time then).[254]

In the late 18th century, the original settlement of Rocky Mount was a small village on the north bank of the Tar River, at the fall line. A high outcrop of stone on that side of the river, which is unusual in the sandy soil of the Coastal Plain, gave the place its name. In 1818, the Rocky Mount Mills (North Carolina's second-oldest cotton mill) were built across the river from the old settlement. In 1840, the Wilmington & Weldon Railroad tracks were placed about a mile east of the cotton mill and the town. Gradually, most of the people of Rocky Mount moved to a new settlement by the tracks, called Rocky Mount Station. The depot, stores, and hotel attracted by the railroad formed the nucleus of the modern city of Rocky Mount.[255]

Riding away from Sparta into the brightening day, Jacobs led his men "... across ditches, through swamps, and through creeks and over bridges none the better for age and rottenness ...." [256]

Around 8:30 a.m., they tore into Rocky Mount like a band of western outlaws, riding at a full gallop and "discharging their pistols in the air to create a panic." "Quite a crowd of men and boys were assembled", wrote a local woman, "and they fired into the crowd – fortunately not one was wounded." Far to the south in Wilmington, Colonel Fremont's fears for his railroad were confirmed at 8:45 a.m. Communication from Rocky Mount was broken off when a Yankee cavalryman cut the telegraph wires.[257]

As soon as the Yankees reached Rocky Mount Station, some of the raiders burst into the hotel near the depot. Inside, they found several Confederate soldiers who were eating breakfast. The soldiers "expected a raid by our cavalry, but thought themselves safe for the present, and concluded to refresh the inner man. The result was a trip to Newbern. One of them had his arm in a sling, and was returning home on a furlough, having been wounded in the Battle of Gettysburg." [258]

The author has not identified any prisoners from this raid who were wounded at Gettysburg. Sgt. William T. Dupree of the 13th North Carolina Infantry, though, make be the man referred to. Dupree was from Edgecombe County. He was wounded in the left shoulder, but at the Battle of Chancellorsville on May 3. Admitted to Chimborazo Hospital in Richmond on May 6, he was transferred to Petersburg (possibly to the North Carolina Hospital there) on May 18. Dupree's records indicate that he was captured at Tarboro on July 21, 1863; however, many Confederates who were captured during Potter's Raid are listed at having been captured at Tarboro on July 21 when they were actually taken at other places or dates during the raid. Dupree was the only prisoner who is definitely known to have been wounded before being taken on

Potter's Raid. It is possible that the southbound mail train, which narrowly escaped falling into Major Jacobs' hands, dropped Dupree off at Rocky Mount that morning. In this case, the unfortunate Dupree would have been waiting for the regular train from Tarboro when he was captured.[259]

Private Andrew J. McIntyre was on guard duty at Rocky Mount Station that day. He was 21 years old, and the son of a prosperous farmer in Colvin's Creek in New Hanover County (now in Pender County). A soldier in the 18th North Carolina, McIntyre was seriously wounded while fighting with his regiment at the Battle of Frayser's Farm in Virginia on June 30, 1862. His recovery was long and difficult, and he remained on light duty for over a year after he was wounded. In May 1863, he was in the Confederate hospital at Wilson, North Carolina, but he had recovered well enough to be detailed as a nurse. Some time later, he was transferred to duty as a railroad guard at Rocky Mount Station. His regiment, which was now in Virginia, had just returned from the Gettysburg Campaign.[260]

McIntyre and two other soldiers were on guard at the depot when they heard the news about the Yankee attack on Tarboro. He wrote later, "Supposing the rumor to be false, I made myself easy, but it was not long before they dashed up to the depot with a shout … I had no chance to escape, and was soon taken into custody, together with about eight or ten other soldiers and two or three officers who were home on furlough, and about the same number of citizens." A report later reached the town of Wilson that a number of Tarboro residents fled to Rocky Mount when news of Potter's Raid reached them on Sunday night. "They had scarcely reached there, when … the enemy made their appearance."[261]

Jacobs Captures a Train

The southbound mail train on the Wilmington & Weldon main line, bound for Wilmington, chugged past Rocky Mount only half an hour before the 3rd New York cavalry got there.[262]

But, the train from Tarboro was not as lucky as the mail train. A Confederate soldier who passed through the area two months before Potter's Raid was not greatly impressed by the Tarboro Branch Railroad train. "The coaches", he wrote, "are light and small, very much like a goodly sized omnibus, and make a rattling, roaring noise, like empty barrels rolling down steps." As of April 1863, the Tarboro Branch Railroad ran "one train a day, and it leaves Tarboro at 2 in the evening and arrives at Rocky Mount by 4, and then leaves Rocky Mount about 7 P. M. and gets here [Tarboro] about 9."[263]

According to Major Jacobs, the Tarboro train carried fifteen soldiers (one captain, four lieutenants, and ten privates), several tons of bacon belonging to the Confederate government, and two cars filled with ammunition. Evidently the officers aboard the train were worried about a raid on Rocky Mount as well.

Delaying their departure, they halted by a government warehouse near the tracks. The soldiers from Tarboro were busy loading more army bacon onto the train when the blue coats of the onrushing enemy cavalry came into sight.²⁶⁴

The train was pointed north on the main railroad line. Although the steam pressure was low, the engineer (probably J. D. Southall, the regular Tarboro Branch Railroad engineer) started the locomotive. Smoke and steam puffed from the engine as the train slid away from the warehouse. The Yankees saw their prize chugging out of their grasp, but Major Jacobs had prepared for this moment. One of his men, Private George A. White of Capt. Rowland M. Hall's Company E, was a former "engineer on the New York Central". In case they had a chance at seizing a Confederate train, Jacobs made sure that the railroader was in the advance, and that he was mounted on a particularly fast horse. White spurred his horse and galloped after the train, which by then was picking up speed and narrowing the distance to the Tar River bridge.²⁶⁵

Capt. Rowland M. Hall, USA
U.S. Army Military History Institute

The engineer had to cover less than two miles to get from the end of Tarboro Branch Line to the railroad bridge. While the engineer sped away, "bullets from our dragoons' carbines began to batter his engine thick and fast, so thickly that he dare not rise up to put on more steam ..." White's horse pulled even with the locomotive cab, and the private "jumped from his horse, swung himself pistol in hand upon the engine, and seized the lever from the driver." White "placed his revolver at the head of the engineer" and brought back the train. The engineer, it seems, was not taken prisoner; someone later saw him "jumping off and making for the woods." White's feat earned him a great deal of admiration. Although Jacobs recommended him for promotion, White finished his wartime service as a private.²⁶⁶

Corporal Chester F. Wakeman, another member of Capt. Hall's Company E, spotted several Confederate soldiers who had jumped off of the train and "started to run for the swamp. I pursued and captured three, and brought them in." Captain Hall then sent Wakeman and Private Hamilton H. Hall some distance away on picket duty.²⁶⁷

This time, the Federals didn't parole the captured Confederate soldiers, but hauled them back to New Bern. Among the prisoners were Capt. P. Nichols and four men of his Company B, 13th Battalion North Carolina Troops; their company, later transferred to the 66th North Carolina, was known as Captain Nichols' Company, Raleigh and Gaston Railroad Guard. Records show that Private Andrew Dozier of the 6th Virginia, who was detailed as a teamster in the forage train of Longstreet's Corps, was captured at Rocky Mount. Also taken prisoner there was Private Reddick Jones of Company B, 12th Battalion, North Carolina Cavalry. It is unclear why Jones was in Rocky Mount, but his records show that he too was sometimes detailed as a teamster.[268]

Robert A. Watson, the Tarboro train conductor, was robbed by the Union troops of "$1,000 in gold and his wearing apparel", according to the *Daily Progress* in Raleigh. Conductor Watson met two of Jacobs' men almost thirty years later in 1892, and told them that "except for a little hindrance in making a switch" they "would not have caught" the train. The two men, Henry J. Knapp and Charles N. D. Mead of Company I of the 3rd New York Cavalry, mentioned to Watson that they'd heard that $15,000 in gold was taken from the Tarboro train. Knapp doubted that "Uncle Sam's treasury ever swelled because of it." Watson told his visitors that the gold was his, and that "he would be very pleased at its return."[269]

Jacobs' men set fire to their captured locomotive, like this one photographed in 1865.
Library of Congress

In 1892, Watson also told his visitors that he escaped from Jacobs' men by climbing onto a cavalry horse, which he "thought belonged to the man who boarded the engine", Private White. The conductor said he was "not expecting to get away with it but he was not watched very closely and in the confusion of burning R. R. buildings, cars, ... etc., he got off to one side and skipped with horse and equipments." The soldier whose horse Watson escaped on "had left his carbine and sabre hanging to the saddle and he got the whole business." Watson still had the saber in 1892, but he was willing to return the weapon if its former owner sent his address.[270]

Private McIntyre watched Jacobs' men destroy the captured train. He wrote, "They run the engine off the track, and burnt the cars. While the car

No wartime photo has been found of the Rocky Mount railroad bridge, but it may have resembled this Neuse River bridge in 1865. National Archives

which was loaded with ammunition was on fire, an explosion took place which blowed one Yankee, who was plundering around inside, a-whizzing outside, but though badly burned, he was not killed, and was doing well when I saw him last; and when some of his comrades expressed sympathy with his mishap, said that was 'narthing'."[271]

Capt. Rowland M. Hall was the company commander of Private Gideon F. Blackman, the man who was hurt in the explosion. Hall's version stated that "the depot of the Railroad & adjoining sheds contained a large amount of cotton, & upon being incautiously fired, a spark blew up the ammunition loaded upon the train, burning one of the sentinels in charge very severely." A Union soldier wrote that the fire consumed "shells, shrapnel, powder cartridges &c.", and "the explosion of which at short intervals as the fire reached them was grand and terrific."[272]

This document notes that Pvt. Gideon Blackman was "blown up and badly burned" while fighting the fire at Rocky Mount. Blackman recovered and returned to duty.

National Archives

"Three coaches and two box cars" of the Tarboro train were destroyed, and the engine was "ruined ... completely". Besides the military property, the fire on the train also destroyed "many trunks, boxes, & c., of fugitives". [273]

Locomotives in those days were given names, just as boats and ships are today. The name of the engine that was "ruined" at Rocky Mount was not mentioned in the reports of the raid. Perhaps it was the *Tarborough*, which was listed as "worthless" in an 1865 U. S. Military Railroad inventory of captured Confederate railroad stock. That *Tarborough* was listed as an "Anderson" locomotive. "Anderson" engines were built in the 1850s at the Tredegar Iron Works in Richmond, Virginia, which was owned by Joseph Reid Anderson.[274]

A Union Army track-wrecking crew at work in Georgia, , 1864. Library of Congress

In 1930, an old Union veteran named Mordecai Knapp talked to a newspaper about his days in Company D of the 3rd New York Cavalry. He amused his audience by telling them that he remembered getting paid only $14 a month. But, probably referring to the raid on Rocky Mount, Knapp added that he once was in on the capture of a "Confederate pay train". Knapp's share was $200 in Confederate money. Captured Confederate money could be sold on the black market. Knapp remembered that one dollar in Rebel bills were worth eight cents in US currency. The $25 he would have received would have been almost two month's pay.[275]

Jacobs' men came to Rocky Mount with a selection of specialized tools for tearing up railroad tracks. Private Alfred Holcombe of the 27th Massachusetts mentioned that he saw the cavalrymen in Swift Creek Village with "their machine for tearing up the railroad". The Union Army also used "U-irons", tools that looked a bit like large horseshoes, which were pried under the iron rail. (These may have been the large iron hooks that Mrs. Atkinson described being used to break open safes in Greenville.) A lever was forced through the U-iron, then pushed so as to twist the rail in a spiral direction. The Yankees had learned that bent rails could be straightened out fairly easily, but a twisted rail was permanently ruined. These would be the same sort of tools mentioned by Capt. H. W. Wilson, the commander of the pioneer detail during the raid on Warsaw by the 3rd New York Cavalry.[276]

While work crews pulled up the tracks, other soldiers set fire to the train depot, telegraph and ticket offices, a woodshed, a water tank, and a nearby warehouse. [277]

Other Federals went door to door through Rocky Mount's homes. The troopers demanded that the residents hand over their firearms, which they "deliberately ... dashed into pieces against the trees."[278]

Another Confederate who fell into the hands of the Yankees in Rocky Mount was Col. Henry A. Dowd, the former commander of the 15th North Carolina. Dowd was wounded at Malvern Hill, Virginia, on July 1, 1862, and resigned from the regiment in February, 1863. He then became the head of the clothing bureau of the North Carolina Commissary Department. Dowd and his wife, with a considerable amount of baggage, were captured by some of Jacobs' men in Rocky Mount. His story was printed in a Charlotte newspaper after the raid. The former colonel, in civilian clothes, inspired little interest in his captors until they opened one of the trunks and found his officer's uniform and his sword.[279]

Dowd was brought before "their Major" (evidently Major Jacobs). The Federals neglected to ask what his current job was. They took his sword, but did not ask where it had come from. The sword

Col. Henry A. Dowd, CSA

was an early war trophy. It was said to have been captured on July 10, 1861, at the Battle of Big Bethel, the first major clash of the war after Fort Sumter in 1861.[280]

Answering his captors' demands, Dowd coolly opened one of his trunks, and showed them a "pile of small children's clothing" on the top tray of the trunk. Before Dowd had to dig any deeper into the trunk, Jacobs figured that they had wasted enough time on his baggage and told him that he "thought that would do". After detaining the Dowds a little longer, Jacobs released them. The Union soldiers never knew that "beneath the bottom tier of the little unmentionables there lay a pile of many thousands of dollars entrusted to the

Colonel for certain purposes." Perhaps because he was by then a civilian, Dowd was released instead of being taken back to New Bern as a prisoner.[281]

The Destruction of the Rocky Mount Mills

Jacobs sent some of his men to burn the railroad bridge over the Tar River. The bridge, which Jacobs described as being "750 feet long" (much of this was trestle-work over the low ground by the river) was about one mile north of the depot. Jacobs personally led a detachment to the Rocky Mount Mills, about one mile northwest of the depot, and a short distance west of the railroad bridge.[282]

At that time, the mills were in Edgecombe County. In 1871, the boundary shared by Nash and Edgecombe Counties was moved to the east, along the tracks of the Wilmington & Weldon Railroad, dividing Rocky Mount and putting the mill site in Nash County. [283]

A view of the Rocky Mount dam and mill circa 1890.
N.C. State Archives

Various relatives of Joel Battle had owned the mills over the past four decades. William S. Battle, a wealthy planter who also owned an impressive brick mansion that was just outside of Tarboro, was the owner at the time of the cavalry raid. Battle unsuccessfully offered the mill complex for sale in 1860. At that time, he described the mill as "one of the best Granite Buildings in the State, 38 by 74 feet, two stories, with basement and attic; with machinery in good order, turning out 300,000 to 350,000 lbs. cotton yarn per annum." There was also a grist mill, which Battle stated was "a large and substantial framed building on granite walls – running five pairs large stones..." Battle went on to list one sawmill, "one large and commodious Dwelling ... three other residences ... fourteen Cottages for operatives; one large ... Store-house; three Ware-houses, [and] Blacksmith and Wood Shops..."[284]

A later newspaper story described the mill dam, which was "constructed of massive blocks of rock hewn out of the large rocks lining the river", which was about "80 yards wide" at that point. This "aquatic monster" of a dam provided the power to run the cotton factory, as well as the grist mill and sawmill.[285]

The mill was originally run by slaves, but the owners switched to paid white labor in the early 1850's. Union army sources stated that the mill employed 150 to 200 hands. Most of the workers were women or girls. Many of the employees lived in "neat white cottages, sufficiently numerous to have the appearance of a village" near the mill. The 1860 census lists a notably large number of women living near the mill; the census, which includes the value of real and personal property for each person, lists not a single dollar in property for any of the names likely to be ordinary mill workers. Hands working at the rebuilt Rocky Mount Mills in 1867 earned $2.50 a week.[286]

The fires set by the raiders "left only black and crumbling walls to mark the remains" of the mills. Captain Hall mentioned that they also destroyed a "large establishment" nearby that supplied "pilot bread" [hardtack crackers] for the Southern army. Jacobs reportedly have made a little speech to the now jobless mill workers: "'Girls, I am sorry to throw you our of work, but', he continued, pointing to a rich store of Rebel provisions, 'go there and help yourselves.'"[287]

The cavalry spared a handsome home built by in 1835 by Joel Battle, the founder of the mills. (The building was later used as offices for the mills.) Also spared was the home of the mill's superintendent. An often-repeated story about the raid says that the superintendent, who was a Mason, found another Mason among the Union officers and persuaded him not to burn these houses. The story may be only folklore. On the other hand, Potter's men didn't target private homes for burning during the raid. For whatever reason, both houses are still standing today.[288]

Many houses and shops in and around Rocky Mount were looted. "Nothing seems to escape them", wrote one Southern newspaper. Some of the raiders "entered private dwellings, broke open bureaus and drawers, [and] stole clothing, petty trinkets and jewelry, in one case known to our informant taking forcibly from a lady's finger her wedding and other rings."[289]

The superintendent's house at the Rocky Mount Mills was spared by the raiders and is still standing today. Photo by Author

The home of Rocky Mount merchant William E. Pope was "ransacked" by soldiers who took $20,000 in cash and bonds, "his bed-clothing, his own and family's personal clothing, including children's clothing" — and even their toothbrushes! Another merchant, W. W. Parker, who lived a short distance east of Rocky Mount, was hard hit by the raid. The Yankees burned his stables and barns, and "robbed him of money and bonds to the amount of $70,000, destroying thirty bales of cotton belonging to him and absolutely stealing his buggy." Some of Potter's men broke open Parker's safe, and they took $7,000 worth of $500 and $1000 North Carolina treasury bonds belonging to William Pope. Private McIntyre, taken along as a prisoner, watched as the raiders "burned Mr. Parker's store, and broke into the bar rooms and took all the liquor." Two horses and a mule were taken from Parker's stables. Parker placed advertisements with detailed descriptions of the animals in several newspapers. He offered rewards of one hundred dollars for the safe return of his mule, and two hundred dollars apiece for the horses. [290]

> **Notice.**
> **N. C. STATE BONDS AND COUPONS.**
> NOTICE IS HEREBY GIVEN THAT the Yankee Raiders who visited Rocky Mount Depot, on the 20th July, 1863, took from the iron safe of W. W. Parker, the following Bonds, to wit: Bonds Nos. 448, 449, 450, 451, 452, and 453, of $1,000 each, dated respectively 1st day of January, 1863, and running 30 years. These were North Carolina State Treasury Bonds, with Coupons, none of which had been collected up to the time of capture. They were made payable to bearer and belong to Wm. E. Pope, of Rocky Mount.
> The public generally, and all Banks and Brokers are hereby notified and requested not to receive said Bonds, or either of them, or their Coupons, without my endorsement in my own hand writing. And the Public Treasurer of the State and his agents, clerks or employees, are hereby forwarned and prohibited from receiving the said Bonds or any part thereof, or paying the Coupons thereto attached. Any information about said Bonds will be thankfully received.
> WM. E. POPE.
> Rocky Mount, July 23, 1863.   jy 24-2w

Pope's newspaper ad seeking the stolen bonds.
Raleigh Register, *July 25, 1863*

William Pope advertised the serial numbers and descriptions of his stolen bonds in newspaper ads, and warned buyers not to accept them. The High Shoals Iron Company of Virginia later placed similar ads in the *Richmond Examiner.* Six 8% Confederate government $500 bonds and one $1000 bond owned by the Virginia firm were also stolen "by the late Yankee raiders in Rocky Mount". [291]

The troops also "plundered a store house of Jordan and Williford, breaking up and giving out a quantity of articles that had been stored there for safekeeping." "John Tillery and others", said a Raleigh newspaper, "also suffered heavy loss." [292]

It is quite possible that the Union cavalrymen were taking women's and children's clothing for their own families. A Union army private was paid only $13 a month. Not only was their pay often late, it much less than many of the family men had been making before the war. The combination of low pay and growing wartime inflation was squeezing many of their families back home.

Wealthy Nash County planter Kenelm Lewis (known also as Kelly Lewis) lived in a fine brick mansion known as "Stonewall", across the river from the Rocky Mount Mills. The house got its name from a granite wall that borders the front lawn. Lewis's wife Elizabeth Herritage Bryan was the sister of Charlotte Emily Bryan, who became the second wife of Confederate brigadier general Bryan Grimes.[293]

Apparently, none of the Union cavalrymen crossed the Tar River at Rocky Mount. Jacobs' men also set fire to the county bridge, which spanned the Tar River near the mill, but local citizens persuaded the Yankees to let them douse the fire.[294]

Because Jacobs' men didn't burn the county bridge, the slaves who lived north of the river had a chance to escape to New Bern with the Union forces. Eighteen of Lewis' slaves, almost one third of the 60 whom he had owned in 1860, were among them. Despite the loss of so many of his slaves, and the accounts that he had heard of the damage that the raiders did at Rocky Mount, Lewis still felt that "from all that I can learn the Scoundrels were more thievish at Tarboro and below than they were here."[295]

The raiders also set fire to "three trains" of Confederate army wagons, totaling 37 wagons loaded with "all manner of stores and supplies". Many of the refugee slaves were given captured mules to ride on their way to New Bern.[296]

The 'Leisurely' Ride to Tarboro

The raiders left Rocky Mount about 11 a.m. Somehow a rumor arose among the townspeople that the Yankees were heading west for Raleigh, but Jacob's men turned to the east, taking the road that followed the south bank of the Tar River to Tarboro. Jacobs summed up the morning's work in his report: "the destruction of property was large and complete." Captain Hall apparently forgot to summon his men Corporal Wakeman and Private Hall back from their post. Jacobs' men left Rocky Mount without them.[297]

Two more of Jacobs' men, Privates Pembroke J. Dunham and Henry H. Eager of Company G, were last seen by their comrades at Rocky Mount. A comrade writing to a New York newspaper wrote of the missing men, it appeared that they were "… over come by fatigue and the want of sleep, they had laid down to rest and were thus left behind and consequently taken prisoners." Dunham was released after spending time in Confederate prisons, including Andersonville. Eager died while he was a prisoner in Richmond. (See Appendix II.)[298]

On their way to Tarboro, the raiders intercepted a "Mr. B. Selby". They "assaulted" him, tore up the contents of his valise, and took the borrowed rockaway and horse he was driving. A woman who knew the horse's owner (someone named only as "Aunt Mae") wrote, "Poor 'John horse', as the children call him. Aunt Mae knows his sad fate."[299]

Jacobs called his march to Tarboro "leisurely". The Federals burned six cotton gins, several wagons, and, according to Jacobs, over 800 bales of cotton at plantations along the road to Tarboro. Newspaper reports stated that the gin houses belonging to "R. S. Petway, Colonel W. R. Cox, Spencer Hart, Mrs. Powell, Robert Norfleet and Jas. S. Battle" were destroyed. One of Petway's slaves left with the raiders, who also took three of his horses. The raiders were said to have burned 100 bales of cotton at the Cox plantation. William Ruffin Cox, later a Confederate general and a postwar three-term congressman, at that time commanded the 2nd North Carolina Regiment in Lee's Army of Northern Virginia. For some reason, newspapers reported that the Yankees spared gin houses along that road that belonged to Kemp P. Battle, Col. Joseph H. Hyman, and Coffield King. [300]

Raiders burned cotton presses like this one.
Library of Congress

On the way from Rocky Mount, the raiders briefly halted at a plantation belonging to Frederick Proctor. Only Celia Proctor, who was sick in bed, and her three daughters were home. Some of the cavalrymen stopped at the plantation, and according to family tradition threatened to burn their home and the farm buildings. The girls begged the soldiers to spare their plantation, and promised to fill their canteens with brandy if they didn't burn them out. The soldiers agreed, riding away with the brandy and leaving the plantation intact. [301]

Private McIntyre chatted with his captors as they rode along the road to Tarboro. They told him that they were the same soldiers who had made the earlier raid on the Wilmington & Weldon Railroad at Warsaw. Also, they told him that one company of their party was made up of "buffaloes". McIntyre was positive that the "buffaloes" acted as "pilots" [scouts or guides] for the expedition. The captive Rebel said of them, "it would not become me to urge any extreme measures with them, since they treated me as well as I could wish while in their hands, but the authorities will know how to deal with them." [302]

Most of the prisoners were mounted onto captured mules, and according to McIntyre the Yankees "asked us how we liked the cavalry service." McIntyre watched as the Union soldiers "pressed every wagon and team they came to, and took all the best horses and mules out of the stables, on which they mounted negroes, most of whom came along voluntarily." [303]

Upon hearing news of the raid, William S. Battle's overseer J. J. Harper rounded up a caravan "with 25 negroes, all the wagons and mules of the farm and some 10 or 12,000 pounds of bacon" to lead them out of the path of the Federals. Unfortunately for Battle, Harper didn't know about the raid on Rocky Mount. Harper took the River Road west from Tarboro and ran right into the enemy force. Jacobs burned the bacon and the wagons, seized the mules, and took Harper prisoner. Battles' slaves joined the Federal column. Kenelm Lewis wrote after the raid, "Mr. Battle estimates his loss at $300,000 ... his operatives did not act well, they concealed his bacon, cotton yarn and other things they got when the Yankees came. The poor people will be in a sad plight here ..."[304]

"I Never Saw a More Frightened Community"

The town of Wilson was on the Wilmington & Weldon Railroad, eighteen miles south of Rocky Mount. Wilson's railroad depot, the Confederate Army's General Hospital No. 2, and the bridge where the railroad crossed Toisnot Creek made the townspeople fear that they were a likely target of a Yankee raid. News of the capture of Rocky Mount reached Wilson by telegraph about 8:30 a.m. on July 20, just before the line was cut.

Deborah Virginia Bonner Warren, wife of state legislator Edward Jenner Warren, was in Wilson when news of Potter's Raid hit the town. She wrote that "I can not imagine a more panic-stricken community than Wilson ... The militia of the town were called out, [and] couriers dispatched to all the different districts in the county ..." [305]

Ironically, after the raid, a "pile of burnt gun and rifle barrels" was found in the ashes of the Rocky Mount depot. The ruined firearms were all that was left of a shipment of civilian weapons that the state of North Carolina had impressed from the citizens of Wilson County. The weapons were intended for the North Carolina militia. The state's desperate efforts to obtain every possible weapon for the regular army had been very thorough. On the day when Potter's men swept into Rocky Mount, the Wilson County militia could scrape up only sixteen muskets "and such other guns as had escaped the officer of the most insufficient quality ..."[306]

Surgeon Solomon S. Satchwell of the Confederate hospital in Wilson wrote a letter about the day of the raid. His description of the experiences of the militia, and the hospital patients who were rounded up and issued arms, was written in the style of a mock epic: "the citizens flew – to their trunks and wardrobes, the militia flew to the woods, and the 'Hospital Defenders' flew to arms ... This glorious band, composed of the halt and the maimed and the blind, of those who had diverse miseries in the bowels ... were stationed where the mighty Tossnot rolls its languid tide, to guard the bridge there placed ... Soon the militia rallied handsomely and reinforced the defenders ..." [307]

N.C. State Archives

Dr. Solomon S. Satchwell (above), and Commodore William F. Lynch, CSN (below), led the defense of Wilson.

Naval Historical Center

Oddly enough, a Confederate naval officer stepped in to take over the defense of Wilson. Commodore William F. Lynch, the commander of the Confederate Navy in North Carolina waters, was in town on navy business. The navy maintained an office in Wilson, which was a good point on the railroad for Lynch to keep an eye on the gunboats under construction on the Roanoke, Tar, and Neuse Rivers.[308]

To build emergency breastworks, "all the able-bodied negroes were called for, to appear with spades and shovels ..." Evidently referring to the Toisnot Creek bridge on the Wilson-Tarboro Road, which was close to the railroad, Satchwell stated that under Lynch's command, the "bridge was destroyed, timber felled athwart the road, and two lines of entrenchments at least sixty yards in length were thrown up."[309]

Satchwell went on to write that Lt.Col. Stephen Decatur Pool, with "one hundred and eighty men" of the 1st North Carolina Artillery reached Wilson between 6 and 7 a.m. on the morning of the raid "with discretionary powers to protect Wilson, Rocky Mount or Tarboro". [310]

Pool's Battalion of was one of the first units that General Martin sent after Potter. Their camp was at Spring Bank "six miles below Goldsboro" on the Neuse River. They might have arrived earlier, except for "a delay of six hours, caused by the absence of the Goldsboro operator from his office". It was their second recent trip to the Tarboro area; they were the troops whose train derailed on the Tarboro Branch Railroad after a fruitless trip to repel Union raiders on July 8.[311]

While Lynch organized the defense of Wilson, Pool was urged to move on to Rocky Mount. Pool left later in the morning, "rode to within eight miles of the place, saw the smoke of the burning property, and retired", to the great disappointment of Satchwell and other Confederates in Wilson.[312]

When the telegraph line from Rocky Mount went dead, Colonel Fremont in Wilmington knew that the Federal raiders were there. At 1 p. m., Colonel Fremont received a telegram from Wilson that confirmed his fears of a strike against Rocky Mount. The message also added the news that the raiders were moving toward Wilson. Luckily for "the Hospital Defenders", that last bit of information was not true.[313]

An 1891 view of Tarboro, looking west on Church Street from the new town hall.

Chapter 9

"May Heaven Deliver Our Beautiful Village"
*Potter's Expedition in Tarboro
Monday Morning and Afternoon,
July 20, 1863*

Tarboro was one hundred years old in 1860. Neatly symbolizing the old and the new in that colonial-era town, the Tarboro Branch Railroad, which linked the riverside town to the Wilmington & Weldon Railroad, was completed in that same year. The modern spelling of "Tarboro" (which sometimes still appeared with an apostrophe as Tarboro') had just about edged out the archaic versions of "Tawboro" or "Tarborough". Local folks liked to say that the new spelling was the one "without the '-ugh'".

Located on high ground along the Tar River, Tarboro was 28 miles by water from Greenville, and just downstream from Shiloh, the head of steamboat navigation on the Tar. 1,048 people called Tarboro home in 1860. The population was broken down into 451 whites (including a number of European immigrant merchants and artisans), 65 free blacks, and 530 slaves.[314]

Visitors to Tarboro in the mid-19th century were charmed by the beauty of the little town. A canopy of hardwood trees shaded the "wide and level" streets. Comfortable homes and elegant mansions rested away from the streets "in the midst of large groves — indeed some of the houses can scarcely be seen, so thickly are they embowered in the foliage of trees and shrubbery surrounding them." Shortly after the war, a visitor was enchanted by the variety of birds that sang in the trees of Tarboro. Mockingbirds sang "all day, and during the beautiful moonlit nights, nearly all night ... the groves resound with the notes of almost every kind of bird to be found in the South."[315]

Civil War-era Tarboro was a busy place. There were ten stores, two hotels, four churches, two drugstores, a bakery, four confectionaries, three milliners, and two jewelers. Artisans who worked in the town included coachbuilders, saddlers, and gunsmiths. The town also was the home of the *Tarboro Southerner*, one of the few newspapers in the region that managed to keep publishing during the Confederacy's wartime shortages of paper, ink, and labor. The business district clustered around the southern end of Main Street, near the bridge that crossed the Tar River. A mile or so north of downtown was the brand new train depot.[316]

Seven blocks north of the river was a large park called the Town Common. The common was a remnant of the original colonial-era common that marked the northern edge of town. Once a place for townspeople to graze their animals, it had become a park shaded by large oak trees by the time of the Civil War. At the west end of the Common was the Tarboro Male Academy. At the east end was the brick building of the Tarboro Female Academy.[317]

In Confederate Tarboro, soldiers tended warehouses filled with quartermaster and commissary supplies. F. L. Bond owned a little factory that made army caps. The Female Academy was closed for the duration of the war, and the building was converted into Way Hospital No. 7 by the state of North Carolina. Way (or wayside) hospitals were set up in locations where they could provide care for sick or wounded soldiers who were on their way home on medical leave. Probably, Tarboro's location as a link between the Wilmington & Weldon Railroad and the Tar River got the hospital placed there. Across the Tar River, carpenters hammered on the framework of what was intended to be an ironclad gunboat for the Confederate Navy.[318]

The most famous Civil War officer from Tarboro was Maj. Gen. William Dorsey Pender, one of the most promising young commanders in the Army of Northern Virginia. Two days before Potter reached his home town, Pender died in Virginia on July 18, 1863 from wounds received at Gettysburg on July 2. His body was on the way home to Tarboro for burial when Potter reached the town.[319]

Potter Leaves Sparta

About 5 a. m. on July 20, one hour after Major Jacobs left for Rocky Mount, the rest of Potter's men left their camp at Sparta. William H. Graves of the 12th New York Cavalry wrote that he only had two hours of sleep before he was awakened. Sgt. Gleason Wellington had been sick since the cavalry crossed the Neuse River at New Bern. He wrote in a letter to his family that on that morning, "I got up from my blanket which was spread in the edge of a corn field but I had hardly got on my feet before down I went." Wellington got a comrade to feed his horse for him, and asked him to bring the surgeon. The surgeon gave the Wellington some medicine, and ordered him to ride in an ambulance. [320]

Sparta was an important spot for Potter because of the three bridges near the little town. One bridge on the River Road crossed Town Creek, which flowed into the Tar River nearby. Another bridge was on a side road that crossed a tributary of Town Creek. A third bridge crossed the Tar River. The river bridge, like the one at Greenville, was "rendered impassible".

It's not known for certain what Potter was planning as his return route to New Bern. Returning on the original route required crossing the bridge over Town Creek again. The Union commanders were also concerned by reports that a company of Confederate cavalry was following them. Potter ordered Companies K and M of the 3rd New York Cavalry to remain at Sparta, to guard the bridges and watch for the enemy cavalrymen. The rest of Potter's men, ten companies of cavalry and three mountain howitzers, turned toward Tarboro. [321]

News Spreads About Potter's Raid

When Potter left Sparta, a detachment of Confederate cavalry was galloping toward Tarboro. It was "early Sunday morning", and Potter was well on his way to Greenville, when news of Potter's raid reached General Martin at his headquarters in Kinston. Martin wrote orders for all of his available troops to intercept the raiders. The orders were telegraphed to Goldsboro, to be relayed from there to Rocky Mount. There was no telegraph line from Rocky Mount to Tarboro, and only one train a day made the round trip. Messages that were too important to wait for the train were sent by courier — provided that a courier was available. Martin's orders didn't reach Tarboro until around ten o'clock Sunday night. Potter was already drawing close to the Edgecombe County line near Sparta.[322]

The nearest Confederate troops available to protect Tarboro were about 25 miles to the northeast at Fort Branch. The fort was in Martin County, two miles south of Hamilton, on the Roanoke River. Begun early in 1862, Fort Branch's walls of sand and soil crowned Rainbow Banks, a 70-foot high bluff on the south bank of the river. From that height, the fort's heavy 24-pounder and 36-pounder guns commanded the Roanoke. Smaller field guns protected the fort from a land assault. Outside the walls of the fort, a cluster of wooden huts sheltered the garrison.[323]

Fort Branch was commanded by Lt.-col. John Calhoun Lamb of the 17th North Carolina. Lamb took command when his superior, Col. William Francis Martin, fell sick. It was "between 1 & 2 o'clock" on Monday morning when a courier galloped into Fort Branch with news of the threat of a raid against Tarboro.[324]

The heavy guns at Fort Branch could not be moved to use against Potter. The fort had only a small regular garrison, part of the 17th North Carolina Infantry and a Virginia battery, the Petersburg Artillery (also known as Graham's Petersburg Battery).[325]

Almost every company of the 17th North Carolina was stationed too far away to be of any help during Potter's Raid. Company I, the company with the most to lose from a raid on Tarboro, was the furthest away. This company, under Capt. John S. Dancy, was from Edgecombe County. Dancy's men were on detached duty over 130 miles away in the Piedmont, rounding up deserters in Moore and Randolph Counties. Seven other companies were scattered over twenty miles to the east, on picket duty keeping an eye on the Federal garrisons at Washington and Plymouth. This left two companies, Capt. J. M. C. Luke's Company D, and Capt. Thomas J. Norman's Company G, at the fort.[326]

Luckily for Lamb, a few days before Potter's Raid, Maj. John T. Kennedy's three companies of the 62nd Georgia Cavalry arrived from their old camp near Greenville. The fort's commander wasted no time in obeying Martin's orders. Within one to two hours, every available man at Fort Branch was on the move. Lamb sent Martin a dispatch around 2 or 3 in the morning on July 20, informing the general that "the two companies of infantry, two pieces of artillery (Graham's) [and] Kennedy's command left camp ... for Tarboro, moving on different roads." [327]

Lamb planned for his cavalry to intercept and delay the Yankees until his foot soldiers and artillery could arrive. After daybreak, Kennedy's three companies pulled up at Daniel's Schoolhouse, about three miles from Tarboro. For most of their journey, the cavalry evidently took the old Plymouth or Hamilton Road, which corresponds to modern-day N. C. 111 (formerly N. C. 44). Kennedy thought that it would be "prudent" to send scouts ahead, so he dispatched Capt. J. B. Edgerton with a five-man detachment to see if the raiders were already in Tarboro. Edgerton's party included at least one local man, "Ed Lewis" (possibly Private Thomas E. Lewis of Company C). The major and the rest of his men stayed behind near the schoolhouse.[328]

Daniel's Schoolhouse stood on the plantation of John Henry Daniel, who was listed in the 1860 Census as an "O. S. Baptist minstr." (O. S. stood for "Old School", that is, Primitive Baptist). The census lists Daniel (born in 1801), and his wife Meniza (born in 1809) as the owners of property valued at $55,000 – quite a fortune at the time. The Daniel home, "Danielhurst" still stands along modern US 64 east of Tarboro. Danielhurst combined a family residence with

An early 20th century view of St. Andrew Street in Tarboro. Potter's men would have tied their horses to fences like those in the photo. Edgecombe Co. Memorial Library

an addition that had been built to accommodate church services. The exact location of the schoolhouse is unknown today, but it was a short distance away from the Daniel home.[329]

"Their Furious Charge into the Town"

At seven that morning, Potter's advance under Maj. Floyd Clarkson "dashed" into Tarboro. A Southern witness described how Potter's men swept into town: "I think this party numbered between 3 and 4 hundred men, some armed with sabres and carbines; most of them armed with Colt's large size pistols only. They rushed into town at a furious rate, and picketed every approach to it as soon as possible, which was the work of only a few minutes."[330]

"The first notification the snuff-dipping denizens of the village" had of the raiders, according to one journalist, "was their furious charge into the town." The raiders rode in on the old Wilson Road (NC 111) to Wilson Street, crossed Hendricks Creek, and then fanned out to cover all of the town's streets and seize the river bridge. When the Yankee soldiers dismounted, many of them tied their horses to the fences which were then a common feature of the front yards in town. "Our movements were so unexpected by the Rebels", wrote Private Graves, "that we were not opposed by the enemy very much …" [331]

The New York *Herald* reported that "a few inhabitants fired upon our men from windows; but that work stopped soon after a few summary examples were made." Southern sources don't mention the names of any of these "summary examples". The shots taken at the Yankees were probably fired by the handful of Confederate soldiers who guarding the town. As they ran toward the Tar River bridge, a few of them squeezed off a shot or two at the enemy. Two Confederate soldiers (one lieutenant and one sergeant) were taken prisoner. The men taken at Tarboro were not specified in Union reports, but the captured officer was probably Lt. Bennett P. Jenkins of Company I, 7th Confederate Cavalry.[332]

Governor Clark's Narrow Escape

Just before they came into town, Potter's men approached the home of a valuable potential prisoner—former North Carolina governor Henry T. Clark. After his term as governor ended in 1862, Clark returned to Hilma, his plantation home just outside of Tarboro. The name "Hilma" was created from the initials of the first names of Clark's five children.[333]

Hilma was conveniently close to Tarboro; indeed, it was only a few hundred yards from the edge of town. Unfortunately for Clark, the same Wilson Road that Potter took to get to Tarboro ran right in front of his home. Clark was getting ready for his usual morning horseback ride when he spotted the approaching Union cavalrymen. Some of the cavalrymen thundered after Clark, but the former governor rode into the woods and managed to lose them.[334]

Hilma, the plantation home of former North Carolina governor Henry T. Clark. Clark is the man on the porch. Courtesy Monika S. Fleming

Once Tarboro was securely in Union hands, Lt.-col. Lewis ordered Maj. Floyd Clarkson across the river with orders to "post a squadron on the Hamilton Road, 1 mile from the bridge."[335]

Years after the war, a recollection of the raid was written by a Tarboro resident who was a child at the time. The anonymous remembrance may have been penned by Dr. Julius M. Baker, who in 1863 was the five-year-old son of Surgeon Joseph Baker of the Tarboro Wayside Hospital. The writer recalled that during Potter's Raid, he sat on his porch and shook his little fist at the enemy troopers as they rode by his house. Later, the lad and his grandmother followed some of the raiders as they made a room to room search of their house. The soldiers confiscated a handgun; it was the first pistol the boy ever remembered seeing. For safety's sake, some of the children in Tarboro were hustled into the cellar of a home on Trade Street. Other townspeople rushed to bury their money, and tried to hide their firearms or other valuables.[336]

Maj. George W. Cole took four companies of the 3rd New York Cavalry to the train depot. (The remaining two companies of Cole's battalion were the ones left behind to guard the bridges at Sparta.) None of the accounts of the raid mention the Confederate hospital at Tarboro, but at the depot, Cole's troopers burned a stockpile of medical supplies. They also destroyed "a large quantity of cotton", and "several" (most likely four) railroad cars. Oddly, they appear to have spared some of the railroad buildings for the moment.[337]

Near the depot was "a large corn-sheller, run by steam." Back in May 1863, the Nottoway Grays (Company G, 18th Virginia) marched to Tarboro after D. H. Hill's unsuccessful siege of Washington. The Grays helped themselves to a generous supply of corncobs, which they stockpiled aboard the flatcars that they were to ride. A soldier of the regiment recalled that "Whenever they passed a person" by the railroad tracks, "they would commence '*shelling him*', as they called it. As rude as it was, it was nonetheless amusing to see men and boys, white and black, as well as horses, running pell-mell to escape the volley of cobs which poured forth with a shout from the passing cars." The fate of the "corn-sheller" during Potter's Raid is uncertain.[338]

The Confederate army commissary (where Winslow's Stables later stood, at 117-119 Granville Street) was burned. One of Cole's officers, Capt. John Ebbs, took his company on "a dash into the country and captured a fine lot of mules and horses." Cole asserted that he posted some men to guard private property and "the various roads".[339]

The Destruction of Tarboro's Steamboats

Major Clarkson sent detachments to burn the two steamboats that were tied up at the steamboat landing, which was "just below the bridge." Lt. William Banta, Jr. of the 12th New York Cavalry, set fire to the *Colonel Hill*. Capt. Emory

Cummings of the 23rd New York Cavalry burned the other steamer, the *Governor Morehead*. These boats were the only two steamers left on the Tar River after the Union occupied Washington in the spring of 1862.[340]

In April 1863, a Confederate soldier wrote that steamboats ran from Tarboro down the Tar River past Greenville as far as Boyd's Ferry "8 miles above Washington". From there, soldiers went on foot to their camps. He added, "the hire for horse and conveyance is enormous. The most certain way is to go on foot, which is tolerably pleasant considering the water is not more than waist deep in some places."[341]

The *Governor Morehead* came to the Tar River in 1853. She was built in Philadelphia for John Myers & Son, a merchant and shipping firm in Washington, North Carolina. An antebellum newspaper described the steamboat as being "100 feet long, and 23 feet wide ... having an extensive salon handsomely furnished ..." She was powered by a pair of 30-horsepower engines. An informant told the Union authorities that she was "fast, and in good order." John Myers & Son still owned the steamboat during the Civil War. A document shows that on July 12, 1862, they were paid $257.98 for transporting the 44th North Carolina from Tarboro to Greenville and back again.[342]

The *Colonel Hill's* longer career reflected quite a bit of North Carolina history. Built at Baltimore in 1846, the original name of the boat was the *Oregon*. In 1848, she became the first steamer to pass through an as yet unnamed inlet that was torn through the Outer Banks by a recent hurricane. The passage was from then on called Oregon Inlet. The *Oregon* ran on the Tar River until her owners went out of business, and the steamer disappeared from the river.[343]

Lt. William Banta, who burned the **Colonel Hill** *during Potter's Raid.*
U.S. Army Military History Institute

When the Civil War broke out, the *Oregon* reappeared with a new, patriotic Southern name. Col. Daniel Harvey Hill had just won fame across the South after his 1st North Carolina Volunteers defeated a larger Union force in a clash at Big Bethel, Virginia, on June 10, 1861. (Big Bethel was the war's first major clash of arms after Fort Sumter.) Apparently, the boat's owners re-named the boat the *Colonel Hill* after the hero of Big Bethel. Hill was made a brigadier

Tarboro's steamboat landing, shown on a postcard mailed in 1907. Author's collection

general soon after Big Bethel. Apparently, some North Carolinians gave the steamboat a promotion as well, because an informant told the Yankees that the boat was named the *General Hill*. The boat was used to haul Confederate troops and supplies in North Carolina's sounds before the Union Navy seized most of the coastal waters in early 1862. By 1863, the *Colonel Hill* was described as "old, slow", and "drawing six feet", which was an inconveniently deep draft for the shallow Tar River. [344]

The Rebels Make Their Appearance

From across the Tar River, Captain Edgerton and his party watched Yankee soldiers water their horses in the river at the foot of Trade Street. None of the Federals even noticed the Rebels until one of the Southerners, against orders, fired at them. The small band of Confederates galloped back toward Daniel's Schoolhouse while the startled bluecoats organized a pursuit. When he rejoined his battalion, Edgerton reported that they were being followed. It looked to him like "their whole force had come over the bridge and were feeling their way and were then two miles" away.[345]

Major Kennedy sent Edgerton back to find the enemy, make sure that the Yankees spotted them, and then draw them back toward the schoolhouse. The rest of Kennedy's men dismounted. With their horses concealed in "a nice old pine field" about 200 yards away from where they planned their ambush, they took up their positions. Hidden in the flat, "pretty well timbered" terrain along both sides of the road near Daniel's Schoolhouse, they waited for Edgerton to bring the Yankees within reach. Lt. John G. Smith remembered that his Company C was stationed "across a large ditch covered with briars and underbrush, partially concealing the men ..."[346]

Back in Tarboro, Maj. Floyd Clarkson of the 12th New York Cavalry reported to Lt.-col. Lewis. Clarkson stated that his pickets across the river along the Hamilton Road had been fired on twice. The major was also concerned because one of the prisoners that his men captured earlier ("one of those who

Potter's men spared the Edgecombe Co. Courthouse. It was demolished in the 1960s.
Author's collection

had fired upon us on our entry into Tarborough") gave out the worrisome information that "160 cavalry were quite near us". [347]

Private Melvin F. Stephens of Company B, 12th New York Cavalry, was possibly part of detachment of Clarkson's that was assigned to watch the Hamilton Road. "Our pickets," he wrote, were "so near to the woods as to draw a fire of musketry from the advance line of the enemy [which was] … placed so as to command the two roads leading from the bridge, and the open field through which they run …." Clarkson asked Lewis if he could take some men and attack the enemy across the river. Lewis agreed to let Clarkson go. It's unclear exactly who was firing on Potter's men at Tarboro after the initial rush into town. They may have been some of the pickets who were chased across the bridge earlier that morning, local militia, or citizens.[348]

Looking back on that day, William H. Graves wrote, "I presume had we returned at once to Newbern it would have been better for us. But, our officers were very anxious to have a brush with the Rebels, so as soon as we could prepare us a cup of coffee which we were sadly in need of we were ordered to mount our horses and away we went."[349]

Clarkson took Companies A, B, and F of his 12th New York Cavalry, along with a mountain howitzer commanded by Lt. John D. Clark of the 3rd New York Artillery. Clarkson had a good deal of experience in handing troops from his previous service in the 6th New York Cavalry. Companies A and B were the best-trained and most reliable in his new regiment, but really, all of his men were still inexperienced compared to the Confederate veterans who lured drawing them across the river. The months of wasted time at Staten Island and a few weeks in the field North Carolina had left the men with little time to learn how to handle their horses and weapons in action.[350]

As Clarkson rode toward the enemy, more of Potter's men burned two large government warehouses. One of them contained commissary stores, such as "bacon, flour, rice, sugar, etc."; the other, a quartermaster warehouse, was filled with "camp equipage, wagons, harness, etc." Union troops also burned the market house and the jail, and some caissons and gun carriages. Potter spared the Edgecombe County Courthouse, which survived until it was demolished in 1964.[351]

With the army equipment that was destroyed was "a box of blankets, caps & shoes" that was intended for Capt. W. H. Spencer's company of rangers. Spencer's company served behind the Union lines in Beaufort County. A box of muskets that Spender had been expecting was thrown into the river, but the captain later had hopes that they could be recovered. Spencer's supplies had been piled up at Tarboro for some time, because of the difficulty in smuggling the equipment to him beyond the Confederate lines.[352]

Besides Confederate army buildings, private businesses with any sort of military application were also in danger of destruction. Newspapers reported that the Union troops burned the shop of Julius Holtzscheiter. Born in Baden, Germany, he was a gunsmith and locksmith who also made and repaired surgical instruments for the Confederate Army. The soldiers also burned three blacksmith shops, including one owned by the firm of Williams & Palamountain. Blacksmith Isaac B. Palamountain and his wife Elizabeth were both from England.[353]

Potter's men also burned a grist mill that was owned by Irish immigrant Michael Cohen. Cohen claimed to have arrived in the U.S. about 1842, and moved to North Carolina around 1857. Before the war, Cohen operated a distillery in Tarboro. The 1860 Census found him at the age of 47, as a resident in the home of the German-born gunsmith Julius Holzeicher. Cohen was listed as a "plumber", with $2,000 in personal property (a substantial amount for an artisan.) In August 1862, Cohen and his partner Reddin Williams contracted to produce two thousand gallons of alcohol "at least ninety degrees above proof", for the Ordnance Department of the Confederate Army.[354]

According to a statement made by Cohen, wartime regulations stopped him from making liquor and he turned his distillery into a steam-powered grist mill. As a miller, Cohen was exempt from conscription into the Confederate army. The destruction of his mill cost Cohen not only his livelihood, but also his draft exemption. His prospects looked so bleak that he willingly left Tarboro with the raiders. After he got to New Bern, Cohen gave Union authorities some detailed information on the Confederate Navy gunboats that were being built in the region. He apparently hoped to appear to be a loyal Unionist, which might have gotten him some sort of compensation for the loss of his mill. His cooperation gained him a job with the quartermaster department in New Bern, but little else.[355]

The Tarboro Gunboat

Cohen provided the Yankees (and incidentally, Civil War history) with a description of one of Potter's major targets in Tarboro — the partly finished gunboat. Apparently, the vessel was never officially named, but it was a sister ship to the *Neuse* and the *Albemarle,* which were being built on the Neuse and Roanoke Rivers. Perhaps if the ironclad had ever been completed, it would have become the *CSS Pamlico*. The Tarboro gunboat was built at a makeshift boatyard, which was across the river and a short distance upstream from the town.[356]

Cohen reported, "The work on the gunboat at Tarborough was begun in September last [1862], continued one month, then stopped (in order to work on the ironclads at Wilmington and afterward on the Roanoke), and was renewed only two weeks before General Potter destroyed it (July 20); at which time, about 20 feet of its amid-ships section had been put up in six parts of the frame (of bottom four parts, making sides and angle and top); more of the frame in sections was ready to put up." The framework of the vessel was reduced to ashes. The Confederate Navy abandoned the Tarboro project to concentrate its regional efforts on the *Albemarle* and the *Neuse*.[357]

An early 20th century view of the Tar River as seen from the bridge at Tarboro. Edgecombe County Memorial Library

General Potter posted guards in front of some of the shops that lined Main Street, but the guards failed to prevent other men from breaking in through the back doors. The business district was "extensively pillaged" by Union soldiers. A bitter Tarboro resident later charged that " ... appeals to General Potter were only answered evasively by saying to the complainant 'identify the man and I will redress you', which was an impossibility in a crowd of licentious soldiers straggling promiscuously. And any one who dared to charge one with a theft would have been murdered."[358]

At least one of Potter's officers kept a tight rein on his men. A woman whose home was overrun by soldiers informed this officer, whose name is not known. The officer confronted the looters, one of whom was obviously drunk, and ordered them out of the house. The drunken soldier was placed under arrest, and the officer even drew his saber when the soldier objected. The same officer inspected some of the stores downtown and poured captured whiskey "out in the gutters" to keep the men from overindulging in it.[359]

Taking Revenge on Governor Clark

A Tarboro resident reported to the *State Journal* that "Ex-Gov. Clark's residence, on the suburbs of the town, was shamefully abused. Mrs. Clark and her niece, Miss Bettie Tool, were compelled to leave their house and take refuge in the kitchen. ... Among the things stolen from them were two gold watches, one belonging to Mrs. Clark, the other to Miss Bettie Tool, and several articles of jewelry belonging to the latter and much prized by her as having been formally worn by her mother." The raiders drank all of Clark's "stock of wines and brandies ... They were in Tarboro eight hours and some of them were in Gov. Clark's house and lot all the while drinking and stealing."[360]

Another Tarboro resident wrote about the "marauders" who ransacked Clark's house, led by a "lieutenant in uniform, who proceeded vigorously to break open and search, without a word of enquiry, every trunk, drawer, lock or latch in the house, taking money, papers, jewelry, clothing of every description and whatever seemed of the most trifling value", even children's' clothing. "Being about to break open the dairy and cellar doors, [Mrs. Clark] sent them the keys, with which they unlocked the doors and threw the keys in the well. They threw the butter and cream on the floor, broke the plates and threw a keg of lard down the well. They took the wagon and mules with about 1200 pounds of bacon and a barrel of sugar, and with what plunder they could, forced his negro man to drive it off, and as a parting remembrance, emptied several papers of snuff into the vinegar barrel. They even robbed two of the negroes they were coaxing to go with them."[361]

A Tarboro citizen wrote to the *State Journal* that, "numberless low, thieving depredations were committed ... by these scoundrels". This anonymous writer stated that at the home of John Rodgers, a neighbor of the Clarks, Potter's troops "stole all Mr. Rodgers clothes and Mrs. R's pins, needles, and handkerchiefs." The writer went on to say that soldiers burst into the home of a "Mrs. Williams", who was a widow, "and took some of her best dresses before her face, searching every drawer." The "straggling rogues" also broke into the house of a "Mrs. Dancy", who was not present, and "helped themselves in a like manner". At the home of a "Mr. Menan", "they broke his furniture and scattered every thing on the floors, selected every thing of value and brought up his cart and carried off a load." At "Mrs. Shurley's 'house, which was also near Governor Clark's, "there were only two ladies, and they attempted to take the jewelry and money from their very persons, and committed depredations on the trunks and drawers."[362]

Some of Potter's men burst into the home of Martha Elizabeth Hoskins Foreman Lewis, who was an Edgecombe County relative of William Foreman of Green Wreath Plantation. One of the soldiers "put his hand on her breast pin and said he must have that." Mrs. Lewis refused to give up her pin; it held a picture of her deceased husband. The soldier "then asked for brandy. She told him there was none, but there was country wine which he drank & left." [363]

"A gentleman from Tarboro", according to a newspaper account, was caught by Potter's men while "trying to escape". "They took his horses and carriage and turned him loose. When acting so meanly, they would say, 'I know this is hard, but your troops did so in Pennsylvania.'" The writer went on to claim that this "you know, is false — so far as our Generals could restrain." [364]

At least three safes in Tarboro were "forced", but not a single one of them yielded any money. John Norfleet was the owner of one of these safes. The disappointed safecrackers retaliated by tearing up and scattering all of Norfleet's papers that they found inside the safe, and by "stealing every article of his wearing apparel." [365]

The Tarboro branch of the Bank of North Carolina must have looked like a tempting source of plunder, but according to a Southern newspaper account, the valuables inside the bank had already been taken away and hidden. The bank's cashier, a Connecticut native named Russell Chapman, was robbed of his watch and his clothes by soldiers while an officer searched the bank. At the same time, other soldiers plundered Chapman's home.[366]

Other raiders broke into the Masonic Lodge and "carried off the fine regalia of the Chapter and all the jewels and emblems even to the common gavel, and damaged what could not be removed." After over a quarter of a century, and a bizarre chain of circumstances, some pieces of the Tarboro Lodge's stolen property would at last be returned to Edgecombe County.[367]

Sheriff Joseph Cobb of Edgecombe County reported that he was robbed of $16,893.53 by Potter's men. The stolen money was part of the year's taxes that he had so far collected in Edgecombe County. More county tax money, amounting to $27,802.48, was deposited in an iron safe in the office of the clerk of the county court in Tarboro. That money was also taken. At the meeting of the Edgecombe County Court in September 1863, the county judges made a point of absolving Cobb of responsibility over the loss of the money. However, the *Tarborough Southerner* later ran an announcement dated October 31, 1863, which notified the public that Cobb had repaid the stolen money "out of my private funds" and was applying to the General Assembly to be reimbursed for it out of state funds. "A resolution in favor of Joseph Cobb, Sheriff of Edgecombe County", was passed by the General Assembly in December. The same legislative session also passed a "Resolution in favor of John W. Hinson, Sheriff of Duplin County". The reader will remember that the 3rd New York Cavalry captured some county funds from the Duplin County sheriff during the Warsaw and Kenansville raid. [368]

Judge George Howard eluded the enemy cavalry. Two days after the raid, the judge dashed off a quick note to his wife: "The Yankees have been here. I left and kept about an hour ahead. Those that were following me, were most all taken ..." The family's main property in town, the Tarboro Hotel, fared much better than he expected. "No damage done to us", he wrote. "They only took one horse and 6 or 700 segars. The Negroes behaved well — even Jane was faithful, not only in staying, but in making such representations that they did not trouble the hotel. Only two came into the house, and they took dinner and left."[369]

The anonymous Tarboro citizens who reported their accounts of Potter's Raid for the *State Journal* viewed their experiences differently. One growled that his account was merely "... a partial recital of the conduct of these fiends and hyenas." Another pleaded, "May heaven deliver our beautiful village from the painful anxieties of another such day as Monday the 20th July, 1863."[370]

Back in Rocky Mount, Wakeman and Hall of the 3rd New York Cavalry realized that while they had been on picket duty, the rest of their detachment had left for Tarboro. "The column", wrote Wakeman, "had marched about three hours before we knew they were gone; we were fourteen miles behind, in the enemy's country." The two men wasted no time in spurring their horses toward Tarboro.[371]

Daniel's Schoolhouse once stood near Danielhurst, the home of planter and minister John H. Daniel. Edgecombe County Memorial Library

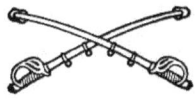

Chapter 10

"Kennedy's Men Did the Work"
The Skirmish at Daniel's Schoolhouse
Monday, July 20, 1863

Fifteen-year-old Lucy Barlow had just spent an enjoyable weekend with her schoolmate Maggie Chesson. Maggie's parents, John B. and Eleanor Chesson, left their Washington County, North Carolina plantation ahead of the Yankees in 1862. The Chessons then lived on a farm that was two miles from Daniel's Schoolhouse. Lucy and Maggie attended a school in Tarboro that was run by Rev. Thomas Owen and his wife Mary. Their weekend over, the girls were ready for the trip back to town. Before they could leave, a Confederate courier who had been stationed between Sparta and Tarboro, dashed up to Mr. Chesson. The courier's name was given as L. C. Lewis; his army unit wasn't mentioned. Lewis brought the shocking news that Yankee soldiers were on their way to Tarboro.[372]

Springing the Trap

Hidden in the woods near Daniel's Schoolhouse, Maj. John T. Kennedy's cavalrymen lay in wait for a Yankee attack. "My recollection", wrote Lt. John G. Smith, "is that it was about 9:30 when we heard firing in front." Captain Edgerton and his decoys kept in sight enough to lure Clarkson's detachment toward the schoolhouse. At last, Edgerton came into view at the bend in the road. Major Kennedy rode out of the woods to join Edgerton's mounted men in the middle of the road. Hidden in the undergrowth along the north side of the road, the 34 men of Edgerton's Company I held their weapons and waited. On the south side of the road were the rest of Kennedy's men: 28 troopers of Capt. William L. A. Ellis' Company C, and 19 men of Capt. William A. Thompson's Company E. [373]

Private Melvin F. Stephens of Company B, 12th New York Cavalry, later described the route taken by Clarkson. Across the bridge, "a general charge was ordered up the river road, which circling half way around ... [an] open field ... bears suddenly to the left and leads for a long distance through woods, in which whole regiments of Infantry might lay concealed on either side of the road, but which are perfectly inaccessible to Cavalry". Pvt. William H. Graves recalled riding down a road running through "a dense strip of timber".[374]

When Major Clarkson stopped to read the directions on a guidepost "to determine our course", he was fired on by "six cavalrymen a short distance down the road." Clarkson ordered up a mountain howitzer, and the Southern horsemen turned around and galloped away down the road. [375]

Perhaps, as Sergeant Cooley of the 3rd New York Cavalry believed, the major was "anxious to gain a good name that day". Pvt. Graves could see Rebels who "formed a line of battle across the road". Clarkson ordered Captain Simeon Church, of Company B, to charge the enemy horsemen. Kennedy had already ordered his men to aim at the enemy's stirrups; this way, their shots were likely to bring down the horses and capture the riders. The New Yorkers galloped about "half a mile" down the road. When the Federals passed the Confederate cavalrymen in the woods, Kennedy ordered, "Fire!" Company E had recently drawn a crate of .58 caliber ammunition; some of the other men fired "double-barrel guns heavily charged with buckshot". Together, they shattered the 12th New York Cavalry's first charge of the war.[376]

A postwar portrait of Maj. Floyd Clarkson, USA

"No sooner had one Troop entered the woods than they seemed saturated with a perfect storm of bullets through which they rode for more than a mile, the enemy firing and falling back further into the woods", wrote Private Stephens of the ambush that cut apart his company. The first volley struck Ordnance Sgt. Stephen Laishly and five other Federal troopers. Seventeen horses were shot down, according to one account. Part of the company was "forced ... into the woods on the left side of the road", and started shooting back. Some of the others, though, went "tilting back to Tarboro".[377]

Clarkson rode forward to see what had happened to Company B. He could only see "about 15 rebels drawn up across the road", who fired a volley in his direction. The major ordered Clark to open fire with the howitzer, and the lieutenant fired three rounds of case shot. Case shot, round, explosive shells packed with lead .69 caliber musket balls, was a good choice to use against the Southerners hidden in the woods. The rounds could be timed to explode just overhead of the enemy, making the most deadly use of the lead shot.[378]

"Immediately on the discharge of the howitzer ... With hearty good will and a stirring yell", the two other companies of the regiment charged. The troopers rode, "discharging their pistols at the Rebels as we passed, and taking their fire." Clarkson wrote, "Owing to the fact that it was the first time that any of these men or officers (with the exception of five or six) had been under fire, their horses also entirely unaccustomed to the report of firearms, very many pistols were discharged while at 'raise pistol', and their fire lost."[379]

Capt. Cyrus Church, USA
U.S. Army Military History Institute

A Confederate officer said of Daniel's Schoolhouse, "the fight lasted but a short while, but while it lasted it was fast and furious". Of Clarkson's men, Captain Cyrus Church's Company A was the hardest by the Confederates' fire, and accounted for most of the 12th New York Cavalry's losses. Sgt. John Miller's horse, which had been difficult to handle all during the expedition, panicked and bolted into the woods. Before he could regain control of his horse, two musket balls struck Miller under the ribs and tore through his body, and knocked him out of the saddle. He crawled a few feet to the base of a tree, and collapsed. Twenty feet away from Miller, one of his boyhood friends who served in the same company also fell wounded. This friend left an anonymous account of Miller's last moments. Later, a hometown friend and fellow sergeant, Gleason Wellington, wrote to dispel the reports that Miller had panicked and was fleeing from the field. Wellington knew about the trouble Miller had been having with his horse.[380]

Both of Church's lieutenants fell wounded. One of them had drawn a bead on Lieutenant Smith with his pistol. The Yankee officer "emptied his Colt revolver at me, then he threw the pistol at me with all his might and ran at me and collared me. About this time he was struck by a bullet. I threw him in the ditch where he remained until the fight was over."[381]

Capt. Cyrus Church was also struck down. There are several versions to his fate at Daniel's Schoolhouse. A Northern account states simply that "... Captain Cyrus Church, while gallantly leading the charge at the head of his company, was instantly killed, eleven bullets entering his body." [382]

Southern accounts tell two different stories about Church. A couple of weeks after the skirmish, a Raleigh newspaper described a dramatic duel between two enemy captains: "... Capt. Church was killed by Capt. Ellis ... each firing deliberately at the other, only a few paces apart with pistols. Several shots were exchanged before Capt. Church fell, Capt. Ellis escaping unhurt." Around the end of the century, in an account co-written by Kennedy, another story is given: "...Major Kennedy had shot out all he had loaded and did not have time to draw saber before the Captain (Church) and others were pressing him, and having his rifle in his hand he raised himself in his stirrups and gave the Captain such a blow as sent him reeling him off his horse."[383]

Among the troopers in Company A of the 12th who escaped was Private Henry A. Harman. His "clothing was cut in many places" by Rebel fire, and his horse was shot from under him. Harman managed to get back to Tarboro, perhaps by catching a riderless horse. [384]

Clarkson passed the Rebels, who were "in a wood with but little underbrush", and rallied his remaining men about a quarter of a mile beyond. He knew that Capt. Cyrus Church and both of his lieutenants of Company A had fallen. Judging from the later casualty lists, Company B probably did little effective fighting after they were scattered by the initial blast of gunfire. They lost one man killed and six wounded — and Clarkson stated that six were hit in the first volley. [385]

Despite the heavy casualties suffered by his detachment, Clarkson still believed there were not more than 40 Confederates in the woods firing at them. "This was a liberal estimate, as I carefully surveyed them as I charged with Captain Church's squadron." One more charge, he thought, would "clean up the enemy". Since most of their pistols were either empty or "incapable of being fired" (the old-style Colt revolvers, using black powder, were easily fouled and clogged by powder residue), they would "charge directly into the woods" with sabers.[386]

"Calling upon my men for a cheer, which was heartily given", Clarkson ordered his men "to draw our sabers and cut their way through them." The major "stood in the road as fair a mark for them as they could ask for and not a bullet touched him", wrote Graves. The major's remaining men formed in column of twos and galloped toward the Confederates hidden in the woods. The New Yorkers, wielding drawn sabers and empty pistols, were turned back by

Kennedy's fire before they reached the woods. Clarkson may have dismissed the Rebel force as numbering only 40 men, but to Graves it felt like they were "surrounded by 1500 Rebels" Many years later, Graves thought, "it has always been a wonder to me how any of our 150 men came out of those two charges alive … the bullets flew as thick as hailstones."[387]

Lieutenant Clark, bringing his gun closer to the action, "charged down the road with the view of throwing in some canister". Canister was a load of lead musket balls packed in sawdust in a sort of tin can. When the gun was fired, the can disintegrated as the shot was hurled from the muzzle, turning the cannon into a huge sawed-off shotgun. While his crew was preparing to fire, Clark "was thrown from his horse by Company B, which had also charged, though without orders", write Clarkson. The major added that a Confederate volley at this time wounded a sergeant and a private of the howitzer detachment.[388]

Faced with mounting casualties and blocked by a large and well-placed enemy force, Clarkson ordered a retreat to Tarboro. Stephens wrote that they withdrew "in good order, but in sorrow and anger" because of the dead and wounded friends they had to leave behind. Their rear guard, made up of a small detail of cavalry and Clark's howitzer, aimed to keep Kennedy at bay while they survivors rejoined Potter. Private Bill Brown of Company F, the recruit who had signed up using the name of the deserter Daniel Mulligan, was later "commended for personal bravery" in the fighting at Daniel's Schoolhouse.[389]

Lieutenant Clark was not seriously hurt when his horse threw him, but the horse ran away in the confusion. Clark was left on foot and was cut off from the rest of his men. Two men from the 3rd New York Artillery, Sgt. Abram H. Hamblin and Private William Miller (possibly the two gunners who Clarkson saw being shot) were captured. As the rest of the gunners and the remnants of Clarkson's command streamed toward safety at Tarboro, Clark "saved himself by dodging into the swamp." [390]

When Clarkson's men began their retreat, some of Kennedy's men rushed 200 yards from the scene of the fighting to retrieve their horses. The major and five men were still on horseback, from their earlier work at decoying the Yankees into the trap. While the dismounted men ran to their horses, "the six of us who were already mounted had some exciting races through the woods and paths adjacent to the school house in running down and catching a number who had got cut off from the Major in his rapid flight in the direction of Mr. John Daniels'."[391]

Daniel's Schoolhouse Becomes a Hospital

As the firing died down, Lieutenant Smith remembered the wounded Federal officer he had left in the ditch, and ordered two his men to help him.

A typical Edgecombe County schoolhouse, circa 1880. Daniel's Schoolhouse probably looked something like this one.

"He was a gallant fellow", recalled Smith, "and I regretted to see him go, but it was war and such was his fate." The Yankee officer, whose name Smith incorrectly recalled as "Herbert" (he probably meant Lieutenant Henry Hubbard), gave Smith his sword and pistol. Smith kept the weapons until they were captured from him at the end of the war.[392]

According to local tradition, one of the wounded officers rode for about a mile along a path, only to collapse near the Daniel house. The officer was cared for until he was fit enough to move.[393]

Many years later, Tarboro historian Mabrey Bass remembered that when he was a boy, one could still peep through the bullet holes that peppered the old school building, which was still standing well into the 20th century. The schoolhouse disappeared by the 1950s. The exact location of the schoolhouse is unknown today, but it was not far from the Daniel home. The battle site is probably now under the pavement of the new US 64.[394]

The wounded soldiers were taken to Daniel's Schoolhouse, which was turned into a makeshift hospital. Captain Church and Sergeant Miller were still alive when they were brought into the schoolhouse. The unidentified friend of Miller, who had been shot down twenty feet away from him, was also brought to the schoolhouse. "Seeing his hopeless condition", wrote Miller's friend, "I asked him if he had any word to send to his friends. His reply was, 'Tell my mother I tried to do my duty'". Miller and Church both died within a few hours. At the same time, the 20-year-old Miller had a brother who was stricken with fever in a Vicksburg, Mississippi hospital; Miller's brother died a few days later.[395]

At least four, and possibly five, other men from the 12th New York Cavalry died at Daniel's Schoolhouse. Private Narcisse Mulway was an 18-

year-old bugler of Company F. Mulway, who born in Montreal, Canada, was a farmer. Private Hiram Rude (also spelled Rood) of Company B, a 31-year-old farmer from Fulton, New York, left behind a widow and five children. His youngest daughter, Lizzie, was born on April 29, 1863. He probably never had a chance to see her before he left camp at Staten Island to go to North Carolina. Private David Corl, of Company A, was a 25-year-old laborer when he enlisted in Fulton, New York, almost a year before. Also among the dead was Company A's Private William Davies, whose roughly-spelled letters had shown his love and concern for his wife and children. After the raid, a quartermaster sergeant made a routine inventory of Davies' effects. The document listed no money and very little property: only a greatcoat, a haversack, and one "pocket book containing letters."[396]

Neither of the two William Thompsons of Company A made it back to New Bern. The elder Thompson was among the prisoners. He arrived at Libby Prison in Richmond on August 8, "on which day he was sunstruck", and died from "either fatigue or sun stroke or both causes" at the prison hospital on August 9, 1863. The younger Thompson was variously reported as captured or killed during the skirmish. One record states that he died "at Richmond Va. Jan. 14 1864". The 12th New York Cavalry returned to Tarboro in 1865 and reburied their dead comrades. They moved six bodies, but no mention was made of the younger Thompson's remains. The burial places of both William Thompsons are unknown.[397]

Sgt. John Miller died of wounds suffered at Daniel's Schoolhouse.
U.S. Army Military History Institute

Several women who lived near the battlefield came to the schoolhouse to tend the wounded. Young Lucy Barlow and her friend Maggie Chesson were among the volunteer nurses who helped bandage the enemy soldiers. According to Lucy, the dead soldiers were buried on a nearby farm that was later owned by Dr. Joe Lawrence.[398]

Clarkson lost eighteen men captured, including Lieutenants Mosher and Hubbard. Fourteen of the men who made it back to Tarboro were wounded. One Confederate account noted that five of Clarkson's horses were killed and "about twenty five [were] captured with their accoutrements on." Major Kennedy, years later, claimed that Clarkson lost "seventeen horses killed", and "forty-five [horses] captured" with "sixty-two saddles and equipments." On July 21, Kennedy's battalion sent a requisition for extra forage to feed 26 horses and four mules which they captured on July 20. Besides the wounded men in the schoolhouse, Kennedy said that ten prisoners were sent to the custody of Lt.-col. Lamb, who was "only a few miles in our rear".[399]

Corporal Billy Cromack, the English-born sailor, was among the captured soldiers. A bullet killed his mount, and Cromack's leg was crushed when he was pinned under the dead horse.[400]

Kennedy's troops were almost unscathed at Daniel's Schoolhouse; one officer and three unnamed men were wounded, by one account. Records mention only that Capt. W. A. Thompson suffered a slight wound in one wrist; and Private William Newton McKenzie, a Georgian from Captain Ellis' company, was shot in the left leg. McKenzie recovered from the wound, and served until the end of the war.[401]

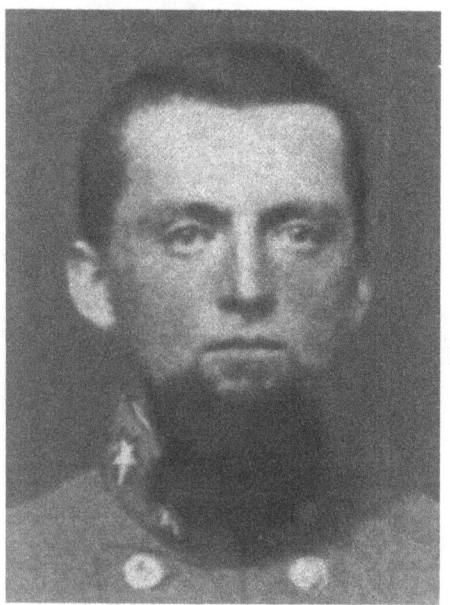

Lt.Col. John C. Lamb, CSA

The noise of the fighting at Daniel's Schoolhouse, with the 62nd Georgia "loading and giving it to them as rapidly as possible" carried back to Tarboro. Sergeant Gleason Wellington heard his comrades in Company A being "all cut up" as he lay in an ambulance in Tarboro. He wrote, "Oh how I begged for my horse and saber as I lay there burning with a fever when I heard the firing ..."[402]

As the noise of the fighting across the river intensified, Potter sent for the two companies at Sparta to rejoin the main force. To relieve Clarkson's men, Potter ordered Major George Cole of the 3rd New York Cavalry to take Companies C, F, and H and join the battle.[403]

Major Cole Gets His Own Battle

Looking for Clarkson, Cole traveled about a mile to the east on what he called the Plymouth Road. Instead of rescuing the 12th New York Cavalry, Cole ran into more Confederates —Lt.-col. John C. Lamb with Companies D and G of his 17th North Carolina, plus two guns from the Petersburg Artillery. Lamb's troops left Fort Branch before dawn. The Petersburg Artillery had horses for pulling their guns. The officers also had horses to ride, but the men had to walk. Like many Southern batteries, the Petersburg Artillery had a mixture of different kinds of guns. A November 1862 receipt shows the battery was issued a mixture of 3-inch rifle shells and 6-pounder spherical case shot. After "a forced march of 25 miles in about 7 hours", Lamb's force neared Tarboro. They took a different route than did Kennedy. There is no mention of Lamb linking up with the Confederate cavalrymen until after the skirmish, and Lamb informed General Martin that the cavalry and the rest of the force were taking different roads.[404]

At 11 a.m., Lamb was at Clark's Mill, about three miles upstream from Tarboro on the opposite bank of the Tar River. (The mill was owned by former governor Henry T. Clark.) Lamb pressed on until he halted about a mile from Tarboro, at the junction of the River Road and the Williamston Road. The latter road was also was called the Hamilton Road or the Plymouth Road. Lamb's men chose a piece of ground that today is in the modern-day town of Princeville. The ground that he picked gave them some strong advantages. Their right flank was safely anchored on the Tar River, and their left was protected by an "extensive and impenetrable swamp". Records state that Company C of the 17th, under Capt. William B. Wise, also joined the fighting that day, although they apparently did not start from Fort Branch but met the other companies outside Tarboro.[405]

Maj. George W. Cole, USA
Roger D. Hunt Collection,
U.S. Army Military History Institute

A Southern account says that the Union position during the skirmish was in a small ravine, three hundred yards in length, that ran perpendicular to the Tar River. On current maps, a small creek flows into the river near the intersection of the roads where this fight took place. Cole "pushed Company C forward as dismounted skirmishers", and sent them forward against the Confederates. Parts of Companies F and H were deployed in the rear as mounted support to cover the road from Tarboro. The North Carolinians pressed forward, but were held back by "a portion of Company C" on the Union left and "some men deployed in an open field on our right."[406]

Cole neither gained nor lost much ground during the next two hours. More Confederate troops (whether they were some of Kennedy's men or another company of the 17th North Carolina is not clear) appeared at the edge of the swamp. Cole sent back to Tarboro for a gun, and Lt. Jasper Myers of the Ordnance Corps brought up a mountain howitzer.[407]

"Almost a Miracle": Lieutenant Clark's Escape

Lieutenant John D. Clark of the 3rd New York Artillery wandered for what seemed to him like "several hours in water waist deep, among 'varmints' and mosquitoes". After flailing his way through the swampy woods, Lieutenant Clark heard the noise of the fighting between Cole and Lamb. Following the sound of gunfire, he at last spotted Cole's detachment. To rejoin the Union troops, Clark had to run a gauntlet of musket fire from the 17th North Carolina. That was bad enough, but then Cole's overanxious men mistook Clark for a Rebel and also shot at him. The "safe escape of this brave lieutenant was almost a miracle", stated one newspaper.[408]

After reporting to Cole, Clark took charge of the gun brought up by Myers. He fired three shells "with remarkable precision" before Cole ordered the "howitzer and support, and dismounted men and led horses "... half a mile to the rear, fearing these discharges might give the enemy a point on which to direct his fire". Indeed, the Petersburg Artillery had gotten the range. The Yankees believed that the enemy guns swept the area with canister and grapeshot, but "with no effect, as there were but three or four of us there". Grapeshot was a load of iron shot attacked to a central metal stem, similar to a bunch of grapes. Although of little use against fortifications, grapeshot and canister were deadly against infantry. Both types of ammunition were often used in mountain howitzers.[409]

Capt. Edward Graham, the son of a British army officer, was born in the north of Ireland. Graham was a merchant in Petersburg before the war. He was one of the officers of the Petersburg Artillery when it was still an antebellum militia company. Despite his years in Virginia, Graham retained a trace of his Irish accent. His men found him a "rigid disciplinarian ... yet he was kind and always looked out for [his men's] welfare." Another veteran of his battery wrote, "... give us Captain G. in a fight. He knew how to carry us in, how to fight us, and how to bring us out ..." Even a Yankee reporter conceded that while the name of the Rebel battery in this skirmish "was not known ... it is certain it was handsomely handled."[410]

The Yankees Began to Skedaddle

Capt. Thomas Norman and Company G of the 17th North Carolina pressed forward. Under the cover of Graham's guns, they partially flanked Cole's line. When Norman's company opened fire, according to the Southern version, the Yankees "began to skedaddle and run for the bridge protecting themselves as well as they could by the dam or levee, which runs parallel to the river half or three-quarters of a mile." [411]

The "Record of Events" section of the July-August 1863 muster roll for Norman's company states that four men were captured at Tarboro. Records at the National Archives, though, provide only two names – Privates Asa W. Snell and Thomas W. Chesson.⁴¹²

Cole ordered his skirmishers "to fall back slowly under cover as much as possible." Myers aimed the gun and fired an occasional shell to cover their retreat, as the Confederates pushed them toward the Tarboro bridge. Graham parked his two guns in a field "about a mile from the bridge." Taking aim at the Yankees, they fired several shells after Cole. They missed the enemy, but killed three cows that were grazing in the field that was swept by the Confederate guns. Myers could do little to protect their retreat. His little smoothbore cannon "could not at all compete" with the longer-range Confederate guns.⁴¹³

Cole's companies and the survivors of Clarkson's detachment, at last rejoined Potter near the Tar River bridge. After the raid, a grateful Tarboro resident praised the troops who drove Potter's men back, "Kennedy's dismounted men, Graham's shells or Norman's rifles did the work."⁴¹⁴

Major John T. Kennedy of the 62nd Georgia Cavalry signed this requisition for extra forage for 26 horses and 4 mules that his men captured at Daniel's Schoolhouse.

National Archives

The Tar River Bridge as it looked at Tarboro in the early 20th century. Edgecombe County Memorial Library

The Thomas Dupree House, near Otter Creek Bridge, before it was modified in the 1930s. When Potter was blocked by Confederate troops at Otter Creek, a ford on the Dupree Plantation offered a way out.
Photo: Amos L. "Bucky" Moore, Jr.

Chapter 11

"The Fun Commenced in Earnest"
Riding Back to New Bern
Monday Afternoon, July 20 – Tuesday Morning, July 21, 1863

Potter was deep in Confederate territory. His force was divided and widely scattered. So far, they had not heard a word from the six companies that were sent to Rocky Mount. Two other companies were miles away at Sparta. The booming echoes of cannon and musket fire from across the river told him that Clarkson's detachment, plus the companies taken by Cole to rescue them, were seriously entangled with enemy forces. After Potter sent Cole's three companies to relieve Clarkson, he had only four companies left.[415]

Before and after the expedition, Potter and Foster wrote little about their plans for the raid. As far as Sergeant Cooley and his comrades in Sparta knew, they were holding three bridges there "until the Regt. came back". But, a Southern witness claimed that before the fighting at Daniel's Schoolhouse, Potter ordered the refugee slaves, captured wagons, and draft animals across the Tar River bridge. From that point, a march of "only 43 miles ... over a hard piney woods road" along the north bank of the river would get them to Washington, the closest Union garrison. At the rate they had been pushing themselves on the raid so far, they could get to Washington on the next day. From there, New Bern would be just an easy steamboat ride away. If that indeed had been Potter's intention, Kennedy and Lamb had forced a sudden change in the general's plans.[416]

Returning to New Bern by their original route was a much longer journey. By that time, there was also the danger that Confederate troops from Kinston and Goldsboro were converging on the area. On the other hand, there were far fewer Confederate soldiers north of the Tar River: only a few companies of the 62nd Georgia Cavalry and the 17th North Carolina, and the small garrison at Fort Branch. The damage to the bridge at Greenville would hinder Confederate forces trying to cross to the north side of the river.

Potter hinted that the sharp defeat at Daniel's Schoolhouse forced him to make a quick change of plans. He wrote, "… having learned that the enemy were in considerable force on the opposite side of the river, I determined to return by the same road we had taken in coming." Clarkson also implied a change in their original plans by saying, "when the enemy, having brought up a piece of ordnance, opened fire upon us, while we were upon the north side of the Tar River, we were ordered to move across the bridge, through the town, and out upon the same road to Sparta by which we had advanced."[417]

Surgeon Albert Potter, USA

Potter sent word for the two companies at Sparta to join him. Cole covered the bridge while Potter's troops, the growing crowd of refugee slaves, and the straggling survivors of the Daniel's Schoolhouse fight gathered in Tarboro. As soon as it looked like everyone who was not dead or captured had crossed the river, Cole ordered his men to set the bridge on fire. A roll call of Clarkson's men was called after they crossed the bridge. It was then that they realized the extent of their losses in their first battle.[418]

Medical officers treated the wounded men who were brought back from Daniel's Schoolhouse. Sgt. James McKenna of the 12th New York Cavalry was brought to Surgeon Albert Potter, who found the patient suffering from a "shot wound of left shoulder, involving bone and artery". Potter could do nothing but amputate McKenna's arm, and get his patient ready to travel on one of the ambulance wagons. Without waiting any longer for Jacobs to get in from Rocky Mount, Potter began pulling out of Tarboro around 4 or 5 p.m. Major Cole stayed behind to guard their retreat, and to keep the townspeople from putting out the fire on the bridge.[419]

Going back to New Bern was a small group of prisoners. In the National Archives' records, most of the Potter's Raid prisoners are listed as being captured at Tarboro on July 21, no matter when or where they were taken, which makes it difficult to determine whether they were captured at Rocky Mount, Tarboro, or elsewhere. The Tarboro prisoners probably included at least ten men: Lt. Bennett P. Jenkins and Private Joshua W. Tucker of the 7th Confederate Cavalry; Lt. Nathan M. Lawrence, an officer of the 8th North Carolina; Lt. Thomas J. Stewart, formerly of the 3rd North Carolina Artillery; Sgt. Ezra S. Moody and Private Robert J. Turner of the Petersburg Artillery; Private Henry G. Jones of the 43rd North Carolina; Private Elisha C. Jones, Company I, 17th North Carolina, and Privates Jones and Snell, who were captured from Company G of the 17th North Carolina during its fighting with Major Cole.[420]

Some of the prisoners were not on active duty when they were picked up. Lieutenant Lawrence, who was from Tarboro, was home on sick furlough. Lieutenant Stewart, who was also of Edgecombe County, belonged to a company that had been disbanded, and was apparently at home awaiting new orders. Private Henry G. Jones is listed in his regimental records as absent in the hospital at Goldsboro during this period.[421]

When Jacobs rode into Tarboro from Rocky Mount, only Cole's rear guard was still in town waiting for him. Cole, upon learning that Jacobs was near, stayed behind for him. The route from Rocky Mount led past the Tarboro railroad depot, at the edge of town. Potter had unaccountably spared some of the railroad buildings, so Jacobs' troopers set fire to the ticket agent's office and two warehouses as they passed by.[422]

"We Showed Them a Clean Pair of Heels"

Confederate cannons, presumably belonging to Petersburg Artillery, fired some parting shots to hasten the Federals on their way, but without hitting anyone. As Sergeant Cooley of the 3rd New York Cavalry put it, "We now started on our homeward track, and now the fun commenced in earnest. Soon after our column got under way, Mr. Reb Artillery commenced to toss us a shell or two but our horses being in good trim we showed them a clean pair of heels getting back to Sparta". Cooley added that before they left Sparta, "all the bridges were ordered to be burned".[423]

Captain Hall wrote that Potter's command was "twelve miles from Tawboro" when the Rocky Mount contingent caught up to the main body of troops. They continued on their way down the River Road in the direction of Greenville.[424]

Potter's rear guard was far down the road when the two lost pickets, Wakeman and Hall, had at last covered the fourteen miles from Rocky Mount to Tarboro. "We expected to join the army at Tarboro", wrote Wakeman. "Judge of our surprise when we found it deserted by the Union troops."[425]

Wakeman later wrote that he and Hall "advanced at a good round pace" through Tarboro. But, according to his account, when they were "about half way through the town" they saw four rebel soldiers blocking the street about one hundred yards in front of them. The Confederates "coolly drew up their pieces, and fired at us as though they were firing at a target." Luckily for the Yankees, all four of the enemy shots missed. Wakeman said that he "loosed my carbine, but it missed fire", so he spurred his horse and drew his revolver. Unable to reload before the horsemen were upon them, the four men dropped their guns. "I should have killed the one that fired at me had they not surrendered", wrote Wakeman, but since they had given up, he felt that he "could not have the heart to shoot them." Hall didn't share Wakeman's kinder instincts; he "snapped his pistol" at the captives, "but it missed fire". The two New Yorkers pressed on for Sparta, bringing the four unidentified prisoners with them.[426]

Meanwhile, Major Kennedy and his three companies reached the end of the burning Tar River bridge. Tarboro's 1886 Sanborn Fire Insurance Map indicates that the bridge in that year was 550 feet long, and that the river itself was 200 feet wide. Kennedy later stated, " ... As we approached the bridge we found a small portion of it torn up and that portion next to town on fire. Dismounting and going as far as we could for the fire on the bridge, we called on the town to aid us with all the help and buckets they could and we would save the bridge. The call met a hearty response from the citizens. The first bucket handed was from Governor Clark ..." Also helping to douse the flames were some of Capt. Norman's infantrymen; Philip Garnett, a Virginia-born brick mason; Dr. Joseph Baker of Tarboro's Confederate hospital; and the English-born blacksmith Isaac B. Palamountain.[427]

By 8 p.m., they had put out the fire and repaired the bridge well enough that Kennedy's horses could get across. But, a superior officer (whom Kennedy did not name, but Lt.-col. John C. Lamb was apparently the only superior officer present) denied the cavalry permission to pursue Potter until the next morning. Kennedy was disappointed, although as a practical matter, it would not have been wise for his 80 or so men to pitch themselves headlong into a fight with a force of over 800.[428]

Although Potter had escaped Kennedy's small force, he was on a collision course with a regiment of Confederate cavalry. Col. William C. Claiborne's 7th Confederate Cavalry had been after Potter since July 19, when General Martin sent them from Goldsboro to intercept the Yankees. At that time, the intelligence available to Martin had the Yankees moving toward Coward's Bridge (present-day Grifton, at the Southern edge of Pitt County). In other words, Martin didn't know by then that Potter had turned north toward Greenville after leaving Swift Creek Village.[429]

Maj. Thomas Claiborne (who was the brother of the regiment's colonel) took 150 men and a mountain howitzer and left ahead of the rest of the regiment. Like the 3rd New York Cavalry, the 7th Confederate Cavalry also had a separate

Potter's Raid

mountain howitzer detachment. The gun with Major Claiborne was under the command of Lt. William D. Matthews. On the night of July 19, Major Claiborne reached Scuffleton, on Contentnea Creek in Greene County, about ten miles from Coward's Bridge. Because Potter's men hadn't shown up at Contentnea Creek, Major Claiborne sent a scouting party to Greenville on Monday morning. His scouts learned that Potter had moved on toward Tarboro on the previous day. The people of Greenville gave the remarkably accurate information that Potter had four guns and "between eight hundred and a thousand" men.[430]

A postwar portrait of Lt. W.D. Matthews, CSA

Major Claiborne took his command along the River Road until they got to the bridge over Otter Creek, which was about one mile north of Falkland (and eight miles west of Greenville). Claiborne figured that Potter would retrace his route, and he settled down to wait for the Yankees on the south bank of the Otter Creek bridge. He sent a few men to scout the road ahead of them to look for Potter, and waited for the rest of his regiment.[431]

After the Federals passed Sparta, the loyalist North Carolina company and Company C of the 3rd New York Cavalry were in the advance, under Major Clarkson. One mile south of Falkland, when the advance rode through the plantation of Charles Vine, about 20 men of the 7th Confederate Cavalry sprang an ambush. The Rebels killed two of the Federal horses, and then they turned and galloped down the road toward Falkland. The Yankee advance troops followed them and kept up a "running skirmish".[432]

Even as the advance troops were fighting with the Confederate cavalry, some of the Union officers found time "to get a good supper at W. B. F. Newton's, who lived at the Swain place.", according to historian Henry King. "While there", added King, "several neighbors tried to get an opportunity to shoot at some of them and one James Dupree, son of Thomas Dupree, a boy about sixteen, was captured with his gun but was released."[433]

A Trap Is Set at Otter Creek

Before Potter's force approached Otter Creek, Major Claiborne ordered his men to tear up the bridge. From 50 to 100 of his men dismounted and scattered under cover, as sharpshooters. The Rebels, with their little mountain howitzer, were in a good position to block the Yankees, due to "the conformation of the country being such as to form a valley just in front" of them. Williams Branch and Kitten Creek both flowed into Otter Creek just west of the bridge. Together, the creeks wove an extensive barrier of wetlands. At the very first sight of a dozen or so of Potter's advance troops, who were "400 or 500 yards" distant up the road, Claiborne gave the order, "Fire!".[434]

Major Claiborne gave himself away too soon. At that long range, the first Confederate volley did no harm, but it alerted the Yankees to the trap waiting for them. Clarkson sent Capt. Alonzo Stearns' company of the 3rd New York Cavalry, Capt. Emory Cummings of the 23rd New York Cavalry, and 30 men of the North Carolina company ahead on foot "into the woods as skirmishers to cover the right flank." The rest of the men were formed into "columns of four by squadrons, and retired ... into the fields on the left side of the road, to keep them out of range of the enemy's skirmishers." Captain Cummings escaped hurt when his horse was killed by a bullet through its forehead. Clarkson sent a messenger back to the main body of troops with a request for a mountain howitzer. Lieutenant-colonel Lewis rode to the scene with the gun and "took command of the skirmish."[435]

Sergeant Cooley wrote that "they now commenced to shell us in earnest several Cos. Of Carbines were sent forward to the front and went to work. Co. M was now sent for to take the advance."[436]

A Confederate witness wrote that at Otter Creek, "the rattling of rifles ... commenced, and a shell from one of their pieces came bursting over us. The little pet, 'Lennox', replied handsomely, and we continued to shell the opposite woods." After an hour of skirmishing, Colonel Claiborne and more of the regiment joined them.[437]

Colonel Claiborne also brought a four-gun battery from Alabama, the Montgomery True Blues. As a military unit, the True Blues dated back to 1836. They were founded as a militia company to take part in the Second Creek War, one of the last of the Indian Wars to be fought in the South. At the start of the Civil War, the company served as part of the 3rd Alabama Infantry before they were detached and changed into an artillery unit. Before they left Montgomery, the True Blues were part of the parade at the inauguration of Jefferson Davis as president of the Confederate States, on February 18, 1861. The artillery company, which included a number of prominent citizens of Montgomery, spent most of the war in eastern North Carolina. They were also known as Andrews' Battery, after their first commander, Capt. W. G. Andrews, although by this time, they were commanded by Lt. Edgar J. Lee. The battery's armament at Otter Creek was not mentioned, but late in 1864, the True Blues had two 6-pounder guns, one 3-inch rifle and one 12-pounder field howitzer.[438]

At first glance, the Confederate position looked strong indeed. Major Claiborne's men were well hidden. The guns of the Montgomery True Blues could maul the Yankees without much danger to the rebels. A mountain howitzer (at a 5 degree elevation) had a range of 900 yards, which was about half of the range of a 3-inch rifle and hundreds of yards less than the 6-pounders or the full-sized howitzer. But, Lt. Van Buren Sharpe, an officer of Company I of Claiborne's regiment, saw a glaring flaw in his colonel's plans. Sharpe, who had lived nearby in Edgecombe County, knew that there was a ford across Otter Creek a short distance upstream from the bridge. This ford, called "the Dupree Crossing", offered an escape route for the Yankees. But, Colonel Claibourne brushed aside Sharpe's suggestion that he dispatch some men to cover the ford.[439]

Potter surveyed the situation and saw that his adversaries were "in considerable strength" at the creek (which he and Clarkson both mistakenly thought was Tyson's Creek rather than Otter Creek), and that "their position was a very difficult one to carry". Things looked even worse to Sergeant Cooley. He believed that "we were some eighty or ninety miles from any support and only twelve hundred men to resist a force nearly twice as large."[440]

Cooley overestimated the size of Potter's force, as well as that of their enemies; Potter's 800-man force probably outnumbered Claiborne two to one. It's uncertain just how many troopers Colonel Claiborne brought with him. Three of Claiborne's companies were unavailable because they were assigned to W. H. C. Whiting's District of the Cape Fear. Besides Company F at Kenansville, Company D was at Snead's Ferry in Onslow County and Company E was at Fort Fisher, south of Wilmington. Although Potter may have had the numbers to push through Claiborne's line, every moment of delay brought the possibility of more Confederate troops marching in to block his way. His men and horses were tired from their lack of sleep and the hard riding of the past couple of days. They could not risk a battle at Otter Creek.[441]

The Road to Dupree's Ford

The Yankees started looking for a way out. Sergeant Cooley, with some of his comrades of the 3rd New York Cavalry, rode back the way they came for a short distance along the Tar River Road. They came back to the house of Thomas Byrd Dupree, the same man whose teenage son had earlier been caught while shooting at them. At the Dupree place, they explored a road that led west, away from the River Road. After riding for half a mile, they stopped at a house where a man told them about an unguarded ford nearby — the very ford that Lieutenant Sharpe was worried about. William H. Graves remembered their benefactor only as "a colored boy". No one seems to have recorded this man's name, nor noted whether he was enslaved or free, but this unknown fellow may have saved Potter's Raid from an inglorious end at Otter Creek.[442]

A Confederate newspaper later accused Claiborne of "an impardonable military blunder" by overlooking the obvious precaution of guarding Dupree's Ford with a few men. Potter left a few pickets in Claiborne's front to keep up the skirmish and draw the Confederates' attentions away from their move toward the ford. Private Graves wrote that "we were cautioned to keep our sabers and everything which could make a noise as still as possible." The route through the creek was "very circuitous and difficult of passage, and its track is about 150 yards in length." Captain Hall of the 3rd New York Cavalry wrote that the men rode "up to our horses' ears in water." [443]

Graves wrote that "I guess when we forded that stream every man was surprised. I know I was for one, for the water was over my horse's back and consequently the water was around my waist. This was an old ford and had not been used for years and the branches of the trees on the other side swept off about every man's hat as we ascertained when morning came." By 11 p.m., the entire force had passed the home of Col. Walter Newton, who lived four miles away from the Otter Creek bridge.[444]

A disgusted Southerner wrote that Colonel Claiborne, oblivious to Potter's escape, "continued shelling from the bridge, the enemy's supposed but abandoned position, until half past five o'clock in the morning, to the destruction of nothing except the limbs of a few unoffending trees that couldn't retreat."[445]

Sergeant Cooley was "scarcely a mile" past Dupree's Ford when "the advance Videttes came to a halt, raised their pieces to their shoulders and fired by the light of their pieces could be seen men lying along side of the road in ambush. Brig'd Gen. Potter now gave the order for M Co. to draw sabres and charge through them. Our Sabres were soon in hand and our spurs in the flanks of our horses and away we went through and pass their ambush as the rear of our Co. was passing and a piece of Light Artillery was coming up, the Rebs opened

Otter Creek, near the Dupree Ford, where Potter escaped from the Confederate cavalry.
Photo: Amos L. "Bucky" Moore, Jr.

The Montgomery True Blues, armed with full-sized field guns like this one, fought at Otter Creek.

fire from the woods and three men fell wounded from their horses upon enquiry they proved to be members of the battery." Records of the 3rd New York Artillery show that four men of Battery H were wounded during Potter's Raid; their casualties that were not inflicted at Daniel's Schoolhouse may have occurred during this nighttime ambush. No records have turned up that show any casualties from the 3rd New York Cavalry's howitzer company.[446]

Cooley and Company M might have found out who ambushed them after they crossed the ford. The ambuscade may be the same one recorded by historian Henry King, who stated that Col. Walter Newton and his nephew W. B. F. Newton fired at the Federal troops after they crossed Otter Creek. The elder Newton was the colonel of the 17th North Carolina Militia; his nephew was a merchant who served as a second lieutenant in the same militia regiment, from the Falkland district. Colonel Newton's home was in the neighborhood of the ford. The Newtons escaped after firing a few shots. If the colonel and his nephew were the men who fired on Cooley and Company M, they evidently never learned that they had hit three of the gunners. Some of Potter's men may have blamed Colonel Newton for the ambush, since they set fire to his house as they passed. Something particularly marked the Newton home for this treatment, because it seems to be the only private dwelling that was deliberately set afire during Potter's Raid. After the Federals left, the Newton slaves put the fire out before it had time to do much damage.[447]

There were units of the North Carolina Militia in each county. The militia was once a form of universal military service, but by 1861, the militia system had declined to the point that it was of little practical use. The antebellum militia met irregularly, and the musters were more social events than training sessions. A few exceptionally well-trained volunteer militia companies, which kept to much higher self-imposed standards, were quickly brought into the army. On paper in 1861, there were 116 militia regiments, with at least one in each county. By mid-1862, heavy volunteering and the strict conscription laws had plucked most of the useful men from the militia, leaving mostly men who were too old or sick to do active service, with a smattering of "exempts" such as government officials.[448]

Other than the Newtons, no names of any militiamen are recorded as attacking Potter's column. The author has found no records of casualties among the militia.

Probably referring to the raiding in Tarboro and the ride through the dark and tangled woods around Otter Creek, Private Oren T. Wooster wrote, "I had about twenty five dollars worth of stuff I had about eight yds of heavy blue silk I had a lot of silk thread we broke into a odfellows lodge I got a nice sash worth about $10 dollars and some other things but that night I lost them all off from my saddle."[449]

During the passage through Otter Creek, Private Andrew J. McIntyre, one of the prisoners taken at the depot in Rocky Mount, rode his mule into the ford. Taking advantage of the darkness and the thick woods, he galloped away from his captors on his mule. McIntyre figured that it was "awhile after midnight" when he got away. After a twelve hour ride that covered well over twenty-five miles, McIntyre and his mule reached Wilson the next morning.[450]

A few of Potter's men were captured during this stage of the raid. The *Daily Progress* in Raleigh reported that "three Yankee stragglers, exhausted, drunk, and indifferent to their fate, were captured by three citizens" near Otter Creek. Claiborne's men possibly rounded up a few more, according to the newspaper. Another report stated that eight Union soldiers were "taken at the bridge". Some of the prisoners gave the Confederates a false report that the first shell fired by Lieutenant Matthews' gun at Otter Creek "killed Major Cole, 3rd N. Y. Cavalry, wounded two men, and killed two horses." The available records do not reveal which of Potter's men were taken around Falkland and Otter Creek.[451]

According to Corporal Wakeman, he and Hall headed for Sparta with their four prisoners after they got out of Tarboro. When they got to Sparta, they learned that Potter had already left there and was still far ahead of them. Although they guessed that they had already ridden fifty miles that day, "there was no alternative" but to fight their hunger and fatigue and "push on, and overtake the column …" When they could go no further, they halted in the dark, nearly moonless night and "bivouacked in a door-yard, and fed our horses on whatever we could find." Wakeman said that by then "there were three of us", but he didn't explain where the third Union soldier of their little band came from. The corporal ordered his comrades and the prisoners to get some sleep while he stood the first watch. I ... tried to think of home and friends, in order to keep awake, but it was of no use; if I'd had Jeff Davis to watch, I couldn't have kept awake." Evidently the prisoners were as tired as he was. Everyone slept until about 3 a.m., when they headed out again to try to catch up with Potter.[452]

Captain Hall wrote that Potter "decided to take to the woods leaving all roads; across which ... the enemy might be supposed to be posted". They chose their route by "trusting to Negro guides". After "taking a very intricate path through a plantation", wrote Potter, they reached a "'piney woods road', on which we marched all night." The Yankees were traveling through some rather thinly settled sections, and if they avoided the roads they would come into contact with even fewer people. And, certainly anyone who had warning of Potter's approach would have put out any lights or fires to avoid attracting unwanted attention. Henry King even mentioned that during another raid, a Pitt County woman was warned of the approach of Federal cavalry because their sound "was not the tread of Confederate horses, the Confederate and Federal cavalry drilling being different".[453]

Potter's exact route that night is hard to determine, particularly the sections where he avoided the roads altogether. His sharp detour around Falkland took him out of Pitt County back into Edgecombe County, and he may have brushed the extreme eastern tip of Wilson County before heading back into western Pitt County. Historian Henry King gave the most definite account of Potter's route that night, stating that the Yankees followed Otter Creek Church Road (part of this road corresponds with modern NC Road 1102 in Edgecombe County; a 1905 map has this road running through the eastern edge of Wilson County for a few yards), and entered Greene County "by way of Fieldsboro". Fieldsboro, two miles east of Walstonburg, was on the old Greenville and Wilson Plank Road.[454]

One possible clue to Potter's route comes from the fate of some silverware that was taken from the home of Caroline Williams, who lived on the River Road between Greenville and Falkland. Some of their silver pieces were picked up by someone who recognized the family's initials on them. The Williams silverware was found after it was dropped along a road near Marlboro, which was five miles east of Fieldsboro on the Plank Road near modern-day Farmville. (Old US 264 follows the route of the Plank Road.) Adding the recovery of the Williams' silver to King's statement, it may be that Potter struck the Plank Road at Fieldsboro, and then headed east either on that road or another road that paralleled it just to the north to briefly reenter Pitt County. At Marlboro, Potter turned south on the old Snow Hill Road (US 258).[455]

Major Cole led the advance while the Federal column rode all night. At one unknown location, Cole was "fired into from an ambuscade on our right very sharply, wounding several. Then I charged past, and fired to the right, soon silencing them." There seems to be no corresponding Confederate report of this ambush; perhaps the unknown adversaries were some more of the local militia.[456]

Another soldier, Private Charles N. D. Mead of Company I, 3rd New York Cavalry, wrote that during that night, they "occasionally received a volley from a cornfield or from the bushes. We traveled at double quick and were so tired and sleepy that half the regiment lost their hats while sleeping on their horses' necks."[457]

These minor ambushes by local citizens or militiamen had little direct effect on the raid. At best, they slightly wounded a few Union cavalrymen or horses and caused some minor delays in their march. But, the psychological toll taken on the Federals, as well as the resulting lack of sleep, weighed heavily on them. It seemed to H. A. Cooley that "...we did not travel ten miles from Tarboro to Street's Ferry, a distance of a hundred miles (by the road we traveled) but we had to fight every step of the way."[458]

All night long back at Otter Creek, the Montgomery True Blues hurled shot and shell into the empty woods that the Yankees had long since abandoned. Risking her life in the face of the cannon fire, "a patriotic and heroic young lady", named Mrs. Drake (her first name is not recorded), "who resided not far from Otter Creek bridge, hastened at the dawn of day" to warn that Potter had already made his escape. Another writer noted that Mrs. Drake "passed through it all" as "the firing was going on and our shot [was] hurling through the Trees", and that her conduct was "illustrative of the indomitable bravery of the women of the South". Claiborne gave the order to cease fire about 5:30 a.m., but held his men back from chasing Potter until 9 a.m.[459]

The first name of Mrs. Drake was not recorded in the newspapers. Possibly she was Louisiana Drake, wife of a farmer named George Drake who appears in the censuses of Edgecombe County in 1860 and 1870. In the latter year, they lived in Sparta Township, which in Edgecombe County but close to the Pitt County Line and the Falkland area.[460]

Corporal Wakeman and his party had no idea that Potter had detoured to the Dupree Crossing. They pressed on in the dark, riding straight down the River Road and expecting to link up once again with Potter. Curiously, in his account, the corporal didn't mention hearing the sound of cannon fire during the night. "Just before daylight", Wakeman wrote, the men "heard talking in front of us. I thought it was a relief picket, and told the boys we might be fired upon, as it was dark." Only a few minutes later they heard a musket shot, "... then a dozen – then a whole volley." Instead of finding his comrades, Wakeman had ridden right into Claiborne's regiment near Otter Creek. The hot situation cooled for a moment when a voice in the darkness ordered, "Don't fire, for God's sake, it is your own men!"[461]

A Union Army ambulance photographed in New Bern. Southern Historical Collection

Wakeman said that he ordered his men ahead with one word: "Forward!" Confederate pickets heard him, and the enemy cut loose with "a perfect shower of Canister, and short-range shell [that] … flew around our ears like hail." Two of the prisoners they took in Tarboro escaped under the cover of the artillery fire. The rest of the small party fell back out of range and tried to pick up Potter's trail.[462]

At daybreak, by the time when Mrs. Drake alerted Claiborne of Potter's escape, Sergeant Cooley was far ahead of them with Cole's advance troops. Cooley was relieved when after "beating a double-quick for several miles morning came to our relief and we found ourselves on the Snow Hill Road". Cole's men "halted and fed at a house on our right", and waited for Potter. They had ridden non-stop for about forty miles since they left Tarboro. Soon, other than Wakeman's party, the rest of the Federal column was reunited with Cole. There was time for only a short rest near Grimsley's Church, about three and a half miles north of Snow Hill, the county seat of Greene County. They were over fifteen miles from Claiborne's regiment and the Montgomery True Blues at Otter Creek.[463]

The raiders halted briefly near the Greene County home of W.P. Grimsley. Mike Edge

Although most of Potter's force remained north of Contentnea Creek, some troops entered the Aquilla Sugg House in Greene County near Snow Hill, south of the creek.
Mike Edge

Chapter 12

"All Sorts of Rumors Are Afloat"
The Raiders at Large in Greene County
Tuesday, July 21, 1863

Potter's troops remained near Grimsley's Church only long enough "to graze their horses and take a short rest." They knew that they were too close to the Confederates around Kinston, and too far from safety at New Bern, to relax for very long. Indeed, one Southern account went so far as to claim that some of Potter's scouts reported that Claiborne's cavalrymen were not far from them. Upon hearing that report, so this account said, "immediately everything was in the utmost confusion, much plunder was thrown away, and all mounted in hot haste." Potter, however, mentioned nothing of any hasty departure and simply stated that "at 8 a. m. the march was continued toward Snow Hill." [464]

After daylight on July 21, Wakeman and Hall learned that Potter had left the River Road to get around the Confederate trap at Otter Creek. Picking up the Federal trail, they finally caught up with the column during the day. Their remaining prisoners were handed over to the expedition's provost-marshal, and the two men rejoined their companies. [465]

Two of the farms near Snow Hill that the Federals passed by were owned by Union sympathizers, according to a Greene County letter that was published in the *State Journal* in Raleigh. This account stated that Potter's advance troops stole two horses that were owned by a Mr. Grimsley, who was "known" to be a "tory". The writer continued, "I understand Mr. Grimsley visited their camp, and, after learning his position, the commander of the raiders gave him *six horses* for the two taken! They told Mr. Grimsley's negroes to *stay at home*, while they took care to carry away all they could get belonging to rebels. How the rest of the tories fared, I know not; but I learn the raiders took nothing from Mr. Patrick except some rye to feed with." W. P. Grimsley, along with a Mr. Patrick and two men named Williams and Dixon, were identified as "tories" who held an anti-war meeting in Greene County after the raid.[466]

The reactions of Grimsley, Williams, and Dixon to these accusations were not recorded. Perhaps Edward Patrick spoke for them when he angrily denied the charge of disloyalty to the Confederacy. When Patrick read that piece in the *State Journal,* he demanded that the editor tell him who had accused him of being a "Tory". The editor claimed that he had "mislaid the communication, and not remembering the name" of the accuser, could not provide it. Patrick could only denounce in print, in a newspaper that was politically opposed to the *State Journal,* the charges that a "cowardly and infamous poltroon and slanderer" made against him.[467]

Edward Patrick died in October 1865, and his executor John M. Patrick filed a claim with the Federal government for the loss of eight horses, eight mules, two yoke of oxen, and four carts. These were taken, though, in 1865 by troops that the Patricks believed to be part of Lt. Gen. William T. Sherman's army. That claim was denied on the grounds that Patrick had served in the state legislature under the Confederacy, and was not eligible for reimbursement as a loyal Unionist.[468]

Among the other Greene County farms hit by Potter's men was that of T. T. Dail. About 4 p.m. on the day that the raiders were in Greene County, Dail's son, M. E. Dail, put a bay mare belonging to his father in a stable. Fifteen minutes later, the younger Dail saw one of Potter's men riding the mare. In 1871, Dail filed a claim against the Federal government for the loss of the mare, which he valued at $200. J.A.D. Phillips, also of Greene County, filed a postwar claim for 400 pounds of fodder, valued at $4.00, which Potter's men seized and fed to their horses "on the premises." The claims of Dail and Phillips were eventually denied by the US government, on the grounds that they could not prove wartime loyalty to the Union.[469]

One Greene County claim that was upheld was filed by W. P. Grimsley. In 1874, he was awarded $1745 as part of the "claims for supplies furnished by loyal citizens during the Rebellion".[470]

By early on Tuesday morning, July 21, alarming reports of Potter's Raid were spread across eastern North Carolina. "All sorts of rumors of their whereabouts are afloat, but nothing definite outside of military circles," worried one newspaper. The *Petersburg Express* fretted that the "raiders have only fallen back to Tarboro. …If allowed to remain at Tarboro, it will be time thrown away to repair the Wilmington & Weldon railroad for the Yankee government will be able to reach it in two hours time whenever they feel disposed…" The *Richmond Dispatch* reported that the confusion caused by the raid was compounded because, "During this raid the wires between Petersburg and Weldon were cut — by some Union man, doubtless." After they left the vicinity of Grimsley's Church in Greene County, the raiders were effectively hidden in a remote area away from major towns, railroads, or telegraph lines. General Martin, guiding the search for Potter from Kinston, did not know exactly where Potter was, nor what the Yankee general's plans were.[471]

Catherine Anne Devereaux Edmonston lived on a Halifax County plantation near Scotland Neck, perhaps 20 miles north of Tarboro. Her wartime diary is packed with detailed records that she made of events of the war in North Carolina, as well as the reactions and opinions of her family and neighbors. Mrs. Edmonston and her father were playing chess when her husband burst in with the first frightening rumors of the raids on Tarboro and Rocky Mount. Her husband then dashed off to find the local militia captain, even though there were few men left in the region to serve in the militia.[472]

The most alarming news was the notion that the Yankees would leave Tarboro for Halifax County, to destroy the ironclad gunboat *CSS Albemarle,* which was under construction on the Roanoke River. No one in Halifax County could know that Potter had turned in the opposite direction and was already in Greene County. One of the Edmonston's neighbors, a Mr. Hill, was determined to pull up the floor planks of every bridge in the area. Mrs. Edmonston in vain tried to point out that pulling up small bridges no more than ten feet long wouldn't stop Yankee cavalrymen, but would merely inconvenience the locals. Despairing of the elderly and inefficient militiamen doing anything practical to stop the Yankees, she started hiding her silverware herself.[473]

In Wayne County, far to the south of Mrs. Edmondston's neighborhood, Goldsboro was gripped by rumors that Potter was heading there. One writer in Goldsboro stated, "I never saw a community more determined, yet more cool than this was, when we expected that they might return by this route on Tuesday night. The oldest citizens we have were out with their muskets — one of the oldest complaining lustily yesterday that *he* was not called upon — and fresh rumors arriving yesterday, I saw him walking briskly down street with his gun in hand, hurrying to the rendezvous." At the Confederate army hospital in Goldsboro, an emergency defense company was formed by the patients who were fit enough to drag themselves from their beds.[474]

Sheriff W. H. High of Wake County left Raleigh on Monday, July 20 "in command of a scouting party". High's party personally inspected the destruction in Rocky Mount, and brought back stories of "other depredations too numerous to mention" in Sparta and Tarboro.[475]

Closing In On Potter

Potter's Raid was just one of the many problems that were piled up on the desk of President Jefferson Davis in Richmond. Davis noted in a letter to General Robert E. Lee on July 21, that "yesterday it was reported that the enemy's cavalry were moving on the R. R. to Wilmington from the direction of Greenville ..." When news of the raid got to Richmond, Confederate Adjutant General Samuel Cooper ordered Brig. Gen. Mathew Ransom to take one of his regiments from Petersburg, Virginia to North Carolina to intercept Potter. Ransom's train pulled into Rocky Mount on Tuesday, one day too late. The general reported that "it is only a raid" and that the Yankees were on their way back to New Bern. The Wilmington & Weldon Railroad was safe for the moment.[476]

During Tuesday, July 21, couriers galloped back and forth across eastern North Carolina, carrying orders from General Martin, who was shuffling his scattered forces to intercept the Yankees. Martin ordered a force of "six hundred infantry" and six cannons from Kinston to move toward Swift Creek, where he hoped they would intercept Potter. The infantry force from Kinston probably included the 50th North Carolina and elements of the 42nd. Company B of the 42nd North Carolina received orders on July 20 to march to Greenville, which they reached the next day. The company marched "8 miles above Greenville and returned." [477]

Besides part of the 42nd North Carolina, the battalion of Maj. William Saunders, with 75 mounted artillerymen and 80 men in wagons, reached Greenville on Tuesday. On Tuesday morning, Major Kennedy of the 62nd Georgia Cavalry finally got permission to leave Tarboro and go after the raiders with his 84 men. In front of Potter, though, were only a few small bands of men from the battalions of Whitford and Nethercutt.[478]

Mary Jane Phillips of Greene County was 13 years old during Potter's Raid. She later recalled that "local militia and part of Whitford's Partisan Rangers" thought that Potter would head from Grimsley's Church along a road that led east across the county. They chose the Forrest Farm as a likely spot to dig some hasty earthworks and wait for the Yankees, not knowing that Potter's men had taken a more southerly route instead. The fortifications were never used. Visible until recent times, these earthworks were lost when a farm pond was dug on the site.[479]

The closest Confederate units to Potter were two companies of the 7th Confederate Cavalry. Capt. Lycurgus J. Barrett of Pitt County, commanded company H, which was made up mostly of men from Wilson County. Company

I, commanded by Capt. Franklin G. Pitt, was made up mainly of Edgecombe County men. Their local origins gave them considerable knowledge of the country. Indeed, Lt. Van Buren Sharpe, the officer who tried to warn Colonel W.C. Claiborne that Potter might escape from across Otter Creek at Dupree's Ford, served in Pitt's company.[480]

Modern-day Edwards' Bridge, over Contentnea Creek. Mike Edge

Only small parties of Confederates actually caught up with Potter on July 21. Potter's troops had no way of knowing exactly how many enemy soldiers were closing in on them, so these small forces seemed much more threatening than they really were. The rear guard soldiers of the Union force felt like they were being "harassed by a swarm of rebel hornets who were now thoroughly stirred up in their nest". William H. Graves of the 12th New York Cavalry remembered that "we met the enemy in every piece of timber we came to and we had to dismount and drive them through the timber only to meet them again in the next timber we came to".[481]

Major Cole's battalion formed the Federal rear guard after the early morning halt near Grimsley's Church. Cole wrote that they were "annoyed all day by the firing of a squadron of rebel cavalry", probably Pitt's and Barrett's companies. At one time, the Confederates were preparing to charge when they were blasted by "a double charge of grape and canister" from a Union mountain howitzer. The Rebel horsemen "still kept following, although more cautiously, and again attacked us while feeding, slightly wounding Lieutenant [Walter F.] Budlong in the face." Another blast of canister "scattered them", and they did not press Cole so closely for the rest of the day. The available records of the 7th Confederate Cavalry do not mention any casualties on that day, making it difficult to trace their movements and losses on Potter's Raid.[482]

Company A of the 12th New York needed considerable reorganization after the heavy losses that they had suffered on the day before at Daniel's Schoolhouse. All three of their officers were lost in the skirmish, and 1st Sgt. Gleason Wellington had been sick and incapacitated in an ambulance since they left Sparta. To replace the missing non-commissioned officers, two corporals and one private were promoted to sergeant as they crossed Greene County on July 21. One of the new sergeants, former Corporal George Palmer, was among the walking wounded. Four privates were promoted to corporal that day. They included William H. Graves. He was once a non-commissioned officer, but had been reduced to the ranks some time before. This second chance at promotion put him in his way to finishing the war as a quartermaster sergeant.[483]

Potter moved south through Greene County until he reached Contentnea Creek near Hookerton, where he took a road that led northeast, toward Scuffleton. Somewhere "near Snow Hill", Corp. Robert Strieback of the 1st North Carolina Union Volunteers was captured. Strieback was born in Brooklyn, New York, and he was a seaman before the war. He had enlisted in Graham's company at the age of 35 in Plymouth, North Carolina on December 27, 1862. His records reveal no details about the circumstances of his capture, his eventual fate, nor, indeed, why a Brooklyn-born sailor enlisted in a Union regiment in North Carolina. Records of Battery H, 3rd New York Artillery, as well as those for Potter's cavalry units, note a skirmish at Hookerton (sometimes misspelled "Hooktown" or "Hookerstown") on July 21. One soldier of the 12th New York Cavalry was reported as wounded at Hookerton, and another was listed as missing.

Contentnea Creek from the Scuffleton Bridge (above), and the Potter's Raid marker at the current Scuffleton Bridge (below).
Photos by Mike Edge

Their names were mixed together with the Tarboro casualties in the regimental reports.[484]

As they rushed toward Greene County, Major Kennedy and his men of the 62nd Georgia Cavalry were worried — worried that Potter and his men would be captured before they had a chance to take part. The major was positive that the Confederates would converge on Potter to trap the Yankees at one of two crucial points: Edwards' Bridge or Scuffleton Bridge.

Kennedy knew that by this time, Potter was hemmed into a triangle of eastern Greene County that was marked off by Big Contentnea Creek to the south and Little Contentnea Creek to the north and east. The creeks and rivers still ran high from the heavy rains of early and mid-July. The Yankees had to cross either Big Contentnea Creek at Edwards' Bridge, or Little Contentnea Creek at Scuffleton Bridge, which was about two miles to the north. Both bridges were protected by earthworks dug by the 42nd North Carolina. Company A of that regiment spent fifteen days at Scuffleton in the first half of June before marching two miles to Edwards' Bridge to dig more fortifications.[485]

The village of Scuffleton reportedly got its name after arguments over a point of doctrine boiled over at a Baptist church. The debate exploded into a tremendous fistfight, and the congregation split in two. The town's name was also spelled "Scupperton" or "Scuppernong" in Civil War reports.[486]

The Rebels, with their knowledge of the "near cuts", got to both bridges ahead of Potter.

Confederate pickets only pulled up the planks at Scuffleton Bridge, like Union troops did to this bridge at Batchelder's Creek near New Bern.

Some of Claiborne's 7th Confederate Cavalry (probably Barrett's and Pitt's companies), two companies of Whitford's Battalion, and the Montgomery True Blues assembled at the bridge at Scuffleton.[487]

The other possible way out of Greene County, Edwards' Bridge, required Potter to cross Contentnea Creek again further downstream (where it was much wider), or to cross the Neuse River itself. Crossing at Edwards' Bridge also put Potter dangerously close to the Confederate troops that the Union Army knew were near Kinston. Dr. William Blow of Greenville, "a gentleman thoroughly acquainted with the country", was on the scene. Blow had a special reason to catch Potter; the reader will recall that the Yankees had taken $2800 in cash from him in Greenville two days before. The doctor "entreated" Colonel Claiborne of the 7th Confederate Cavalry to wait for Potter at Scuffleton Bridge. Claiborne brushed off the doctor's pleas. He moved almost all of his men to cover Edwards' Bridge, and left only a token force at Scuffleton.[488]

The men who were ordered to hold the Scuffleton Bridge were a few dozen soldiers of Whitford's Battalion, under Capt. D. W. Edwards of Company C. They had orders to burn the bridge. Many of them were from Greene County, so perhaps they did not want to burn a bridge that they and their families depended on. Or, perhaps, they believed as Claiborne did, that the Yankees would cross at the other bridge. For whatever reason, they merely pulled up some of the floor planks instead of burning the bridge.[489]

Sgt. Henry S. Lee of the 1st North Carolina Artillery had been guarding Edwards' Bridge with a squad of ten men (acting as infantry) for two days. Lee got word that the Yankees were near Snow Hill, and he sent some pickets to watch the road north of the bridge. About 5 pm, Claiborne got to Edward's Bridge and settled down to wait for the enemy. The works dug by the 42nd North Carolina back in June, unfortunately for them, were on the south side of the creek, while they would have to defend the bridge from the north bank to keep Potter away from it.[490]

Near nightfall on July 21, Potter's advance troops under Major Jacobs reached eastern Greene County. Precisely as Doctor Blow had warned, the Federals avoided Edwards' Bridge and went straight for Scuffleton. As the Yankee horsemen charged toward the bridge, the Confederates fired a volley, then scattered. "A dozen" Confederates from Whitford's Battalion were taken prisoner: six from Company A, five from Company C, and a corporal from Company D. (Their names are recorded in Appendix II.) At the cost of only two dead horses, Potter now grasped the key to his escape.[491]

Meanwhile, in the rear of Potter's expedition, Company A of the 23rd New York Cavalry "arrived at dusk at a place said to be Hookerton. Burned bridge across creek; continued marching ..."[492]

At Scuffleton, the Yankees filled the gaps in the flooring with fence rails. Claiborne's force two miles away at Edwards' Bridge did not move to stop Potter, even though, it was alleged, a soldier from Whitford's Battalion escaped with the news that Potter was crossing at Scuffleton. Sergeant Lee recorded that around midnight, they learned that the enemy forces were near them, and Claiborne ordered Lee to burn Edwards' Bridge. Lee followed his orders. Apparently none of them knew that Potter was already well into Pitt County, and that they had burned the bridge for nothing.[493]

The crossing at Scuffleton seems to have taken some time. Historian Henry T. King related that Josiah Dixon and two other men on the west side of the creek fired at the last bluecoats who were crossing into Pitt County. Dixon, a farmer from Greene County, joined the 1st North Carolina Cavalry on July 4,

1861. He was discharged from the army in May 1862 because of his "frequent attacks of inflammatory rheumatism following typhoid fever". On December 20, 1862, he reenlisted, this time joining Company C of Whitford's Battalion as a sergeant. "It was early in the morning" by the time Dixon and his companions sprang their ambush. "The raiders thinking they were attacked fled, leaving some horses and baggage, which the three took." [494]

Black civilian scouts worked for the Union Army in North Carolina.

Chapter 13

"I Regret the Manner of Their Leaving"
The Experiences of the Slaves Who Escaped During Potter's Raid
July 19-23, 1863

By the time that Potter crossed the Scuffleton Bridge, the Federals had picked up a large contingent of slaves who were following them to find freedom in New Bern. Piled into farm wagons and fine carriages, or mounted on mules and horses captured from their former masters, they numbered several hundred by the time they reached Little Contentnea Creek. According to Col. Walter Newton of the Pitt County militia, the column of escaping slaves was so long that the last group of them passed his house "two hours after sunrise" on the morning of Tuesday, the 21st, while the last Union troops had passed his house at 11 the night before.[495]

By the middle of 1863, thousands of former slaves swelled the population of Union-occupied New Bern. Many "contrabands" found work with the Union army as teamsters, laborers, servants, laundresses, and in other civilian jobs. Others joined the new black regiments that were being recruited for Brig. Gen. Edward A. Wild's brigade. Still other contrabands from eastern North Carolina enlisted in the Union Navy, which unlike the army had never had a policy of excluding black enlistments.[496]

Only a few glimpses of the experiences of individual slaves who were drawn into Potter's Raid are briefly recorded in contemporary letters and newspaper articles. In the records found so far, the slaves do not speak for

A 1940s photo of Stonewall, home of planter Kenelm Lewis during Potter's Raid. Eighteen slaves from here escaped to Union troops. Library of Congress

themselves; they are seen only from the points of view of angry Confederates, or patronizing Union soldiers and reporters. The author was able to discover the names of only five of the many slaves whose lives were affected by Potter's Raid. Only their first names were recorded, and my attempts to identify them further have so far been unsuccessful.

All of the slaves who were owned by a "Dr. King" of Edgecombe County joined Potter, but at some point, two of the children were left behind along the road. The children were found and were sent back. After the raid, wealthy planter Kenelm Lewis of Rocky Mount wrote to his wife that " ... I have heard nothing of my Negroes who escaped to the Yankees; I suppose they are safe in Newberne ..." Touching upon Potter's visit to the home of his sister-in-law Martha Foreman Lewis of Edgecombe County, Lewis wrote, "Harvey, Sister Martha's carriage driver, hitched up her horses to a waggon & took off his wife & child (Raney). The horses are at Kinston, Harvey has not been heard from — Wm. Foreman says he will certainly hang him if he gets him." Lewis also mentioned that a slave named "Ephraim left with the Yankees at Tarboro. I reckon he & Harvey will put up a shoe shop in Newberne."[497]

Lewis lost 18 of his slaves. He felt that at least the slaves who remained were "behaving very well." Of those who left, he claimed, "I regret the manner of their leaving more than I do their actual value in money."[498]

Potter's Raid

Many slaveholders professed to believe that their slaves did not really want to leave them. Southern newspaper accounts of Potter's Raid routinely refer to blacks being "kidnapped", "carried off", "decoyed", or "forced" to accompany the Yankee raiders to New Bern. [499]

There are a few instances of slaves who chose not to leave with the raiders. George Howard of Tarboro seemed mildly surprised that "even Jane" remained "faithful" during the raid, and that she made "such representations" to the Federal troops that they spared Howard's hotel from damage. One newspaper claimed that the slaves of ex-governor Henry T. Clark refused to reveal his hiding place to the Union soldiers looking for him near Tarboro. When the raiders set fire to the home of Colonel Walter Newton near Falkland, Newton's slaves stayed behind and put out the fire.[500]

Many slaves took the first chance they had to escape to Union forces.

On the other hand, Potter was given valuable help by black guides who knew the local country. Little is known of the men of the 1st North Carolina Colored Volunteers who accompanied the expedition, but it is likely than at least some of the men were chosen particularly because they were familiar with the area they would be passing through. A Confederate newspaper account stated that at Rocky Mount, "two negroes were with the Yankees, their pilots we presume". The most valuable black guide was the man who lived near Falkland, who showed the 3rd New York Cavalry the location of their escape route through Dupree's Ford. Indeed, if the Federals had not found that way to get around the 7th Confederate Cavalry at Otter Creek, Potter's Raid might have ended right there.[501]

Leaving the Contrabands Behind

Until Potter's expedition was near Scuffleton, Major Cole's men protected the rear of the entire Union column, including the crowd of "contrabands" that they had picked up. Lt.-col. George Lewis then ordered Cole to "pass the negro column" and "close up on Major Clarkson". Cole obeyed his

"Contrabands" (escaped slaves) accompany Union troops into New Bern in 1863.

orders, and his troops left their followers behind. Lt. Henry S. Joy, the regimental quartermaster, stopped Cole and asked for a detail to help guard the ambulances. Cole assigned a platoon for that duty.[502]

Potter's cavalry rode all night after crossing the Scuffleton Bridge. They headed for Swift Creek Village, where they had left their camp three days before. Unlike their slow progress through Greene County, they were now covering ground as quickly as they could push themselves and their horses. After riding through the settlement of Johnson's Mills in southern Pitt County on the night of July 21-22, the Federals learned that there were some Confederates waiting in ambush along their intended route. They chose a different road and reached Swift Creek after a grueling but uneventful night's ride on the morning of Wednesday, July 22, 1863.[503]

Potter's luck still held, but luck ran out for many of the contrabands who were trailing the Federal troops. Around dawn on Wednesday, as Potter drew near Swift Creek, the rear of the refugee column was several miles behind them at a plantation in southern Pitt County known as the Burney Place. (The current St. John's Episcopal Church stands on the site of the Burney Place, in the community of St. John's, at the intersection of State Roads 1917 and 1753.) In the dim predawn light, the contrabands were moving toward an ambush laid by the 50th North Carolina Infantry – possibly the very ambush that Potter had avoided.

The 50th North Carolina was ordered out of their camp near Kinston on July 19. "Our object", wrote Lt. J. C. Ellington, of Company C of the regiment, "was to get between Potter and New Bern, cut off his retreat if possible, or at least harass and delay his return until reinforcements might reach us by way of Kinston and effect his capture." There was not enough Confederate cavalry available to track Potter and alert the infantry to his likely path. The foot soldiers maneuvered blindly back and forth, following contradictory intelligence reports. They burned several bridges, pointlessly as it turned out, that they thought Potter might cross. The 50th marched "without rest, sleep, or anything to eat ...for two days and nights ..." of endless exertion in the summer heat.[504]

Almost forty years later Ellington wrote, "On reaching the 'Burney Place', we opened fire on the column with a small brass cannon mounted on the back of a mule, the shock being so unexpected to the enemy that the effect was indescribable". He is obviously describing a mountain howitzer, but it isn't known whether this was the same gun that the 7th Confederate Cavalry used at Otter Creek. Historian Henry King, who drew heavily upon Ellington's account, wrote that the cannon "had little effect other than to completely demoralize the followers..." Ellington described what happened after they opened fire: "The great cavalcade, composed of men, women, and children, perched on wagons, carts, buggies, carriages, and mounted on horses and mules ... was suddenly halted by our fire upon the bridge ... In the excitement and confusion which ensued many of the vehicles were upset in attempting to turn around in the road and many others were wrecked by the frightened horses dashing through the woods."[505]

Ellington wrote that "This fire was upon some negro troops who were in the rear of Potter's column". He remembered that "one negro captain, who was driving a pair of spirited iron-gray horses, attempted to rush past three of our men who were lying in the yard [at the Burney place] and was shot dead as he stood up in the buggy firing at them as he drove past . ... others were either killed or wounded in attempting to escape through the woods near by. ". Black troops were rarely promoted to officer rank during the Civil War. The only black officers who ever served in the black North Carolina Union regiments were an assistant surgeon and a chaplain. This unidentified "captain" at the Burney Place could have been a sergeant, or he may have been a private, a civilian Federal scout, or even an armed contraband who had taken on a leadership role in the refugee column.[506]

A Raleigh newspaper printed a letter from a soldier who claimed that the prisoners taken on Potter's Raid included "seven Yankee soldiers (white) and two blacks, wearing the unmistakable uniform of their brother Abolitionists." Despite these statements, no records of any casualties at all from the 1st North Carolina Union Volunteers during Potter's Raid have come to light. Perhaps these witnesses were describing contrabands or civilian scouts who were given captured weapons by Potter's troops. On the other hand, if more documents come to light, they may show that the first combat action by black troops in North Carolina occured at the Burney Place.[507]

At and around the Burney Place, Confederate soldiers captured a large number of fugitive slaves. Some of them were children who were lost in the woods after being separated from their families. Captain Charles White of Whitford's Battalion and "some six or eight of his men, mounted on pressed horses" captured a party of "contrabands" at Jackson's Crossroads, about five miles from the Burney Place. They also recovered several carts loaded with tools, clothing, tobacco, and other things taken during the raid. One man, a slave who had belonged to a Mr. Dosier of Tarboro, was said to have been "mortally wounded" by White's men. About 75 captured slaves were seen on their way to Kinston, under guard, on July 23. [508]

The Union military reports of Potter's Raid make scant mention of the attack on the contraband column at the Burney Place. Somewhere in that vicinity, Major Cole left two companies of his men behind with orders to burn a certain bridge after the contrabands had crossed; unfortunately, Cole does not explain which bridge he meant. The men waited "at least an hour for the Negroes to cross, and none approaching, as they were ... gobbled up by the Rebel squadron in the rear ... about one-third or one-half of the whole number of negroes and mules were lost at this place."[509]

There was no official Union or Confederate total for the number of slaves who were recaptured from Potter's column. A North Carolina newspaper alleged that 150 slaves from Edgecombe County alone "escaped from the Yankee raiders ...at Burney's Place." At Rocky Mount, Kenelm Lewis saw a train carrying "about 50 contrabands" sent from Goldsboro after their recapture. Lewis personally knew some of the people that he saw on the train; their number included three who had escaped from the Foreman plantation near Falkland, "'to wit' Rainy & child & Little Dennis". Lewis noted that although Rainy and her child had been recaptured, "the horses are at Kinston, [and] Harvey [Rainy's husband] has not been heard from ..." 17 slaves of John Rogers of Tarboro "left with the Yankees. They also took 11 mules, 3 horses, and some bacon ..." At some point later during the raid, 8 of the Rogers slaves and "one or two of the mules" were recaptured. The *State Journal* reported that on July 24, 160 recaptured slaves were held in Kinston. [510]

Southern newspapers tell of other bands of runaway slaves arrested after the raid: five taken near Kinston on July 26; forty, "mostly women and children ... that had been left behind by the Abolitionists" near Greenville; and six, taken with "eight abolitionist prisoners" near Snow Hill. These numbers may reflect slaves from distant farms and plantations who heard about the raid and were intercepted before being able to reach the Union column. Little was written about those slaves who were arrested and sent back. A Mr. Myers, probably of

Many freed slaves found work with the Union Army, like these warehouse workers in New Bern. U.S. Army Military History Institute

Tarboro or Edgecombe County, "sold all of his negroes that ran away except two children."[511]

"About 8 a.m.", the 50th North Carolina finally started after Potter. The trail of the Federal cavalry was easy to follow. A witness wrote, "So many things are strewn along the road; there were carriages that had been upset, throats of horses cut to prevent falling into our lines. ...for miles and miles the road and woods on either side were strewn with all kinds of wearing apparel, table ware, such as fine china and silver ware, blankets, fine bed quilts and all sorts of ladies' wearing apparel which had been taken from the helpless, unprotected women at the plantations ..."[512]

The time lost by the Confederates in arresting fugitive slaves enabled Potter to draw far ahead of his pursuit. By the time the 50th North Carolina again set out after the Yankees, Potter was several miles ahead of the "excitement and confusion" at the Burney Place. Some of the 50th North Carolina were mounted on recaptured horses, and joined Pitt's and Barrett's troopers in pressing Potter. Their added pressure induced the Federal soldiers to toss aside much of the heavy plunder they had taken on the raid. This, in turn, had the double effect of speeding up Potter's force, and further slowing down the pursuit. Whether mounted or on foot, Confederate soldiers made frequent halts to help themselves

Headquarters of Vincent Collyer, Superintendent of the Poor in New Bern. Among his accomplishments was organizing a spy service of freed slaves who brought information from deep inside Confederate territory. Their work may have been instrumental in the planning of Potter's Raid.

to the plunder they found, while Potter drew further down the road toward safety. Even after the raid, citizens looking for their stolen property were held back by Claiborne's cavalrymen until the horse soldiers were "satisfied" with their pick of the lost loot. According to a civilian who was trying to recover lost property, the cavalrymen reasoned that their regiment had "frightened the enemy, and the men should have whatever they wished before the owners should be allowed to assert their rights."[513]

Chapter 14

"The Way They Piled From Their Horses Was a Caution"
The Skirmish at Street's Ferry
Afternoon, July 22, 1863

After crossing the bridge at Scuffleton, Sergeant H. A. Cooley recalled, "after beating around the bush for several hours we found it dark again and we charging into the settlement known as Johnson's Mills" [in southeastern Pitt County, near the Craven County line]. When they rode away from Johnson's Mills, they learned of "several ambushes on the road to Swift Creek so take another was the order of the night. We took another road but before taking it we shelled their ambushes and left them to their glory."[514]

Federal reports mention few specifics of the route they took, and Southern sources are also vague. Contemporary maps show a road leading from Johnson's Mills to Swift Creek, which ran parallel to the Neuse a few hundred yards from the river as the River Road or the Street's Ferry Road. About one mile south of the Burney Place, another route called the Piney Neck Road branched to the east from the River Road. Piney Neck Road ran close to Swift Creek, and would have brought the cavalry to a point opposite Swift Creek Village. Alternately, there was also an unnamed side road, branching off the River Road near Pitchkettle Landing on the Neuse that could also have taken Potter to Swift Creek. The Confederate maps show the area between Johnson's Mills and Swift Creek mostly as thinly settled pocosin. Few farms are indicated on the maps, and the Yankees were not likely to have been seen by many witnesses during that stage of the raid.[515]

Disappointment at Swift Creek Village

Potter reached Swift Creek Village on the morning of July 22, after riding non-stop all night from Scuffleton. Apparently, they planned to cross Swift Creek and continue to New Bern along the road they had taken on Saturday. On the east bank of the deep creek, they would be safe from Rebel pursuit while an easy ride took them to the welcome protection of Fort Anderson, on the north bank of the Neuse. Their long-awaited respite would have to wait a little longer. Cooley noted that they captured "a Rebel Pickett or two", but they could not cross the creek, "the bridge being destroyed."[516]

Potter pressed on to the Neuse River at Street's Ferry, which was only about eight miles from Swift Creek instead of the seventeen miles it would take to reach Fort Anderson, opposite New Bern. Lieutenants Charles C. Kromer and William H. Burke of the 3rd New York Cavalry, and five men, were sent on from Swift Creek to Fort Anderson with a message to have gunboats and transport steamers meet Potter at Street's Ferry. [517]

Potter's men grabbed about four hours of much-needed rest before rousing themselves and their mounts for a final ride to Street's Ferry. More than

Potter's force crossed the Neuse on a pontoon bridge at Street's Ferry. It would have been similar to this one on the Appomattox River in Virginia. Library of Congress

likely, they took a minor road that appears on old maps, which connected with the Piney Neck Road across the stream from Swift Creek Village. This unnamed road intersected with the Street's Ferry Road, or Neuse River Road, about one and a half miles northwest of the ferry site.[518]

Street's Ferry was on the north bank of the Neuse River, about eight miles upstream from New Bern. This place was the last major crossing point before the Neuse widened from a small river into a broad estuary. The first ferry service here was established by Richard Graves before 1730. George Washington crossed the Neuse at Street's Ferry during his Southern Tour on April 20, 1791. The state of North Carolina later operated a small motorized two-car ferry there. In 1961, the last ferry was replaced by the bridge that takes NC Highway 43 across the Neuse.[519]

General Potter himself arrived at Street's Ferry about midday, and the rest of his command rode in during the afternoon. Potter's men had kept up a terrific pace since breaking camp on Sunday morning. Cooley wrote that his comrades had avoided two more Rebel traps since they escaped from the sharpshooters and artillery waiting for them at Otter Creek. The men were exhausted. Frequent ambushes made by Confederate soldiers and militia kept their nerves on edge. "The general opinion of both Officers and men of the Regt. was that there was a prospect of our going to Richmond."[520]

Private Oliver Spoor, of Company A, 3rd New York Cavalry, felt that " ... the raid was the severest, and most tedious, that I have had the honor of participating in ... During the whole six days raid, I did not sleep over five hours. The men were so overcome with fatigue, and the want of sleep, that they would sleep on their horses while marching — and the last night out they had to gallop now and then, to keep the command awake…"[521]

Surgeon William H. Palmer of the 3rd New York Cavalry, speaking about the men suffering from hallucinations after days of sleep deprivation on the raid, said "it was not unnatural for the men to have visions on the Tarboro' raid; I was afflicted in the same way."[522]

It was possible that Confederate soldiers could capture Burke and Kromer before they could get to Fort Anderson, so another plea for help was sent to New Bern from Street's Ferry. Sergeant Cooley wrote: "... A messenger was dispatched to Newbern finding a boat he swam his horse across and brought the news to N.[ew Bern] that the old 3rd was entirely surrounded and if they did not receive reinforcements in half an hour we would be on our way to Richmond." Another source relates that messenger crossed the river in a "dug-out" while his horse swam alongside him.[523]

There was no chance of Potter's force getting across the river without help. Cooley thought that the river was "nearly half a mile wide". Corporal W. H. Graves saw that the Neuse "was very deep and running swift [and] besides the bank on [the] opposite side was abrupt." The corporal wrote that he watched two volunteers swim their horses across the river. "They went a long way down the river before their horses could find a place where they dared attempt to climb out. But at last the leading horse made for the bank and the other one followed suit and now it was only a question of time when we would be relieved."[524]

Private Oren Wooster was sent with about twenty men "out on scout". Wooster wrote that he "got asleep and my horse got out of the ranks and went out in a field of grass he lay down and went to eating and I on his back asleep ..."[525]

The Fight at Street's Ferry

Graves was relieved when he saw the messengers spur their horses up on the opposite bank, but Potter's men were not out of the woods yet. "Scarcely had we stretched our exhausted bodies on the ground", wrote Captain Rowland M. Hall, "when the enemy reached our rear, and began a fierce attack". "We had only just got the bridles from our horses", wrote Cooley, "before the Rebs opened fire upon our rear guard and pickets, they succeeded in wounding one man by their first fire he being shot acrost the breast from right to left the ball first burning the flesh all the way. Co. after Co. went back to the support of the Rear Guard and in less time it takes me to write you the engagement became general."[526]

Because Company L of the 3rd New York Cavalry was "not ... armed with carbines", Company K was sent to relieve them. A mountain howitzer was sent back to cover the skirmishers. When it appeared that the Confederates were going to charge the gun, the skirmishers sent a message to Lt.-col. Lewis, who responded by sending "the whole carbine force".[527]

About fifty men of the 7th Confederate Cavalry, led by Major Claiborne, were the first to attack Potter's forces. They soldiers were probably from Barrett's and Pitt's companies. The major left Edwards' Bridge in Greene County and picked up the trail of the raiders. The Montgomery True Blues accompanied Claiborne with their field guns. The path of the raiders was plain to follow, since "the road was completely strewn with things thrown away in their flight." About ten miles below Scuffleton, the road became so rough that the large guns of the Alabama battery could not travel any further. Major Claiborne left the True Blues behind, and rode ahead with his men and a mountain howitzer.[528]

The fighting at Street's Ferry, centered around the Union mountain howitzers, continued through the afternoon. The section of the Street's Ferry or Neuse River Road held by Potter was near the southeastern edge of a stretch of high ground. South of the road, the land dropped off into swamps and the Neuse

River; about half a mile north of the road, the high ground again gave way to swamps, which stretched to Swift Creek.[529]

Major Jacobs and Companies A, E, I, and L of the 3rd New York Cavalry were "warmly engaged" with the Rebel cavalry. Private Spoor of Company A wrote, "when companies A and E were ordered to support our cannons, we advanced, after having dismounted, with carbines in hand, a mile beyond our pieces and deployed as skirmishers ... soon the enemy opened up on our line with his cannon, dropping his shell exactly among us, but the moment we heard the report, we dropped on our faces. We advanced steadily until we were within 1/2 m[ile] of their pieces — concealed in the woods, behind trees at this point, one of the Boys from our Company was struck by a piece of shell in the shoulder." [530]

At Street's Ferry, Private James R. Shaw of Company L, 3rd New York Cavalry, was "dangerously wounded in right shoulder". The next day, Asst. Surgeon J. W. Gray of the 98th New York operated on Shaw in New Bern. Gray reported that the injury was caused by a "conoidal ball" [that is, a minie ball] that "perforated the head of right humerus and fractured the neck of the scapula." Gray removed "the head and two and half inches of [the] humerus." Shaw remained in the army until he was discharged in September 1864.[531]

Major Cole's battalion also fought at Street's Ferry. At first, Cole was attacked "by cavalry, infantry, and a small piece of artillery, but not too severely". His companies supported two other mountain howitzers against Rebel attacks. H. A. Cooley fought near one of these guns: "The Reb Cavalry made a charge upon one of our little howitzers ... the Rebs came charging up within pistol shot when all of a sudden the Carbines raised themselves from the ground and made them welcome with a dose of balls almost the same time the Howitzer made good their welcome by a double dose of Canister and Case shot. And the way they piled from their horses was a Caution they soon beat a retreat formed a new line of battle and began to advance again but they found the little piece waiting for them."[532]

Capt. Rowland M. Hall's men, "lying prostrate on the ground", held off the Confederates with their carbines, although the troopers were "... ready to sink with fatigue ..." Hall's men lured the Confederate cavalrymen in close. The captain reported that the enemy soldiers saw one of the mountain howitzers "apparently abandoned (the gunner Corporal Vandervoort of Co. 'E' lying between the wheels of the piece.)" The Rebels charged "in columns of fours. The corporal waited coolly, & when they were within 50 yards pulled the lanyard. The charge of canister destroyed the head of the column, & the rest retreated in confusion." Hall claimed that on the next morning, "15 horses killed by the single discharge lay in the road."[533]

Probably describing the same incident, Sergeant Graves wrote, "the gunner had been ordered to hold the charge until just before the Rebel cavalry reached us. The reason this order was given was because we were out of ammunition only the one charge left. Their cavalry came on and probably thought they would capture our howitzer but what a fearful slaughter was made of them. This howitzer was charged with what was called Spherical case a tin can or case which held at least one hundred and seventy five balls ..." Although Graves made a technical mistake here (canister and spherical case shot are two different kinds of artillery ammunition), he was right to say of either sort of load, "when it left the gun [it] spread like water from a watering pot ..." Graves asserted "in this instance there were at least one hundred saddles emptied". Private Charles N. D. Mead wrote of seeing a "double charge of grape and canister—keeling over 42 of the grey jackets at one lick". 534

Major John N. Whitford, CSA

Private Oren Wooster noted later that "I can stand bullets pretty well but when the shells come whyning by it made me prick up my ears some of the men was pretty scared ..."535

During the afternoon, more Confederates trickled in to join the skirmish. Kennedy knew he had to get his battalion of the 62nd Georgia Cavalry in front of Potter's column to stop them. Unfortunately for him, finding reliable information "in that locality was bad to do, as nearly all the parties you met down there were doubtful until you had time to understand them fully." Like Claiborne's men, Kennedy's troopers were delayed by arresting contrabands who were trying to catch up with Potter, or stopping to take "vehicles of various kinds with varied supplies." It was about "half an hour before sundown" when Kennedy got to Street's Ferry. He combined with Claiborne to "make a dash or two" at the Yankees. Major John N. Whitford and a few of his men also got there in time for some of the fighting that day. 536

The Confederate horsemen and their little mountain howitzer were strengthened when the Wilmington Horse Artillery arrived from Kinston. Officially designated 1st Company A of the 2nd North Carolina Artillery, the company was then known as Bunting's Battery, although Capt. Samuel Bunting had resigned a few days before. Bunting turned over command to newly promoted Capt. Thomas J. Southerland. Southerland's Battery would be the name of the unit until the end of the war. Their armament at this time is uncertain; in 1865, Southerland's Battery was equipped with five 6-pounders and one 12-pounder gun.[537]

With their growing force, the Confederates pressed their attacks as the sun sank lower in the sky. Around 7 p.m., Lt. James Allis repelled a Confederate attack on one of his guns with the help of Company K of the 3rd Cavalry. [538]

Allis' other mountain howitzer was positioned "about a mile in advance, posted to cover some cross-roads leading to Swift Creek ... and our camps". "About 8 o'clock", this forward howitzer came under fire, by a "heavy rifled gun", evidently one of the pieces from Southerland's Battery. Cole wrote that the enemy "threw grape at our skirmishers, advancing his line, and making a desperate attempt to press back our small force within shelling distance of our camp ..." Cole noted that the Confederate artillery shelled his position "with great rapidity and accuracy, excepting that the fuses were too long, and most of the shell exploding just beyond us."[539]

Lt. J.C. Ellington, CSA

Cole was holding his line against the Confederates when he was surprised to see his pickets fall back from their position on his right. His men claimed that they were following his orders to pull back, but Cole had never given such an order. It turned out that the opposing lines were so close together that a creative Rebel simply shouted at them, and ordered them to retreat. Cole sent them back to their old position. Before darkness brought an end to the firing, two Union soldiers were captured near Allis' forward gun. One of them, Private Edgar Taylor, managed to escape the next morning.[540]

About 70 men from the 50th North Carolina straggled in about two hours after dark (sundown that night was at 7:20), "broken down with fatigue, heat, and hunger". Perhaps about one fourth of the regiment made it to Street's Ferry that evening. The rest of the men were struggling to catch up, or had collapsed from the oppressive July heat. Lt. J. C. Ellington commanded soldiers from four different companies who reached Street's Ferry. The soldiers were not only worn out, but they had outrun their rations and had nothing to eat. But, "after a rest of about two hours nearly every man and officer was in his place".[541]

Only a few casualties were reported from the clash at Street's Ferry. Although the Union soldiers who were fighting around their embattled mountain howitzers felt hard-pressed by the enemy fire, there were not really enough Confederates there to give a serious threat to Potter's 800 men. Potter did not separate his casualties at Street's Ferry from the total losses on the raid. Records of the 3rd New York Cavalry specify the names of three men who were wounded (see Appendix II), and three who were captured (including Private Taylor, who later escaped.) It is unclear whether any men from Potter's other units became casualties at Street's Ferry.

The available Confederate sources mention few specifics about the skirmish at Street's Ferry. Despite several Federal claims of frightful destruction before the muzzles of their mountain howitzers and carbines, the available records of the 7th Confederate Cavalry (the most likely victims of this incident) or other units in the area reveal not one single casualty attributed to this skirmish. The Kenansville Raid resulted in a flurry of claims for reimbursement for captured horses, but apparently no one even filed a claim for a horse that was lost during Potter's Raid. The records of the 62nd Georgia Cavalry are likewise silent on Street's Ferry. It is possible that some of Whitford's men were killed or wounded; many of the records of Whitford's Battalion at this time are missing.

One estimate of the Rebel forces present listed "Major Kennedy's cavalry, about seventy-five; Major Claiborne's cavalry, he said, about fifty; and of the 50th about 75; there were also a few men of Whitford's Battalion." Even including Southerland's Battery, there could not have been many more than 250 or 300 Confederates there, all told. Regardless of their numbers, the Southern officers got together after supper — "such as we had", as one man described the meal. While eating, they hammered out their plans for a final assault on the enemy camp in the morning. Kennedy and Whitford looked forward to the pleasure of "marching the enemy out to our own headquarters." [542]

Help Arrives for Potter

Late on the night of July 22-23, Potter's men heard the welcome sounds of steamboat engines chugging toward the ferry landing. Some said it was midnight, but Corporal Graves thought it was about 3 a.m. when he heard a steamer "puffing up the river". The relief force that arrived at Street's Ferry was two gunboats from New Bern, accompanied by a pair of steamboats carrying the pieces of a pontoon bridge. Federal sources name three of the vessels: the gunboat *Bombshell* and the steamers *Allison* and *Port Royal*. Potter's men were safe now.[543]

Confederate pickets and local residents brought word of the reinforcements to the senior officers at Street's Ferry, who were now "in very great danger of being captured." Soon after, a courier arrived with orders from a superior officer. These orders might have come from General Martin, although his name was tactfully omitted by Whitford and Kennedy in their postwar reminiscences. The officers were ordered to break off the attack and fall back immediately from Street's Ferry. The weary foot soldiers of the 50th North Carolina would have to endure one more long march. Reluctantly slipping away, the Southerners left their "campfires brightly burning, and retiring in the midnight darkness, marched the balance of the night, in the direction of Kinston ...."[544]

Maj. John T. Kennedy planned and led the only truly effective resistance to Potter. After fighting a sharp skirmish outside Tarboro and enduring a long ride to Street's Ferry, he was fired up with the prospect of bagging the entire Federal expedition. The sudden arrival of the orders to let Potter go was to Kennedy "a blow entirely unexpected and well calculated to vex and perplex troops who had been doing faithful duty ..." Lt. John G. Smith, though, noted that Kennedy's men "during two days ... had no rest and hardly any feed for man or horses." Private Kinchen Jahu Carpenter of the 50th North Carolina also took a practical point of view, figuring that the Confederates at Street's Ferry were as tired as the Yankees, but were much smaller in numbers.[545]

Union army engineers and laborers built a pontoon bridge across the Neuse. Pontoons were small floating hulls, across which a wooden roadway was laid. First, soldiers rowed the pontoons out into the river, positioned them in a line, and then dropped anchors to hold them in place. The pontoon hulls were connected by ropes, and then timbers called balks were installed to connect the pontoons. The balks in turn were covered with perpendicular floor planks, called chesses. A pontoon bridge capable of supporting loaded wagons and heavy guns could be thrown together in a few hours.[546]

This pontoon bridge was assembled with great difficulty. H. A. Cooley noted that "the river being so swollen it took the [steam]boats to keep it in place." A strong current could push a pontoon bridge into a dangerous arc, possibly causing it to break. To prevent pontoon bridges from snapping in two, steamboats were maneuvered into the middle of the river to gently nudge the bridge slightly upstream, so it would be straight. Cooley wrote that "several blacks were drowned by the pontoon flying around in the stream." These men who were Cooley said were killed while building the bridge may have been from the pioneer detail under Captain Wilson that accompanied the expedition, or civilian laborers brought from New Bern. However, the author has found no other mention of the accident with the pontoon bridge, and has found no names of any men who were lost at this stage of the raid.[547]

Captain Ebbs' company of the 3rd New York Cavalry stayed in the saddle all night on guard duty while the bridge was completed. The night passed with mounting tension, but no Confederate assault materialized out of the darkness. The Union soldiers clearly heard the sounds of Southern troops in the distance, not knowing that they were just making a show to cover the sounds of their withdrawal toward Kinston.[548]

The pontoon bridge was finished by about 7 a.m. on Thursday, July 23rd. Potter's men and the refugee column trudged across during the morning. By noon, nearly everyone was safely on the south bank of the Neuse. Cooley and his lighthearted comrades were relieved that at last they "could now laugh at the Rebs and their pieces."[549]

After the last soldiers stepped off of the walkway, the bridge was taken apart. The pontoons and timbers were loaded back onto the steamboats, along with the Confederate prisoners, the contrabands, and some of the captured horses. Major Clarkson, the officer of the day, supervised these final preparations. Clarkson boarded the last of the pontoon flats, and was rowed out to board the steamboat *Port Royal* for the trip back to New Bern.[550]

While the bridge was being dismantled, "the line of Reb skirmishers began to show themselves again" on the north bank of the river. Cooley wrote that Major Cole ordered his men "to keep our fire arms by our sides" and not waste any ammunition on the distant Rebels. Potter's Raid was over.[551]

Potter's Raid

Wounded Union soldiers from Potter's Raid were treated in New Bern at Foster General Hospital (above), or at Stanly General Hospital (below). U.S. Army Military History Institute

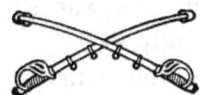

Chapter 15

"Our Raid Was Eminently and Gloriously Successful"
The Raiders Return to Camp
Afternoon, Wednesday, July 23, 1863

Potter's men plodded back to their quarters. Before the troops reached camp, Maj. George W. Cole gave way to exhaustion and fell from his horse. A sergeant found him "lying asleep on the ground." Cole "remained in camp for some time sick and suffering pain". The major suffered not only from the effects of the harsh conditions of the raid, but also because falling from his saddle aggravated a previous injury. Surgeon Palmer gave Cole a leave of absence after the major "spoke of having seen visions" during the sleepless nights on the raid.[552]

In the next few days, many of the men reflected on their experiences during the raid as they wrote letters to family and friends. H. A. Cooley of the 3rd New York Cavalry wrote, "By noon, we were back at Camp Grove, nearly worn out, where we got a chance to look back and see through what we had passed and it made me shudder to think of it." They had been through "six days and five nights or marching with only two feed of oats and three days' rations for their men." All through that time, asserted Cooley, they could not dare "get half a mile in the rear of the column for fear of getting a ticket through to Richmond." Cooley marveled that they escaped with the loss of less than one hundred casualties and without "the loss of a single wagon". He concluded in this letter to his father, "... this I consider the greatest cavalry raid ever made by so small a force in this war."⁵⁵³

Corporal William H. Graves wrote, "You may believe we were a pretty tired lot of boys when we arrived home again." During the whole five day raid, he had only two solid hours of sleep at Sparta early on July 20. Other than that, the only sleep that Graves had was "what we got in the saddle." Another veteran of the 12th remembered that during the entire expedition they had halted "only at intervals long enough to feed their horses and cook coffee."⁵⁵⁴

Capt. Rowland M. Hall's Company E of the 3rd New York Cavalry was among those that rode the extra distance to Rocky Mount during the raid. Hall lamented, "... my old horse, I think, will never recover. I had to leave him to be walked home five miles from camp. He was reeling under me — almost all our horses are spoiled, I fear permanently —."⁵⁵⁵

Potter's Raid took a heavy toll on the cavalry's horses. Clarkson's battalion (which was only one third of Potter's eighteen companies) lost 24 horses killed in action. 89 more of the battalion's horses were abandoned along the route as unfit to travel. One of Clarkson's men, Private Oren Wooster, wrote that "we lost a good many horses on the march there were lots of them dropt down dead the first day mine stood it all through he is as good a horse as there is in this regiment I think a good deal of him ..." ⁵⁵⁶

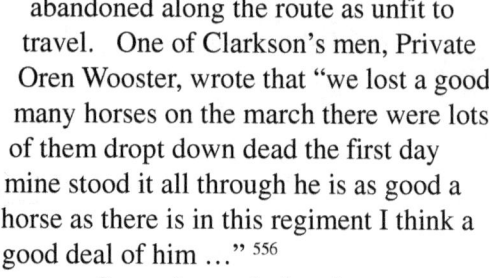

Five days of hard riding took a heavy toll on the Union raiders' horses.

Seven horses belonging to Lieutenant Clark's section of the 3rd New York Artillery were killed in action or abandoned. Company A of the 23rd New York Cavalry lost Captain Cummings' horse when it was shot dead at Otter Creek Bridge, and twelve more of their horses were "worn out and abandoned." A report from Company H of the 3rd New York Cavalry indicated that they had 41 serviceable horses just before the raid on July 17. A report on July 29 stated that three of their horses had died on the raid. 35 more mounts were rendered "unserviceable", leaving only three horses fit for duty. Losses of Union horses, of course, were eased by using captured mounts. No report has been located on the losses of Confederate horses in the raid.⁵⁵⁷

Yet, despite the loss of so many horses, Hall was pleased with the results of the raid. "Our raid to Rocky Mount was eminently and gloriously successful ..." he wrote to his father. "It was made at a cost of hardship and fatigue you

This photo, believed to have been taken in New Bern, may include some who escaped during Potter's Raid. U.S. Army Military History Institute

could not estimate ... We destroyed over $2,000,000 worth of Rebel property, thus paying for the regiment by this raid alone."[558]

General Potter wrote, "... the behavior of the officers and men of the command was excellent. They bore with cheerfulness the fatigue of long marches, and the loss of food, sleep, and rest. They displayed great dash and courage in all our encounters with the enemy."[559]

The eventual escape of the expedition should not let one underestimate Potter's accomplishment. "The Yankees had it all their own way", as one New York newspaper put it. The Federal cavalry slashed through Tar River region and halted traffic on the Wilmington & Weldon Railroad. The destruction of the *Governor Morehead* and the *Colonel Hill* ended Confederate steamboat traffic on the Tar River. The Tarboro gunboat was a charred ruin; it would be the last attempt to build a Confederate gunboat to break the North's grip on the Tar and Pamlico Rivers. The Rocky Mount Mills were reduced to smoking ruins, along with a fortune in military supplies and provisions. General Foster claimed that the expedition brought in 100 Confederate prisoners and 300 horses and mules. He added that 300 contrabands followed Potter back to New Bern. There was apparently no official criticism for the expedition's failure to prevent the capture of so many contrabands at the Burney Place on the morning of July 22.[560]

Potter's men had found themselves in some tight spots during the raid, but their casualties were quite low, apart from the drubbing given to Clarkson's detachment at Daniel's Schoolhouse. Only seven Union soldiers, all from

Clarkson's command, lost their lives on the raid. The total list of dead, wounded, missing and captured men was less than 75. Potter claimed only 64 casualties in his report.[561]

A journalist who watched the contrabands straggle into New Bern with Potter saw them "mounted on animals so poor that their 'traps' might have been suspended from the protruding bodies." Yet, they "appeared as happy as they only can appear when to them the great Millennium, the total abnegation of slavery shall come." They told anyone who questioned them that they had run away from the "Rebs", and were "gwine to fight 'dem soon".[562]

Because no telegraph lines connected the Union-held parts of North Carolina with the North, news of Potter's Raid was carried to the North by the steamers that ran from New Bern to Fort Monroe. From there, telegraph lines sped news of the raid to newspapers across the country. Another major source for details of the raid in the North was the *Petersburg Express*. Evidently a copy of this Confederate newspaper quickly got across the Union lines; their July 23 story of the raid was reprinted in the *Baltimore Sun* two days later, and appeared in other Northern papers over the next few days. Sped by the transcontinental telegraph, news of Potter's Raid reached California by July 25, as shown by a notice in the *San Francisco Evening Bulletin*. An account of the raid that was reprinted from the *Petersburg Express' July* 23 article appeared in *The Times* of London, England on August 7.[563]

Perhaps the greatest distance that the news traveled is best shown by this short notice: "The Federal cavalry have destroyed property worth 5,000,000 dollars, in the shape of cotton factories and bridges in North Carolina." Obviously referring to Potter's Raid, that brief statement appeared in *The Herald,* of Melbourne, Australia on October 9, 1863.[564]

Back in camp, the saddle-sore riders of the 12th New York Cavalry were granted a little time to recuperate from their first long raid. "We will have a few days rest now", wrote Private Oren Wooster. "We have got infantry to stand guard for us." Wooster wrote a couple of letters home, enclosing two captured Confederate newspapers for his father and some silk thread for his mother.[565]

Yet, all in all, perhaps the New York *Herald* best summed up the raid from the Northern point of view, calling the affair " ... a pretty good week's work for the little but noble band of heroes who are serving their country *en cheval* in North Carolina."[566]

Private Profits and an Army Investigation

Besides their pride in the "brilliant success of the expedition", some soldiers came out of Potter's Raid with other, more tangible rewards. Captain Hall wrote wistfully that, "I wish I could make money on these raids consistently with honor and duty, but I cannot." Not everyone on the raid was as scrupulous as Hall, and some men evidently made a great deal of profit from the expedition. Hall noted in one of his letters home that Confederate money sold for fifteen cents on the dollar in United States money at New Bern. Brig. Gen. Innis N. Palmer, who succeeded Foster in command at New Bern in late July 1863, was appalled at the conduct of some Union officers regarding captured Rebel property. "With regard to the funds captured on the late raid, and placed in the hands of Lieutenant Cardner", wrote Palmer, "I can only say that the whole matter was conducted in a very irregular manner ... this money ($2,600) had been turned over by Lieutenant Cardner to Colonel Lewis, who was to turn it over to General Potter. Why, then, did not Colonel Lewis do so? He was here for several days with General Potter, and as soon as General Potter left, he (Colonel Lewis) applied for and received a leave of absence to go direct to New York, taking the money with him. Besides, I think I can show that Lieutenant Cardner sold a considerable sum of money, either North Carolina state or Confederate money — as much as $1,100 to one person — all of which was money captured in the raid. The matter is in the hands of the Provost Marshal, who, will, I hope, be able to throw more light on this matter". [567]

Despite Palmer's anger and his call for an investigation, the *Official Records* has nothing more on this matter. Lewis apparently managed to stay out of serious trouble. His compiled service record mentions nothing about Palmer's call for an investigation. Lewis succeeded to command of the regiment after Colonel Mix was killed near Petersburg, Virginia on June 15, 1864.[568]

The matter did not end with suspicions of Cardner and Lewis. Maj. Gen. Benjamin F. Butler took over the Department of Virginia and North Carolina after General Foster was transferred to another region. On his first inspection tour of eastern North Carolina, Butler was outraged to discover widespread malfeasance in the handling of the money that was captured on Potter's Raid. Butler's reports revealed in detail how some of the Confederate money that was seized on the Warsaw Raid and Potter's Raid was exchanged for US currency. A great deal of it, according to Butler's investigation, went through the hands of Isaiah Respress (whose name is spelled "Respess" in the 1870 Census). He was a merchant who had once been the mayor of Washington, N.C. After professing his loyalty to the Union, he was allowed to do business in New Bern.[569]

During the summer of 1863, a "Private Horn" of the 3rd New York Cavalry let some of his comrades know that Respress would buy Confederate currency. Respress admitted that soldiers brought the Confederate money to his room at the Gaston House, a New Bern hotel. A "Corporal or Sergeant" unloaded $10,000 in Confederate bills (ranging from $5 to $100 notes) in a single transaction. Respress paid him $1,000 in United States greenbacks. Although he agreed to pay the fellow another $100 "in case the money should all prove genuine", the soldier never returned for that last payment. A lieutenant accompanied the seller, but he claimed that the money belonged to the non-commissioned officer and that he himself "had nothing to do with it".[570]

Another non-commissioned officer exchanged $1500 in Confederate money with Respress, openly taking care of business in the "sitting-room" of the Gaston House. Neither man even bothered to conceal what they were up to. Through a "Mr. Curry of the Gaston House", Respress paid a soldier with a $300 draft on a Philadelphia bank for $6,000 in Confederate bills. A merchant named "Smith" sold another $1,000 worth of Southern currency to him, which was probably obtained in trade with Union soldiers who had been on the raids. In all, Respress admitted to acquiring "$20,000 and $30,000 in all, at prices ranging from 5 to 10 cents on the dollar". He used the Confederate money to pay debts that he owed in the Confederacy, and also to buy 2,000 pounds of chewing tobacco. The tobacco, which was bought in Richmond, got to New Bern by a mysterious process that Respress vaguely referred to as "the underground railroad". [571]

General Butler moved to file charges against Respress for "buying Confederate money stolen from our soldiers", and illegally using the profits to buy tobacco, cotton, and naval stores, which was smuggled through the Union lines. Butler believed that "hundreds of thousands of dollars" in Confederate money had been taken from the vault of the Bank of Tarboro by Potter's men. (Confederate newspapers claimed that the valuables had been removed from the bank just before the raid.) The general also thought that other citizens of Washington were buying stolen Confederate currency, and that "certain of the officers had been embezzling it." [572]

Former Massachusetts congressman Charles R. Train visited the camp of the 3rd New York Cavalry in February 1864, searching for further evidence in the case after a team of "Special Commissioners" had investigated the matter. Train told Butler that "the affidavits are very wide apart in their statements of facts [and] much of the statement is hearsay." The former congressman concluded that "I do not believe the public service would be promoted by a trial before a Court Martial, or Military Commission."[573]

Butler ended the matter by dropping the proceedings against Respress after a frustrating and inconclusive investigation. Although he was dead sure that the prisoner was guilty, he wrote Secretary of War Edwin M. Stanton, "I will discharge him … if for no other reason than that which the unjust judge granted the widow's suit, because Respress' friends 'by continual coming weary me.'"[574]

Chapter 16

"The Raiders Escaped Back to Their Dens"
Southern Reaction to Potter's Raid
Late July to September 1863

The number of Confederate casualties from Potter's Raid is difficult to determine. This is partly due to the lack of official reports by the 62nd Georgia Cavalry and the 7th Confederate Cavalry, the Confederate units that were the most heavily involved in the raid. The writer of a letter to the *State Journal* in Raleigh, who was obviously unaware of the capture of a dozen Confederate soldiers at Scuffleton bridge, stated that Southern losses "did not exceed six killed, wounded, and missing". Another informant, writing from Kinston on July 23, 1863, told the same newspaper that "we have lost two killed, and four or five wounded." It is unknown where these Confederate soldiers were killed or wounded, but this writer did not know about the fighting at Street's Ferry when he wrote this estimate. If this account is accurate, these losses may reflect militia losses, or otherwise unrecorded casualties from the skirmishing between the 7th Confederate Cavalry and Potter's men in Greene County. The Union's Maj. Gen. John Gray Foster claimed that Potter's expedition returned with 100 prisoners. Appendix II of this book contains the names of four officers, thirty enlisted men, and seven civilians who were taken prisoner by Potter. Of these forty-one men, Private Andrew McIntyre escaped, and at least two of the civilians were released before the raiders returned to New Bern. Only two Confederates, both members of the 62nd Georgia Cavalry who were hit at Daniel's Schoolhouse, are known to have been wounded on the raid.[575]

In the weeks after Potter's Raid, outraged newspaper editors and readers sharpened their pens. They filled the columns of North Carolina's newspapers with sharp opinions and heated accusations. Anger at the "depredations" by Yankee "barbarians" was equaled only by the resentment and fury directed at the Confederate government and military, which allowed the "scoundrels" to escape "back to their dens without punishment".[576]

One typical lament asked, " ... how can the brave boys of Carolina, scattered over the whole Confederacy, be but despondent, when they see her perfectly denuded of troops, their homes left open to every little chicken-stealing party of the enemy that stick their heads out of Newberne, and their mothers and sisters liable daily to insults. North Carolina, with 90,000 men in the field, has not enough left her to stand guard or protect a potato patch ... our state is not receiving justice." [577]

The *Wilmington Journal* thought that "This raiding requires some vigorous measures to be adopted. General Martin staying at Kingston (sic) and supposing that the enemy is going towards Wilson, don't stop the enemy from going to Tarboro and Rocky Mount ..." The *Journal* cast a covetous eye on the cavalry of Maj. Gen. James E. B. "Jeb" Stuart. One or two of Stuart's regiments, thought the editor, "held well in hand ready to launch at a moment's warning, would do much to protect" the Wilmington & Weldon Railroad and eastern North Carolina from further raids. The editor fatalistically suspected, though, that after the Yankees returned "to Newbern or Washington, of wherever they came from ... The wires will be put up, the railroad communication restored, and the public, excepting the immediate sufferers, will begin to forget this raid, when, lo and behold, the raiders will make their appearance in a fresh place."[578]

Adding the effects of Potter's Raid to the mounting misfortunes of the Confederacy, one North Carolina newspaper asked, "Are we likely to recapture Vicksburg, Port Hudson, Memphis, Nashville, or either of them? We fear not. Can we even drive the enemy from Newbern, in our own State?"[579]

The *Tarborough Southerner,* which was then owned by Judge George Howard (who had barely escaped capture by Potter's men), remained defiant after the raid. The newspaper insisted that when the South gained its independence, the peace treaty must include a requirement that the North "pay for all private property which they have stolen or wantonly destroyed during the prosecution of the war." [580]

Ardent Confederates called loyal Unionists "tories", placing them in the same category as the pro-British faction during the Revolution. This of course implied that the secessionists were fighting in a worthy cause, just as had their Revolutionary War ancestors. A good bit of the blame for the success of Potter's Raid went to the disloyal "tories" of the region. Several witnesses noted the presence of their fellow North Carolinians of Company L of the 1st North

Carolina Volunteers in Potter's ranks. The notion of civilian Unionists, operating in secret, worried the Confederates. A Greene County resident asserted that "it is a prevalent notion in the neighborhood that these tories are in regular communication with the enemy. ... They will bear watching, and I would suggest to General Martin that he keep an eye on them." Lt. John M. Smith of the 62nd Georgia Cavalry blamed the whole raid on information brought to New Bern by "tories", whom he considered to be "Judases". "I have always felt that the Potters Raid was made on information furnished by the Brook gang or some of their people, as it would have been hardly possible for the enemy to know the disposition of our troops without such information." So far, the identity of the members of the "Brook gang" is unknown.[581]

In newspaper articles, several Confederate officers were accused of incompetence or cowardice for letting Potter get away. Col. William C. Claiborne of the 7th Confederate Cavalry, Maj. John N. Whitford of the 1st Battalion, Local Defense Troops, Col. James Washington of the 50th North Carolina, and Brig. Gen. James G. Martin were lambasted in North Carolina newspapers for several weeks.

On the other hand, Maj. John T. Kennedy of the 62nd Georgia Cavalry and Lt.-col. John C. Lamb of the 17th North Carolina were warmly praised for their efforts in repulsing the Union cavalry across the river from Tarboro. One grateful writer claimed, "I have not met a citizen of Edgecombe who does not believe that if Major Kennedy had had command of all the cavalry, not a Yankee would have escaped." A resident of Tarboro wrote, "we are under many and lasting obligations to the officers and men of Kennedy's troop, Col. Lamb's two companies of the 17th, and Capt. Graham's Battery."[582]

Two Broken Careers

Colonel James Washington, of the 50th North Carolina, was "a good man, but not a good disciplinarian", remembered one of his men, Private Kinchen Carpenter. Carpenter wrote that Washington's career ended because of the way his regiment straggled and fell apart during its pursuit of Potter. At a court "convened at the instance of Lt.-col. S. D. Pool", Washington was censured for his "conduct in the late Yankee raid upon Tarboro." Possibly to avoid a court-martial, he resigned his commission on October 30, 1863.[583]

The most sustained criticism was aimed at Col. William C. Claiborne of the 7th Confederate Cavalry. He was blamed for letting Potter slip by him at Otter Creek Bridge, and again by holding Edwards' Bridge while Potter crossed Little Contentnea Creek nearby at Scuffleton. Several witnesses reported that Claiborne's men stopped pursuing Potter on the way to Street's Ferry, in order to grab their pick of the loot that had been dropped along the road by the Union cavalry. One angry writer, identified only as "Edgecombe", asked bitterly, "what protection can we hope for from our troops with such inefficient commanders as Gen. Martin and Col. Claiborne?" The writer, after enumerating Claiborne's failures, went on to hint that he had "other facts much more damaging to the reputation" of Claiborne, which he declined to reveal at that time.[584]

Like Colonel Washington's, Claiborne's army career was nearly over. On August 17, General Martin ordered Claiborne's arrest. General W. H. C. Whiting, Martin's superior, wrote from Wilmington on August 20 that "I wish that they would push Claiborne's case and get rid of him." The available records do not state the reason that the colonel was arrested, but Whiting wrote on the back of a document concerning the case, "... the only question in regard to this man is whether he should be kept for trial on charges that if true prove him to be a scoundrel or to get rid of him by accepting his resignation."[585]

On August 28, Claiborne wrote to President Davis from Kinston. The colonel claimed that he had been arrested without cause, and no action had been taken on his request for a court of inquiry. Davis noted on the back of the letter (which also included Whiting's remarks, and brief notes from Martin and a staffer at the office of the Secretary of War), "No officer can be kept in arrest without charges duly preferred."[586]

Years later, John W. Sanders, a former lieutenant in Company H of Pool's Battalion wrote that "... a court of inquiry was asked for to determine the cause of failure and place the blame where it justly belonged. The court convened, and after a thorough investigation the officers and men of the battalion were completely exonerated and the failure charged to the [telegraph] operator's absence from his office and to the officer whose regiment had the raiders hemmed in between Neuse River and Contentnea Creek and delayed to attack them until next morning." Sanders mentions no names, but certainly one could get the impression that he was referring to Claiborne.[587]

On September 12, Claiborne was allowed to resign his commission; the official reason was because "of the illness of his child". Thereafter, William C. Claiborne drops out sight until after the end of the war. He later filed an application for a pardon from President Andrew Johnson, which was granted on November 17, 1865. Generals, high officials, and some other Confederates had to apply directly to the president for their pardons; Claiborne was affected by the rule that required pardons for men worth over $20,000.[588]

Getting rid of Claiborne didn't solve General Martin's problems. As the commander of the District of North Carolina, Martin came in for a large share of the recriminations that resounded from angry North Carolinians after Potter's Raid. Typical of these reactions to Martin's leadership during the "late disgraceful Yankee raid" was one writer who felt that because of the "apparent indisposition of those in command of the troops of that section to meet and punish the Yankee thieves", a Union raid on Raleigh was imminent. He urged the people of the state to prepare to "defend the capital", as "the command at Kinston and vicinity seems indisposed to interfere with such pleasure excursions of the enemy."[589]

One of North Carolina's Confederate senators, Goldsboro resident William T. Dortch, wrote to Secretary of War James Seddon of his reservations about Martin. Although Dortch claimed that Martin was "a personal friend, who I like very much, it is that I should inform you that he has not the confidence of the army or of the people. I think he is not sufficiently active, and I learn from good authority that his troops are very much demoralized, and that both officers and men believe he will not fight, and for that reason want a change of commander."[590]

Rocky Mount planter Kenelm Lewis's friend "Mr. Pippin" of Tarboro helped to spread a rumor that was circulated through the Tar River region after the raid. "Pippin says there is certainly treachery somewhere and he don't hesitate to say Genl. Martin is unsound. He states that Mrs. Martin is in Newberne and sends her husband various articles of luxury and necessity. He says that Martin and Potter married sisters and that there is an understanding between them." Lewis personally believed that General Martin was "inefficient", rather than "traitorous". A few miles down the river from Tarboro, Mrs. Peyton Atkinson wrote to Governor Vance to express "the sentiment of the community" after the raid. She repeated to the governor the same story of Martin and Potter being married to sisters. Actually, General Potter was a lifelong bachelor.[591]

N.C. Gov. Zebulon B. Vance

On the other hand, in dismissing a severe newspaper critique of Martin, Major John N. Whitford responded, "I wonder if the writer was in the advance after the enemy to Street's Ferry?"[592]

Martin retained the complete confidence of his commander, General Whiting. Whiting sympathized with Martin; after all, both men were responsible for guarding a vast region with nowhere near enough troops. Whiting sent a dispatch to Martin on the same day that Potter reached Street's Ferry. The commander hoped that Martin had intercepted the raiders, but he thought " ... without effective cavalry force I do not see how either their depredations can be arrested or punished ... I do not see anything undone on your part that it is possible for us to do in our present circumstances." Indeed, Martin's few cavalrymen available were scattered over such a wide area (and away from access to a telegraph) that it was virtually impossible to assemble them in time to meet a threat such as Potter's Raid.[593]

Had a telegraph line been in place as far as Tarboro, news of Potter's Raid would have reached Fort Branch sooner. Potter might then have been greeted at Tarboro by an entrenched and ready Confederate force. Former governor Henry T. Clark pointed out that the expense of the telegraph line would have been less than the county tax receipts that the raiders took from the Edgecombe County sheriff. Clark believed that the pine woods along the Tarboro Branch Line would easily yield enough poles for the telegraph line; indeed, "the trees themselves could be used *temporarily* until poles could be set up". The Confederacy, though, was hard-pressed to come up with wire and equipment for new telegraph lines, and a remote town such as Tarboro would just have to wait. [594]

As some North Carolinians searched for scapegoats, others labored to repair the damage left in Potter's wake. Jesse Brown, an Edgecombe County miller, was working long into the nights to grind corn meal after Potter's men burned two other local mills during the raid. Brown wrote to Governor Vance, explaining that he had "another set of runners at my mill". He could relieve much hardship in Edgecombe County if an exemption to conscription was granted to an experienced hand to work at his mill. The slaves who were good at mill work, he wrote, were always "going off to the Yankees", and otherwise "it is almost impossible for me to get a miller whose age the militia law will not reach …" Brown even asked if a few soldiers could be sent to help him temporarily.[595]

Repairing the Rocky Mount Bridge

Restoring rail traffic across the Tar River was the Confederacy's top priority. Colonel S. L. Fremont, the superintendent of the Wilmington & Weldon Railroad, arrived at Rocky Mount on the day after the raid and took charge of the reconstruction of the bridge. Fremont told Brig. Gen. Matthew Ransom, who arrived from Virginia with a regiment of infantry, that the bridge at Rocky Mount could be replaced in a week.[596]

Fremont came up from Wilmington aboard a train that carried a disassembled pontoon bridge, which was being shipped to Petersburg. It was a Yankee-made bridge that was captured near Fredericksburg, Virginia, in December 1862. Samuel Cooper, the Adjutant General of the Confederates States Army, telegraphed from Richmond with permission to keep the pontoons at Rocky Mount for a temporary railroad bridge. By July 27, two daily trains were again running each way on the Wilmington & Weldon. Passengers were still delayed at Rocky Mount by a five-minute walk across the pontoon bridge over the Tar to switch trains. Laborers were by then building a replacement bridge. Kenelm Lewis, of Stonewall Plantation, sent six of his remaining slaves to work on the job.[597]

The body of Maj. Gen. William Dorsey Pender was aboard one of the southbound trains that was held up while the Tar River bridge was being replaced. Pender, who was mortally wounded at Gettysburg, died at Staunton, Virginia on July 18. His body was placed in the Capitol in Richmond (the old Virginia State Capitol building served as the capitol building for the Confederacy) on July 19 – the day before Potter's men reached Pender's home town. Pender's remains were then sent home for burial in the graveyard at Calvary Episcopal Church in Tarboro.[598]

The Wilmington & Weldon, like other 19th century railroads, kept a large force of laborers on hand to keep up with the constant repair work needed to keep the tracks in order. Railroad ties on those days were laid directly in the dirt, rather than on a bed of gravel as is the practice today; consequently, the ties rotted quickly and needed constant replacement. Wooden railroad bridges were often washed away or damaged by floods. So, railroads were prepared to make quick repairs. Northern newspapers reported that the Rocky Mount railroad bridge would take "weeks, perhaps months" to rebuild, but that trains were crossing the Tar River at Rocky Mount again by August 1. The railroad was satisfied enough with the "temporary" bridge to keep it for the rest of the war.

MajGen. William Dorsey Pender, CSA

There was little point in building a more permanent bridge in a place that was so vulnerable to enemy raids.[599]

In the middle of August 1863, a member of the 56th North Carolina passed through Tarboro. He noted that "the bridge is burned in several places, but not unfitted for use."[600]

Temporary repairs made the fire-damaged bridge at Tarboro useable, at least for the adventurous. In September 1863, the Edgecombe County Court appointed three citizens to a committee to see that "necessary" repairs were made to the bridge. (At this time, the judges of North Carolina's county courts were empowered as county administrators as well as magistrates.) The bridge committee included former governor Henry T. Clark, who had helped put out the fire on the bridge after Potter left Tarboro.[601]

$500 REWARD.

TWO HORSES AND ONE MULE TAKEN FROM my Stables by the 3d New York Cavalry, the 30th July, 1863, one horse about seven years old, a sun-burnt, yellow sorrel, thick, heavy set, short tale, with tale and main a little wavy ; had on shoes before ; hind feet white and very tender footed, and is gentle in all work, but rough under the sadde. The Filly is about three years old, blood bay, with white in her forehead about the size of a half dollar, with a long tale with a few white hairs in the end of it, and a roan spot on her side. The mule is a very small-horse mule, three years old, rather a mouse color, with main and tail cropped, and has a dark stripe down his back. I will pay one hundred dollars for the Mule and two hundred dollars each for the Horses, provided they are not injured.   W. W. PARKER,
Aug 5-1w*   Rocky Mount, N. C.

W.W. Parker of Rocky Mount advertised descriptions of two horses and a mule that were stolen during Potter's Raid. The fate of Parker's animals is unknown. State Journal, *August 5, 1863*

While workmen labored on the Rocky Mount bridge, many of the victims of the raid tried to recover their lost property. The *State Journal* reported that "50 horses and mules, wagons, carts, clothing, arms of all sorts and sizes, clothing, tobacco, brandy and money" that were cast aside by the raiders were being held at Kinston, along with recaptured slaves and some Federal prisoners. Some victims followed the path of the raiders all the way to Street's Ferry, looking for anything of theirs that might have been dropped along the way. Early in September, Maj. Adam Gordon (General Martin's brigade quartermaster) notified the public that he still held in Kinston "about twenty horses and six mules, belonging to citizens, which were captured from the Yankee raiders. Their owners are respectfully requested to call for them with as little delay as possible. If not claimed before the end of the month they will be taken for the public service."[602]

Kenelm Lewis sent someone to get "the remains of my waggon (sic), three of the wheels are perfectly good ..." However, Lewis wrote that he "had not succeeded in getting any of my mules yet." Lewis heard that there were "a great many stray mules in Greene County" left behind by the raiders, and he hoped to get some of them. Others were less lucky in recovering their losses. A "Mr. Rose", an acquaintance of Lewis, "went as far as Otter's Creek and returned yesterday", presumably empty-handed.[603]

The raid also made Lewis worry about the future of the Confederacy. In the same letter in which he told his wife about Potter's Raid, he said that the

$40,000 in cash and bonds that they owned "had better be exchanged for something else. I think Confederate bonds & notes will be worthless in six months unless there is a great change for the better."[604]

Lewis' friend Mr. Pippin followed the path of Potter "as far as Scuffleton, but found nothing. He says he is going to Newbern to try and recover his papers." Pippin tried for months to recoup at least some of his losses. In October 1863, he was a passenger aboard a "flag-of-truce boat", a vessel that carried mail and passengers between Confederate territory and the Union enclave at New Bern. The New York *Herald* reported that Pippin "desires to see what can be done about the recovery of twelve thousand dollars in gold and a large amount of government bonds, captured in one of our raids last summer." The outcome of Pippen's desperate effort is unknown.[605]

Lieutenants Henry Hubbard and Henry E. Mosher of the 12th New York Cavalry, captured at Daniel's Schoolhouse, were sent to Libby Prison in Richmond. Author's collection

Chapter 17

"A Ticket Through to Richmond"
*The Experiences and Fates of the Prisoners, Blue and Gray,
Captured during Potter's Raid*

Although most of Potter's men made it safely back to New Bern, around 40 Union soldiers ended up in Confederate prisons. Potter's report states that 43 of his men were missing. Five men who Potter thought were missing were among the seven men who were killed at Daniel's Schoolhouse. For the rest of the missing, their fears of getting "a ticket through to Richmond" came true. Some of the Yankee prisoners were brought through Tarboro on their way to military prisons. Capt. George Brown, the Confederate quartermaster officer at Tarboro, had what he considered "the pleasure of seeing some of the mean low looking villains. They were sent to Petersburg. I think one of them certainly had as bad looking [a] face as any living..."[606]

A Perilous Journey to Rocky Mount

On July 25, just two days after Potter's return, two Union officers who were "on a pleasure excursion" were captured outside of New Bern by soldiers of the 5th North Carolina Cavalry, whom they called "guerillas." The officers, Maj. John R. Houstain and Capt. William A. Avery of 132nd New York Infantry, were taken to Kinston on the first stage of their journey to a military prison. On July 27, they arrived in Goldsboro, where they were put on a train to Virginia.

Their train was delayed at Rocky Mount, because the railroad bridge that was burned during Potter's Raid was still under repair. Houstain and Avery were taken off the train to await the completion of the temporary pontoon bridge.[607]

Houstain and Avery were placed under guard with the two officers of the 12th New York Cavalry who were wounded and captured at Daniel's Schoolhouse, Lieutenants Henry A. Hubbard and Henry Ephraim Mosher. Houstain told the New York *Herald* that the captives went through a terrifying experience when "an attempt to hang the prisoners was made by the inhabitants of Rocky Mount", who "were fully bent in carrying out their hellish designs ..." Warning the lynch mob that if they hanged him and his companions, the Union government would "retaliate two for one", Houstain demanded protection from the Confederate officer who was in charge of the prisoners. Houstain also pleaded with the officer in charge to give guns to the Union captives so that they could protect themselves.[608]

It's not surprising that the Confederate officer refused to hand weapons to the Union officers. But, he did go out to face the mob. He warned the rioters that his charges were prisoners of war, and that he was "duty bound to shield them from all harm, come what may." Houstain added that "the reply of the demons to this humane speech was 'hang the Yankee sons of bitches, never mind the retaliation.'" The unnamed Southern officer drew his revolver and announced to the mob that he would "kill the first man who dared lay a finger on the prisoners." The crowd sullenly dispersed after that threat. Soon afterwards, the prisoners crossed a new pontoon bridge over the Tar River, on their way to Petersburg. Houstain considered that the "delectable and humane neighborhood of Rocky Mount" was named "in honor of the flinty substance composing the hearts of the inhabitants."[609]

Houstain, Hubbard, and Mosher might have been among the "fifteen or twenty of the Yankee raiders who have lately been... burning public and private property, stealing Negroes, horse and cattle and robbing people generally" who were seen passing through Petersburg on their way to prison in Richmond. "These fellows were captured in the neighborhood of Rocky Mount", noted the *Petersburg Express*, and more were expected to follow.[610]

Hubbard and Mosher were listed among the "nearly one hundred prisoners" from various points who arrived at Richmond's Libby Prison on July 30. Houstain, too, was imprisoned there. A former warehouse and ship's chandlery, Libby Prison is one of the most famous prisons of the Civil War. Major Houstain later escaped and made his way to the Union lines, where he told his story to the newspapers.[611]

Lieutenant Mosher remained in Southern prisons. On June 6, 1864, he sent a letter to his brother from the Confederate prison at Macon, Georgia. "I continue to have tolerably fair health", he wrote. "The change of water, & c. did not agree with me at first, but as I get accustomed to it I think the change will be for the better." However, Mosher was transferred to Charleston, South Carolina, where he died of yellow fever on October 6, 1864.[612]

Lt. Henry A. Hubbard was exchanged in 1864, rejoined the 12th New York Cavalry in North Carolina, and was promoted to captain. Early in April 1865, his regiment was operating in Greene County. Near Hookerton on April 8, Hubbard and an orderly were riding alone from their picket line to headquarters. "Suddenly,", according to one of Hubbard's hometown newspapers, "several men sprang from the bushes, and ordered them to surrender. Capt. Hubbard, however, did not propose to acquiesce in the demand, but grasped his pistol, when, the enemy fired, and he fell, pierced by two balls and several buckshot. He died in a few hours." Hubbard was one of the last Union soldiers to die in North Carolina.[613]

Corporal William "Billy" Cromack, another soldier who was captured at Daniel's Schoolhouse, later told the story of how he got back to the North. He ended up in the prison at Belle Isle, in the James River near Richmond. Maj. John E. Mulford, later a brevet general, was the assistant commissioner of exchange for prisoners. Cromack was a sailor on Lake Erie before the war, and said he recognized the officer because Mulford had been the captain of a Great Lakes steamer. Cromack renewed their acquaintance with the plea, "for God's sake, get me out of here". The next morning, Cromack's name was on the exchange list and he was on his way to the Union base at City Point, Virginia.[614]

Maj. John E. Mulford (right) was in charge of the prisoner exchange that released the Confederate enlisted men captured on Potter's Raid. Library of Congress

Cromack transferred to the navy as a master's mate. Again, he was taken prisoner when the *USS Shawsheen* was captured on the James River on May 7, 1864. Before his release in October 1864, Cromack met two old comrades from his company of the 12th New York Cavalry. At Macon, Georgia, he saw Lieutenant Mosher. Cromack also reported that another officer of the regiment, Lt. Alonzo Cooper of Oswego (who was captured at Plymouth, North Carolina in 1864), was in prison at Columbia, South Carolina.[615]

Most of the enlisted men who were captured at Daniel's Schoolhouse were exchanged within a few weeks or months. However, not all of the men who were captured during Potter's Raid were exchanged. Records indicate that at as many as ten Union enlisted men or non-commissioned officers who were captured during the raid died without being released from Confederate prisons.[616]

After their release, many of the other Potter's Raid captives became prisoners again. When Plymouth, North Carolina fell to Confederate forces under Brig. Gen. Robert F. Hoke on April 20, 1864, about 115 men from Companies A and F of the 12th New York Cavalry were taken prisoner. Many of the men who were captured at Plymouth ended up at the prison at Andersonville, Georgia. This time, exchange and parole did not come quickly. By some accounts, 85 men of the 12th New York Cavalry died at Andersonville.[617]

The Fates of the Confederate Prisoners

The Confederate soldiers who were captured during Potter's Raid may have been aboard the side-wheel steamer *S. R. Spaulding,* which arrived at Fortress Monroe, Virginia on July 25, 1863. A list of prisoners who were paroled at Fort Monroe, Virginia on August 4, 1863 includes twenty-seven Confederate enlisted men who were taken prisoner during the raid. (The list includes a mistaken listing for a prisoner who was captured elsewhere.) For their return, the Potter's Raid prisoners were very likely aboard the Union steamship *New York,* which on August 4 left Fort Monroe for City Point, Virginia, with "about 300 prisoners under Maj. Mulford" (the same officer who Cromack credited with his release). It was a standard practice for Confederates who were being released from Northern prisons to board a "flag of truce boat" at Fortress Monroe, which took them to City Point, from where they traveled overland to the Southern lines.[618]

The steamer **New York** *delivered exchanged Confederate prisoners from Potter's Raid.* Library of Congress

One of the Potter's Raid prisoners, Private Andrew Dozier of the 6th Virginia Infantry, was crossed off the August 4 list of paroled prisoners. The November-December 1863 muster roll of his company states, "taken prisoner while serving as a teamster at Rocky Mount, N. C. July 20/63 & has since gone to his home in Norfolk."[619]

Potter's Raid

The Confederate officers who were captured on the raid probably also expected to be paroled soon. But, the enlisted men were lucky to be released, because the old system by which men were routinely paroled and exchanged was breaking down. The *New York Times* on August 8, 1863, stated, "All the rebel officers in our hands are being gathered at Johnson's Island, Sandusky, where they will be kept until a satisfactory reply is received from the Rebel authorities in answer to the President's order of retaliation, which has been forwarded by our government." The "order of retaliation", which came into effect to the bad luck of the prisoners, referred to a Confederate refusal to agree to Northern demands about treating captured black Union troops as regular prisoners of war. At any rate, by mid-1863, the exchange system was seen as being too helpful to the Confederacy's smaller army, which could not afford to permanently lose men as prisoners. Pressure grew in the North to stop all paroles and exchanges.[620]

Four Confederate officers who were captured by Potter were temporarily quartered in New Bern's "Pollock Street Jail", which was also called "the Sesesh Jail." This jail, also known as the Jones House, was a two-story residence that was built at the corner of Pollock and Eden Streets in 1809. The Union authorities in New Bern used it as a prison. Military and civilian prisoners, including spies, spent time there during the war. The famous Confederate spy Emeline Pigott of Carteret County was imprisoned there in 1865. In 1963, the Tryon Palace Commission purchased the Jones House. Currently, it serves as a gift shop and offices for Tryon Palace.[621]

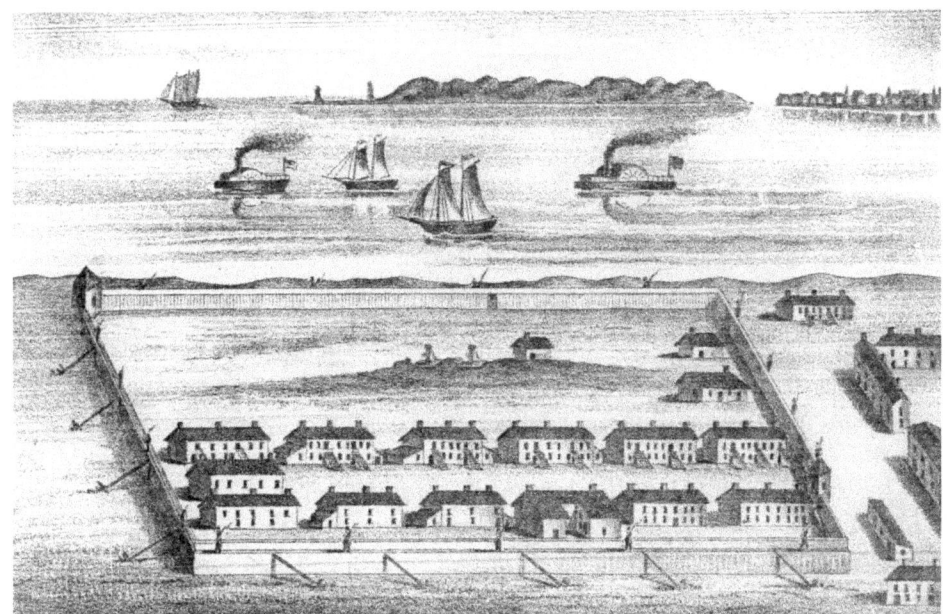

Confederate officers captured on Potters' Raid were sent to the prison at Johnson's Island, on Lake Erie near Sandusky, Ohio.

The officers – Lt. Bennett P. Jenkins of the 7th Confederate Cavalry, Lt. Nathan M. Lawrence of the 8th North Carolina Infantry, Lt. Thomas J. Stewart of the 3rd North Carolina Artillery, and Capt. P. Nichols of the 13th Battalion, North Carolina Infantry – requested their release in a petition that they sent to General Foster. The petition, which was drafted by Lawrence on July 30, asserted that each man "was at home on furlough, some on sick furlough, unable to perform military duty [and] without arms of any kind. We were told when we were taken that we would be released on parole …"[622]

The petition went to Brig. Gen. Sullivan Amory Meredith, the "agent for exchange of prisoners" at Fort Monroe, Virginia. One of Foster's staff officers, Lt.-col. Southard Hoffman, jotted on the back, "there is no way these officers can be released, I presume?" Without explaining further, Meredith replied, "I can see no way in which the within named officers can be released at present."[623]

The gravestone of Capt. P. Nichols. Captured during Potter's Raid, he died on February 27, 1864 in the prison at Johnson's Island, Ohio.
Photo by the author.

Long after the war, Captain Nichols' brother told an acquaintance that after his capture, the captain befriended some Union officers who were Masons. Learning that Captain Nichols was going to be sent to a prison deep in the "cold country" of the North, they "provided him with new shoes, a warm overcoat, two blankets, and some money …"[624]

After confinement at Fort Norfolk, Virginia, and Fort McHenry at Baltimore, Maryland, the four officers were sent to the prison for Confederate officers on Johnson's Island, in Lake Erie off Sandusky, Ohio. Captain Nichols died at Johnson's Island of chronic diarrhea on February 27, 1864. He still lies buried today in the prison's Confederate Cemetery, his grave marked by a standard marble tombstone. The other three officers were released after they took the Oath of Allegiance to the Union after the end of the war in 1865.[625]

In August 1863, Major John N. Whitford traveled to New Bern on a "flag of truce boat." Reportedly, Whitford was investigating reports that his captured men were being held "in irons". Union authorities denied that Whitford's men were being mistreated. On the contrary, they told the major that two thirds of his captured men wanted to take the Oath of Allegiance to the

Union and remain in New Bern, rather than return to their old unit. Most of the soldiers of Whitford's Battalion who were captured during Potter's Raid were "exchanged at Fort Monroe, Virginia" on August 4, 1863 (see Appendix II). A less fortunate captive was Private Furnifold Powell, the man who was taken at Swift Creek Village on July 18, at the beginning of the raid. For unknown reasons, Powell was imprisoned at Point Lookout, Maryland and Elmira, New York until February 1865. After his release, Powell went to a hospital in Richmond, where he received a furlough. By the time he had recuperated from his imprisonment, the war was over.[626]

Lieutenant Commmander Charles W. Flusser pleaded in vain with Gen. Foster to destroy the CSS Albemarle. <small>Naval Historical Center</small>

Chapter 18

The Bungled Follow-Up to Potter's Raid
The Battle of Boon's Mill
July 28, 1863

Just as Foster had planned an attack on Wilmington if the December 1862 Goldsboro Expedition had panned out for him, he had plans for another raid after Potter's return to New Bern. Before eastern North Carolina had time to recover from Potter's Raid, a larger Union force bore down on the Wilmington & Weldon Railroad. General Foster personally led this expedition. Unlike Potter's Raid, where a single force diverged against two targets, Foster drew two separate forces together in a complex plan for a devastating final blow to the Wilmington & Weldon.

Potter's men were still at Street's Ferry late on the night of July 22 when Lt.-com. Charles W. Flusser received orders from Acting Rear Admiral S. P. Lee to cooperate with a secret expedition planned by General Foster. Flusser took three steamers from Plymouth to Winton, where he remained to guard Foster's transports.[627]

Foster personally led a large force of infantry by steamboat from New Bern to Winton, on the Chowan River in Hertford County. Leaving New Bern around 6 a.m. on July 25, they arrived at Winton on Sunday, July 26. The expedition waited for a large cavalry force from southeastern Virginia under Col. Samuel P. Spear to join them. Foster expected the horsemen would already be at Winton. The cavalry companies involved in Potter's Raid remained on duty around New Bern; their horses were still too exhausted for them to endure another long raid.[628]

Meanwhile, "to divert the attention of the rebel forces", another Union force left Plymouth and marched west as if to threaten Williamston. Under the command of Col. Theodore F. Lehmann of the 103rd Pennsylvania, the expedition also included Company E of the 12th New York Cavalry. Lehmann's men briefly occupied Williamston, and fought a skirmish at Foster's Mills, on Sweetwater Creek in Martin County on July 27 before returning to Plymouth.[629]

A postwar photo of Brig. Gen. Matthew Ransom. Library of Congress

Spear's cavalry arrived across the Chowan from Winton on July 27. Their crossing was delayed because a storm in the Albemarle Sound had destroyed the pontoon bridge that the expedition was depending on. (It's tempting to wonder whether this was the same bridge used by Potter to cross the Neuse at Street's Ferry.)[630]

Foster headed west toward Weldon, the site of a vital bridge and a crucial rail junction just south of the Virginia line. A successful attack against Weldon and the nearby junction of Garysburg would cut Virginia off from rail communication with the rest of the Confederacy.[631]

On July 28, Spear's cavalry passed through Jackson, the county seat of Northampton County, on their way to Weldon. They stirred up a small party of Confederate officers, who turned out to be Brig. Gen. Matthew Ransom and his staff. Ransom had been sent from Virginia to deal with Potter. Although they got to Rocky Mount too late to go after Potter's men, Ransom's troops were still in the area when news came of Foster's approaching raiders. The general and his staff were looking for the Yankees, and indeed found them. Ransom and his men spurred their horses down the road just ahead of a flock of Yankee cavalrymen. A short distance away at Boon's Mill were Ransom's nearest troops, four companies of the 24th North Carolina, and the Macon Light Artillery, a battery from Macon, Georgia. Ransom had posted them around the mill when he rode into Jackson to look for the enemy.[632]

On this hot day, most of Ransom's men shed their uniforms and went skinny-dipping in the millpond. They saw their general galloping up the road, shouting a warning as the advance of Spear's cavalry thundered behind them. Many of Ransom's men had time to pick up only their muskets and cartridge boxes, and had to leave their clothes by the pond. Ransom's 200 men and the two guns potentially faced about 5,000 troops. The Rebels held off Spear for a couple of hours, until a "terrific storm" ended the fighting by drenching everyone. Rather than wait for the Federal infantry to come up and renew the battle, Spear withdrew to the main Union camp. With the unexpected resistance and the mucky condition of the roads, Foster ordered his troops to return to New Bern and Virginia.[633]

Flusser wrote that during the expedition, he asked Foster to detach a party to Edward's Ferry on the Roanoke River, to destroy the Confederate gunboat *CSS Albemarle*, which was under construction. To Flusser's regret, he "did not succeed in impressing him with the importance of the move, and it was not done."[634]

The fiasco at Boon's Mill abruptly ended Foster's mini-campaign against the Wilmington & Weldon. Although Potter's Raid was already planned when Foster stepped into the post of commander of the Department of Virginia and North Carolina on July 15, after that date, his attention was less focused on North Carolina. Maj. Gen. John J. Peck took command of the Union District of North Carolina on August 14. Peck continued to send small expeditions and scouting parties into Confederate territory, but there would not be anything to match the scale of Potter's Raid. (See page 228, "More Union Raids on Pitt County"). [635]

Potter's Raid, and the Union failure at Boon's Mill, indirectly contributed to the South's greatest victory in North Carolina. At last awakened to the danger posed to the Wilmington & Weldon Railroad and the *CSS Albemarle,* (which was being built at Edwards' Ferry on the Roanoke, in Halifax County), the Confederates strengthened their forces in the region. Brig. Gen. John J. Peck wrote to Foster to explain that the Confederate reinforcements "have resulted from your late raids, and will make it a matter of some difficulty to destroy the ironclad at Edwards' Ferry." [636]

By late August 1863, Foster had decided that further action against the Roanoke River gunboat was impossible because "the force at my disposal is not adequate to overcome the resistance I would meet by the concentration of troops from Richmond, Petersburg, and North Carolina. Any military movement would, I fear, induce the enemy to strengthen their works and so, perhaps, block future movements intended for farther up."[637]

The Union would regret Foster's decision. In April, 1864, the *CSS Albemarle* steamed down the Roanoke. The ironclad rammed and sank the *USS Southfield*. Lieutenant-commander Flusser, who had tried in vain to persuade

Foster to destroy the *Albemarle,* was killed aboard the *USS Miami.* Flusser was killed by a shell that he'd fired himself; the shell bounced off the ironclad's hull and exploded over the *Miami.* The fragile wooden navy steamers were no match for the Albermarle, and they withdrew after Flusser's death. With the gunboats driven away from Plymouth, the *Albemarle* was free to turn her guns toward the land defenses. With the *Albemarle's* help, Confederate troops under Brig. Gen. Robert F. Hoke captured Plymouth on April 20. Washington was abandoned after Plymouth fell, and New Bern itself was threatened until the Confederate troops were ordered to Virginia to strengthen Lee's army.

Chapter 19

"Southern Hospitality Has Improved Since Then'
*What Happened to the People Who Were Involved in Potter's Raid
1863 — 1940*

Many of the units that took part in Potter's Raid, including the 3rd New York Cavalry and Battery H of the 3rd New York Artillery, along with the Confederacy's Petersburg Artillery, the 7th Confederate Cavalry, the 17th North Carolina and part of the 62nd Georgia Cavalry, were sent to Virginia. Some of these units were fated to meet again later in the war. The Petersburg Artillery and the 7th Confederate Cavalry together manned Fort Harrison, near Petersburg, Virginia against a Union onslaught on Sept. 30, 1864.

The Petersburg Artillery Saves Their Home Town
Capt. Edward Graham's Petersburg Artillery also had another run-in with the 3rd New York Cavalry, their adversaries in the fighting along the Plymouth Road near Tarboro on July 20, 1863. The 3rd New York Cavalry was part of an expedition under Brig. Gen. August V. Kautz that menaced Petersburg on June 9, 1864. Kautz' force came close to capturing the lightly defended city, after overwhelming some hastily mustered militia and home guard units from Petersburg.

As the Federal cavalry halted in a little valley at the edge of town, the horse-drawn guns of the Petersburg Artillery rumbled through the city. Crowds of frightened civilians milled in the streets. Graham, single-minded in his rush to get at the Yankees, roared, "God damn them! If they won't get out of the way, run over them!"[638]

Their guns rolled to a stop at the crest of Reservoir Hill, and they looked down at the approaching enemy cavalry. When the guns were "in battery", Captain Graham ordered, "Give 'em hell, boys!" The Yankee cavalrymen had just halted to water their horses in a small creek when the four guns of the Petersburg Artillery opened fire. It stunned the horsemen, who had believed that Petersburg was undefended. While the Federals hesitated, Confederate reinforcements rushed to join Graham's Battery on the hill. Kautz, who had expected no more resistance at that point, called off the attack. Graham's men saved their home town from capture, and kept a vital Confederate stronghold in Lee's hands. When Petersburg fell on April 2-3, 1865, both Richmond and Lee's army were lost within two weeks.[639]

After the Petersburg Artillery disbanded at the end of the war, Graham returned to Petersburg and went back into the dry goods business. He died in 1887.[640]

John G. Harris, of North Carolina, served in the 3rd New York Cavalry.
U.S. Army Military History Institute

The 3rd New York Cavalry

The 3rd New York Cavalry was sent piecemeal to Virginia until the whole regiment was there by May, 1864. The colonel of the regiment, Simon H. Mix, was killed on June 15, 1864. (Mix had not personally taken part in Potter's Raid.) Lt.-col. George Lewis was promoted to colonel, and took command of the regiment.[641]

Maj. Jephtha Garrard left the regiment when he was promoted to colonel of the 1st US Colored Cavalry, the first black cavalry regiment in the Union Army. At least twelve other officers or sergeants of the 3rd New York Cavalry accompanied Garrard to posts as officers in his regiment. Maj. George W. Cole later became the commander of the 2nd US Colored Cavalry, and other men transferred with him from the old regiment.[642]

Potter's aide, Capt. George Gouraud, is seated at the right in this postwar photo. Seated in the center is his business associate, Thomas Edison. Library of Congress

Capt. George Edward Gouraud, Potter's aide-de-camp during the raid, finished the war as a lieutenant-colonel. In 1893, he was awarded the Medal of Honor for "rescuing a wounded comrade from within 30 yards of the enemy's ranks" at the Battle of Honey Hill, South Carolina, on November 30, 1864. [643]

After the war, Gouraud lived in England. He was a business associate of Thomas Edison, and helped introduce the phonograph, electric light, and other inventions to Britain and Europe. When Gouraud joined a GAR post at the behest of his wartime comrade Floyd Clarkson in 1890, Gouraud summoned the veterans to dinner with a recording of bugle call that he had made in England. The voice of George Gouraud can still be heard today on a number of early Edison recordings. Some of them are available online on the sounds page in the "Edisonia" section of the website of the National Park Service's Edison National Historic Site. Gouraud died in 1912. [644]

Brig. Gen. Edward E. Potter served as Foster's chief of staff for much of the rest of the war. He followed Foster on assignments to Virginia, the Department of the Ohio, and South Carolina. In April 1865, the brigadier led another "Potter's Raid", a devastating slash through South Carolina that lasted three weeks. Although it was successful in the sense of destroying much Confederate property at little cost to the Union, the raid came too late to affect the course of the war. It served only to make Reconstruction that much more bleak for the people of a large section of South Carolina. Potter retired from the army with a brevet rank of major general. He was listed as a lawyer in the 1880 census of Morris County, New Jersey.[645]

Potter died of pneumonia on June 1, 1889. He was buried in the New York City's Marble Cemetery, in lower Manhattan. The cemetery was the resting place of many prominent New Yorkers. Two very famous men were buried there, both temporarily. Former US president James Monroe died in New York and was buried in his son-in-law's vault in the cemetery until his body was moved for reburial in Virginia in 1858. Only a few weeks before Potter died, John Ericsson, the designer of the pioneer ironclad *USS Monitor* was buried in the Marble Cemetery on March 11, 1889. Ericsson's body was soon moved to his native Sweden.[646]

George W. Lewis finished the war as the colonel of the 3rd New York Cavalry. He was awarded a $12 a month pension in 1890. Lewis died of pernicious anemia in 1896. His widow, Elfrida C. Lewis, was born in Virginia and had married Lewis during the Civil War.[647]

Ferris Jacobs, Jr., who led his battalion to Rocky Mount during the raid, retired from the army at the end of the war with a brevet (acting) rank of brigadier general. Jacobs returned to the practice of law in peacetime. From 1881-1883, he was a Republican congressman from New York. He died On August 30, 1886 and was buried in his home town of Delhi, New York.[648]

George W. Cole's Spectacular Murder Trials

Maj. George Cole left the 3rd New York Cavalry early in 1864 to take up the post of colonel of the newly formed 2nd United States Colored Cavalry. He was promoted to the rank of brevet brigadier general by the end of the war. Before the war, Cole had given up the practice of medicine to become a lumber dealer. After the war, he was "attached to the detective service of the Internal Revenue Department" in New York.[649]

In 1867, delegates from across New York were assembled at the state capital of Albany to write a new state constitution. On the evening of June 4, Cole was seated in the lobby of the Stanwix House, a fine hotel that was popular with politicians. About 8:30, Cole rose from his seat. He approached a New York state senator, and drew a pistol. Without saying a word, he fatally shot the senator in the head. Both men were long-time acquaintances from Syracuse, New York. Cole claimed that the victim, L. H. Hiscock, had carried on an affair with his wife during the war. Two spectacular trials followed. Cole's trials were widely covered in newspapers across the United States because of the notoriety of the crime, and his status as a minor celebrity. Not only could he claim the title of general, but his brother Cornelius Cole was a U. S. senator from California. Another brother was a US consul in Acapulco, Mexico.[650]

Oddly enough, Hiscock was a cousin of US senator Ira Harris. The 12th New York Cavalry, a regiment that Cole would have known well in North Carolina, had been called "the 3rd Ira Harris Cavalry" in honor of that senator.[651]

Among the witnesses who were called into court to testify about Cole's mental state was Rowland M. Hall. Hall was one of Cole's company commanders on the Rocky Mount portion of Potter's Raid. In 1867, Hall was practicing law in New York City. Hall "testified to the general sanity of the accused", but noted that when he saw Cole again after the war, "he remarked something wild and singular in the expression of his face ..." Cole's first trial ended in a mistrial. In the second trial, he was acquitted on the grounds of temporary insanity, which was still a new (and controversial) legal defense at the time. His wartime wounds, and the injury suffered from a fall from his horse at the end of Potter's Raid, were used by his defense attorneys as contributing toward his state of mind at the time of the murder.[652]

After his acquittal, Cole found a position in the post office at New York City, and then moved to the west and started a medical practice in New Mexico. Cole became a member of the Union Lodge, the Masonic lodge at Fort Union. His fellow lodge members conducted his funeral after Cole died of pneumonia in Mora, New Mexico on December 11, 1875. He was buried in the private family cemetery of Ceran St. Vrain, a legendary fur trader and explorer. The verdict in Cole's second trial was never accepted by much of the American public. A newspaper pointed out upon Cole's death that "the insanity which the jury decided was the cause of his crime never showed itself afterward".[653]

The 3rd New York Cavalry lost 207 men during the war; 51 were killed in battle, and the rest lost to "disease and other causes". As with other Civil War

A ribbon from a reunion of the 3rd New York Cavalry in 1884.

regiments, germs killed many more soldiers than did bullets and bayonets. One man of the 3rd was quite lucky. Private Gideon Blackman, the man who was sent "a-whizzing outside" the exploding ammunition car at Rocky Mount, recovered and returned to duty in October, 1863.[655]

Private John G. Harris, the Hyde County, North Carolina native who served in Company F, 3rd New York Cavalry, made the news long after the war. Uncle Sam had neglected to pay Harris for some travel expenses, clothing, and rations, as well as 67 cents for his last day in the army in 1865. In 1902, Harris' patience was rewarded when the Army sent him a check for $53.00. (It's not clear whether this included 37 years' worth of interest.) [656]

Harris paid a high price for his loyalty to the Union. He lost all of his property in North Carolina. While he never met any of his three Confederate brothers on the battlefield during the war, he never saw them or his parents again. "It was fully twenty years" after the war "before he saw a relative".[657]

After the war, Harris lived in New Hamburgh, in Dutchess County, New York. The transplanted Southerner found remarkable respect in his new home. Harris was listed on the 1910 census as a postmaster. In 1913, he retired from a term as the president of the veterans' association of the 3rd New York Cavalry. When German names became unpopular during World War I, a suggestion was made to change the name of New Hamburgh to Harrison. Naming the town in honor of Harris, a "veteran soldier, former postmaster and present town official" would "prove a good American substitute" for the town's German-sounding name. The war ended soon after, though, and the town's name remained unchanged. Harris died in New Hamburgh in 1923.[658]

In contrast with a Southerner like Harris who found a new life in the North, at least one of the raiders from New York stayed on in North Carolina. Sgt. Abram H. Hamblin of the 3rd New York Artillery was one of the men who was captured at Daniel's Schoolhouse. Hamblin was soon released for exchange. He was transferred to the 1st North Carolina Volunteers and promoted to lieutenant in September 1863. In the 1880 Census, Hamblin appears as "A. H. Hamblin" in Pamlico County, North Carolina. His wife is not listed, but Hamblin had two daughters, 12-year-old Florence and 9-year-old Lavinia. His occupation was listed as "teaching". By 1890, Hamblin was living in Beaufort County, according to the Civil War Veterans Census. Beginning in 1865, he received an invalid's pension for his wartime service. Hamblin died at Norfolk, Virginia on June 9, 1915. [659]

George W. Graham's Double Life

Lt. George Wallace Graham, who led Company L of the 1st North Carolina Union Volunteers on Potter's raid, went on to lead several small but successful raids in eastern North Carolina. (See page 228, "More Union Raids in Pitt County".) He was a captain when he mustered out of the service in June

1865. Graham exchanged a career of leading "buffalos" (white eastern North Carolina loyalists), for leading "buffalo soldiers", the famous black troops who served in the postwar West. In July 1866, Graham went back into the army as a first lieutenant in the 10th US Cavalry, one of the two black cavalry regiments that served on the frontier.[660]

Promotion was usually slow in the small postwar army, but Graham was promoted to captain in May 1867. For his "gallant and meritorious service" at the Battle of Big Sandy in Colorado on September 17, 1868, he won the brevet rank of major. In his autobiography, Buffalo Bill Cody mentioned that he scouted for hostile Indians with Graham. For all the promise hinted at by his successful postwar career, Graham was destined to become, if anything, more notorious than his former comrade George W. Cole. Graham was arrested at Fort Leavenworth, Kansas and charged with "speculating with government funds and other misconduct." After a court martial, he was cashiered on August 16, 1870.[661]

Graham was soon well-known in Colorado as "a genteel loafer and blackguard, who ... frequented the saloons and gambling houses of Denver." The former raider, though, was getting ready to gamble with more than cards and the roulette wheel. On September 10, 1873, shocking news reached Denver by telegraph. Graham was wounded and arrested after he and an accomplice tried to rob an army paymaster near River Bend, Colorado. Denver newspapers reported that Graham had been planning a robbery of the United States Mint in that city, and that after those plans fell through, tried the payroll robbery instead.[662]

For the holdup, and for wounding two army officers and a female passenger on the ambulance wagon that was carrying the payroll, Graham got two years in the Colorado State Prison. In 1874, Graham led a breakout of seven prisoners. After weeks of hunting by law enforcement officials, the escapees were surrounded in a miner's cabin at Rosita, Colorado. The convicts were captured after a shootout with a posse of prison guards and miners, and Graham once again survived some severe bullet wounds. After his release in 1875, Graham returned to Rosita and opened a saloon. His last scheme was a takeover of the Pocahontas Mine at Rosita, Colorado. Graham at last "met his desserts", shot over twenty times by a posse of miners. He was buried in a five-dollar coffin.[663]

The 12th New York Cavalry spent the rest of the war in North Carolina. Two of the companies battered at Daniel's Schoolhouse, A and F, were captured when the Confederates took Plymouth, North Carolina on April 20, 1864. Three men of the 12th were killed at Plymouth, and 118 were taken prisoner. New York newspapers reported that 85 of these men died at Andersonville Prison in Georgia. Among them was Sgt. Gleason Wellington, the soldier who heard the fighting at Daniel's Schoolhouse while lying delirious in an ambulance. Wellington's body was brought home to Oswego, New York for a funeral and reburial in January 1866. In all, the 12th New York Cavalry lost 222 men during the war. 39 died in battle, and 183 of "disease and other causes", including the men who died at Andersonville and other military prisons.[664]

Floyd Clarkson ended the war as a brevet lieutenant-colonel. He had a postwar career as a banker in New York City. Clarkson was also heavily involved in veterans' organizations. He took part in the ceremonies for the grand funerals of Ulysses S. Grant (in 1885) and William Tecumseh Sherman (in 1890). Also in 1890, Clarkson was elected as New York's Department Commander of the Grand Army of the Republic. He died on January 2, 1894. Alonzo Cooper of the old 12th Cavalry recalled that his comrades said that on the "Tarborough Raid", Clarkson "led the advance and was always called the 'Custer' of the Twelfth Cavalry." Cooper apparently meant the Custer remark as a compliment to Clarkson's leadership, not a criticism of his tactics at the costly charge at Daniel's Schoolhouse.[665]

The 12th New York's Cavalry Returns to Daniel's Schoolhouse

Late in August 1863, the father of Sgt. John Miller planned "to send a man to try and find poor Johnny's remains" from his burial site near Daniel's Schoolhouse. Sgt. Gleason Wellington wrote to his family to tell Miller that "it is no use. It cannot be done." Capt. Simeon Church "has tried ... to get his brother's body which is buried with John cannot the Rebs are as thick as hops there now and will not receive a flag of truce."[666]

After the fall of Plymouth, North Carolina, the Union captives were marched to Tarboro on their way to prisons in the South. On their way to Tarboro, some of prisoners of Company A of the 12th were allowed to briefly visit the graves of their fallen comrades near the schoolhouse.[667]

In May 1865, the 12th New York Cavalry again rode into Tarboro. This time, they were on their way home for discharge. The regiment had orders to spend a few days in Tarboro "in forming Home Guards, and securing peace and quiet until the re-establishment of the civil government". They were "quietly but cordially welcomed by the citizens of the town". The troopers camped across the river from town, in a large open field surrounded by two segments of the River Road. Many of the men remembered riding around the field on their way to Daniel's Schoolhouse, and also remembered the shells of the Petersburg Artillery hurtling at them over that field as they began to leave Tarboro.[668]

The regiment also reburied their dead comrades and gave them a military funeral. Lt. Alonzo Cooper supervised their exhumation and reburial. Cooper recognized the bodies of two of his fellow townsmen from Oswego, John Miller and William Davies. Capt. Simeon Church was there to identify the

Alonzo Cooper wrote **In and Out of Rebel Prisons** *about his days in the 12th New York Cavalry, but he was on recruiting duty during Potter's Raid.* Author's collection

body of his brother, Cyrus, and other men were able to identify Privates Corl, Mulvey, and Rude. Cooper charged that the men had been placed in a single grave "in a perfectly nude state, the fiendish brutes having appropriated to their own use every article of wearing apparel." Nothing was ever mentioned about finding the body of "William Thompson 1st" of Company A, who was reported killed at Daniel's Schoolhouse.[669]

The soldiers made coffins, "small enough to be placed in other coffins for removal", for their dead comrades. Their bodies were brought to the cavalry camp for their funeral on May 17, 1865. The day of the funeral was, wrote Sgt. Melvin F. Stephens of Company B, "a bright and beautiful May day, when the air was laden with the perfume of roses and the many flowers of this semi-tropical clime …" The procession was led by the regimental band. Behind the band followed forty men riding white horses and carrying drawn sabers, the pallbearers, ambulances bearing the coffins, and then the rest of the regiment. The procession "moved with sabres reversed, the band playing a solemn dirge, and marched to a beautiful burying ground in the village, where the Episcopal burial service was read by Chaplain Palmer of our regiment", wrote Cooper.[670]

Sergeant Stephens eulogized those "whose remains we followed" as "the first offering of our regiment to the cause for which we had left homes and friends and all that men hold dear in social life …" Although many others in the regiment died later in battle, prisons, and hospitals in the next two years of the war, "these seemed peculiarly Our Dead, from the fact that they had first fallen, and that we were now, on the first dawning of peace, permitted thus to pay them this tribute of respect."[671]

The bodies were reburied in Tarboro's Public Cemetery, which was downtown in the block bounded by St. James, Pitts, St. David's, and St Patrick's Streets. Their new graves were marked by wooden headboards, with "name, troop, place of residence, time and manner of death, and age, painted on each". Lieutenant Cooper clipped a lock of John Miller's hair for his father, and lock of Davies' hair for his wife. After the funeral, the regiment proceeded to Raleigh, where they turned over their horses and equipment before being mustered out of the army.[672]

Over the next few months, grieving relatives made the trip to North Carolina to reclaim the bodies of three of the men who died at Daniel's Schoolhouse. Samuel Miller went to Tarboro in August 1865 to bring back his son. In December 1865, Mrs. William Davies returned to Oswego with the body of her husband. An Oswego newspaper wrote that Mary Davies, "with a true woman's devotion, has alone sought out her husband's resting place, and brought the remains this great distance, that his grave may be watered by the tears of affection, in his early home. It was a great undertaking, but a woman's determination and love has been found equal to it."[673]

Captain Church's body was returned to New York in March 1866. "A large concourse of citizens", wrote a newspaper, "accompanied by a brass band" took his remains from the depot in his home village of Fulton to the cemetery.[674]

The other three men of the 12th New York Cavalry who were killed on Potter's Raid, Privates David Carl and Hiram Rude, and Bugler Narcisse Mulway are still in North Carolina. They were later reburied at the Raleigh National Cemetery. Oddly enough, the place where these men were temporarily buried in Tarboro is near the area of the cemetery later chosen as the Confederate plot.[675]

The 23rd New York Cavalry apparently also passed through Tarboro on their way home after the war. Thomas J. Paul, the Irish-born private who was captured while charging against Confederate troops at Tarboro in 1863, died at that same town of typhoid fever on July 8, 1865.[676]

Half a century later, James M. Himes, a veteran of Company A of the 12th New York Cavalry and of the Daniel's Schoolhouse fight, answered a telephone call in Oswego. At the other end of the line was Billy Cromack. Himes had not seen his old comrade since the skirmish in 1863, when Cromack was left behind on the field, his leg crushed underneath his dead horse. They spent an enjoyable time together, remembering that afternoon when "the supply of Confederates was so much greater than the demand, just at that moment, that the Twelfth departed in considerable haste ..."[677]

Sgt. William "Billy" Burr of the 12th New York Cavalry finished the war as a lieutenant. After the war, he returned to his home town of Oswego until 1881, when he moved to Texas. He sold his interest in a cotton gin company to invest in Texas' oil fields in 1901. It was a good move. At the time of his death in 1915, Burr owned several productive oil wells, including "Burr Well No. 1", which gushed forth 2,500 barrels a day.[678]

Private William Brown, who was still using the alias of Daniel Mulligan, was among the members of Company F who were captured at Plymouth. Brown spent about one year in Confederate prisons, including Andersonville, before the end of the war. When Brown, returned to his home town of Fort Covington, "one of his thighs was permanently crippled, rheumatism racked him, and his body was beginning to cramp forward so that he walked bent half double, unable to stand straight again." He was 23 years old.[679]

Despite his painful condition, Brown worked on farms for several years until he was unable to do any work at all. For his wartime service, he was awarded a pension of $24 a month, which was later increased to $50 a month. The census of Union veterans of 1890 listed him as "William Brown, alias Daniel Mulligan". But, in 1897, someone with a grudge against him wrote to the Pension Department, telling them that "Daniel Mulligan" was a deserter. The pension was revoked. He was caught in a bureaucratic nightmare. Daniel Mulligan was a deserter, and so was not entitled to a pension, but there was no enlistment record under his real name of William Brown. Brown lived until 1917. Despite considerable sympathetic newspaper coverage, he was never able to get his pension restored.[680]

About fifty years after Potter's Raid, Dr. Russell H. Conwell, a famous lecturer of the day (and the founder of Temple University), gave a well-attended talk in Tarboro. Conwell surprised his listeners with the news that he had last visited Tarboro as a Yankee cavalryman in 1863, and that he was one of those who had burned the Rocky Mount Mills. He amused the audience with his observation that "Southern Hospitality has improved since those days." Conwell's story, alas, was no more than a good yarn to grab the attention of his audience. He was stationed in New Bern as a captain with the 46th Massachusetts Infantry, but he did not take part in Potter's Raid.[681]

Michael Cohen, the Irish mill owner who "defected" to the Yankees at Tarboro, was unable to put his life back together again. During the raid, his Tarboro grist mill was reduced to ashes, costing him his job and his exemption from conscription. He accompanied Potter back to New Bern, and gave the Union authorities some information on the Confederate Navy's Tarboro gunboat, and the *CSS Albemarle*."At the request of General Potter", Cohen was given a job as a plumber with the Quartermaster Department in New Bern. His co-operation with the Union Navy netted him nothing in the way of financial compensation for his losses. He was sent to New York City, where he took the Oath of Allegiance. Cohen traveled back to New Bern to work for a time, and then returned to New York.[682]

Back in New York, Cohen was "noticed by his family to behave in a manner that led them to believe that he was not in his right mind." On a Saturday night in 1864, Cohen entered a "porter-house" owned by a Patrick McGinn in Williamsburg, New York (now part of Queens). Witnesses saw the pair talking for some time. Then, "without any provocation", Cohen stabbed McGinn and escaped from the building. Several days later, in history's last glimpse of Cohen, he was still on the run from the police. Immediately after the attack, McGinn's injuries were believed to be fatal, but he later began to recover.[683]

Confederate Participants in Potter's Raid

The Montgomery True Blues finished out the war when they blew up the magazine at Fort Branch on April 10, 1865, to prevent its capture. After an unsuccessful attempt to join General Joseph E. Johnston's army before it surrendered, they disbanded at Ridgeway, North Carolina. In 1874, the company was revived as an Alabama militia unit. Their postwar uniforms of dark blue, with white cross belts and tall plumed shakos, harked back to the pomp and splendor of the Napoleonic era. At national drill competitions, they were recognized as one of the "old 'crack companies'", and one of the best-drilled units in the country. In the late 1800s, they were chosen to be in a series of collectible cigarette cards that showed fancily-attired American and foreign soldiers. The revived Montgomery True Blues served in the Spanish-American War (as Company D, 2nd Alabama Volunteers) in 1898; the 1916 Border Campaign against Pancho Villa, and during World War I. Records document the continuation of the company as late as 1939.[684]

John T. Kennedy's success at Daniel's Schoolhouse won him a promotion to lieutenant colonel four days after the skirmish. On June 9, 1864, Kennedy was shot and captured near Petersburg, Virginia. While he was still imprisoned, he was promoted to colonel of the 16th Battalion, North Carolina Cavalry in May, 1864. His new battalion was made up of the North Carolina companies of the 62nd Georgia Cavalry and the 7th Confederate Cavalry. Kennedy was exchanged and took up his new post in November, 1864.[685]

Kennedy had a long and varied public career after the war. He served as the sheriff of Wayne County, and as a North Carolina state senator. He was a founder of the State Hospital for the Colored Insane in Goldsboro, which was the forerunner of today's Cherry Hospital. Late in life, he was an assistant curator for the Museum Section for the North Carolina Department of Agriculture, which later became the North Carolina Science Museum. Half a century after "Kennedy's men done the work" in driving Potter away from Tarboro, Kennedy died at the Confederate Soldiers' Home in Raleigh on January 13, 1913. He is buried in Raleigh's Oakwood Cemetery.[686]

Kennedy's superior, Col. Joel R. Griffin, became the commander of the 8th Georgia Cavalry in July 1864. Griffin's new regiment combined the Georgian companies of the old 62nd Georgia Cavalry and the 7th Confederate Cavalry. He returned to his native Georgia after the end of the war. While he was still on parole, Griffin was appointed by Maj. Gen. James H. Wilson to serve as the first superintendent of the cemetery at the Andersonville Prison. Among those helping Griffin was Clara Barton, who compiled a list of the 13,000 Union soldiers who were buried near the abandoned prison. Griffin directed the reburial of bodies washed from their shallow graves by heavy rains, and also began fencing in the cemetery. He also stopped Benjamin Dykes, the former owner of the land, from planting a vineyard on the cemetery property. Griffin later became a Republican and served in the Georgia Legislature during Reconstruction, a move that prompted one newspaper to call him "a monstrous Confederate scalawag". In 1890, Griffin was living in Nashville, Tennessee. A special census was made that year of Union veterans; Griffin's name was entered by mistake and then crossed out on the census form. Among the deleted words was the notation "suffering from wound".[687]

John N. Whitford's battalion was enlarged into a full regiment, the 67th North Carolina, and he became its colonel on January 18, 1864. After the war, Whitford was elected to the North Carolina General Assembly. He died on June 26, 1890, and was buried at Cedar Grove Cemetery in New Bern.[688]

Kenelm Lewis, the Rocky Mount planter who wrote about the raid, lost most of his fortune in the war. He died in 1868. His widow, Elizabeth Herritage Bryan Lewis, lived in "Stonewall" until her death in 1916. The restored house stands today near Rocky Mount, just north of the Tar River.[689]

William S. Battle rebuilt the Rocky Mount Mills in 1865. Fire destroyed the new buildings again on November 10, 1869. Once again, Battle built a new mill complex. The Rocky Mount Mills continued in operation until they closed in 1996. The historic nature of the site has encouraged plans for restoration and adaptive reuse of the mill buildings and the surrounding mill houses.[690]

The Flags of Potter's Raid

Several flags survive from units that were involved in Potter's Raid. The national flag and the regimental standard of the 12th New York Cavalry, as well as seven guidons (company flags with a swallowtail shape) are held by the New York State Military Museum at Sarasota Springs, New York. Among their collections is also a guidon of Battery H of the 3rd New York Artillery. Flags of the 17th and 50th North Carolina Regiments are in the North Carolina Museum of History in Raleigh. The Alabama Department of Archives and History in Montgomery has a flag of the Montgomery True Blues.[691]

The Long Journeys of Some Stolen Property

Some of the property looted from the Masonic Hall in Tarboro was returned more than twenty years later, "after having passed through many hands and being carried great distances." In 1886, a Masonic lodge in Delhi, New York, informed the lodge in Tarboro that they had one of their silver "jewels" that was taken in 1863. It was sent back in May of that year. Another stolen Masonic object was also returned during that decade.[692]

Strangest of all, a lost Masonic piece from Tarboro was returned in 1891 after an Apache raid in Arizona. "Four or five men", whose names were not given in the newspapers, were killed in the raid. One of the dead men had a silver piece that was stamped with "Concord Lodge No. 58", the lodge in Tarboro. A man who found the bodies recognized the sterling silver object "belonging to the office of treasurer", as Masonic property. The finder handed it over to a Mason in Arizona, who sent it back to Tarboro. Apparently, the names of the people who held these Masonic pieces over the years were not publicly revealed. It is interesting to note, however, two odd coincidences that may explain the travels of these long-lost jewels to New York and the Southwest. Ferris Jacobs, Jr., who led a battalion during Potter's Raid, was from Delhi, New York and died only a few months after the lodge in that town gave the Tarboro piece back. No one knows how the piece that was recovered in Arizona ended up in the Southwest. But, it has already been noted in this chapter that George W. Cole, the battalion commander who raided Tarboro in 1863, died in New Mexico in 1875.[693]

In 1898, a Louis Graton of Ithaca, New York, wrote to the *Eastern Reflector* in Greenville that he had an edition of Shakespeare's works that was captured there during Potter's Raid. Two wartime inscriptions were written inside the volume. The first read "Capt. T. (or G.) S. Barton, January, 1862." The other inscription read, "captured July 19, 1863 at Greenville, N. C. from a Rebel ordby (sic) by E. B. W.". Graton wanted to find Barton, or anyone from his family, so he could return the book. The book evidently belonged to Capt. Thomas Scott Barton, who was sent as a commissary officer to Greenville in May 1863. Barton, the brother of Brig. Gen. Seth Barton, was the post sutler at Fort Cobb, Indian Territory when the war began in April 1861. After the war, Barton became a cotton broker in New Orleans. There was apparently no answer to Graton's query.[694]

John H. Daniel, who owned the land where the skirmish at Daniel's Schoolhouse took place, died on April 16, 1872. His wife Meniza died on November 5, 1871. Both were buried in the John Henry Daniel Graveyard, which is near old US 64 east of Tarboro.[695]

John G. Smith of the 62nd Georgia Cavalry finished the war as a captain. Years after the war, Smith visited the resort of Buffalo Lithia Springs in Mecklenburg County, Virginia. Because Meniza Daniel died in 1871, before her husband's death, it's strange for Smith to state that at the springs, he met Mrs. John Daniel, the widow of the builder of Daniel's School House. (Perhaps Smith met a daughter or another relative of the family.) Smith went on to say that while he and this "Mrs. Daniel" were at the springs, some mutual friends "put a job on us." They told Mrs. Daniel that Smith was one of the *Yankee* officers from the fight at Daniel's Schoolhouse. The joke "exploded when I was presenting a prize to some young ladies and making them a short address, while Mrs. Daniel, unbeknown to me, was at my back holding a Confederate flag over my head." For a short time, Mrs. Daniel was "greatly mortified" when she learned of joke that had been played on her, but she and Smith became friends after the embarrassment wore off.[696]

William Newton McKenzie of the 62nd Georgia Cavalry, the only Confederate soldier who was seriously wounded at Daniel's Schoolhouse, lived until 1915. Kinchen Jahu Carpenter of the 50th North Carolina, who was present at the Burney Place and Street's Ferry, lived until 1928 in his home town of Rutherfordton.[697]

Perhaps the last surviving soldier of Potter's Raid was Johnson Abbott. He was a corporal in Company B of the 12th New York Cavalry when he took part in the fight at Daniel's Schoolhouse in 1863. Abbott returned to New York and farmed after the war. He long outlived most of his contemporaries, and by the 1930s was noted several times in area newspapers as one of the dwindling number of living Civil War veterans in his region.

Abbott kept his enlistment paper in a frame with a Confederate $10 bill in one corner. A neighbor remembered even when Abbott was in his nineties, his eyes lit up when talking to younger folks about his days during the Civil War in North Carolina. Just the same, the old veteran cavalryman told his listeners that hoped that there would never be another war.[698]

On June 28, 1940, he died in Oswego County, New York at the age of 98. The newspaper page with Abbott's obituary also carried a story about Nazi air raids on Great Britain. Mordecai Knapp, a veteran of the 3rd New York Cavalry who captured a good deal of Confederate money at Rocky Mount, lived until 1932.[699]

Traces of the Confederate earthworks that once surrounded Greenville survived decades of wind and rain. For many years, children who lived in the neighborhoods near the western edge of the East Carolina College campus played army in a remaining section of these genuine Civil War trenches. The earthworks were obliterated in early 1960, when new dormitories were built on the western edge of East Carolina University, near downtown.[700]

Potter's Raid was overshadowed by far more famous events that took place the same month of 1863 – the Battle of Gettysburg on July 1-3, the surrender of Vicksburg on July 4, the New York City Draft Riots of July 13-17, and the Union attacks on Battery Wagner near Charleston on July 18. The small affairs such as Potter's Raid, though, were as much a part of that war as the famous large battles. Perhaps they were truly more typical of the kind of experiences faced by Civil War soldiers and civilians. A close look at this raid in a relatively quiet part of the Confederacy shines a light on the lives of people who might have been "ordinary", had not extraordinary efforts been demanded from them during that war.

Appendices

Units Involved in Potter's Raid

July 19-23, 1863
Union Army

Cavalry Expedition under Brig. Gen. Edward E. Potter

3rd New York Cavalry (all 12 companies, plus a howitzer section)
12th New York Cavalry, Companies A, B, and F
23rd New York Cavalry, Companies A and B
3rd New York Artillery, Battery H, one section
1st North Carolina Union Volunteers, Company L
Pioneer detachment, 1st North Carolina Union Volunteers

Col. James Jourdan's Brigade
(only as far as Swift Creek Village, July 18-20)

25th Massachusetts Infantry
27th Massachusetts Infantry
158th New York Infantry

Confederate Army

Confederate District of North Carolina
Brig. Gen. James G. Martin, at Kinston

Whitford's Battalion (1st North Carolina Local Defense Troops)
62nd Georgia Cavalry (Companies C, E, and I)
7th Confederate Cavalry (especially Companies H and I)
Nethercutt's Battalion (8th North Carolina Cavalry Battalion, Partisan Rangers)
Petersburg Artillery, (Graham's Virginia Battery), one section

Saunders' Artillery Battalion
Andrews' Battery (Montgomery True Blues, of Alabama)

Bunting's Battery (1st Company A, 2nd North Carolina Artillery)
Cummings' Battery (1st Company C, 2nd North Carolina Artillery; also known as Southerland's Battery and the Wilmington Horse Artillery)
Dickson's Battery (2nd Company G, 3rd North Carolina Artillery)

Pool's Battalion, 1st North Carolina Artillery (Companies B, G and H)

13th Battalion, North Carolina Infantry (Company B)
17th North Carolina, Companies D and G (and possibly C)
50th North Carolina

Appendix II

Casualties and Prisoners from Potter's Raid

Union Army

Union casualties are drawn from regimental muster rolls, contemporary newspaper articles and letters, the *Official Records,* and records of the New York State Adjutant General's Department. Apparently, all of the Union soldiers who were wounded on the raid survived.

12th New York Cavalry
Company A – Capt. Cyrus Church
Killed:

Capt. Cyrus Church
Mortally wounded at Daniel's Schoolhouse, July 20, 1863. Probably died in the schoolhouse, which was used as a field hospital. Church's body was returned to Fulton, New York for burial in 1866.[701]

Sgt. John P. Miller
Mortally wounded at Daniel's Schoolhouse, July 20, 1863. Probably died in the schoolhouse, which was used as a field hospital. Miller's father came to Tarboro just after the war and brought his son's body back for burial in Oswego, New York.[702]

Private David Corl (also spelled Carl, Carrol, or Carryl)
Killed at Daniel's Schoolhouse, July 20, 1863. Buried in the Raleigh National Cemetery, Raleigh, N. C.[703]

Private William Davies (also spelled Davis)
Killed at Daniel's Schoolhouse, July 20, 1863. Davies' widow came to Tarboro and brought her husband's body home to Oswego, New York for burial in December 1865.[704]

Corporal William Thompson
Also known as "William Thompson 1st" in regimental records. Listed as a corporal in the casualty list in the *New York Times,* August 26, 1863, but regimental records show that he was reduced to the ranks on May 20, 1863. New York State Adjutant General's Department records show him as "captured at Tarboro, NC, July 20, 1863" but also as "killed 20 July '63." An Oswego newspaper reported "Mr. Thompson" was killed during Potter's expedition. His burial site is unknown.[705]

Wounded:

Cpl. George Palmer
Still "In General Hospital at New Berne", August 31, 1863.[706]

Private John Grison
Appears in a casualty list, *New York Times,* August 26, 1863. Probably a clerical error; his name does not appear in other regimental records.

Private John Green
Still "In General Hospital at New Berne", August 31, 1863. Green was unable to resume active service after his wound, but was "employed in the care of horses." He was granted an invalid's pension in 1866; he drew four dollars a month in 1883. His pension was raised to $12 a month in 1890 due to "gunshot wound of the right forearm, partial loss of second and third fingers of left hand", evidently suffered during Potter's Raid. A board of surgeons in Jacksonville, Florida examined him in 1897, and his pension was increased to $20 a month. He died in 1917.[707]

Private William Lipkin
Still "In General Hospital at New Berne", August 31, 1863. Granted an invalid's pension, November 1, 1869. Died December 17, 1878.[708]

Missing (Captured)

1st Lt. Henry A. Hubbard
Wounded and captured at Daniel's Schoolhouse, July 20, 1863. Sent to Libby Prison, Richmond, Virginia. Paroled 1864. Rejoined his company. Mortally wounded near Hookerton, Greene County, North Carolina on April 8, 1865.[709]

2nd Lt. Henry Ephraim Mosher
Wounded and captured at Daniel's Schoolhouse, July 20, 1863. Sent to Libby Prison, Richmond, Virginia. Later, died of yellow fever while still a

prisoner at Charleston, South Carolina, October 6, 1864. His burial site is unknown.[710]

Sgt. Henry Wilson

Captured at Tarboro, N.C. on July 20, 1863. Returned to duty, October 31, 1863.[711]

Cpl. Michael Quinn

Captured at Tarboro, N.C., July 20, 1863. Paroled on an unstated date. Captured at Plymouth, N.C., April 20, 1864. Reportedly died at Andersonville Prison, Georgia; another record states that he died in prison at Florence, South Carolina, October 23, 1864. His widow filed a pension in 1865.[712]

Cpl. William Cromack

Wounded and captured at Daniel's Schoolhouse on July 20, 1863. Imprisoned at Belle Isle, Virginia, then exchanged at an unknown date and returned to duty.[713]

William Thompson

Also known as "William Thompson 2nd". Captured at Daniel's Schoolhouse, July 20, 1863. The New York *Herald* reported that he died at the Libby Prison Hospital in Richmond on August 9, 1863. His widow Amanda Thompson's pension claim states that Thompson "was taken to Libby Prison in Richmond on the 8th day of August 1863 on which day he was sunstruck and died in said prison on the 9th day of August 1863 either from fatigue or sunstroke or both causes." Amanda Thompson drew eight dollars per month from her widow's pension in 1883.[714]

Private John Dannison (or Dennison)

Released or exchanged on an unknown date. Later captured at Plymouth, NC on April 20, 1864. Died at Andersonville Prison, Georgia on July 28, 1864. Buried at Andersonville National Cemetery.[715]

Private Collins Martin

Records state that he was captured at Tarboro, July 20, 1863; evidently he was never paroled or exchanged. Private Collins Martin died of 'anasarca" at Andersonville Prison, Georgia, on April 8, 1864. Buried at Andersonville National Cemetery.[716]

Private Truman Mitchell

Captured at Tarboro on July 20, 1863. Released; date not stated. Arrested April 1864; claimed as a deserter from the 81st New York, but remained in the regiment.[717]

Private Myron Taylor

Records state that he was captured at Tarboro on July 20, 1863. Evidently never exchanged. Died at Andersonville Prison, Georgia, of scorbutus (scurvy) on December 15, 1864. Buried at Andersonville National Cemetery.[718]

Private Roswell Taylor
Captured at Tarboro, July 20, 1863. Released for exchange. "Died at Annapolis, August 4, 1863." Buried at the Annapolis National Cemetery, Maryland.[719]

Private Lester Taylor
Captured at Tarboro, N. C., July 20, 1863. "Died while a prisoner at Richmond". Taylor's mother was granted a pension in 1873."[720]

Private James Jones
Captured at Tarboro, July 20, 1863. Released or exchanged at an unknown date. Captured again at Plymouth, N. C. on April 20, 1864. Spent some time at the Andersonville prison. Survived the war.[721]

Private John Riley
Born in Ireland; occupation: butcher. Promoted to corporal May 20, 1863; reduced to private June 20, 1863. "Missing in action and captured near Tarboro, N. C. July 20, 1863." Later confined at Andersonville Prison. Released April 21, 1865. Mustered out July 6, 1865 at New York City.[722]

Company B – Capt. Simeon Church
Killed:

Bugler Hiram C. Rude (Also spelled Rood, Reed, or Rudr)
Killed at Daniel's Schoolhouse, July 20, 1863. Buried in Raleigh National Cemetery, Raleigh, N.C. Pensions for Rude's widow and a child were granted in 1865.[723]

Wounded:

1st Sgt. Stephen Lashley (or Laishley)
As of August 31, 1863, "In Gen. Hospt. At New Berne, N. C. since July 23/63." Granted an invalid's pension in 1865.[724]

Cpl. Abial W. Laws
Muster roll dated August 31, 1863 states, "In Gen. Hospt. Newberne, N. C. since July 23rd/63. Rec'd. sick furlough from hospt. for 30 days from Aug. 24/63." Laws was drawing a seven dollar a month pension in 1883, for wartime wounds in his thigh and left foot.[725]

Cpl. Josiah Burnette
As of August 31, 1863, "In Gen Hospt. At New Berne N. C. since July 22nd/63."[726]

Private John Tracy
Still "in Gen. Hospt. at Newbern", as of August 31, 1863.[727]

Missing (Captured)
Quartermaster Sgt. Henry G. Breede
Listed as missing in action, July 21, 1863, near Tarboro, N.C. Date returned to company not stated. Reduced to ranks, November 26, 1863; in arrest as deserter, since February 20, 1864.[728]

Private David Wilson
Reported missing in action, at Tarboro, N.C. Paroled at Annapolis, Maryland. Returned to duty, May 21, 1864.[729]

Company F – Lt. Thomas T. Bruce
(in the absence of Capt. John W. Flinn)

Killed:

Private Narcisse Mulway
"Taken prisoner or supposed to have been killed during the skirmishing of July 20th/63." Buried at the Raleigh National Cemetery, Raleigh, N. C. [730]

Wounded:

Sgt. James McKenna
Received "shot wound of left shoulder, involving bone and artery" at Daniel's Schoolhouse. Left arm amputated at Tarboro, July 20, by Surg. Albert Potter, 5th Rhode Island Artillery. "Sick in Stanly Gen. Hospital Newbern N. C." as of August 31, 1863. He was discharged on account of his disability on November 26, 1863. He was granted an invalid's pension in 1864.[731]

Private Charles Dermoulin (also spelled Demonlin)
As of August 31, 1863, "Sick in Regimental Hospital of 132nd N Y Vols. (Infy.)" Later captured at Plymouth, April 20, 1864 and died while a prisoner at Florence, South Carolina.[732]

Private Louis Beckstein
Later captured at Plymouth, N. C., April 20, 1864. Died September 18, 1864, while imprisoned. Buried at Andersonville National Cemetery.[733]

Private James Devlin
Later captured at Plymouth, N. C., April 20, 1864. Died August 13, 1864, while imprisoned. Buried at Andersonville National Cemetery.[734]

Private Riley Lincoln
Later captured at Plymouth, N. C., April 20, 1864. "Reported to have died at Andersonville", November 1, 1864.[735]

Missing (Captured)

Private Hubert Kelly

Captured at Tarboro, N.C., July 20, 1863. Returned to company, November 30, 1863. Captured at Plymouth, N. C., April 20, 1864. Records state that he "escaped from prison, June 1865".[736]

Private Adolphus Kahlbaum

Captured at Tarboro, N.C., July 20, 1863. July-August 1863 muster roll notes "Now on Bell's Island ... Richmond" [There was a Confederate prison on Belle Isle, in the James River at Richmond.] Returned to company, November 30, 1863. Captured at Plymouth, N. C., April 20, 1864, at Plymouth, N.C. Died at Andersonville Prison, Georgia, August 10, 1864.[737]

Private George Pentland

Captured during the Tarboro raid, paroled on unstated date and returned to company, November 11, 1863. Captured at Plymouth, N.C. on April 20, 1864. Confined at Andersonville Prison, Georgia; records various state that he died there, or that he survived the war. [738]

Private Charles Smith

Captured on the Tarboro raid, July 20, 1863. Exchanged, date not known. Captured at Plymouth, N. C., April 20, 1864. Died at Andersonville Prison, Georgia.[739]

Private Thomas Rogers

Captured at Tarboro, N. C., July 20, 1863. Paroled at Annapolis, Maryland, November 30, 1863. Captured again, date not stated (possibly at Plymouth, N. C., April 20, 1864.) Died at Andersonville Prison.[740]

Saddler Charles Rote

Captured at Tarboro, N.C., July 20, 1863. July-August muster roll states "Paroled and now at Annapolis, Md.", as of August 31, 1863. Captured at Plymouth, N. C., April 20, 1864. Temporarily held at Andersonville Prison. Died in prison at Charleston, S.C., December 10, 1864.[741]

Private John McCue

Born in Ireland. Listed as captured at Tarboro, July 21, 1863; paroled in August 1863; deserted from Camp Parole at Annapolis, Maryland on August 18, 1863. No further record.[742]

3rd New York Cavalry
Company A – Capt. James R. Chamberlin
Wounded:

Private Patrick Clarke

"Sick in Regt. Hosp. Newberne", July-August 1863.[743]

Missing (Captured)

Cpl. Addison G. Henry
Captured at Street's Ferry, according to a letter by Private Oliver Spoor. Muster roll states "Taken prisoner by the enemy July 25/63". Released on August 29 or November 14, 1863; place of release not stated. Commissioned first lieutenant, December 22, 1864. In 1909 he was living in the Soldier's Home in Danville, Illinois and drawing a pension of $24 a month.[744]

Company D – Capt. Harvey W. Brown
Wounded:

Private Peter E. Borst
Recovered. Borst became a lieutenant in the 3rd New York Cavalry on December 7, 1864.[745]

Missing (Captured)

Private Phillman Winchell
Taken prisoner on raid, July 21, 1863. Died April 7 or April 24, 1864. Place of death not stated. Buried at Marietta National Cemetery, Marietta, Georgia.[746]

Private Timothy Corkry (also Corckery or Cokey)
Served as saddler for Company D. "Taken prisoner on raid between Tarboro and New Bern July 21/63." Place of confinement and date of release not stated. Returned to duty during November-December 1863. Mustered out at Bermuda Hundred, Virginia, August 11, 1864 "by reason of expiration of term of service".[747]

Company E – Capt. Rowland M. Hall
Wounded:

Private Gideon Blackman
Private Blackman was "blown up" when a burning carload of ammunition exploded at Rocky Mount Station on July 20, 1863. Reported "sick in Stanly General Hospital since July 24th." He recovered, and was returned to duty by September-October 1863.[748]

Missing (Captured)

Private William Cormack
"Captured by enemy on raid to Rocky Mount July 21, 1863." Paroled October 29, 1863 (place not stated).[749]

Private John L. Smith+
"Captured by enemy on raid to Rocky Mount July 21, 1863." Held at Andersonville Prison; exchanged at Savannah, Georgia on November 20, 1864. Mustered out on April 13, 1865 at Elmira, New York. His pension was raised to $36 a month in 1910 because of his seriously impaired health.[750]

Company G – Capt. Newton Hall
Wounded:

Bugler Joseph F. Massett
Wounded "slightly in the thigh by a musket ball at Street's Ferry". Sent to hospital in New Bern. [751]

Missing (Captured)

Private Henry H. Eager
Muster roll states he was "missing since July 21. Supposed taken prisoner near Rocky Mount." Died while a prisoner of war at Richmond, Virginia (date not stated).[752]

Private Pembroke J. Dunham
Muster roll states he was "missing since July 21, 1863. Supposed to have been taken prisoner near Rocky Mount." He was imprisoned at Andersonville, Georgia during part of 1864. Reported at "Camp Parole Apl 30, '64" Returned to company January 20, 1865. Mustered out on June 7, 1865.[753]

Company I – Capt. Gustavus F. Jocknick
Wounded:

Private John H. Barnes
"Slightly" wounded on July 22, 1863, probably at Street's Ferry.[754]

Missing (Captured)\+

Private David Kinney
Reported missing on July 22, 1863, "with horse and equipments, arms, and accoutrements complete. Supposed to have deserted." Died of disease March 9, 1864, while a prisoner of war at Richmond, Virginia.[755]

Company L – Capt. George Gouraud
Lieutenant George F. Dern was in command during the raid, while Gouraud was detached for duty as General Potter's aide.[756]

Wounded:

Private James R. Shaw
    Enlisted at Cincinnati, Ohio. Wounded in right shoulder at Street's Ferry, July 22, 1863. "Conoidal ball perforated head of right humerus and fractured the neck of the scapula." Sent to Stanly General Hospital in New Bern. "Head and two and a half inches of humerus excised, by Ass't. Surg. J. W. Gray, 98th New York" on July 23, 1863. Discharged because of wounds at Dennison Hospital, Columbus, Ohio, September 15, 1864. Received a pension because of his wound, September 1873.[757]

Regimental Howitzer Battery

Private Edgar Taylor
    Enrolled in Company K; assigned to duty with battery. Captured at Street's Ferry, July 22, 1863; escaped the next morning.[758]

23rd New York Cavalry

Company A – Capt. Emory Cummings
Wounded

Lt. Walter F. Budlong
    Slightly wounded in Greene County, July 21, 1863.[759]

Missing (Captured)

Private Thomas John Paul
    Born in Ireland. Listed as "missing in action" at Tarboro on July 20, 1863. "Private Paul captured with horse when charging enemy second time." Released at an unspecified date and sent to parole camp at Annapolis, Maryland; officially exchanged and returned to duty November 7, 1863. While his unit was en route back to New York after the end of the war, Paul died of typhoid fever in Tarboro on July 8, 1865. He is now buried at the Raleigh National Cemetery.[760]

Company B – Capt. Alfred Spann
Missing (Captured)

Private Thomas Yearney
    Born in England and enlisted in New York City, April 13, 1863. "Taken prisoner by the enemy July 22, 1863. Reported for duty to the company Oct. 26/63." Died at Foster General Hospital at New Bern, October 13, 1864.[761]

Private Joseph Sheriden (or Sheridan)

Born in Ireland. Recorded as "captured on a road [raid?] to Tarboro", July 22, 1863. Recorded as "absent, prisoner of war" throughout the war until the regiment was mustered out. No further records.[762]

Private Harman Wolf

Also borne on company records as "Hermann Wolf 2nd" (another Hermann Wolf had enlisted and then deserted from the same company in March 1863.) Listed as "taken prisoner by the enemy the 22nd of July 1863". Evidently exchanged late in 1863 or early in 1864. In General Hospital, Annapolis, Maryland, January-February 1864. "Deserted May 18 1864 from U. S. Hospital Annapolis Md."[763]

Private David Kaemmerer

Born in Germany. Occupation butcher. "Taken prisoner by the enemy July 22, 1863 on road to Tarboro N. C." Recorded as prisoner of war through April 30, 1865.[764]

1st North Carolina Union Volunteers

Company L
Wounded

Private Caleb Gaylord

Listed as wounded during Potter's Raid, but available records do not state exactly when or where; perhaps it was at Falkland, where his company was sent forward to skirmish with Claiborne's regiment.

A Caleb Gaylord, age 24, who was born in Virginia, is listed as a grocer in Raleigh on the 1870 US Census of Wake County.[765]

Missing (Captured)

Cpl. Robert Strieback *(or Striebeck)*

Born in Brooklyn, New York. Prewar occupation: seaman. Enlisted at Plymouth, N.C., December 27, 1862. Previous service, if any, unknown. Regimental records have contradictory notations "taken prisoner of war July 20/63 at or near Snow Hill", as well as "Captured by the Enemy at Snow Hill Aug. 2nd/63". Promoted to sergeant while still in captivity. The regiment's muster-out roll, dates June 27, 1865, states "died in enemy's hands", with no place or date given. Confederate records that mention him have not been located. His widow, "Nancy Streeback" was granted a widow's pension, which she filed on July 24, 1865. The author, while curious about the reasons that brought a Brooklyn-born sailor to Plymouth to enlist in a Unionist North Carolina regiment, has been unable to locate further information about him or his wife.[766]

3rd New York Artillery
Battery H, Detachment under Lt. John D. Clark

Regimental records state that Battery H "was engaged with the enemy a short time" near Tarboro. Four men were "slightly wounded" (all of whom recovered) and two men were captured. No casualties were recorded in the skirmishes at Hookerton and Street's Ferry. Maj. Floyd Clarkson of the 12th New York Cavalry said that at the fight at Daniel's Schoolhouse, Lt. Clark was thrown from his horse, and that he "received one volley, by which he lost his sergeant and 1 rider", presumably Sergeant Abraham H. Hamblin and Private William W. Miller.[767]

Captured

Sgt. Abraham H. Hamblin
Enlisted at age 25 on August 6, 1862, in Auburn, New York. Occupation: student. "Missing in action … at Tarboro." Date of parole or release not stated. Promoted to 2nd lieutenant and transferred to Company H, 1st North Carolina Union Volunteers on September 7, 1863. Discharged June 29, 1865. Also appears as "Abram H. Hamblin."

Appears in the 1880 Census as "A. H. Hamblin", living in Pamlico County, North Carolina. That census indicates that this Hamblin, age 43, was born in New York; his occupation was listed as "teaching". Included was the additional notation "in war wounded". In 1890, "Abram Hamblin" appears on the Civil War Veterans Census in Beaufort County, North Carolina.[768]

Pvt. William W. Miller
Captured near Tarboro, July 20, 1863. Date of parole or release not stated. Reported "in Gen'l Hospital, New Berne, N. C., since Aug. 21, 1863". Discharged "with co. at Richmond, Va.", on June 24, 1865.[769]

Confederate Army

Maj. Gen. John Gray Foster claimed that Potter's expedition captured "about 100" prisoners. No official Confederate army tally of the casualties of Potter's Raid has been found. The writer of a letter to the *State Journal* in Raleigh stated that Southern losses "did not exceed six killed, wounded, and missing". Another writer told the same newspaper, before knowing of the fighting at Street's Ferry, that "we have lost two killed, and four or five wounded." It is unknown where these losses took place, nor indeed whether this report was accurate. The casualties may have occurred during the skirmishing between the 7th Confederate Cavalry and Potter's men in Greene County on July 21.[770]

Unfortunately, many records of the Southern units that were the most directly involved in confronting Potter's Raid are unpublished, incomplete, or missing. Some of the men who were captured during Potter's Raid were home on sick leave or furlough from regiments that were stationed out of state. It is possible that other prisoners included members of the militia, or soldiers from non-regimental organizations not found in published rosters. The following names have been drawn from available sources.[771]

Whitford's Battalion, 1st North Carolina Local Defense Troops
(Later, 67th North Carolina Regiment)
Maj. John N. Whitford

Several men of Company E, under the command of Capt. Charles A. White, were captured at a place called "Four Corners" or "the Chapel" in Pitt County on July 19, 1863. A small but unknown number of Confederates were captured in Greenville that day. They were paroled on the same day they were captured, but a list of their names has not been found. At the same time that these men were captured, one man was reportedly shot in the leg, but his name also was not recorded.[772]

Company A – Capt. James H. Tolson

Private Furnifold Powell
Captured at Swift Creek on July 18, 1863. Confined at Fort Norfolk, Virginia, where he refused to take the Oath of Allegiance. Transferred to Point Lookout, Maryland. For some reason, unlike the other Confederate enlisted men who were captured on Potter's Raid, Powell was not paroled. Transferred to the prison at Elmira, New York on August 16, 1864. Appears on a roll of prisoners at Elmira who desire to take the Oath of Allegiance; a remark notes that he "Desires to go to his [home?] in Newbern N.C. where his family resides." Paroled at Elmira on February 20, 1865. Admitted to Howard's Grove Hospital at Richmond, Virginia on March 1, 1865. Given a furlough on March 6, 1865. Also known as "Furnie" Powell. Died in 1870.[773]

The following seven men of Company A were listed as captured at "Tarboro" on "July 21, 1863", according to records; all were paroled at Ft. Monroe, Virginia on August 4, 1863.

Private William Adkinson[774]
Private Dennis Destrall[775]
Private Andrew J. Donaldson[776]
Private William H. Dudley[777]
Private A. L. Heath[778]
Private William H. Hill[779]
Private Addison P. Whitford[780]

Company B – Capt. Stephen G. Barrington

Cpl. John H. Powers
 Captured at "Tarboro, July 21, 1863"; paroled at Fort Monroe, Virginia on August 4, 1863.[781]

Company C – Capt. D. W. Edwards

 The following five men of Company C were listed as captured at "Tarboro" on "July 21, 1863", according to records; all were paroled at Ft. Monroe, Virginia on August 4, 1863.

Corporal Thomas Thorn[782]
Private B. B. Bowden[783]
Private Newet S. Potter[784]
Private William I. Price[785]
Private Henry Shirley[786]

Company D – Capt. Daniel A. Cogdell

Cpl. James H. Satterthwaite
 Captured at Tarboro on "July 21, 1863"; paroled at Ft. Monroe, Virginia on August 4, 1863.[787]
 Except for Powell, most of the Potter's Raid prisoners taken from Whitford's Battalion may have been part of the small detail sent to guard the bridge at Scuffleton, on Little Contentnea Creek in Greene County. Potter reported capturing "a dozen" troops after a brief skirmish at the bridge around sunset on July 21.

3rd North Carolina Artillery (40th North Carolina Regiment)
1st Lt. Thomas J. Stewart
 Company G. Captured in Edgecombe County, July 20, 1863. Imprisoned temporarily at the Jones House ("the Sesesh Jail") at New Bern.

Transferred to the prison at Johnson's Island near Sandusky, Ohio, where he remained until he was released after taking the Oath of Allegiance on June 11, 1865.[788]

6th Virginia Infantry

Private Andrew J. Dozier, Company B
Captured. July-August 1863 muster roll notes him detailed as a "teamster in forage train in Longstreet's Corps" since December 25, 1862. Name appears on a list of prisoners paroled at Ft. Monroe, Virginia on August 4, 1863. November-December 1863 muster roll states, "taken prisoner while serving as a teamster at Rocky Mount, N. C. July 20/63 & has since gone to his home in Norfolk."[789]

7th Confederate Cavalry

Lt. Bennett P. Jenkins, Co. I
Captured at Tarboro, July 20, 1863. Imprisoned temporarily at the Jones House ("the Sesesh Jail") at New Bern. Sent to Norfolk, Virginia. Arrived at Fort McHenry, Baltimore, Maryland, on August 10, 1863. Sent to the prison at Johnson's Island, Sandusky, Ohio on August 22, 1863. Confined at Johnson's Island until taking the Oath of Allegiance on June 11, 1865.[790]

Private Joshua W. Tucker, Co. H
Captured at Tarboro; date given as "July 21". Paroled at Fort Monroe, Virginia on August 4, 1863. September-October muster roll lists him as "present".[791]

8th North Carolina Infantry

2nd Lt. Nathan M. Lawrence, Co. C.
Lawrence's service file reports he was captured at Rocky Mount on July 20, 1863. Imprisoned temporarily at the Jones House ("the Sesesh Jail") at New Bern. Transferred from Fort Norfolk, Virginia to Fort McHenry, Baltimore, Maryland on August 10, 1863. Sent to the prison at Johnson's Island near Sandusky, Ohio on August 22, 1863. Confined at Johnson's Island until released after taking the Oath of Allegiance, June 11, 1865. After the war, he worked as an accountant in Tarboro and later moved to Charlotte. Died March 11, 1916. Buried in Elmwood Cemetery, Charlotte.[792]

12th Battalion, North Carolina Cavalry

Private Reddick Jones, Company B.
Appears as "R. Jones" on a list of Confederate prisoners who were paroled at Fort Monroe, Virginia on August 4, 1863. The roll states that he was captured at Rocky Mount on "July 21", 1863. Jones' Compiled Service File states that he was "on parole" from November 1862 through August 1863, but his company's muster rolls were captured at Hill's Bridge, N.C. on July 26, 1863, and were rewritten later with apparent mistakes.[793]

13th North Carolina Infantry

Sgt. William T. Dupree, Co. G.
Resident of Edgecombe County before enlisting in the same county on May 8, 1861. Received gunshot wound "in the left shoulder" at Chancellorsville, Virginia on May 3, 1863. Admitted to Chimborazo Hospital No. 3, Richmond, Va. On May 6. July-August 1863 muster roll states "absent wounded May 3 without leave." Evidently, he was home on sick leave when he was "captured by the enemy at Tarboro on June 21, 1863" (erroneous date). Paroled at Fort Monroe, Virginia on August 4, 1863. Rejoined company, September-October 1863.[794]

13th Battalion, North Carolina Infantry
(Later part of the 66th North Carolina)

Company B (Captain Nichols' Company, Raleigh and Gaston Railroad Guard)

Captain P. Nichols
Was captured at Rocky Mount on July 20, 1863. Imprisoned temporarily at the Jones House ("the Sesesh Jail") at New Bern. Nichols died at the prison on Johnson's Island near Sandusky, Ohio, of "chronic diarrhea" on February 27, 1864. His grave is marked by a stone, inscribed "P. Nichols Capt. Co. B. 11th Bat. N. C. Inf'y", at the prison cemetery. Nichols' first name, spelled as "Possum" in Volume 5 of *North Carolina Troops,* was "probably Passun, Parson, or Parsons." [795]

Cpl. J. J. Griffin[796]
Captured at Rocky Mount, July 20, 1863. Still a prisoner of war when his company was transferred to the new 66th North Carolina in October 1863. Exchanged at an unknown date; reported for duty in Company B, 66th North Carolina Infantry, in December 1863.

Private Thomas B. Bunting
   Captured "at or near Tarboro on or about July 21, 1863." Exchanged at Fort Monroe, Virginia, August 4, 1863.[797]

Private James M. Culpepper
   Captured "at or near Tarboro on or about July 21, 1863." Exchanged at Fort Monroe, Virginia, August 4, 1863.[798]

Private James H. Wood
   "Captured at Tarboro or Rocky Mount on or about July 20, 1863. Paroled at Fort Monroe, Virginia, August 4, 1863."[799]

17th North Carolina Infantry

Company G, Capt. Thomas Norman

The "Record of Events" section of this company's July-August muster roll states that four men of the company were captured in the skirmishing near Tarboro during Potter's Raid. Of these four, only Private Asa Snell's name is recorded in *North Carolina Troops,* and only Snell and Chesson have entries in their Compiled Service Files at the National Archives indicating that they were captured at Tarboro.[800]

Private Thomas W. Chesson
   Captured at Tarboro, "July 21" [1863]. Name appears on a list of prisoners "paroled until exchanged, at Ft. Monroe, Va., Aug. 4, 1863." "Absent on parole" through September-October 1863.[801]

Private Asa W. Snell
   "Captured at or near Tarboro on July 21, 1863." Imprisoned at Fort Monroe, Virginia until August 4, 1863, when he was paroled and sent for exchange.[802]

Company I

Private Elisha C. Jones
   "Captured near Tarboro on July 21, 1863." Jones' company was on detached duty in Moore and Randolph Counties, N. C.; Jones was from Edgecombe County and was perhaps on leave during Potter's Raid. Paroled at Fort Monroe, Virginia, on August 4, 1864. Appears on a September 15, 1863 muster roll of "detached and exchanged prisoners at Camp Lee, near Richmond, Va." Rejoined his company. Killed near Petersburg, Virginia, on June 16, 1864.[803]

18th North Carolina Infantry

Private Andrew J. McIntyre
Wounded at Frayser's Farm, Virginia on June 30, 1862. Placed on light duty during an extended recovery, he was assigned as a guard at the depot in Rocky Mount, where was captured on July 20, 1863. During the night of July 20-21, he escaped from Potter's men at Otter Creek, in Pitt County, and made his way to Wilson.[804]

43rd North Carolina Infantry

Private Henry G. Jones
Muster rolls mark him as absent at the hospital at Goldsboro from June-October, 1863. Records of the Union Army's provost marshal at Fort Monroe Virginia note that while absent from his regiment, Jones was captured at "Tarboro, N.C." on "July 21" [1863]. Paroled at Fort Monroe, Virginia on August 4, 1863. Present for duty November-December, 1863.[805]

62nd Georgia Cavalry

Company E, Capt. William A. Thompson
Wounded

Capt. William A. Thompson
Wounded in the wrist at Daniel's Schoolhouse, near Tarboro, on July 20, 1863. Reported on sick furlough at the end of August 1863; "present" in November-December, 1863.[806]

Company C, Capt. William L. A. Ellis
Wounded

Private William Newton McKenzie
"Wounded in left leg in North Carolina July 21, 1863".[807]

Company I, Capt. J. B. Edgerton
No casualties reported.

The Petersburg Artillery
(Capt. Edward Graham's Battery)

Sgt. Ezra S. Moody
Captured at Tarboro; date given as July 21, 1863. Paroled at Fort Monroe, Virginia on August 4, 1863. September-October muster roll lists him as "present".[808]

Private Robert J. Turner
Captured at Tarboro; date given as July 21, 1863. Paroled at Fort Monroe, Virginia on August 4, 1863. September-October muster roll lists him as "present".[809]

Civilians

George Greene
A North Carolina state official. Captured near Swift Creek Village (Vanceboro), July 19, 1863. Released the same day on the Tar River Road (Highway 43), "four miles above" Greenville.[810]

J. J. Harper
William S. Battle's overseer. Captured by Maj. Jacobs' detachment on the River Road between Tarboro and Rocky Mount, July 20, 1863.[811]

"Mr. Potts"
Civilian, reportedly taken prisoner on July 20, 1863. No further information.[812]

John B. Daniel
John B. Daniel was employed as a civilian clerk in the Quartermaster Department in Tarboro, in the office of Capt. George Brown. Daniel stated "that he was captured near Tarboro, North Carolina, by the forces under General Edward Potter, and paroled on the field." He requested, apparently to the Confederate Army's agency for handling prisoner exchanges, that he be exchanged. Daniel's request was answered on July 29, 1863. The Union authorities decided that "the parole given by you on the battlefield is invalid, not binding, and cannot be recognized. You are released from it, and free to enter the service at once." Daniel's regiment is not specified. The phrase "free to enter the service" instead of "free to return" implies that this was a man, such as a civilian clerk, who was not in the army.[813]

"Mr. Hatton"
Civilian, reportedly taken prisoner on July 20, 1863. No further information.[814]

Tom Blount

Civilian, reportedly taken prisoner on July 20, 1863. No further information.[815]

Henry Fowler

Civilian wagon driver, reportedly taken prisoner on July 20, 1863. Fowler "made his escape, and walked here [to Wilson] and was the first to give the details & c ..."[816]

Fatalities at the Burney Place

"One negro captain, who was driving a pair of spirited iron-gray horses, attempted to rush past three of our men [of the 50th North Carolina] who were lying in the yard and was shot dead as he stood up in the buggy firing at them as he drove past". Available Federal records reveal nothing about the identity of this man. Although a detachment of the 1st North Carolina Colored Volunteers accompanied Potter, the author has been unable to find records of any casualties from that regiment during the raid.[817]

Unidentified refugee slave

A man "belonging to a Mr. Dosier" of Tarboro was reported as mortally wounded by Capt. Charles A. White's company of Whitford's Battalion on July 22, 1863, while they were capturing a party of contrabands at Jackson's Crossroads, in southern Pitt County. [818]

Appendix III

[819]

Casualties on the Kenansville-Warsaw Raid, July 3-7, 1863

Union Army

3rd New York Cavalry
Company B
Missing:

Private John F. Baker

Muster roll for July-August 1863 lists him as "deserter July 6 ... on march from Warsaw, N. C." It was noted on the roll that he owed the army for "1 Colt's revolver, 1 lt. cavly sabre ... 1 cartridge box and cap pouch ... 1 pistol holster" and other items.[820]

23rd New York Cavalry
Company A
Captured:

Private Emmett Haggerty
Released and returned to company; date not stated. Mustered out on July 22, 1865, at Raleigh, N. C.[821]

Private Jefferson Moore
Released and returned to company; date not stated. Mustered out on July 22, 1865, at Raleigh, N. C.[822]

Private James Mitchell
Released and returned to company; date not stated. Mustered out on July 22, 1865, at Raleigh, N. C.[823]

Company B

Private John Laetsch
Listed as missing in the *New York Times,* August 26, 1863. No further records found.

Confederate Army

5th North Carolina Cavalry
Company E
Captured:

Private Manly Lane
Captured "on Cav. Expn. To Wmton & Warsaw R.R. July 3, 4 & 5" [1863]. "Name appears as a signature on a Roll of Prisoners of War, paroled, until exchanged at Fort Monroe, Va., July 16, 1863".[824]

7th Confederate Cavalry
Company F
Captured

Private Gabriel Aycock
Captured "July 3, 4 +5 … on Cav. Expn. To Wmton & Warsaw R. R." Exchanged at Fort Monroe, Virginia, July 16, 1863. Aycock's file also contains a claim for $550 as reimbursement for "a horse unavoidably captured … by the enemy at Kenansville on the 4th day of July 1863." [825]

Private G. W. Bumpass
    Captured at Kenansville. Paroled at Fort Monroe, Virginia, July 16, 1863.[826]

Private William H. Oliver.
    Captured "July 3, 4 +5 … on Cav. Expn. To Wmton & Warsaw R. R." Exchanged at Fort Monroe, Virginia, July 16, 1863.[827]

Private William K. Parker
    Captured at Kenansville. Paroled at Fort Monroe, Virginia, July 16, 1863. Appears on a muster roll of paroled and exchanged prisoners at Camp Lee, near Richmond, Virginia, dated July 23, 1863.[828]

Private Alexander Potts
    Captured: Kenansville. Paroled: Fort Monroe, Virginia, July 16, 1863.[829]

Private William Price
    Captured at Kenansville. Paroled at Fort Monroe, Virginia, July 16, 1863. Price's file contains a claim asking for a reimbursement of $600 for his horse, which was also captured as Kenansville.[830]

Company I

Private H. G. Worsley
    Captured on "Exp. To Wmton & Warsaw RR July 3, 4 & 5." Paroled at Fort Monroe, Virginia, July 16, 1863.[831]

17th North Carolina Infantry
Company L
Captured:

Private Cullen P. Turner
    Captured "July 3-5" at "Wilmington & Weldon Railroad". Confined at Fort Monroe, Virginia before being taken to City Point, Virginia, for exchange on July 17, 1863. Turner was near the end of a 10-day furlough when he was captured.[832]

61st North Carolina Infantry
Company K

Private David Craft
    Captured "on Cav. Expn. To Wmton & Warsaw R.R. July 3, 4 & 5" [1863]. "Name appears as a signature on a Roll of Prisoners of War, paroled, until exchanged at Fort Monroe, Va., July 16, 1863".[833]

Additional Regional Actions

The 1862 US Navy Raid on Greenville

The first Federal raid against Greenville was a naval expedition, which captured the town for a couple of hours on November 9, 1862. The expedition was led by Second Assistant Engineer John L. Lay. Lay, a talented inventor, later designed the explosive device that Lt. William B. Cushing used to destroy the *CSS Albemarle* in Plymouth, North Carolina on the night of October 27-28, 1864. After the war, Lay designed the first modern self-propelled torpedo.

Lay made his first attempt to attack Greenville, a point much further upriver than the Federal Navy had ever been before, early in November 1862. He was assigned Gunner Edwin A. McDonald and twenty men, "partly armed with Sharps rifles", and Assistant Paymaster William W. Williams was sent "to take care of the wounded." One reason for the raid was to destroy a gunboat that the Confederates were thought to be building on the Tar River. But the raid misfired when the steamer *North State* ran aground "some 2 or 3 miles below Greenville". The Federals seized six horses and three mules, and returned to Washington. They did bring back some information, including a statement that the Confederates were building two vessels at Tarboro, "to be ironclad".[834]

The Navy's second attempt to raid Greenville came after Col. Edward E. Potter, who then was in command of the Union forces at Washington, planned to send the steamer *North State* back up the Tar River "for forage, etc." Acting Lt. R. T. Renshaw of the Navy learned of the plan, and proposed that Lay and the North State be used for another raid on Greenville.[835]

The second attempt by the Navy was on a larger scale than the first. On the *North State*, Lay had fourteen men from the navy and a boat howitzer, under Gunner McDonald. A "Captain Greenwood" was the commander of "the little craft". Also aboard was a detachment of six men from the 1st New York Marine Artillery who manned a 24-pounder howitzer. The Marine Artillery was an army regiment that wore naval-style uniforms and handled artillery aboard river gunboats. Pulled behind the *North State* were a launch from the *USS Chasseur*, with seventeen sailors and a 12-pounder boat howitzer, and a flatboat with another seventeen men from the 1st North Carolina Union Volunteers, under Lt.

John B. McLane of Company A. They left Washington at 4:30 p.m. on November 8.[836]

The Tar River itself was the biggest obstacle that faced the Yankee sailors. A prewar traveler described this stretch of the Tar River, with "the dark-colored water, and low, swampy shores common to all the streams in the lower country. ... The river is narrow, crooked, shoaly, and only navigable for flat-bottomed boats." After halting for the night, they got underway in the morning. About 9 am, the *North State* ran aground about a mile below Greenville. The steamer had reached a point called the old lock, where the Corps of Engineers had built a wing dam before the war to back up water upstream to improve navigation. The raiders used poles and oars to push their smaller craft the rest of the way up to Greenville.[837]

Lay landed bearing a flag of truce, perhaps at the steamboat landing which was at the eastern edge of the Town Common. The mayor of Greenville surrendered the town. Just after the takeover of Greenville, Lay heard a flurry of gunshots. The only Southern troops in town were a handful of cavalrymen, possibly from the 3rd North Carolina Cavalry. These Rebel horsemen were on the bridge and firing at the launch from the *Chasseur*. Lay aimed one of his howitzers at the bridge and "fired several stands of grape". One of the Confederates, whose name was given by historian Henry King as "W. C. Richardson", shot and killed Private George Smith, of Company I of the Marine Artillery. In November 1862, a Corporal William Richardson was serving with Company I, 3rd North Carolina Cavalry, a unit that was stationed at "Camp Baker, near Greenville" at the time of the raid. Richardson and the other troopers escaped.[838]

The Federals "made many threats of vengeance." Lay stated in his report that "as they had disregarded a flag of truce, I deemed it advisable to destroy the bridge, and detailed Mr. McDonald with a party to proceed and fire it." Southern sources, though, say that the townspeople persuaded the raiders that they had nothing to do with the soldiers who fired the fatal shot, and the Federals let them put the fire out.[839]

After firing the bridge, the Yankees checked the jail, but found that there were no prisoners. They also asked to see "the head men" of Greenville. Dr. William J. Blow was "mentioned as one of them, [and] they had an interview with him, telling him they did not intend to interfere with private property, unless fired upon ..." Blow was warned that if they were fired on, "they had orders to burn the town." To the locals, Lay's small party seemed "considerably alarmed" during their brief stay. Unlike Potter's Raid, Southern sources mention little about the Federals looting the town.[840]

Even more of a surprise than the naval raid itself was the sight of what the people of Greenville thought were black Union soldiers "in uniforms with belts, swords, and pistols. They drew the artillery through the streets ..." These black "soldiers" were really sailors. The Union Army at that time had no black soldiers in North Carolina, and indeed was only beginning to enlist any black troops at all. On the other hand, the US Navy had never prohibited the enlistment of black sailors. When assigned to landing parties, sailors carried revolvers and cutlasses. The guns that they landed were boat howitzers, special guns mounted on light iron carriages that the sailors drew by means of special harnesses.[841]

The black sailors, "when leaving gave a general invitation to all the negroes to go with them", according to Henry King. But, says King, "none went at that time."[842]

Lay's party spent perhaps two hours in Greenville. They filled the flatboat with wagons, horses, mules, and "stores and provisions." After taking "ten of the citizens" as prisoners, they headed back to Washington. Although Doctor Blow was pointed out as one of the "head men" of Greenville, the Federals did not take him.[843]

There are at least three lists of the names of the prisoners, each varying in its details. "Joel Hodges", variously described as a "jailor" and as an "ex-sheriff", may have been Josiah Hodges, who was the sheriff of Pitt County in 1860. Joseph Dancy was identified as the clerk of superior court. Ed Hoell was a prosperous grocer, and Alfred Forbes was a prominent businessman. One list named James Forbes instead of Alfred. James Cobb was a "bar keeper". Allen Tyson (or Allen Tice) also appears on the list of prisoners. Other men on one or more lists included William Stocks, "B. Albritton" (or B. G. Albriton), "Benj. Corry" (or B. A. Corey), and one variously identified as Bob Green or Charles Green.[844]

The locals were taken hostage "to prevent the sharp shooters from firing on them on their return down the river." Struggling back downriver was not much easier than going up. The *North State* got stuck on another sand bar for four hours. At 10 p.m., Lay stopped for the night at Yankee Hall, which was on the north bank of the Tar only about ten miles downstream from Greenville. Lay received information that an enemy force intended to stop him at Boyd's Ferry, but no such attack materialized the next day. Still, it was 2:30 p.m. on Tuesday, November 11, before the Federals were back in Washington. The prisoners were released after a few days. Like everyone else in Greenville, the freed captives wondered when the Yankees would be back.[845]

The prospect of a Rebel ironclad steaming down the river to sweep the Union's wooden gunboats away from Washington and the Pamlico alarmed the Federal navy. But, the repeated grounding of even a small river steamboat such as the *North State* warned the navy that it was too dangerous for them to risk steaming that far up the shallow Tar River. It was up to the army to handle any Union strikes in that area again.

More Union Raids in Pitt County

When General Potter's force rode out of Greenville on July 19, 1863, the Confederates in town hoped they'd seen the second and last Yankee raid of the war. While Union forces didn't reach Edgecombe or Greene Counties again until near the end of the war, they would be back for several more visits to Pitt County. Each time, one of the leaders among the Union officers was Capt. George W. Graham of Company L, 1st North Carolina Union Volunteers.

On November 25, 1863, detachments from the 12th New York Cavalry, 23rd New York Cavalry, and Company L of the 1st North Carolina Union volunteers, struck a Confederate camp at Haddock's Crossroads (about seven miles south of Greenville). In the camp were Companies E and I of Whitford's Battalion. The attack was evidently a complete surprise. Union officers reported 52 Confederates were captured, and a Confederate lieutenant and four enlisted men were killed. Federal losses were one man killed and three wounded. The expedition was under Capt. George W. Graham; the higher-ranking Capt. R. R. West of the 12th New York Cavalry ceding command to Graham because of "familiarity with the country to be traversed". A "Mr. Horn" acted as a guide for the Federals.[846]

Another raid, on December 17, 1863, struck a camp of the 3rd North Carolina Cavalry, east of Greenville. A force of the 1st North Carolina Union Volunteers, under Maj. Charles C. Graves, left Washington at two a.m. on December 17. About 5:30 a.m., they halted at Chicod Creek and waited for a signal from a 100-man force of the 58th Pennsylvania Infantry, which had left Washington before them.[847]

At 8 a.m., Graves' men heard horses approaching. It was the detachment of the 58th Pennsylvania, under Capt. Theodore Blakely. Somewhere east of Greenville, they had captured the camp of Company H, 3rd North Carolina Cavalry, taking 35 prisoners including company commander Capt. Julius W. Moore. Blakely's men also captured 30 horses and 4 mules; there were no Federal losses.[848]

A sharper clash occurred in Pitt County on the night of December 30-31, 1863. Union raiders burned Red Banks Church, east of Greenville on December 30. About 11:30 p.m., a one-gun detachment from Starr's Battery (Company B, 13th Battalion, North Carolina Artillery) under Lt. James H. Myrover set out from Greenville to intercept the raiding party. Moving east along the Washington Road (or River Road), they met "fifty or sixty" men of Companies E, G, and K of the 3rd North Carolina Cavalry under Maj. Roger Moore.[849]

The Confederate force marched east for "six miles" before turning right on a road that led to Red Banks Church. After midnight, the Confederates received word that the raiders were about one mile behind, and turned around to intercept them. In a spot "where the road led through a swamp, and was fringed by dense undergrowth", wrote Myrover years later, the Union cavalry surprised them with a volley of carbine fire. "The surprise was complete", Myrover continued, and "the Confederates, utterly bewildered, and ignorant of the size of the force pouring its fire into them, retreated ..."[850]

"Amid sharp firing in close contact", wrote a veteran of the 3rd North Carolina Cavalry, "and the clash of contending sabres", the Confederate cavalrymen cut their way through the enemy and avoided capture. The Federals were so close behind that the gunners couldn't fire without hitting their own men. "Private John H. Dobbin ... made great efforts to fire it", but it was too late and the gun and crew were overrun.[851]

The six-pounder gun and caisson were taken back to Washington with 12 artillery horses. Lt. David Camp and Private Francis B. Ferral of Company G, 3rd North Carolina Cavalry, were killed and "several" men were wounded. Four members of Starr's Battery and three men of Company G, 3rd North Carolina Cavalry were captured.[852]

Federal losses included Lt. William K. Adams of Graham's Company L of the 1st North Carolina Union Volunteers, who "fell while making a charge at the head of his command". The 12th New York Cavalry had one man wounded and by one account, listed four men as missing.[853]

Brig. Gen. John J. Peck's report on the Red Banks Church raid commended a "Mr. Hahn ... in the 2nd North Carolina Union Volunteers", who "was a guide on this occasion, and did us great good service". It is quite possible that "Hahn" was the same "Mr. Horn" who served as a guide on the November 25 raid on Haddock's Crossroads. A "Jacob H. Horn" is recorded as serving in Company G of the 1st North Carolina Union Volunteers, and Company A of the 2nd North Carolina Union Volunteers. No one named Hahn seems to have served in either unit.[854]

There's an interesting postscript to Horn's life, which is mentioned in Chris E. Fonvielle Jr.'s *The Battle of Forks Road*. In January 1865, Jacob Horn was a corporal, and was attached as a guide to Brig. Gen. Alfred Terry's corps. After the Battle of Fort Fisher, as Union forces were advancing north toward Wilmington, the *Philadelphia Inquirer* reported that a Union corporal requested permission to visit a nearby house. The story reported that the corporal wanted to visit "the residence of his parents and the home of his youth". "Clasped in the arms of his overjoyed mother", the Union corporal was told that only yesterday, his Confederate soldier brother had visited their home. The Philadelphia reporter didn't mention the corporal's name, but evidence suggests that it was Corporal Jacob Horn, brother of Hosea Lewis Horn of the Wilmington Horse Artillery. In 2006, the US government placed new military gravestones for

Jacob Horn and Hosea Lewis Horn. The two brothers are both buried in the Horne Family Cemetery, south of Wilmington.[855]

Only a small postscript of the raid on Red Banks Church cheered up the Confederates. At dawn on the morning after the fight, Lt. William Slade of Company K, 3rd North Carolina Cavalry was astounded to find a Federal cavalryman asleep in his camp! One Union soldier, possibly of the 12th New York Cavalry, became separated from his command in the dark. Apparently he fell in with some horse troops and followed them to camp. Not realizing that his new companions were from the 3rd North Carolina Cavalry, he bedded down after tending to his horse. Slade captured the man before he could react.[856]

On March 26, 1864, Federal raiders struck Pitt County again. Led by Capt. George W. Graham, mounted troops of the 1st North Carolina Union Volunteers conducted "a reconnaissance toward Greenville". Moving "with the utmost rapidity and secrecy", Graham's detachment attacked a Confederate picket post at Black Jack Church. The attack resulted in the "complete surprise of the enemy's pickets and reserve at and near" the church. Graham's men burned the church, which had been used for shelter by Confederate soldiers.[857]

The picket post belonged to Capt. Patrick Gray's Company G of the 62nd Georgia Cavalry. At the time of Potter's Raid, Gray's company was stationed down the Tar River from Greenville, but they were too far away from there to take part in the pursuit of the raiders.

A Union report overstated Confederate losses at "1 officer and 8 men killed and several wounded, besides prisoners". The Federals lost only "a few horses wounded." Confederate records show that Lt. Carlton J. McKenzie was killed; Private Charles A. Miller was wounded; and Privates David M. Stripling and John W. Taylor, all of Company G, 62nd Georgia Cavalry, were captured.[858]

The Last Raid on Greenville

On February 17, 1865, a Union raiding party left New Bern. Once again, the raiders were led by Capt. George W. Graham. Graham's force included his own Company L of the 1st North Carolina Union Volunteers, and Company G of the 12th New York Cavalry, under Capt. John W. Horn. Graham and his men, it will be recalled, were part of Potter's 1863 raid; Captain Horn's troopers were not. Another detachment of the 12th New York Cavalry, under Maj. Rowland R. West, also set out on their own expedition into Confederate territory.[859]

On the second day of the raid, Graham's men were at a point "six miles" from Greenville when they overran a Confederate cavalry camp, at Haddock's Crossroads in Pitt County. Like the camp Graham surprised at Black Jack, it belonged to Captain Gray's company, which by that time had been transferred to become Company G of the 8th Georgia Cavalry.[860]

Company G was called "Capt. Gray's company of Georgia ruffians" by a Unionist newspaper in New Bern. They had recently "fired into the *Mystic* [a Union gunboat] at Washington a few days ago ..."[861]

Some of Gray's company scattered into the woods and escaped. Records show that two officers, Lieutenants B. Arnold Northen and Daniel Vinson, and at least 15 men were captured. One Confederate, Private A. C. Holt, was wounded in the left wrist. Holt escaped capture, and was reported to be in a hospital in Greenville as late as April 26. Although the wound caused his arm to "wither away", he lived until 1926.[862]

One Union soldier, Private Francis McKenna of Company G, 12th New York Cavalry, was listed as missing on that day. Records do not state the exact place where he was captured. McKenna was released at an unknown date, and he was discharged from the army in May 1865.[863]

Graham left behind a detail under "Lieutenant Turner" (probably Lt. William S. Turner of Company D, 12th New York Cavalry) to guard the prisoners. The rest of the force pressed on to Greenville and seized the town. Just as it was on Graham's first visit to Greenville in 1863, the town was practically undefended. The raiders destroyed some government supplies and took some more prisoners. Among the men who they captured was Maj. William Demill, who had served as a commissary officer at Greenville since 1863.[864]

Graham's force was "considerably reduced by the number required to guard the prisoners, and captured property." The captain "thought it advisable" to leave before the Confederates in the area had time to block his escape. By one account, they took 28 prisoners in all. They headed back to Washington, where Graham dropped off the prisoners. The Federals then rode back to Fort Anderson, near New Bern, by way of Blount's Mill.[865]

At Washington, the captives were placed on board the steamer *Escort* to take them to Northern prisons. The officers were sent to Fort Delaware, and the enlisted men ended up imprisoned at Point Lookout, Maryland. Demill was released from Fort Delaware on June 3, 1865.[866]

Notes

Chapter 1

1. *Daily Dispatch* (Richmond, Virginia), July 16, 1863.
2. George Howard to Wife, July 14, 1863, George Howard Papers, Collection #197, Container #197.1, East Carolina Manuscript Collection, Special Collections Department, J. Y. Joyner Library, East Carolina University, Greenville, NC, USA.
3. George Howard to Wife, July 9, 1863, George Howard Papers.
4. George Howard to Wife, July 14, 1863, George Howard Papers.
5. George Howard to Wife, July 9, 1863, George Howard Papers.
6. George Howard to Wife, July 9, 1863, George Howard Papers.
7. J. W. Sanders, "Tenth Regiment (same Companies)" in Walter Clark, ed., *Histories of the Several Regiments and Battalions from North Carolina in the Great War, 1861-'65*, 5 vols. (Goldsboro, N.C., 1901), 1:523-524. (Hereafter cited as Clark, *Histories of the Regiments*.)
8. J. W. Sanders, "Tenth Regiment (same Companies)", Clark, *Histories of the Regiments.*, 1:523-524.
9. J. W. Sanders, "Tenth Regiment (same Companies)", Clark, *Histories of the Regiments*, 1:523-524; George Howard to Wife, July 9, 1863, George Howard Papers.
10. George Howard to Wife, July 9, 1863, George Howard Papers; J. W. Sanders, "Tenth Regiment (same Companies)", Clark, *Histories of the Regiments*, 1:523-524. A check of the available records of the 1st North Carolina Artillery, however, has failed to turn up the name of a single casualty of the train wreck.
11. George Howard to Wife, July 15, 1863, George Howard Papers.
12. George Howard to Wife, July 12, July 15; 1863, George Howard Papers.
13. *The War of the Rebellion: A Compilation of the Official Records of the Union and Confederate Armies,* ser. 1, 18:1027-1028. (Hereafter cited as *Official Records*.)
14. *Official Records,* ser. 1, 18:872, 891, 1051 John G. Barrett, *The Civil War in North Carolina* (Chapel Hill: University of North Carolina Press, 1963), 151.
15. Ezra J. Warner, *Generals in Gray* (Baton Rouge: University of Louisiana Press, 1959), 334-335.
16. Barrett, *The Civil War in North Carolina,* 151-162.
17. *Official Records,* ser. 1, 27, pt. 3:1006.
18. Warner, *Generals in Gray,* 213-214, *Official Records*, ser. 1, 9:480.
19. *Official Records,* ser. 1, 27, pt. 3:1068.
20. *Official Records,* ser. 1, 27, pt. 3:1067-1068.
21. John G. Smith, "The Tarboro Raid", *Carolina and the Southern Cross,* February 1914, 250; *Raleigh* (N.C.) *Register* (semi-weekly), August 8, 1863.
22. *Official Records,* ser. 1, 27, pt. 3:1067-1068.
23. *Macon Telegraph* (Macon, Georgia) January 26, 1861, October 31, 1862; *Macon Daily Telegraph*, May 31, 1862; Clark, IV, 73.
24. John T. Kennedy and W. Fletcher Parker, "Seventy-fifth Regiment (Seventh Cavalry)", in Clark, *Histories of the Regiments* 4:74; John T. Kennedy, 62nd Georgia Cavalry, Compiled Military Service Record, Record Group 109, National Archives.

25. Kennedy and Parker, "Seventy-fifth Regiment (Seventh Cavalry)", in Clark, *Histories of the Regiments* 4:77; Henry T. King, *Sketches of Pitt County* (Raleigh: Edward and Broughton, 1911), 135.
26. Kennedy and Parker, "Seventy-fifth Regiment (Seventh Cavalry)", in Clark, *Histories of the Regiments* 4:, 77; King, *Sketches of Pitt County,* 135; Mrs. P. Atkinson to Governor Zebulon Vance, July 28, 1863, Zebulon B. Vance, Governors' Papers, North Carolina State Archives, Division of Archives and History, Raleigh; William L. A. Ellis, 62nd Georgia Cavalry, Compiled Military Service File, Record Group 109, National Archives; Lillian Henderson, comp., *Roster of the Confederate Soldiers of Georgia,* 6 vols. (Hapeville, Ga.: Longina & Porter, 1959), 6:297; Janet B. Hewett, ed., *Supplement to the Official Records of the Union and Confederate Armies* 100 vols. (Wilmington: Broadfoot Publishing Company, 1994—), serial vol. 17:653-656, 660.
27. Kennedy and Parker, "Seventy-fifth Regiment (Seventh Cavalry)", in Clark, *Histories of the Regiments* 4:77; Henry T. King, *Sketches of Pitt County,* 35.
28. *Macon Daily Telegraph* (Macon, Georgia), May 31, 1862; Eighth Census of the United States, 1860: Pittsylvania County, Virginia.
29. *Carolina Watchman,* (Salisbury, North Carolina), May 4, 1863; *Tarboro Southerner* (Tarboro, North Carolina)*,* January 17, 1863.
30. *Tarboro Southerner,* January 17, 1863.
31. Kennedy and Parker, "Seventy-fifth Regiment (Seventh Cavalry)", in Clark, *Histories of the Regiments* 4:73; Warner*, Generals in Gray,* 259-260; *Official Records,* ser 1, 18: 051.
32. *Official Records,* ser 1, 18:1089; Kennedy and Parker, "Seventy-fifth Regiment (Seventh Cavalry)", in Clark, *Histories of the Regiments* 4:76.
33. *Official Records,* ser. 1, 27, pt. 3:1067-1068; *State Journal* (Raleigh), August 5, 1863; Louis Manarin and Weymouth T. Jordan, Jr., comps, *North Carolina Troops 1861-1865: A Roster,* 15 volumes to date, (Raleigh, North Carolina: North Carolina Office of Archives and History, 1966-), 1:113, 174, 218.
34. *North Carolina Troops* 6:201-202.
35. David A. Norris, "The Men of the Stalwart Petersburg Artillery Served from the Beginning of the War to the End", America's *Civil War*, March 1995; *Ripley Bee* (Ripley, Ohio), November 26, 1859.
36. *Official Records,* ser. 1, 27, pt. 3:1068.
37. *North Carolina Troops,* 3:84.
38. Walter Clark, "Eighth Battalion. (Nethercutt's Partisan Rangers.)", in Clark, *Histories of the Regiments,* 4:302.
39. Rufus W. Wharton, "Sixty-seventh Regiment", in Clark, *Histories of the Regiments* Clark, 3:703; *North Carolina Troops,* 2:584.
40. *North Carolina Troops,* 3:84.
41. *Philadelphia Inquirer,* September 3, 1863.
42. W. P. Derby, *Bearing Arms in the Twenty-seventh Massachusetts Regiment of Volunteers Infantry during the Civil War* (Boston: Wright and Potter Printing Company, 1883), 214-215.
43. *Official Records,* ser. 1, 18:1022.

44. John G. Smith, "The Tarboro Raid", *Carolina and the Southern Cross,* February 1914, 250.
45. J. W. Sanders, "Tenth Regiment (same Companies)", in Clark, *Histories of the Regiments* 3:524.
46. George Howard to Wife, July 18, 1863, George Howard Papers.

Chapter 2

47. Ezra J. Warner, *Generals in Blue: Lives of the Union Commanders* (Baton Rouge: Louisiana State University Press, 1964), 157-158.
48. Vincent Colyer, *Brief report of the Services Rendered by the Freed People to the United States Army, in North Carolina, in the Spring of 1862, after the Battle of New Bern* (New York: Vincent Colyer, 1864), 26; *Official Records,* ser. 1, 18:415.
49. *Official Records,* ser. 1, 18:457.
50. *North Carolina Standard* (Raleigh), September 10, September 17, October 18, 1862; *Official Records,* ser. 1, 18:6.
51. *Philadelphia Inquirer,* September 16, 1862; *Evening Courier and Republic* (Buffalo, New York), September 12, 1862; Barrett, *The Civil War in North Carolina,* 134.
52. *Official Records,* ser. 1, 18:4-10.
53. *Official Records,* ser. 1, 18:9.
54. Letters and Applications for US Passports, NARA M1372, National Archives.
55. Ezra J. Warner, *Generals in Blue,* 380; *Brooklyn Daily Eagle,* October 3, 1842; *The New York Spectator,* October 3, 1842; Eighth Census of the United States, 1860: Morris County, New Jersey.
56. *Official Records,* ser. 1, 18:86, 88, 208.
57. *Official Records,* ser. 1, 18:385.
58. *Official Records,* ser. 1, 18:21,447.
59. *Official Records,* ser. 1, 18:21.
60. Barrett, *The Civil War in North Carolina,* 136-138.
61. Barrett, *The Civil War in North Carolina,* 139; *Official Records,* ser. 1:18:22.
62. Barrett, *The Civil War in North Carolina,* 139-146.
63. *Official Records,* ser. 1, 18:58-59; 93.
64. *The Civil War in North Carolina,* 147-148; *Official Records,* ser. 1, 18:60.
65. Warner, *Generals in Blue*: 380; *Official Records,* ser. 1, 18:59, 512.
66. Barrett, *The Civil War in North Carolina,* 150n., 152n.
67. *Official Records,* ser. 1, 18:541, 549-550.
68. Barrett, *The Civil War in North Carolina,* 159-160.
69. Barrett, *The Civil War in North Carolina,* 161.
70. *Official Records,* ser. 1, 27, pt. 3:36-37; Barrett, *The Civil War in North Carolina,* 162-164.

Chapter 3

71. *Herald* (New York), June 23, 1863; *Official Records,* ser. 1, 27, pt. 3:513.
72. *Brooklyn Daily Eagle,* August 7, 1863.
73. Seventh Census of the United States, 1850: Monroe County, New York; *Rochester City Directory,* 1851, 1855, 1859, at Monroe County Library System at http://

www2.libraryweb.org/orgMain.asp?orgid=468; George W. Lewis, 3rd New York Cavalry, Compiled Military Service File, Record Group 94, National Archives.
74. *Official Records,* ser. 1, 27, pt. 2:860.
75. Frederick Phisterer, *New York in the War of the Rebellion* (Albany: Weed and Parson, 1890), 299.
76. *New York Times,* April 27, 1862.
77. Phisterer, *New York in the War of the Rebellion* (1890), 298.
78. William Jewett Tenney, *The Military and Naval History of the Rebellion in the United States: With Biographical Sketches* (New York: D. Appleton and Company, 1866), 784; Frederick Phisterer, *New York in the War of the Rebellion* 5 vols. (Albany: J. B. Lyon and Company, 1912), 1:797; Eighth Census of the United States, 1860: Schoharie County, New York.
79. *Quinquaennial Catalogue of the Officers and Graduates of Harvard University 1636 - 1915 Cambridge, Massachusetts, Harvard University Press in the Two Hundred and Seventy-Ninth Year of the College 1915*; Rowland M. Hall to My Dear Father, June 16, 1862, Julia Ward Stickley Papers, North Carolina State Archives.
80. Rowland M. Hall to My Dear Father, June 16, 1862, Julia Ward Stickley Papers.
81. Eighth Census of the United States, 1860: Essex County, New Jersey; Gustavus W. Jocknick, 3rd New York Cavalry, Federal Pension Application Records, National Archives.
82. Muster Roll, July-August 1863, Company F, Company K, 3rd New York Cavalry, Record Group 94, National Archives; *New York Times,* January 31, 1902; *Official Records,* ser. 1, 18:157-158; 180-182. The 1900 United States Census of Dutchess County, New York listed a John G. Harris, who was born in North Carolina in 1844.
83. *Watertown Daily Times,* (Watertown, New York), October 27, 1920.
84. William Davies to My Dear Wife, June 17, 1863, William Davies Correspondence, Oswego County Historical Society, Oswego, New York; Frederick Phisterer, *New York in the War of the Rebellion* (1890), 299-300.
85. Frederick Phisterer, *New York in the War of the Rebellion* 5 vols. (Albany: J. B. Lyon and Company, 1912), 1:797; 2:1079-1080; Eighth Census of the United States, 1860: Fort Laramie Reservation, Nebraska Territory.
86. Phisterer, *New York in the War of the Rebellion* (1912), 2:1079-1080. John Mix became a captain in the 2nd U. S. Cavalry after the war. Ninth Census of the United States, 1860: Cheyenne County, Nebraska, 1870; *Official Records,* Series I, 29, pt. 3, 143.
87. Francis B. Heitman, *Historical Register and Dictionary of the United States Army From Its Organization, September 29, 1789, to March 2, 1903,* (Washington, D. C.: U. S. Government Printing Office, 1903), 467; *Denver Mirror* (Denver, Colorado), November 23, 1873.
88. *Denver Mirror*, November 23, 1873; Muster Roll, July-August 1863, Company L, 1st North Carolina Union Volunteers, Record Group 94, National Archives; *Union Advance Picket* (Washington, N.C), May 15, 1862; *New York Times,* August 26, 1863.
89. Regimental Special Order No. 11, July 2, 1863, Regimental Order Book, 1st North Carolina Colored Troops (35th United States Colored Troops), Record Group 94, National Archives.
90. *Official Records,* ser. 1, 27, pt. 2: 863.

91. W. W. Howe, *Kinston, Whitehall, and Goldsboro Expedition December 1862* (New York: W. W. Howe, 1890), 10.
92. *Official Records,* ser. 1, 18:127-130; *Herald* (New York), January 30, 1863.
93. *Herald* (New York), January 30, 1863.
94. *The Liberator* (Boston, Massachusetts), June 12, 1863; July 3, 1863.
95. *Official Records,* ser. 1, 27, pt. 2:86-861.
96. *Official Records,* ser. 1, 27, pt. 2:864.
97. *Official Records,* ser. 1, 27, pt. 2:861.
98. *Official Records,* ser. 1, 27, pt. 2:861.
99. *Official Records,* ser. 1, 27, pt. 2:861.
100. Catherine W. Bishir and Michael T. Southern, *A Guide to the Historic Architecture of Eastern North Carolina* (Chapel Hill: University of North Carolina Press, 1996), 413-414; Faison Wells McGowan and Pearl Canady McGowan, *Flashes of Duplin's History and Government* (Kenansville, North Carolina: 1971), 258.
101. Rowland M. Hall to Dear Father, July 17, 1863, Julia Ward Stickley Papers.
102. The phase of the moon is confirmed by the US Naval Observatory's Complete Sun and Moon Data for One Day at http://aa.usno.navy.mil/data/docs/RS_OneDay.html. Rowland M. Hall to Dear Father, July 17, 1863, Julia Ward Stickley Papers; *North Carolina Standard,* July 15, 1863; McGowan and McGowan, *Flashes of Duplin's History and Government,* 325.
103. *Christian Recorder,* Philadelphia, July 11, 1863.
104. *Official Records,* ser. 1, 27, pt. 2:859, 861; Rowland M. Hall to Dear Father, July 17, 1863.
105. For instance, see Sgt. R. G. Best, 7th Confederate Cavalry, Compiled Military Service File, Record Group 94, National Archives. *Official Records,* ser. 1, 27, pt. 2:859, 861; *North Carolina Standard,* July 15, 1863; Rowland M. Hall to Dear Father, July 17, 1863, Julia Ward Stickley Papers.
106. Rowland M. Hall to Dear Father, July 17, 1863, Julia Ward Stickley Papers.
107. William A. Albaugh III, *Confederate Edged Weapons* (Wilmington, North Carolina: Broadfoot Publishing Company, 1993), 23-30; A. Bruce Hartung, "Swordmaker for the Confederacy", *The State,* January 1981.
108. *Official Records,* ser. 4, 1:987. Estvan's book, *War Pictures from the South,* was published under the name "B. Estvan" in New York by D. Appleton and Company in 1863.
109. *Wilmington Journal,* February 21, March 12, 1863; April 28, 1864.
110. *Official Records,* ser. 1, 27, pt. 2:859, 861; *Richmond Daily Dispatch,* July 9, 1863.
111. *Official Records,* ser. 1, 27, pt. 2:861-862; 27, pt. 3, 863.
112. *Official Records,* ser. 1, 27, pt. 2:862; *North Carolina Standard* (Raleigh), July 15, 1863.
113. A. C. Myers to S. D. Wallace, July 14, 1863, National Archives, Record Group 109.7.3, Records of the Quartermaster Department [Confederate].
114. *North Carolina Standard,* July 15, 1863; *Daily Progress,* July 8, 1863.
115. *Herald* (New York), July 12, 1863.
116. *North Carolina Standard,* July 15, 1863; *Daily Progress,* July 8, 1863; *Richmond Daily Dispatch,* July 9, 1863.
117. *Carolina Watchman* (Salisbury, N.C.), July 27, 1863.

118. *Official Records,* ser. 1, 27, pt. 2:862; Rowland M. Hall to Dear Father, July 17, 1863, Julia Ward Stickley Papers.
119. *North Carolina Standard,* July 8, 1863; *Official Records,* ser. 1, 27, pt. 3:978-979.
120. *Official Records,* ser. 1, 27, pt. 3:972.
121. *Official Records,* ser. 1, 27, pt. 3:1067; Robert K. Krick, *Lee's Colonels: A Biographical Register of the Field Officers of the Army of Northern Virginia* (Dayton, Ohio: Morningside Books, 1992), 206; Warner, *Generals in Gray,* 153-154.
122. *North Carolina Standard,* July 15, 1863.
123. Undated newspaper clipping, 3rd Regiment Cavalry, NY Volunteers, Civil War Newspaper Clippings at the Unit History Project, New York State Military Museum and Veterans Research Center, New York State Division of Military and Naval Affairs; URL: http://www.dmna.state.ny.us/historic/reghist/civil/cavalry/3rdCav/3rdCavCWN.htm.
124. *North Carolina Standard,* July 15, 1863; *Daily Progress,* July 8, 1863.
125. *Official Records,* ser. 1, 27, pt. 2:862.
126. *Official Records,* ser. 1, 27, pt. 2:862.
127. *Official Records,* ser. 1, 27, pt. 2:862.
128. *Official Records,* ser. 1, 27, pt. 2:862, 865.
129. *Official Records,* ser. 1, 27, pt. 2:863, 865; *North Carolina Standard,* July 15, 1863; *San Francisco Evening Bulletin,* July 11, 1863.
130. Charles E. Thorburn, Compiled Service Records of Confederate General and Staff Officers, and Nonregimental Enlisted Men, Record Group 109, National Archives; *Wilmington Journal,* July 8, 1863; *Official Records,* ser. 1, 18:866; *Official Records,* ser. 1, 27, pt. 2:946; Robert K. Krick, *Lee's Colonels: A Biographical Register of the Field Officers of the Army of Northern Virginia,* 372.
131. *New York Times,* August 26, 1863; Muster Roll, Company B. 3rd New York Cavalry, July-August 1863, Record Group 94, National Archives.
132. *Official Records,* ser. 1, 27, pt. 2:860, 862.
133. *Official Records,* ser. 1, 27, pt. 2: 863.
134. *Official Records,* ser. 1, 27, pt. 2:864.
135. *North Carolina Standard,* July 22, 1863; *Wilmington Journal,* July 8, 1863; *Official Records,* ser. 1, 27, pt. 2:977.
136. *Wilmington Journal,* July 6, 1863; *Official Records,* ser. 1, 27, pt. 2:978.
137. Leon H. Sikes, "The Swords of Kenansville", *Footnotes,* Number 58, November 1995; Michael Hill, ed., *Guide to North Carolina Historical Highway Markers* (Raleigh: Division of Archives and History, 2001), 76.
138. William K. Lane and William F. Parker, Company F, 7th Confederate Cavalry, Compiled Military Service Files, Record Group 109, National Archives.

Chapter 3

139. Charles McCool Snyder, *Oswego County, New York in the Civil War* (Oswego, New York: Oswego County Historical Society and the Oswego County Civil War Committee, 1962), 85-86.
140. W. H. Graves, *A True Narrative of the Incidents Which Happened in the Life of W. H. Graves* (typescript of a 1901 manuscript), Colorado Historical Society, Denver, Colorado, 93.

141. W. H. Graves, *A True Narrative of the Incidents Which Happened in the Life of W. H. Graves*, 95.
142. W. H. Graves, *A True Narrative of the Incidents Which Happened in the Life of W. H. Graves*, 96-97.
143. W. H. Graves, *A True Narrative of the Incidents Which Happened in the Life of W. H. Graves*, 97; *Commercial Times* (Oswego, New York), November 13, 1862.
144. W. H. Graves, *A True Narrative of the Incidents Which Happened in the Life of W. H. Graves*, 100-101.
145. Charles McCool Snyder, *Oswego County, New York in the Civil War*, 86; W. H. Graves, *A True Narrative of the Incidents Which Happened in the Life of W. H. Graves*.[102]
146. Gleason Wellington to Dear Mother, April 13, 1863, Gleason Wellington Correspondence, Oswego County Historical Society, Oswego, New York.
147. *Commercial Times* (Oswego, New York), May 29, 1863.
148. Frederick Phisterer, *New York in the War of the Rebellion* (1912), 2:965; *Commercial Advertiser and Times*, June 5, 1865.
149. Frederick Phisterer, *New York in the War of the Rebellion* (1912), 2:961; *Oswego Daily Palladium,* November 12, 1910; *Oswego Daily Times,* August 26, 1921; *Times and Journal* (Oswego, New York), June 17, 1856.
150. *Oswego Daily Times,* August 26, 1921; Gleason Wellington to Dear Mother, June 28, 1863, Gleason Wellington Correspondence.
151. Oswego County census, 1860; American Civil War Research database, civilwardata.com.
152. W. H. Graves, *A True Narrative of the Incidents Which Happened in the Life of W. H. Graves*, 103.
153. *Utica* (N.Y) *Saturday Globe,* April 18, 1904.
154. *Utica Saturday Globe,* April 18, 1904.
155. *Utica Saturday Globe,* April 18, 1904.
156. *Utica Saturday Globe,* April 18, 1904.
157. *Utica Saturday Globe,* April 18, 1904.
158. W. H. Graves, *A True Narrative of the Incidents Which Happened in the Life of W. H. Graves*, 104-105.
159. W. H. Graves, *A True Narrative of the Incidents Which Happened in the Life of W. H. Graves*, 105-106.
160. W. H. Graves, *A True Narrative of the Incidents Which Happened in the Life of W. H. Graves*, 106-108.
161. *Commercial Times*, August 26, 1863.
162. William Davies to My Dear Wife, July 8, 1863, William Davies Correspondence.
163. William Davies to My Dear Wife, June 17, 1863, William Davies Correspondence.
164. Gleason Wellington to Dear Mother, June 28, 1863, Gleason Wellington Correspondence.
165. William Davies to My Dear Wife, June 17, 1863. William Davies Correspondence
166. Gleason Wellington to Dear Mother, June 28, 1863; Gleason Wellington to Dear Mother, July 16, 1863, Gleason Wellington Correspondence.
167. W. H. Graves, *A True Narrative of the Incidents Which Happened in the Life of W. H. Graves*, 108.

168. Muster rolls, Companies A, B, and F, 12th New York Cavalry, July-August 1863, Record Group 94, National Archives.
169. Janet B. Hewett, ed., *Supplement to the Official Records of the Union and Confederate Armies,* serial vol. 41:513.

Chapter 5

170. *Official Records*, ser. 1, 27, pt. 2:723.
171. *Utica (N.Y.) Morning Herald and Gazette,* May 23, 1863.
172. *Official Records of the Union and Confederate Navies in the War of the Rebellion,* ser. 1, 8:192-193, 204, 245.
173. Complete Sun and Moon Data for One Day at http://aa.usno.navy.mil/data/docs/RS_OneDay.html.
174. *Official Records*, ser. 1, 27, pt. 2:967; Francis B. Heitman, *Historical Register and Dictionary of the United States Army...,* 584; Alfred Holcomb to Brother, July 21, 1863, United States Army Military History Institute, Carlisle Barracks, Pennsylvania.
175. William Seagrave Diary, United States Army Military History Institute, Carlisle Barracks, Pennsylvania; Alfred Holcomb to Brother, July 21, 1863, United States Army Military History Institute. The *Bombshell* was captured by Confederate forces at Plymouth, North Carolina, on April 18, 1864. The little steamer served the South until it was recaptured on May 5, 1864 during the Battle of the Albemarle Sound. *Dictionary of US Naval Fighting Ships,* online at http://www.history.navy.mil/danfs/cfa2/bombshell.htm.
176. *Official Records,* ser. 1, 27, pt. 2:967; Newton Wallace Diary, United States Army Military History Institute, Carlisle Barracks, Pennsylvania.
177. Newton Wallace Diary, United States Army Military History Institute; *Brooklyn Daily Eagle,* August 7, 1863.
178. *New York Tribune,* July 8, 1863; *Brooklyn Daily Eagle,* August 7, 1863.
179. *North Carolina Troops,* 3: 90, 15:433-434.
180. *Official Records,* ser. 1, 27, pt. 2:967.

Chapter 6

181. William H. Powell, *List of the Officers of the Army of the United States from 1779 to 1900 (*New York: L. R. Hamersly & Co, 1900), 500.
182. Powell, *List of the Officers of the Army of the United States from 1779 to 1900,* 306; *Official Records,* ser. 1, 18:175.
183. Regimental Order Books, July-August 1863, 12th New York Cavalry, Record Group 94, National Archives.
184. Gleason Wellington to Mother, July 16, 1863, Gleason Wellington Correspondence.
185. Rowland M. Hall to Father, July 17, 1863, Julia Ward Stickley Papers.
186. *Official Records,* ser. 1, 27, pt. 2:965
187. Undated clipping, *Republican Advocate* (Batavia, New York), 3rd Regiment Cavalry, NY Volunteers Civil War Newspaper Clippings ... URL: http://www.dmna.state.ny.us/historic/reghist/civil/cavalry/3rdCav/3rdCavCWN.htm; Special Orders No. 200, July 15, 1863, Regimental Order Book, 1st North Carolina Union Troops (35th United States Colored Troops), Record Group 94, National Archives.

188. *National Cyclopedia of American Biography,* s.v., Clarkson, Floyd; Gleason Wellington to Sister, April 13, 1863, Gleason Wellington Correspondence; Eighth Census of the United States, 1860: New York City Census (which spells his name as "Floyde Clarkson").

189. Phisterer, *New York in the War of the Rebellion* (1912), 1:790; *Chicago Tribune,* January 16, 1876; *Biographical Directory of the United States Congress* at http://bioguide.congress.gov/scripts/biodisplay.pl?index=C000607; *New York Daily Reformer* (Watertown, New York), July 22, 1863.

190. Phisterer, *New York in the War of the Rebellion* (1912), 1:795; P. C. Headley, *Public Men of Today: Being Biographies of the President of the United States* ...(Hartford: S. S. Scranton, 1882), 436; *Plain Dealer* (Canton, New York), October 12, 1881.

191. *Official Records,* ser. 1, 27, pt. 2:965.

192. July-August 1863 muster rolls of the 3rd New York Cavalry show that a number of men were detailed with "Allis' Regimental Howitzer Battery".

193. Phisterer, *New York in the War of the Rebellion* (1912), 1:788; *Official Records,* ser. 1, 18:390.

194. *Utica* (N.Y) *Morning Herald,* August 4, 1863.

195. David A. Norris, "Confederate Gunners Affectionately Called Their Hard-working Little Mountain Howitzers 'Bull Pups'", *America's Civil War,* September 1995.

196. David A. Norris, "Confederate Gunners Affectionately Called Their Hard-working Little Mountain Howitzers 'Bull Pups'".

197. United States Surgeon General's Office, *Medical and Surgical History of the Civil War* (Washington, D. C.: U. S. Government Printing Office, 1875-1888), 10: 626; Wellington to Mother, September 5, 1863, Gleason Wellington Correspondence; Thomas J. Cummins and Thomas Dunphy, *Remarkable Trials of All Countries with the Evidence and Speeches of Counsel, Court Scenes, Incidents, & c. Compiled Military from Original Sources. Vol. II.* (New York: S. S. Peloubet & Company, 1882): 288.

198. H. A. Cooley to Father, July 26, 1863, Herbert Arthur Cooley Papers, #2431, Southern Historical Collection, Wilson Library, University of North Carolina at Chapel Hill.

199. Undated clipping, *Republican Advocate* (Batavia, New York), 3rd Regiment Cavalry, NY Volunteers Civil War Newspaper Clippings ... URL: http://www.dmna.state.ny.us/historic/reghist/civil/cavalry/3rdCav/3rdCavCWN.htm

200. Gleason Wellington to Dear Mother, June 28, 1863; September 5, 1863, Gleason Wellington Correspondence.

201. *New York Herald,* July 26, 1863; *Official Records,* ser. 1, 27, pt. 2:964-965; H. A. Cooley to Father, July 26, 1863, Herbert Arthur Cooley Papers.

202. Undated clipping, *Republican Advocate* (Batavia, New York), 3rd Regiment Cavalry, NY Volunteers Civil War Newspaper Clippings ... URL: http://www.dmna.state.ny.us/historic/reghist/civil/cavalry/3rdCav/3rdCavCWN.htm

Chapter 7

203. H. A. Cooley to Father, July 26, 1863, Herbert Arthur Cooley Papers; Undated clipping, *Republican Advocate* (Batavia, New York), 3rd Regiment Cavalry, NY Volunteers Civil War Newspaper Clippings ... URL: http://www.dmna.state.ny.us/historic/reghist/civil/cavalry/3rdCav/3rdCavCWN.htm.

204. *Buffalo* (N.Y.) *Express,* October 16, 1895; *Western Democrat,* July 28, 1863.
205. *Western Democrat,* July 28, 1863.
206. *Western Democrat,* July 28, 1863.
207. *State Journal* (Raleigh), July 29, 1863; *Greensboro Patriot,* July 23, 1863; *Field Map of Lieut. Koerners' Military Survey between Neuse and Tar Rivers, North Carolina* (Raleigh: North Carolina Office of Archives and History, c. 1863, reprint, n. d.); John G. Duncan, *Pitt County Potpourri* (Greenville, North Carolina: East Carolina College Library, 1966).
208. Elizabeth Copeland, ed., *Chronicles of Pitt County* (Greenville, NC: Pitt County Historical Society, 1982): 115.
209. *North Carolina Troops,* 3:84; Undated clipping, 3rd Regiment Cavalry, NY Volunteers Civil War Newspaper Clippings ... URL: http://www.dmna.state.ny.us/historic/reghist/civil/cavalry/3rdCav/3rdCavCWN.htm. Whitford's unit was officially designated as 1st Battalion, North Carolina Local Defense Troops. On January 8, 1864, the unit was re-designated as the 67th North Carolina Infantry. In this book, I will follow the unofficial but commonly used designation, Whitford's Battalion.
210. *Herald* (New York), July 27, 1863; *Buffalo Express,* October 16, 1895.
211. *Official Records,* ser. 1, 27, pt. 2:965
212. King, *Sketches of Pitt County,* 141.
213. *Western Democrat,* July 28, 1863.
214. *Population of the United States in 1860 Compiled Military from the Original Returns of the Eighth Census* (Washington, Government Printing Office, 1864); King, *Sketches of Pitt County,* 114.
215. King, *Sketches of Pitt County,* 114; Michael Cotter, ed., with Kate Ohno and Mary Hollis Barnes, *The Architectural Heritage of Greenville* (Greenville, North Carolina: Greenville Area Preservation Association, 1988), 4-7, 11.
216. *Daily Progress,* March 15, 1864.
217. Michael Cotter et al, *The Architectural Heritage of Greenville, North Carolina,* 5, 10; *Wilson Ledger* (Wilson, North Carolina), February 26, 1861. The Tar River bridges are marked on *Field Map of Lieut. Koerners' Military Survey between Neuse and Tar Rivers, North Carolina.*
218. Elizabeth Copeland, ed., *Chronicles of Pitt County*: 13.
219. Nancy Smith Midgette, "Forgotten Hero", Our *State,* May 1999; *Official Records,* ser. 1, 18:1064, 1089.
220. *The State* (Columbia, South Carolina), January 27, 1895; *Macon Daily Telegraph,* November 11, 1907.
221. *Official Records,* Series I, 18: 1064, 1089; 27, (pt. 2): 898-899; Clark, *Histories of the Regiments* Clark Clark, III: 173; *Daily Reflector* (Greenville, North Carolina), February 25, 1960.
222. *Official Records,* ser. 1, 27, pt. 2:965; *Buffalo Express,* October 16, 1895.
223. H. A. Cooley to Father, July 26, 1863, Herbert Arthur Cooley Papers.
224. *Buffalo Express* (Buffalo, New York), October 16, 1895.
225. Undated clipping, 3rd Regiment Cavalry, NY Volunteers Civil War Newspaper Clippings ... URL: http://www.dmna.state.ny.us/historic/reghist/civil/cavalry/3rdCav/3rdCavCWN.htm

226. *New York Times,* August 5, 1863; Undated clipping, *Republican Advocate* (Batavia, New York), 3rd Regiment Cavalry, NY Volunteers Civil War Newspaper Clippings ... URL: http://www.dmna.state.ny.us/historic/reghist/civil/cavalry/3rdCav/3rdCavCWN.htm.
227. *New York Times,* August 5, 1863.
228. Undated clipping, 3rd Regiment Cavalry, NY Volunteers Civil War Newspaper Clippings ... URL: http://www.dmna.state.ny.us/historic/reghist/civil/cavalry/3rdCav/3rdCavCWN.htm.
229. Rowland M. Hall to Father, August 1, 1863, Julia Ward Stickley Papers.
230. Gleason Wellington to Mother, July 16, 1863, Gleason Wellington Correspondence, New York.
231. Maj. William Demill, Compiled Military Service Records of Confederate General and Staff Officers, and Non-regimental Enlisted Men, Record Group 109, National Archives.
232. Loy, Ursula Fogleman and Worthy, Pauline Marion, *Washington On The Pamlico* (Washington, N.C.: Washington-Beaufort County Bicentennial Commission, 1976) 253, 441-442.
233. *Wilmington Journal,* July 30, 1863; *State Journal (Weekly),* November 26, 1862; *Daily Progress,* August 20, 1863. In 1860, Dr. William J. Blow (1818-1864), was a physician living in Greenville. He was appointed as surgeon of the 27th North Carolina "on or about October 8, 1862", but was "dropped" on April 22, 1862, "by reason of 'having refused to appear for examination before the Medical Board at Goldsboro.'" *North Carolina Troops,* 8:8; Eighth Census of the United States, 1860: Pitt County, North Carolina.
234. *Wilmington Journal,* July 30, 1863.
235. James H. Jackson, 2nd North Carolina Artillery, Compiled Military Service File, Record Group 109, National Archives; Tenth Census of the United States, 1880: Pitt County, North Carolina; *Eastern Reflector* (Greenville, North Carolina), April 22, 1891.
236. Mrs. P. Atkinson to Zebulon B. Vance, July 28, 1863, Zebulon B. Vance, Governors' Papers, North Carolina Department of Archives and History, Raleigh.
237. Oren T. Wooster to Dear Mother, July 25, 1863, on the Twelfth New York Cavalry Page at http://web.cortland.edu/woosterk/ltr_toc.html.
238. *Herald* (New York), July 27, 1863.
239. *Official Records,* ser. 1, 27, pt. 2:965; King, *Sketches of Pitt County,* 141; John G. Smith, "The Tarboro Raid", *Carolina and the Southern Cross,* February 1914, 251. The *Utica Morning Herald and Daily Gazette,* August 5, 1863 also states that the bridge was burned.
240. King, *Sketches of Pitt County,* 141; Oren T. Wooster to Dear Mother, July 25, 1863, Twelfth New York Cavalry Page.
241. *Official Records,* ser. 1, 27, pt. 2:965; King, *Sketches of Pitt County,* 138; Mrs. P. Atkinson to Zebulon B. Vance, July 28, 1863, Zebulon B. Vance, Governors' Papers.
242. *Western Democrat,* July 28, 1863.
243. Kenelm Lewis to Wife, July 27, 1863, Lewis Family Papers #427; Southern Historical Collection, Wilson Library, University of North Carolina at Chapel Hill.
244. *Official Records,* ser. 1, 27, pt. 2:972.
245. Henry T. King, *Sketches of Pitt County,* 189.

246. Timothy Copeland to author, e-mail, November 4, 2006.
247. Mrs. P. Atkinson to Zebulon B. Vance, July 28, 1863, Zebulon B. Vance, Governors' Papers.
248. Rowland M. Hall to Father, August 1, 1863, Julia Ward Stickley Papers; William S. Powell, *The North Carolina Gazetteer* (Chapel Hill: University of North Carolina Press, 1968), 362, 468; *Spirit of the Age* (Raleigh), July 27, 1863.
249. H. A. Cooley to Father, July 26, 1863, Herbert Arthur Cooley Papers.

Chapter 8

250. *Official Records*, ser. 1, 27, pt. 2:976.
251. *Official Records*, ser. 1, 27, pt. 2:976.
252. *Official Records*, ser. 1, 27, pt. 2:968.
253. *Official Records*, ser. 1, 27, pt. 2:976; *Western Democrat*, July 28, 1863.
254. *Official Records*, ser. 1, 27, pt. 2:976; U. S. Naval Observatory, "Complete Sun and Moon Data for One Day" at http://aa.usno.navy.mil/data/docs/RS_OneDay.html.
255 Richard C. Mattson, *History and Architecture of Nash County, North Carolina* (Nashville, North Carolina: Nash County Planning Department, 1987), 49.
256. *Herald* (New York), July 27, 1863.
257. *Herald* (New York), July 27, 1863; *Wilmington Journal,* July 30, 1863; Deborah Virginia Bonner Warren to Dear Daughter, July 21, 1863, Edward Jenner Warren Papers, #3692, Folder 8, Southern Historical Collection, Wilson Library, University of North Carolina at Chapel Hill.
258. *New York Times,* August 5, 1863; *Western Democrat*, July 28, 1863. The author has been unable to determine the names of the soldiers who were captured at the hotel.
259. William T. Dupree, 13th North Carolina Infantry, Compiled Military Service File, Record Group 109, National Archives.
260. Eighth Census of the United States, 1860: New Hanover, North Carolina; *North Carolina Troops 1861-65,* 4:408; Hugh Buckner Johnston (comp.), *Records of the Wilson Confederate Hospital* (Wilson, N. C., 1954):33.
261. *Wilmington Journal,* July 30, 1863; Deborah Virginia Bonner Warren to Dear Daughter, July 21, 1863, Edward Jenner Warren Papers, #3692.
262. *Wilmington Journal,* July 30, 1863.
263. *Fayetteville Observer* (Semi-weekly, Fayetteville, North Carolina), April 9, 1863.
264. *Richmond Whig,* July 23, 1863; *Official Records,* ser. 1, 27, pt. 2:968.
265. *New York Times,* August 5, 1863; *Official Records,* ser. 1, 27, pt. 2:968-969; Rowland M. Hall, Manuscript history of the 3rd New York Cavalry, Julia Ward Stickley Papers, Private Collections, North Carolina Department of Archives and History, Raleigh; Private George White, Co. A, 3rd New York Cavalry, Compiled Military Service File, Record Group 94, National Archives.
266. *Utica Morning Herald and Daily Gazette*, August 5, 1863; *New York Times,* August 5, 1863; Rowland M. Hall, manuscript history of the 3rd New York Cavalry, Julia Ward Stickley Papers; Private George White, 3rd New York Cavalry, Compiled Military Service File, Record Group 94, National Archives.
267. Lydia Minturn Post, ed., *Soldiers' Letters, From Camps, Battle-fields, and Prisons* ... (New York: Bunce & Huntington, 1865), 278.

268. See list of Confederate prisoners in Appendix II.
269. *Daily Progress,* July 23, 1863; *Weekly Recorder* (Fayetteville, New York), November 5, 1892.
270. *Weekly Recorder*, November 5, 1892.
271. *Wilmington Journal,* July 30, 1863.
272. Rowland M. Hall, Manuscript history of the 3rd New York Cavalry, Julia Ward Stickley Papers; Undated clipping, 3rd Regiment Cavalry, NY Volunteers Civil War Newspaper Clippings ... URL: http://www.dmna.state.ny.us/historic/reghist/civil/cavalry/3rdCav/3rdCavCWN.htm.
273. *Daily Progress,* July 23, 1863; *Western Democrat,* August 11, 1863.
274. *Official Records,* ser. 3, 5:35; E. P Alexander, *Iron Horses: American Locomotives 1829-1900.* (New York: Dover Publications, 2003), 233.
275. *Oneonta Daily Star* (Oneonta, New York), November 11, 1930.
276. Alfred Holcombe to Brother, July 21, 1863, United States Army Military History Institute; *Official Records,* ser. 1, 27, pt. 2:863; Mrs. P. Atkinson to Zebulon B. Vance, July 28, 1863, Zebulon B. Vance, Governors' Papers.
277. *Official Records,* ser. 1, 27, pt. 2:863; *Daily Progress,* July 23, 1863.
278. *Western Democrat,* July 28, 1863.
279. H. C. Kearney, "Fifteenth Regiment", *Histories of the Regiments* 1:733; *Western Democrat,* July 28, 1863.
280. *Western Democrat,* July 28, 1863.
281. *Western Democrat,* July 28, 1863.
282. *Official Records,* ser. 1, 27, pt. 2:968; *Herald* (New York), July 27, 1863.
283. Monika S. Fleming, *Echoes of Edgecombe County, 1860-1940* (Dover, New Hampshire: Arcadia Publishing, 1996), 8-9.
284. *North Carolina Standard*, April 11, 1860.
285. *Wilmington Journal*, February 19, 1869.
286. *Wilmington Journal*, July 27, 1867; February 19, 1869.
287. *Wilmington Journal*, February 19, 1869; Rowland M. Hall, Manuscript history of the 3rd New York Cavalry, Julia Ward Stickley Papers; *Herald* (New York), July 27, 1863
288. Richard C. Mattson, *History and Architecture of Nash County, North Carolina* (Nashville, North Carolina: Nash County Planning Department, 1987), 297-298; Eighth Census of the United States, 1860: Nash County, North Carolina.
289. *Western Democrat,* July 28, 1863
290. *State Journal*, July 29, July 30, 1863; *Wilmington Journal*, July 30, 1863; *Daily Progress*, July 23, 1863, August 5, 1863.
291. *Raleigh Register,* July 25, 1863; *Richmond Sentinel*, November 4, 1863.
292. *Western Democrat,* August 11, 1863; *Daily Progress,* July 23, 1863.
293. Finding aid to the Lewis Family Papers at Southern Historical Collection, Wilson Library, University of North Carolina at Chapel Hill, http://www.lib.unc.edu/mss/inv/htm/00427.html ; Helen R. Watson, "A Bright Future for Stonewall", *The State*, November 1971.
294. *Western Democrat,* July 28, 1863
295. Kenelm Lewis to Wife, July 27, 1863, Lewis Family Papers; Slave Schedule, Eighth Census of the United States, 1860: Edgecombe County, North Carolina.

296. *Official Records,* series 1, 27, pt. 2:968; *Herald* (New York), July 27, 1863.
297. *Official Records,* series 1, 27, pt. 2:968; Lydia Minturn Post, ed., *Soldiers' Letters, From Camps, Battle-fields, and Prisons ...,* 278.
298. 3rd Regiment Cavalry, NY Volunteers Civil War Newspaper Clippings ... URL: http://www.dmna.state.ny.us/historic/reghist/civil/cavalry/3rdCav/3rdCavCWN.htm
299. Deborah Virginia Bonner Warren to Dear Daughter, July 21, 1863, Edward Jenner Warren Papers, #3692.
300. *Official Records,* ser. 1, 27, pt. 2:968; *Western Democrat,* July 28, Aug. 11, 1863; Kenelm Lewis to Wife, July 27, 1863, Lewis Family Papers; Warner, *Generals in Gray,* 64-65. Cox's Brigade is often credited with firing the last shots of Lee's Army of Northern Virginia at the Battle of Appomattox. Before his death in 1919, Cox was one of the last surviving Confederate generals.
301. T. E. Ricks, ed., *Nash County Historical Notes: A Bicentennial Tribute* (Rocky Mount, North Carolina: Nash County Historical Society, 1976), 96.
302. *Wilmington Journal,* July 30, 1863.
303. *Wilmington Journal,* July 30, 1863.
304. Western Democrat , Aug. 11, 1863; *Daily Progress,* July 23, 1863; Kenelm Lewis to Wife, July 27, 1863, Lewis Family Papers.
305. Deborah Virginia Bonner Warren to Dear Daughter, July 21, 1863, Edward Jenner Warren Papers.
306. A. J. Battle to Zebulon Vance, July 29, 1863, Zebulon B. Vance, Governors' Papers.
307. S. S. Satchwell to Surgeon Graves, July 24, 1863, William A. Holt Papers, #2516, Southern Historical Collection, Wilson Library, University of North Carolina at Chapel Hill.
308. S. S. Satchwell to Surgeon Graves, July 24, 1863, William A. Holt Papers.
309. S. S. Satchwell to Surgeon Graves, July 24, 1863, William A. Holt Papers; Deborah Virginia Bonner Warren to Dear Daughter, July 21, 1863, Edward Jenner Warren Papers.
310. S. S. Satchwell to Surgeon Graves, July 24, 1863, William A. Holt Papers.
311. J. W. Sanders, "Tenth Regiment (same Companies)", in Clark, *Histories of the Regiments* Clark, 3:524. See also Chapter 1 of this book.
312. S. S. Satchwell to Surgeon Graves, July 24, 1863, William A. Holt Papers.
313. *Official Records,* ser. 1, 27, pt. 2:976.

Chapter 9

314. *Population of the United States in 1860 Compiled Military from the Original Returns of the Eighth Census* (Washington, Government Printing Office, 1864).
315. *Tarboro Southerner* , June 3, 1869; May 11, 1871; April 4,1872; Gaston Lichtenstein, *Recollections of My Teacher Frank S. Wilkinson By Gaston Lichtenstein. Reprinted from The Daily Southerner, Tarboro', North Carolina.* (Richmond: Masonic Home Press, 1953), 2.
316. *Tarboro Southerner,* May 3, 1862.
317. *Tarboro Southerner,* June 3, 1869; May 11, 1871; April 4, 1872.
318. *Tarboro Southerner,* May 3, 1862.
319. Warner, *Generals in Gray,* 233-234.

320. W. H. Graves, *A True Narrative of the Incidents Which Happened in the Life of W. H. Graves*, Colorado Historical Society, Denver, Colorado, 114; Gleason Wellington to Mother, Sept. 6, 1863, Gleason Wellington Correspondence.
321. H. A. Cooley to Father, July 26, 1863, Herbert Arthur Cooley Papers.
322. Henry T. Clark to Governor Vance, December 30, 1863, Zebulon B. Vance, Governors Papers.
323. Fort Branch has been restored and is open for visitors. The original guns of the fort were pushed over the cliff into the Roanoke River in 1865. Most of the guns were later recovered and can be seen at the fort today. See the Fort Branch Battlefield Commission website at http://www.fortbranchcivilwarsite.com/commissary/index.htm
324. Henry T. Clark to Governor Vance, December 30, 1863, Zebulon B. Vance, Governors Papers; Krick, *Lee's Colonels: A Biographical Register of the Field Officers of the Army of Northern Virginia*, 227, 265.
325. *North Carolina Troops 1861-65,* 2:201-202.
326. *North Carolina Troops 1861-65,* 2:201-202.
327. *Greensboro Patriot,* July 23, 1863.
328. Kennedy and Parker, "Seventy-fifth Regiment (Seventh Cavalry)", in Clark, *Histories of the Regiments*, 4:73-74, 77; Henry T. Clark to Governor Vance, Dec. 30, 1863, Zebulon B. Vance, Governors Papers; Roland Taylor, ed., *Mabrey Bass's Tarboro: from 1950 to 1990: Including Twenty-two Articles of Historical Interest by Dr. Spencer P. Bass* (Fuquay-Varina, North Carolina: Research Triangle Publishing, 1997), 429; *Greensboro Patriot,* July 23, 1863; *State Journal*, August 5, 1863.
329. Eighth Census of the United States, 1860: Edgecombe County, North Carolina. My thanks to Monika S. Fleming for information about the approximate location of the school house.
330. *Western Democrat*, August 11, 1863.
331. W. H. Graves, *A True Narrative of the Incidents Which Happened in the Life of W. H. .Graves*, 114; *Utica Morning Herald and Daily Gazette*, August 5, 1863; Jo Webb, "Troops Raided Tarboro, 1863 Recollections of Raid Given by Local Resident", *Lines and Pathways of Edgecombe,* May 1997:10.
332. *Herald* (New York), July 27, 1863; *Official Records,* ser. 1, 27, pt. 2:956, 972; Bennett P. Jenkins, 7th Confederate Cavalry, Compiled Military Service File, Record Group 94, National Archives.
333. Gary Carnell Mercer, *The Administration of Governor Henry Toole Clark* (Thesis, East Carolina University, 1965), 77.
334. *State Journal*, August 5, August 12, 1863.
335. *Official Records,* ser. 1, 27, pt. 2:972.
336. Jo Webb, "Troops Raided Tarboro, 1863 ..." 10.
337. *Official Records,* ser. 1, 27, pt. 2:969.
338. Richard Irby, *Historical Sketch of the Nottoway Grays: Afterwards Company G, Eighteenth Virginia Regiment, Army of Northern Virginia* (Richmond: J. W. Fergusson and Son, 1878), 24-25.
339. Jo Webb, "Troops Raided Tarboro, 1863 ..."10; *Official Records,* ser. 1, 27, pt. 2:969.
340. *Official Records,* ser. 1, 27, pt. 2:973.
341. *Fayetteville Observer,* April 16, 1863.

342. *Official Records,* ser. 1, 29, pt. 2:71; *North State Whig* (Washington, NC), Sept. 21, 1853; John Myers & Son, Confederate Papers Relating to Citizens or Business Firms, 1861-65, National Archives.
343. David Stick, *Outer Banks of North Carolina* (Chapel Hill: University of North Carolina Press, 1958), 280. Richard W. Lawrence of the Underwater Archaeology Unit, Division of Archives and History, provided some useful information on the *Oregon/Colonel Hill,* letter to author, May 9, 1990.
344. Stick, *Outer Banks of North Carolina,* 280; *Official Records,* ser. 1, 29, pt. 2:71. A report by the U. S. Army Corps of Engineers, which removed the wreck of a steamboat near Tarboro years after the war, named the boat as the *Oregon.* ("Surveys of Certain Rivers in Virginia and North Carolina", House Executive Document No. 68, Feb. 5, 1878, 45th Congress, 3rd Session, Vol. XVI.)
345. *Official Records,* ser. 1, 27, pt. 2:972; Roland Taylor, ed., *Mabry Bass's Tarboro,* 429; Clark, Clark, *Histories of the Regiments* Clark IV, 78-79.
346. Kennedy and Parker, "Seventy-fifth Regiment (Seventh Cavalry)", in Clark, *Histories of the Regiments,* 4:78-79; John G. Smith, "The Tarboro Raid", *Carolina and the Southern Cross,* February 1914, 250.
347. *Official Records,* ser. 1, 27, pt. 2:972.
348. Undated newspaper clipping at 12th Regiment Cavalry, NY Volunteers, Civil War Newspaper Clippings at the Unit History Project, New York State Military Museum and Veterans Research Center, New York State Division of Military and Naval Affairs; URL: http://www.dmna.state.ny.us/historic/reghist/civil/cavalry/12thCav/12thCavCWN.htm.
349. W. H. Graves, *A True Narrative of the Incidents Which Happened in the Life of W. H. Graves,* 115.
350. *Official Records,* ser. 1, 27, pt. 2:972; David A. Norris, "The Gallant but Ill-fated 12th New York Cavalry Paid a Steep Price for its Fidelity to the Union", *America's Civil War,* January 1997.
351. *Herald* (New York), July 27, 1863; *State Journal,* August 12, 1863; Monika S. Fleming, *Echoes of Edgecombe County, North Carolina,* 12.
352. W. H Spencer to D. M. Fowle, August 22 [1863], Records of the Quartermaster Department, CSA, Military Collection, Civil War Section, North Carolina State Archives; *North Carolina Troops* 1:718.
353. *Western Democrat,* August 11, 1863; *State Journal,* Aug. 12, 1863; Eighth Census of the United States, 1860: Edgecombe County, North Carolina.
354. Eighth Census of the United States, 1860: Edgecombe County, North Carolina; *Official Records,* ser. 1, 29, pt. 2:71; Michael Cohen File, Confederate Papers Relating to Citizens or Business Firms, 1861-65, National Archives.
355. *North Carolina Times* (New Bern), July 11, 1864; *Official Records,* ser. 1, 29, pt. 2:71.
356. *Official Records (Navies),* ser. 1, 9:164.
357. *Official Records (Navies),* ser. 1, 9:164.
358. *State Journal,* Aug. 12, 1863.
359. Jo Webb, "Troops Raided Tarboro, 1863 …":10.
360. *State Journal,* Aug. 5, Aug. 12, 1863.
361. *State Journal,* Aug. 5, Aug. 12, 1863.
362. *State Journal,* August 12, 1863.

363. Kenelm Lewis to Wife, July 27, 1863, Lewis Family Papers.
364. *Carolina Watchman,* July 27, 1863.
365. *State Journal,* August 5, 1863.
366. *State Journal,* August 12, 1863; *Tarboro Southerner,* May 3, 1862; Eighth Census of the United States, 1860: Edgecombe County, North Carolina.
367. *State Journal,* August 12, 1863.
368. *Tarboro Southerner,* Nov. 14, 1863; *North Carolina County Court Minutes (Edgecombe County) 1757-1868.* Three rolls, microfilm. Reel 3, 1857-1868. (Raleigh: North Carolina Department of Archives and History, 1961); *North Carolina Standard,* December 16, 1863.
369. George Howard to Wife, July 22, 1863, George Howard Papers; *Tarboro Southerner,* May 3, 1862.
370. *State Journal,* August 5, August 12, 1863.
371. Lydia Minturn Post, ed., *Soldiers' Letters, From Camps, Battle-fields, and Prisons* ..., 278.

Chapter 10

372. Eugene Viverette, "The Skirmish at Daniel's Schoolhouse", *The Connector,* Fall, 1998:5.
373. Kennedy and Parker, "Seventy-fifth Regiment (Seventh Cavalry)", in Clark, *Histories of the Regiments,* 4:78; John G. Smith, "The Tarboro Raid", *Carolina and the Southern Cross,* February 1914, 251.
374. Undated newspaper clipping at 12th Regiment Cavalry, NY Volunteers Civil War Newspaper Clippings ... URL: http://www.dmna.state.ny.us/historic/reghist/civil/cavalry/12thCav/12thCavCWN.htm; W. H. Graves, *A True Narrative of the Incidents Which Happened in the Life of W. H. Graves,* 115.
375. *Official Records,* ser. 1, 27, pt. 2:972.
376. H. A. Cooley to Father, July 26, 1863, Herbert Arthur Cooley Papers; *Official Records,* ser. 1, 27, pt. 2:972; Kennedy and Parker, "Seventy-fifth Regiment (Seventh Cavalry)", in Clark, *Histories of the Regiments,* 4:79. A receipt for 1000 rounds of .58 caliber ammunition is in W. A. Thompson, Company C, 62nd Georgia Cavalry, Compiled Military Service File, Record Group 109, National Archives. A few weeks before at a skirmish at Red Hill, near Washington, North Carolina, some of Kennedy's men had been armed with shotguns. (Kennedy and Parker, "Seventy-fifth Regiment (Seventh Cavalry)", in Clark, *Histories of the Regiments,* 4:75).
377. *Official Records,* 1, 27, pt. 2:972; New York State Military Museum, Undated newspaper clipping at 12th Regiment Cavalry, NY Volunteers Civil War Newspaper Clippings ... URL: http://www.dmna.state.ny.us/historic/reghist/civil/cavalry/12thCav/12thCavCWN.htm. Kennedy and Parker, "Seventy-fifth Regiment (Seventh Cavalry)", in Clark, *Histories of the Regiments,* 4:79.
378. *Official Records,* ser. 1, 27, pt. 2:972.
379. *Official Records,* ser. 1, 27, pt. 2:972-973.
380. John G. Smith, "The Tarboro Raid", *Carolina and the Southern Cross,* February 1914, 251; Gleason Wellington to Mother, Sept. 6, 1863, Gleason Wellington Correspondence; *Commercial Times,* August 29, 1863.

381. John G. Smith, "The Tarboro Raid", *Carolina and the Southern Cross,* February 1914, 251.
382. Crisfield Johnson, *History of Oswego County, New York: with Illustrations and Biographical Sketches of Some of its Prominent Men and Pioneers* (Philadelphia: L. H. Everts, 1877), 111.
383. *State Journal*, Aug. 5, 1863; Kennedy and Parker, "Seventy-fifth Regiment (Seventh Cavalry)", in Clark, *Histories of the Regiments*, 4:79.
384. *The National Tribune* (Philadelphia), June 22, 1893.
385. *Official Records,* ser. 1, 27, pt. 2:973.
386. *Official Records,* ser. 1, 27, pt. 2:973.
387. *Official Records,* ser. 1, 27, pt. 2:973; W. H. Graves, *A True Narrative of the Incidents Which Happened in the Life of W. H. Graves*, 116-117.
388. *Official Records,* S ser. 1, 27, pt. 2:973.
389. *Official Records,* S ser. 1, 27, pt. 2:973; New York State Military Museum, Undated newspaper clipping at 12th Regiment Cavalry, NY Volunteers Civil War Newspaper Clippings ... URL: http://www.dmna.state.ny.us/historic/reghist/civil/cavalry/12thCav/12thCavCWN.htm; *Utica Saturday Globe,* April 18, 1904.
390. *Utica Daily Herald and Morning Gazette*, August 5, 1863.
391. Kennedy and Parker, "Seventy-fifth Regiment (Seventh Cavalry)", in Clark, *Histories of the Regiments,* 4:79.
392. John G. Smith, "The Tarboro Raid", *Carolina and the Southern Cross,* February 1914, 251.
393. Roland Taylor, ed., *Mabrey Bass's Tarboro,* 429.
394. Roland Taylor, ed., *Mabrey Bass's Tarboro,* 429; Eighth Census of the United States, 1860: Edgecombe County, North Carolina. My thanks to Monika S. Fleming for information about the location and fate of the school house.
395. Gleason Wellington to Mother, Sept. 6, 1863, Gleason Wellington Correspondence; *Commercial Times*, August 29, 1863; John G. Smith, "The Tarboro Raid", *Carolina and the Southern Cross,* February 1914, 251.
396. Information on these men came from their service and pension files at the National Archives.
397. *New York State Adjutant General's Office Registers of the 9, 10, 11, 12 Regiments of Cavalry, New York Volunteers, in the War of the Rebellion* (Albany, 1895), 1290; *Oswego Commercial Times*, August 8, 1863; *Herald* (New York), Sept. 14, 1863; William Thompson, 12th New York Cavalry, Federal Pension Application Records, National Archives; Alonzo Cooper, *In and Out of Rebel Prisons* (Oswego, New York: O. J. Oliphant, 1888), 256.
398. Eugene Viverette, "The Skirmish at Daniel's Schoolhouse", *The Connector,* Fall, 1998, 5.
399. Regimental Letter Book, July 1863, 12th New York Cavalry, Record Group 94, National Archives; *Western Democrat,* August 11, 1863; Kennedy and Parker, "Seventy-fifth Regiment (Seventh Cavalry)", in Clark, *Histories of the Regiments*, 4:80; John T. Kennedy, 62nd Georgia Cavalry, Compiled Military Service File, Record Group 109, National Archives.
400. *Oswego Daily Times,* April 17, 1914.

401. *State Journal*, August 5, 1863; Lt. Col. John C. Lamb to Governor Vance, July 21, 1863, Governors' Papers, Zebulon B. Vance, North Carolina Department of Archives and History, Raleigh; Lillian Henderson, ed., *Roster of the Confederate Soldiers of Georgia*, 6:297-307.
402. *Western Democrat*, August 11, 1863; Gleason Wellington to Mother, Sept. 6, 1863, Gleason Wellington Correspondence.
403. *Western Democrat*, August 11, 1863; H. A. Cooley to Father, July 26, 1863, Herbert Arthur Cooley Papers; *Official Records,* ser. 1, 27, pt. 2:970.
404. *State Journal*, August 5, 1863; *Official Records,* ser. 1, 27, pt. 2:Series I, 27 (pt. 2), 969; information on the Petersburg Artillery from Section 24, Grinnan Family Papers, Virginia Historical Society, Richmond, Virginia; Edward Graham, Capt. Edward Graham's Battery, Compiled Military Service File, Record Group 109, National Archives; *North Carolina Troops*, 2:202.
405. *State Journal*, Aug. 5, 1863; *Official Records,* ser. 1, 27, pt. 2:970; *North Carolina Troops*, 2:202; *Western Democrat*, August 11, 1863.
406. *Western Democrat*, August 11, 1863; *Official Records,* ser. 1, 27, pt. 2:970.
407. *Official Records,* ser. 1, 27, pt. 2:970.
408. *Utica Daily Herald and Morning Gazette*, August 5, 1863.
409. *Official Records,* Series I, 27 (pt. 2), 970.
410. *Western Democrat*, August 11, 1863; Norris, "The Men of the Stalwart Petersburg Artillery Served from the Beginning of the War to the End".
411. *North Carolina Troops*, 6:173, 254; *Western Democrat*, August 11, 1863
412. Asa W. Snell and Thomas W. Chesson, 17th North Carolina, Compiled Military Service Files, Record Group 109, National Archives.
413. *State Journal*, August 5, 1863; *Official Records,* ser. 1, 27, pt. 2:970.
414. *State Journal*, August 5, 1863

Chapter 11

415. *Official Records,* ser. 1, 27, pt. 2:965, 970; H. A. Cooley to Father, July 26, 1863, Herbert Arthur Cooley Papers.
416. H. A. Cooley to Father, July 26, 1863, Herbert Arthur Cooley Papers.
417. *Official Records,* ser. 1, 27, pt. 2:965; *State Journal*, August 5, 1863.
418. *Official Records,* ser. 1, 27, pt. 2:968, 970; *State Journal,* August 5, 1863; W. H. Graves, *A True Narrative of the Incidents Which Happened in the Life of W. H. Graves*, 117.
419. J. J. Woodward and George A. Otis, *Medical and Surgical History of the Civil War* (Reprint, Wilmington, North Carolina: Broadfoot Publishing Company, 1991), 10:626; *Official Records,* ser. 1, 27, pt. 2:968, 970.
420. *Herald* (New York), July 27, 1863; *Official Records,* ser. 1, 27, pt. 2:956, 972; *North Carolina Troops*; 1:437-438; 4:543. See also the list of Confederate prisoners in Appendix B of this work.
421. *Confederate Military History, a Library of Confederate States History, Written by Distinguished Men of the South, and Edited by Gen. Clement A. Evans of Georgia*. 12 vols. (Atlanta: Confederate Publishing Company, 1899), 4:598; *North Carolina Troops* 5:349; list of prisoners in Appendix II.

422. *Official Records,* ser. 1, 27, pt. 2:968, 970; *Western Democrat,* August 11, 1863.
423. H. A. Cooley to Father, July 26, 1863, Herbert Arthur Cooley Papers.
424. Kennedy and Parker, "Seventy-fifth Regiment (Seventh Cavalry)", in Clark, *Histories of the Regiments,* 4:80; Rowland M. Hall, manuscript history of the 3rd New York Cavalry, Julia Ward Stickley Papers.
425. Lydia Minturn Post, ed., *Soldiers' Letters, From Camps, Battle-fields, and Prisons,* 278.
426. Lydia Minturn Post, ed., *Soldiers' Letters, From Camps, Battle-fields, and Prisons,* 278.
427. Kennedy and Parker, "Seventy-fifth Regiment (Seventh Cavalry)", in Clark, *Histories of the Regiments,* 4:80; F. L. Bond Papers, Collection #296, East Carolina Manuscript Collection, Special Collections Department, J. Y. Joyner Library, East Carolina University, Greenville, NC, USA.; Eighth Census of the United States, 1860: Edgecombe County, North Carolina; H. H. Cunningham, *Doctors in Gray: the Confederate Medical Service* (Baton Rouge: Louisiana State University Press, 1958), 287.
428. Kennedy and Parker, "Seventy-fifth Regiment (Seventh Cavalry)", in Clark, *Histories of the Regiments,* 4:80
429. *State Journal,* July 30, 1863.
430. *State Journal,* July 30, 1863.
431. *State Journal,* July 30, 1863.
432. *Daily Progress,* August 20, 1863; *Official Records,* ser. 1, 27, pt. 2:956, 973.
433. King, *Sketches of Pitt County,* 139.
434. *Wilmington Journal,* August 27, 1863; *State Journal,* July 30, 1863.
435. *Official Records,* ser. 1, 27, pt. 2:973.
436. H. A. Cooley to Father, July 26, 1863, Herbert Arthur Cooley Papers.
437. *State Journal,* July 30, 1863.
438. *State Journal,* July 30, 1863; Alice V. D. Pierrepont, *Reuben Vaughan Kidd: Soldier of the Confederacy* (Petersburg, Virginia: privately published, 1947), 415. "Montgomery True Blues (1836-1939) Collection" description of collection, Alabama Department of Archives and History.
439. Jack Coggins, *Arms and Equipment of the Civil War* (Reprint: Broadfoot Publishing Company, Wilmington, NC, 1990): 66, 75, 77; King, *Sketches of Pitt County,* 139.
440. *Official Records,* ser. 1, 27, pt. 2:965; H. A. Cooley to Father, July 26, 1863, Herbert Arthur Cooley Papers.
441. Muster rolls for July-August 1863 are missing for the 7th Confederate Cavalry. Records for May-June 1863 and September-October 1863 place Company D at Snead's Ferry in Onslow County; Company E at Camp Jackson, near Fort Fisher, and what was left of Captain Lane's Company F was still at Kenansville. Record of Events Cards, 7th Confederate Cavalry, Record Group 109, National Archives.
442. H. A. Cooley to Father, July 26, 1863, Herbert Arthur Cooley Papers; W. H. Graves, *A True Narrative of the Incidents Which Happened in the Life of W. H. Graves,* 117.
443. *Daily Progress,* August 20, 1863; W. H. Graves, *A True Narrative of the Incidents Which Happened in the Life of W. H. Graves,* 117; Rowland M. Hall, manuscript history of the 3rd New York Cavalry, Julia Ward Stickley Papers.

444. *Daily Progress,* August 20, 1863; W. H. Graves, *A True Narrative of the Incidents Which Happened in the Life of W. H. Graves,* 117.
445. W. H. Graves, *A True Narrative of the Incidents Which Happened in the Life of W. H. Graves,* 117.
446. H. A. Cooley to Father, July 26, 1863, Herbert Arthur Cooley Papers; Phisterer, *New York in the War of the Rebellion* (1912), 2:1268.
447. King, *Sketches of Pitt County,* 139; *Chronicles of Pitt County,* 559; Stephen E. Bradley, Jr., *North Carolina Confederate Militia Officers Roster as Contained in the Adjutant-General's Officers Roster* (Wilmington: Broadfoot Publishing, 1992):44-45; Eighth Census of the United States: 1860: Pitt County, North Carolina.
448. Greg Mast, *State Troops and Volunteers: A Photographic Record of North Carolina's Civil War Soldiers,* Vol. I (Raleigh: Division of Archives and History, 1995); Barrett, *The Civil War in North Carolina,* 8, 20.
449. Oren Wooster to Dear Mother, July 25, 1863, Twelfth New York Cavalry Page.
450. *Wilmington Journal,* July 30, 1863.
451. *State Journal,* July 30, 1863; *Daily Progress* (Raleigh), August 20, 1863.
452. Lydia Minturn Post, ed., *Soldiers' Letters, From Camps, Battle-fields, and Prisons,* 278-279.
453. Rowland M. Hall, manuscript history of the 3rd New York Cavalry, Julia Ward Stickley Papers; King, *Sketches of Pitt County,* 136; *Official Records,* ser. 1, 27, pt. 2:966.
454. King, *Sketches of Pitt County,* 139; *Field Map of Lieut. Koerners' Military Survey between Neuse and Tar Rivers, North Carolina.*
455. Elizabeth Copeland, ed., *Chronicles of Pitt County,* 715.
456. *Official Records,* ser. 1, 27, pt. 2:970.
457. Undated clipping, *Republican Advocate* (Batavia, New York), 3rd Regiment Cavalry, NY Volunteers Civil War Newspaper Clippings ... URL: http://www.dmna.state.ny.us/historic/reghist/civil/cavalry/3rdCav/3rdCavCWN.htm
458. H. A. Cooley to Father, July 26, 1863, Herbert Arthur Cooley Papers.
459. *Wilmington Journal,* July 30, 1863; August 27, 1863; *Daily Progress,* August 20, 1863.
460. Eighth Census of the United States, 1860: Edgecombe County, North Carolina.
461. Lydia Minturn Post, ed., *Soldiers' Letters, From Camps, Battle-fields, and Prisons,* 279.
462. Lydia Minturn Post, ed., *Soldiers' Letters, From Camps, Battle-fields, and Prisons,* 279.
463. *Official Records,* ser. 1, 27, pt. 2:970; H. A. Cooley to Father, July 26, 1863, Herbert Arthur Cooley Papers; *Wilmington Journal,* August 27, 1863.

Chapter 12

464. *Wilmington Journal,* August 27, 1863; *Official Records,* ser. 1, 27, pt. 2:966.
465. Lydia Minturn Post, ed., *Soldiers' Letters, From Camps, Battle-fields, and Prisons,* 279.
466 *State Journal,* August 5, 1863.
467 *North Carolina Standard,* August 26, 1863.

468. Edward Patrick File, Barred and Disallowed Case Files of the Southern Claims Commission, NARA M1407, National Archives.
469. T. T. Dail and J. A. D. Phillips Files, Barred and Disallowed Case Files of the Southern Claims Commission, NARA M1407, National Archives. (Thanks to Mike Edge for steering me toward these Greene County claims.)
470. U.S. Congress. House *Serial Set Vol. No. 2028, Session Vol. No.20 47th Congress, 1st Session H.Exec.Doc. 97, An Account of the Receipts and Expenditures of the United States for the Fiscal Year Ending June 30, 1875,* 357, 361.
471. *Richmond Daily Dispatch,* July 23, 1863; *Wilmington Journal,* July 25, 1863; *Zanesville Daily Courier,* (Zanesville, Ohio), July 25, 1863.
472. Beth G. Crabtree and James W. Patton, *Journal of a Secesh Lady: The Diary of Catherine Ann Devereaux Edmondston, 1860-1866,* (Raleigh: Division of Archives and History, 1979), 436.
473. Beth G. Crabtree and James W. Patton, *Journal of a Secesh Lady: The Diary of Catherine Ann Devereaux Edmondston, 1860-1866, 436-440; Eighth Census of the United States, 1860:* Halifax County, North Carolina.
474. *Carolina Watchman,* July 27, 1863; S. S. Satchwell to Surgeon Graves, July 24, 1863, William A. Holt Papers.
475. *Spirit of the Age,* July 27, 1863.
476. *Official Records,* ser. 1, 27, pt. 3:1031, 1033.
477. General Martin to Gov. Vance (telegram), July 21, 1863, Governors Papers, Zebulon B. Vance; Record of Events, July-August 1863 Muster Roll, 42nd North Carolina, Record Group 109, National Archives.
478. General Martin to Gov. Vance (telegram), July 21, 1863, Governors Papers, Zebulon B. Vance.
479. Mike Edge to Author (e-mail), January 19, 2007.
480. Eighth Census of the United States, 1860: Pitt County, North Carolina.
481. *Utica Morning Herald and Daily Gazette,* August 5, 1863; W. H. Graves, *A True Narrative of the Incidents Which Happened in the Life of W. H. Graves,* 117.
482. *Official Records,* ser. 1, 27, pt. 2:970.
483. July-August 1863 Muster Roll, Company A, 12th New York Cavalry, Record Group 94, National Archives.
484. Robert Streaback, 1st North Carolina Union Volunteers, Compiled Military Service File, Record Group 94, National Archives; Frederick Phisterer, *New York in the War of the Rebellion* (1912), II: 781, 960, 1268.
485. Record of Events, May-June 1863 Muster Roll, Company A, 42nd North Carolina, Record Group 109, National Archives. The description of the local geography is drawn from a look at the *Field Map of Lieut. Koerners' Military Survey between Neuse and Tar Rivers, North Carolina.*
486. Powell, *The North Carolina Gazetteer: A Dictionary of Tar Heel Places,* 444.
487. *Daily Progress,* Aug. 20, 1863.
488. *Daily Progress,* August 20, 1863; *Wilmington Journal,* July 30, 1863.
489. *Daily Progress,* August 20, 1863.
490. John Dixon Davis, ed., *A Civil War Diary, January 1, 1863 - May 31, 1864 / by Sergeant Henry S. Lee, Co. B 10 Regt., Arty & Engrs, Kinston, N.C.* (Black Mountain,

North Carolina: Craggy Mountain Press, 1997), 39; Record of Events, May-June 1863 Muster Roll, Company A, 42nd North Carolina, Record Group 109, National Archives.
491. *Official Records,* ser. 1, 27, pt. 2: 966; *Daily Progress,* August 20, 1863; *Wilmington Journal,* July 30, 1863. Volume III of *North Carolina Troops 1861-1865* lists 12 men from three different companies of Whitford's Battalion who were recorded as captured at "Tarboro" on July 21, 1863. It seems likely that these entries refer to the men captured at Scuffleton during the raid on Tarboro.
492. Janet B. Hewett, ed., *Supplement to the Official Records of the Union and Confederate Armies,* serial vol. 41:693.
493. *Daily Progress,* Aug. 20, 1863; John Dixon Davis, ed., *A Civil War Diary, January 1, 1863 - May 31, 1864 / by Sergeant Henry S. Lee, Co. B 10 Regt., Arty & Engrs, Kinston, N.C.,* 39-40.
494. *Daily Progress,* Aug. 20, 1863; King, *Sketches of Pitt County*:140; *North Carolina Troops* 2:73.

Chapter 13

495. *Daily Progress,* Aug. 20, 1863; J. C. Ellington, "Fiftieth Regiment", in Clark, *Histories of the Regiments,* 3:174-175.
496. Colyer, *Brief Report of the Services Rendered by the Freed People...,* 9, 26; Frederick H. Dyer, *A Compendium of the War of the Rebellion Compiled Military and Arranged from the Official Records of the Union and Confederate Armies* ... (Des Moines, Iowa: Dyer Publishing Company, 1908), 1472; National Park Service, Civil War Sailors Index at http://www.itd.nps.gov/cwss/sailors_index.html . The latter index contains numerous African-American Union sailors from Pitt, Greene, and Edgecombe Counties, but linking particular men to Potter's Raid has not been possible.
497. Kenelm Lewis to Wife, July 27, 1863, Lewis Family Papers; G. H. Brown to Wife, July 25, 1863, William Howard Hooker Collection: Martha Gregory Brown Family Papers, 1862-1865. (Manuscript Collection #472.004), East Carolina Manuscript Collection, Special Collections Department, J. Y. Joyner Library, East Carolina University, Greenville, NC, USA. The 1890 census of Union Civil War veterans in North Carolina contains a listing in Belvoir Township, Pitt County, for "Martha widow of Ephraim Foman [Foreman?]", however, instead of listing a regiment or date of enlistment, there is a notation reading "No information to be gained." Eleventh Census of the United States, 1890 Civil War Veterans Census: Pitt County, North Carolina.
498. Kenelm Lewis to Wife, July 27, 1863, Lewis Family Papers.
499. For example, the *Western Democrat,* July 28, Aug. 11, 1863.
500. George Howard to Wife, July 22, 1863, George Howard Papers; *Western Democrat,* July 28, 1863; King, *Sketches of Pitt County,* 139.
501. *Western Democrat,* July 28, 1863.
502. *Official Records,* ser. 1, 27, pt. 2:970.
503. H. A. Cooley to Father, July 26, 1863, Herbert Arthur Cooley Papers.
504. J. C. Ellington, "Fiftieth Regiment", in Clark, *Histories of the Regiments,* 3:174.
505. J. C. Ellington, "Fiftieth Regiment", in Clark, *Histories of the Regiments,* 3:175; King, *Sketches of Pitt County,* 140.

506. J. C. Ellington, "Fiftieth Regiment", in Clark, *Histories of the Regiments,* 3:175; David A. Norris, "Black Union Soldiers of North Carolina", *The State*, December 1993.
507. J. C. Ellington, "Fiftieth Regiment", in Clark, *Histories of the Regiments,* 3:175; *Daily Progress,* July 29, 1863; *Western Democrat,* July 28, 1863; undated clipping from the *Republican Advocate* (Batavia, New York), 3rd Regiment Cavalry, NY Volunteers Civil War Newspaper Clippings ... URL: http://www.dmna.state.ny.us/historic/reghist/civil/cavalry/3rdCav/3rdCavCWN.htm.
508. *State Journal,* July 29, 1863; Aug. 4, 1863.
509. *Official Records,* ser. 1, 27, pt. 2:970.
510. *Western Democrat,* July 28, 1863; Kenelm Lewis to Wife, July 27, 1863, Lewis Family Papers; John Dixon Davis, ed., *A Civil War Diary, January 1, 1863 - May 31, 1864 / by Sergeant Henry S. Lee, Co. B 10 Regt., Arty & Engrs, Kinston, N.C.,* 40; *State Journal,* July 29, 1863.
511. *State Journal,* July 29, Aug. 5, 1863; G. H. Brown to Wife, July 25, 1863, William Howard Hooker Collection: Martha Gregory Brown Family Papers.
512. J. C. Ellington, "Fiftieth Regiment", in Clark, *Histories of the Regiments,* 3:175.
513. J. C. Ellington, "Fiftieth Regiment", in Clark, *Histories of the Regiments,* 3:174; *Wilmington Journal,* Aug. 27, 1863.
514. H. A. Cooley to Father, July 26, 1863, Herbert Arthur Cooley Papers.
515. *Field Map of Lieut. Koerners' Military Survey between Neuse and Tar Rivers, North Carolina.*
516. H. A. Cooley to Father, July 26, 1863, Herbert Arthur Cooley Papers; *Wilmington Journal,* Sept. 3, 1863.
517. Undated clipping from the *Union and Advertiser* (Rochester, New York), 3rd Regiment Cavalry, NY Volunteers Civil War Newspaper Clippings ... URL: http://www.dmna.state.ny.us/historic/reghist/civil/cavalry/3rdCav/3rdCavCWN.htm.
518. *Field Map of Lieut. Koerners' Military Survey between Neuse and Tar Rivers, North Carolina.*
519. Rowland M. Hall to Father, Aug. 1, 1863, Julia Ward Stickley Papers; Barbara M. Howard Thorne, ed., *The Heritage of Craven County, North Carolina, Volume I* (New Bern: Eastern North Carolina Genealogical Society, 1984), 49; King, *Sketches of Pitt County*: 99-100; Michael Hill, ed., *Guide to North Carolina Highway Historical Markers,* 61.
520. H. A. Cooley to Father, July 26, 1863, Herbert Arthur Cooley Papers.
521. Oliver Spoor to Father, August 16, 1863, Oliver C. Spoor Papers, East Carolina Manuscript Collection, Special Collections Dept., J.Y. Joyner Library, East Carolina University, Greenville, N.C.
522. Cummins and Dunphy, *Remarkable Trials of All Countries with the Evidence and Speeches of Counsel, Court Scenes, Incidents, & c. Compiled Military from Original Sources. Vol. II,* 288.
523. H. A. Cooley to Father, July 26, 1863, Herbert Arthur Cooley Papers; Undated clipping, *Union and Advertiser* (Rochester, New York), 3rd Regiment Cavalry, NY Volunteers Civil War Newspaper Clippings ... URL: http://www.dmna.state.ny.us/historic/reghist/civil/cavalry/3rdCav/3rdCavCWN.htm.

524. W. H. Graves, *A True Narrative of the Incidents Which Happened in the Life of W. H. Graves,* 119.
525. Oren Wooster to Dear Mother, July 25, 1863, Twelfth New York Cavalry Page.
526. H. A. Cooley to Father, July 26, 1863, Herbert Arthur Cooley Papers; Rowland M. Hall, manuscript history of the 3rd New York Cavalry, Julia Ward Stickley Papers.
527. Undated clipping from the *Union and Advertiser* (Rochester, New York), 3rd Regiment Cavalry, NY Volunteers Civil War Newspaper Clippings ... URL: http://www.dmna.state.ny.us/historic/reghist/civil/cavalry/3rdCav/3rdCavCWN.htm
528. *Wilmington Journal,* Sept. 3, 1863; *Daily Progress,* July 29, 1863; *State Journal,* July 30, 1863.
529. The terrain is described from Koerner's map and modern topographic maps.
530. *Official Records,* series 1, 27, pt. 2: 969, Oliver Spoor to Father, August 16, 1863, Oliver C. Spoor Papers; *Herald* (New York), Aug. 30, 1863.
531. *New York Times,* August 26, 1863; J. J. Woodward and George A. Otis, *Medical and Surgical History of the Civil War,* 10: 560.
532. H. A. Cooley to Father, July 26, 1863, Herbert Arthur Cooley Papers.
533. Rowland M. Hall, manuscript history of the 3rd New York Cavalry, Julia Ward Stickley Papers.
534. W. H. Graves, *A True Narrative of the Incidents Which Happened in the Life of W. H. Graves,* 119-120; Undated clipping, 3rd Regiment Cavalry, NY Volunteers Civil War Newspaper Clippings ... URL: http://www.dmna.state.ny.us/historic/reghist/civil/cavalry/3rdCav/3rdCavCWN.htm.
535. Oren Wooster to Dear Mother, July 25, 1863, Twelfth New York Cavalry Page.
536. Kennedy and Parker, "Seventy-fifth Regiment (Seventh Cavalry)", in Clark, *Histories of the Regiments,* 4:81.
537. Kennedy and Parker, "Seventy-fifth Regiment (Seventh Cavalry)", in Clark, *Histories of the Regiments,* 4:81; Thomas J. Southerland, 2nd North Carolina, Compiled Military Service File, Record Group 109, National Archives; Chris E. Fonvielle, *The Wilmington Campaign: The Last Rays of Departing Hope,* 396.
538. *Official Records,* ser. 1, 27, pt. 2:971.
539. *Official Records,* ser. 1, 27, pt. 2:971.
540. *Official Records,* ser. 1, 27, pt. 2:971.
541. J. C. Ellington, "Fiftieth Regiment" in Clark, *Histories of the Regiments,* 3:176; Kennedy and Parker, "Seventy-fifth Regiment (Seventh Cavalry)", in Clark, *Histories of the Regiments,* 4:81; *Wilmington Journal,* Sept. 3, 1863. Time of sunset is drawn from the US Naval Observatory's "Complete Sun and Moon Data for One Day" at http://aa.usno.navy.mil/data/docs/RS_OneDay.html.
542. *Wilmington Journal,* Sept. 3, 1863; Kennedy and Parker, "Seventy-fifth Regiment (Seventh Cavalry)"in Clark, *Histories of the Regiments,* 4:81.
543. H. A. Cooley to Father, July 26, 1863, Herbert Arthur Cooley Papers; Undated clipping, 3rd Regiment Cavalry, NY Volunteers Civil War Newspaper Clippings ... URL: http://www.dmna.state.ny.us/historic/reghist/civil/cavalry/3rdCav/3rdCavCWN.htm.
544. *Wilmington Journal,* Sept. 3, 1863; J. C. Ellington in Clark, *Histories of the Regiments,* 3:186; Kennedy and Parker, "Seventy-fifth Regiment (Seventh Cavalry)"in Clark, *Histories of the Regiments,* 4:81.

545. J. C. Ellington, "Fiftieth Regiment" in Clark, *Histories of the Regiments*, 3:176; Kennedy and Parker, "Seventy-fifth Regiment (Seventh Cavalry)"in Clark, *Histories of the Regiments*, 4:81; John G. Smith, "The Tarboro Raid", *Carolina and the Southern Cross,* February 1914, 251; Kinchen Jahu Carpenter, *War Diary of Kinchen Jahu Carpenter Company I, Fiftieth North Carolina Regiment War Between the States, 1861-1865.*" (Rutherfordton, N.C.: 1955), 13.
546. Francis Trevelyan Miller, *The Photographic History of the Civil War* 10 vols. (New York: Review of Reviews Company, 1912), 5:223, 260; J. C. Duane, *Manual for Engineer Troops* (New York: D. Van Nostrand, 1862), 17-33.
547. H. A. Cooley to Father, July 26, 1863, Herbert Arthur Cooley Papers.
548. *Official Records,* ser. 1, 27, pt. 2:971.
549. H. A. Cooley to Father, July 26, 1863, Herbert Arthur Cooley Papers.
550. *Official Records,* ser. 1, 27, pt. 2:974.
551. H. A. Cooley to Father, July 26, 1863, Herbert Arthur Cooley Papers.

Chapter 15
552. Cummins and Dunphy, *Remarkable Trials of All Countries with the Evidence and Speeches of Counsel, Court Scenes, Incidents, & c. Compiled Military from Original Sources. Vol. II.,* 243, 287-288.
553. H. A. Cooley to Father, July 26, 1863, Herbert Arthur Cooley Papers.
554. W. H. Graves, *A True Narrative of the Incidents Which Happened in the Life of W. H. Graves*, 114; *The Palladium*, October 28, 1912.
555. Rowland M. Hall to Father, Aug. 1, 1863, Julia Ward Stickley Papers.
556. *Official Records,* series 1, 27, pt. 2:974; Oren Wooster to Dear Mother, July 25, 1863, Twelfth New York Cavalry Page.
557. July 1863 Morning Reports, Company H, 3rd New York Cavalry, Record Group 94, National Archives; Janet B. Hewett, ed., *Supplement to the Official Records of the Union and Confederate Armies,* serial vol. 41:693, 42:187-188.
558. Rowland M. Hall to Father, Aug. 1, 1863, Julia Ward Stickley Papers.
559. *Official Records,* ser. 1, 27, pt. 2:966.
560. *Lowville Journal* (Lowville, New York), July 28, 1863; *Official Records,* ser. 1, 27, pt. 2:964; 966.
561. *Official Records,* Series I, 27 (pt. 2): 964; 966; *Herald* (New York), August 30, 1863.
562. *Utica Morning Herald and Daily Gazette*, August 5, 1863.
563. *Baltimore Sun,* July 25, 1863; *San Francisco Evening Bulletin,* July 25, 1863; *The Times* (London, England), August 7, 1863.
564. *Herald* (Melbourne, Australia), October 9, 1863.
565. Oren Wooster to Dear Mother, July 25, 1863, Twelfth New York Cavalry Page.
566. *Herald* (New York), July 24, 1863.
567. *Herald,* (New York), July 24, 1863; Rowland M. Hall to Father, July 17, 1863, Aug. 1, 1863, Julia Ward Stickley Papers; *Official Records,* ser. 1, 29, pt. 2:35.
568. George W. Lewis, 3rd New York Cavalry, Compiled Military Service Record, Record Group 94, National Archives.

569. Jessie Ames Marshall, *Private and official correspondence of Gen. Benjamin F. Butler, During the period of the Civil War ... Privately issued.* 5 vols. (Norwood, Massachusetts: Plimpton Press, 1917), 3:161.
570. Jessie Ames Marshall, *Private and official correspondence of Gen. Benjamin F. Butler, During the period of the Civil War ... Privately issued,* 3:161.
571. Jessie Ames Marshall, *Private and official correspondence of Gen. Benjamin F. Butler, During the period of the Civil War ... Privately issued,* 3:161-162.
572. Jessie Ames Marshall, *Private and official correspondence of Gen. Benjamin F. Butler, During the period of the Civil War ... Privately issued,* 3:389; 442; *State Journal,* August 12, 1863.
573. Jessie Ames Marshall, *Private and official correspondence of Gen. Benjamin F. Butler, During the period of the Civil War ... Privately issued,* 3:442.
574. Jessie Ames Marshall, *Private and official correspondence of Gen. Benjamin F. Butler, During the period of the Civil War ... Privately issue,* 3:390.   Here, Butler refers to a parable that was told by Jesus in Luke 18:1-8.

Chapter 16

575. *State Journal,* July 29, 1863, July 30, 1863; *Official Records* ser. 1, 27, pt. 2:966.
576. *State Journal,* August 5, 1863.
577. *Wilmington Journal,* July 30, 1863.
578. *Wilmington Journal,* July 21, 1863.
579. *North Carolina Standard,* August 26, 1863.
580. *North Carolina Standard,* September 9, 1863.
581. *State Journal (weekly),* August 5, 1863.
582. *Daily Progress,* Aug. 20, 1863; *State Journal,* August 5, 1863.
583. Carpenter, *War Diary of Kinchen Jahu Carpenter,* 13; James Washington, 50th North Carolina, Compiled Military Service File, Record Group 109, National Archives; *North Carolina Troops* 12:149.
584. *Daily Progress,* August 20, 1863.
585. William C. Claiborne, 7th Confederate Cavalry, Compiled Military Service File, Record Group 109, National Archives.
586. *Official Records,* ser. 1, 29, pt. 2:676; William C. Claiborne, 7th Confederate Cavalry, Compiled Military Service File, Record Group 109, National Archives.
587. Kennedy and Parker, "Seventy-fifth Regiment (Seventh Cavalry)"in Clark, *Histories of the Regiments,* 4:524.
588. William C. Claiborne, 7th Confederate Cavalry, Compiled Military Service File, Record Group 109, National Archives; United States Congress, *Pardons by the President. Message from the President of the United States, transmitting final report of the names of persons engaged in rebellion who have been pardoned by the President. December 4, 1867.* (1867), 51.
589. *Carolina Watchman,* July 27, 1863.
590. *Official Records,* ser. 1, 27, pt. 2:751.
591. Kenelm Lewis To Wife, July 27, 1863, Lewis Family Papers; Mrs. Peyton Atkinson to Zebulon Vance, July 28, 1863, Governors' Papers, Zebulon B. Vance.
592. *Daily Progress,* September 7, 1863.
593. *Official Records,* ser. 1, 17, pt. 3:1034.

594. Henry T. Clarke to Zebulon Vance, Dec. 30, 1863, Governors' Papers, Zebulon B. Vance.
595. Jesse P. Brown to Zebulon B. Vance, July 25, 1863, Governors' Papers, Zebulon B. Vance; John C. Lamb to Zebulon Vance, July 21, 1863, Governors' Papers, Zebulon B. Vance.
596. *Official Records,* ser. 1, 27, pt. 2:975.
597 Kenelm Lewis to Wife, July 27, 1863, Lewis Family Papers; *Official Records,* ser. 1, 27, pt. 2:975; *New York Times,* July 31, 1863; *Richmond Whig,* August 1, 1863.
598. *North Carolina Standard,* July 29, 1863; Warner, *Generals in Gray,* 233-234; *Fayetteville Observer,* July 27, 1863.
599. Wilmington & Weldon Railroad Annual Report, 1864; *Herald* (New York); *Philadelphia Inquirer,* July 29, 1863.
600. *Fayetteville Observer,* August 24, 1863.
601. *North Carolina County Court Minutes (Edgecombe County) 1757-1868.* Three rolls, microfilm. Reel 3, 1857-1868. Raleigh: North Carolina Department of Archives and History, 1961.
602. Kenelm Lewis to Wife, July 27, 1863, Lewis Family Papers; *State Journal,* July 29, 1863; September 3, 1863; Krick, *Staff Officers in Gray*:139.
603. Kenelm Lewis to Wife, July 27, 1863, Lewis Family Papers.
604. Kenelm Lewis to Wife, July 27, 1863, Lewis Family Papers.
605. *Herald* (New York), Oct. 15, 1863
606. G. H. Brown to Wife, July 25, 1863, William Howard Hooker Collection: Martha Gregory Brown Family Papers.
607. *Fayetteville Observer,* August 3, 1863; *Richmond Dispatch,* July 30, 1863; *Herald* (New York), Nov. 8, 1863.
608. *Herald* (New York), Nov. 8, 1863.
609. *Herald* (New York), Nov. 8, 1863.
610. *Wilmington Journal,* Aug. 6, 1863 quoting the *Petersburg Express.*
611. *Herald* (New York), Nov. 8, 1863.
612. *Oswego Daily Palladium,* July 28, 1864; Henry E. Mosher, 12th New York Cavalry, Federal Pension Application Records, National Archives.
613. Frederick Phisterer, *New York in the War of the Rebellion* (1912), II: 117; *Oswego Commercial Times* (Oswego, New York), April 21, 1865.
614. *Oswego Daily Times,* August 26, 1921; *Oswego Daily Palladium,* July 28, 1864.
615. *Dictionary of American Naval Fighting Ships* online at http://www.history.navy.mil/danfs/s11/shawsheen.htm ; *Oswego Daily Palladium,* July 28, 1864; *Oswego Commercial Advertiser,* October 25, 1864.
616. See Appendix II.
617. See Appendix II.
618. *New York Times,* July 28, 1863; August 7, 1863; Appendix II; "Roll of Prisoners of War Paroled at Fort Monroe, Va. Augt. 4, 1863", Record Group 249, National Archives.
619. Andrew Dozier, 6th Virginia Infantry, Compiled Military Service File, Record Group 109, National Archives.
620. *New York Times,* August 8, 1863.
621. Peter B. Sandbeck, *The Architectural History of New Bern and Craven County* (New Bern: Tryon Palace Commission, 1988), 421-422.

622. The petition is in Nathan M. Lawrence, 8th North Carolina Infantry, Compiled Military Service File, Record Group 109, National Archives.
623. Nathan M. Lawrence, 8th North Carolina Infantry, Compiled Military Service File, Record Group 109, National Archives.
624. Edward S. Ellis, *Low Twelve: "By Their Deeds They Shall Know Them" A Series of Striking and Truthful Incidents Illustrative of the Fidelity of Free Masons to One Another in Times of Stress and Danger* (New York: F. R. Niglutsch, 1907), 131.
625. Warner, *Generals in Blue,* 320-321; Service files of Nichols, Lawrence, and Jenkins, National Archives; *North Carolina Troops 1861-65* 15:328. The author photographed Nichols' gravesite in the Confederate Cemetery at Johnson's Island during a visit to Ohio in 1995.
626. *North Carolina Troops 1861-1865*, 3:86-90, 100-101, 106; *Official Records,* ser. 1, 29, pt. 2:36; Herald (New York), Aug. 18, 1863.

Chapter 18

627. *Official records of the Union and Confederate Navies in the War of the Rebellion*, ser. 1, 9:135-136.
628. Barrett, *The Civil War in North Carolina,* 166-167; *Official Records,* ser. 1, 27, pt. 2:980.
629. *Official Records,* ser. 1, 27, pt. 2:985-987.
630. *Official Records,* ser. 1, 27, pt. 2:980-981.
631. Barrett, *The Civil War in North Carolina,* 168.
632. David A. Norris, "Battle in the Buff", *Civil War Times*, December 1998.
633. David A. Norris, "Battle in the Buff", *Civil War Times*, December 1998.
634. *Official Records of the Union and Confederate Navies in the War of the Rebellion*, ser. 1, 9:135-136.
635. *Official Records,* ser. 1, 29, pt. 2:49.
636. *Official Records,* ser. 1, 29, pt. 2:64.
637. *Official Records of the Union and Confederate Navies in the War of the Rebellion*, ser. 1, 9:180.

Chapter 19

638. David A. Norris," The Men of the Stalwart Petersburg Artillery Served from the Beginning of the War to the End".
639. David A. Norris, "The Men of the Stalwart Petersburg Artillery Served from the Beginning of the War to the End".
640. *Petersburg Express,* July 28, 1865; *Baltimore Sun,* September 12, 1887.
641. George W. Lewis, 3rd New York Cavalry, Compiled Military Service File, Record Group 94, National Archives.
642. *Philadelphia Inquirer,* December 12, 1863.
643. Heitman, *Historical Register and Dictionary of the United States Army...,* 466.
644. *Auburn Bulletin,* (Auburn, New York), April 4, 1890; *The Times* (London, England), February 17, 1912. The National Park Service's Edison National Historic Site's Sounds page can be accessed at http://www.nps.gov/edis/edisonia/sounds.html

645. Warner, *Generals in Blue*: 380-381; Tenth Census of the United States, 1880: Morris County, New Jersey.
646. *New York Times,* March 12, 1889.
647. *House of Representatives, 54th Congress, 1st Session, House Report No. 1669, Mrs. Elfrida C. Lewis;* Ninth Census of the United States, 1870: Suffolk County, Virginia; Fourteenth Census of the United States, 1920: Suffolk County, Virginia.
648. *Dictionary of the United States Congress,* s.v., Jacobs, Ferris, Jr.
649. *Evening Courier and Republic* (Syracuse, New York), June 7, 1867.
650. *Evening Courier and Republic,* June 7, 1867.
651. *Evening Courier and Republic,* June 7, 1867.
652. *Brooklyn Daily Eagle,* June 6, 1867; *New York Times,* June 4, 1867; April 26, 1868; *Idaho Tri-Weekly Statesman,* (Boise, Idaho), February 5, 1876; *Auburn Daily Bulletin,* January 18, 1876; Cummins and Dunphy, *Remarkable Trials of All Countries with the Evidence and Speeches of Counsel, Court Scenes, Incidents, & c. Compiled Military from Original Sources. Vol. II.,* 338.
653. *Idaho Tri-Weekly Statesman,* February 5, 1876; *Auburn Daily Bulletin,* January 18, 1876.
654. Phisterer, *New York in the War of the Rebellion* (1912), 2:789-793, 797, 799, 1080.
655. Phisterer, *New York in the War of the Rebellion* (1912), 2:779; Gideon Blackman, 3rd New York Cavalry, Compiled Military Service File, Record Group 94, National Archives.
656. *New York Times,* January 31, 1902.
657. *Rochester Democrat and Chronicle,* August 25, 1911.
658. Fourteenth Census of the United States, 1920: Dutchess County, New York; *Rochester Democrat and Chronicle,* August 25, 1911; *Middletown Times-Press* (Middletown, New York), August 1, 1918; John G. Harris, 3rd New York Cavalry, Federal Pension Application Records National Archives.
659. New York State Adjutant General's Office, Civil War Muster Roll Abstracts of New York State Volunteers, United States Sharpshooters, and United States Colored Troops, [ca. 1861-1900], New York State Archives; Tenth Census of the United States, 1880 Census: Pamlico County, North Carolina; Sandra Lee Almasy, *North Carolina Civil War Veterans Census* (1990), 17; Organization Index to Pension Files of Veterans Who Served Between 1861 and 1900, database at Footnote.com.
660. Francis B. Heitman, *Historical Register and Dictionary of the United States Army* ... 467.
661. Chapter 8 of William F. Cody, *The Life and Adventures of Buffalo Bill* (1917) mentions Graham several times. Francis B. Heitman, *Historical Register and Dictionary of the United States Army* ... 467; *Colorado Banner* (Boulder, Colorado), November 11, 1875; *Denver Mirror,* October 12, 1873.
662. *Rocky Mountain News,* Sept. 10, 1873; Sept. 17, 1873.
663. *Denver Daily Times,* May 28, 1874; *Colorado Daily Chieftain* (Pueblo, Colorado), June 17, 1874; *Rocky Mountain News,* June 14, 1874; *Colorado Daily Chieftain,* October 13, 1875; *Colorado Banner,* November 11, 1875; *Denver Daily Times,* October 22, 1875; October 27, 1877.

664. Phisterer, *New York in the War of the Rebellion* (1912), 2:959; *Commercial Advertiser and Times*, January 29, 1866.
665. Phisterer, *New York in the War of the Rebellion* (1912), 2:959; *Auburn Bulletin*, February 27, 1890; *Oswego Daily Palladium,* January 4, 1894.
666. Gleason Wellington, undated note on the back of "Will" to Gleason Wellington, August 27 186[3], Gleason Wellington Correspondence.
667. Undated clipping, 12th Regiment Cavalry, NY Volunteers, Civil War Newspaper Clippings ... URL: online at http://www.dmna.state.ny.us/historic/reghist/civil/cavalry/12thCav/12thCavCWN.htm.
668. Undated clipping, 12th Regiment Cavalry, NY Volunteers, Civil War Newspaper Clippings... URL: online at http://www.dmna.state.ny.us/historic/reghist/civil/cavalry/12thCav/12thCavCWN.htm.
669. Undated clipping, 12th Regiment Cavalry, NY Volunteers, Civil War Newspaper Clippings... URL: online at http://www.dmna.state.ny.us/historic/reghist/civil/cavalry/12thCav/12thCavCWN.htm.
Alonzo Cooper, *In and Out of Rebel Prisons*: 256.
670. Cooper, *In and Out of Rebel Prisons,* 256-257; Undated clipping, 12th Regiment Cavalry, NY Volunteers, Civil War Newspaper Clippings... URL: http://www.dmna.state.ny.us/historic/reghist/civil/cavalry/12thCav/12thCavCWN.htm.
671. Undated clipping, 12th Regiment Cavalry, NY Volunteers, Civil War Newspaper Clippings... URL: http://www.dmna.state.ny.us/historic/reghist/civil/cavalry/12thCav/12thCavCWN.htm.
672. Cooper, *In and Out of Rebel Prisons,* 257; Undated clipping, 12th Regiment Cavalry NY Volunteers, Civil War Newspaper Clippings... URL: http://www.dmna.state.ny.us/historic/reghist/civil/cavalry/12thCav/12thCavCWN.htm.
673. *Commercial Advertiser and Times*, August 8, 1865; December 16, 1865.
674. *Daily Palladium*, March 29, 1866.
675. Raleigh National Cemetery page of the Veterans' Administration National Gravesite Locator, online at: http://www.cem.va.gov/nchp/raleigh.htm; Jo Webb, "Troops Raided Tarboro, 1863", *Lines and Pathways of Edgecombe,* May 1997.
676. New York State Adjutant General's Office, Civil War Muster Roll Abstracts of New York State Volunteers, United States Sharpshooters, and United States Colored Troops, [ca. 1861-1900], New York State Archives.
67.7 *Oswego Daily Times*, April 17, 1914.
678. *Dallas Morning News,* January 31, 1915.
679. *Utica Saturday Globe,* April 18, 1904.
680. Eleventh Census of the United States, Veterans' Census, 1890: Franklin County, New York; *Plattsburg Sentinel,* January 14, 1898; *Utica Saturday Globe,* April 18, 1914; *Fort Covington Sun,* September 6, 1917.
681. *Rocky Mount Mills: A Case History of Industrial Development 1818-1943* (Rocky Mount: Rocky Mount Mills, 1943); Russell Conwell Service File, 46th Massachusetts Infantry, Civil War Soldier Database at www.civilwardata.com.
682. *North Carolina Times,* June 11, 1864. A "plumber" in the 1860s would have been a mechanic or artisan.
683. *North Carolina Times,* June 11, 1864.

684. "Montgomery True Blues (1836-1939) Collection" description of collection, Alabama Department of Archives and History; *Auburn Morning Dispatch*, October 25, 1886; *Auburn Bulletin*, June 24, 1887.
685. Krick, *Lee's Colonels,* 221-222.
686. Krick, *Lee's Colonels,* 221-222.
687. William Marvel, *Andersonville: The Last Depot* (Chapel Hill, 1994), 241-242, 248; *Macon Weekly Telegraph*, January 11, 1870; March 25, 1873; Eleventh Census of the United States, Veteran's Census, 1890: Davidson County, Tennessee.
688. Krick, *Lee's Colonels:* 394.
689. Richard L. Mattson, *The History and Architecture of Nash County, North Carolina,* 274.
690. *Rocky Mount Mills, a Case History of Industrial Development, 1818-1943*, 20-21.
691. "Conserved Flags" at New York State Military Museum and Veterans Research Center, http://www.dmna.state.ny.us/historic/btlflags/electronindex.htm; Alabama Civil War Period Flag Collection, Alabama Department of Archives and History, http://www.archives.state.al.us/referenc/flags/083.html.
692. *Tarboro Southerner,* March 5, 1886; May 7, 1886.
693. *Tarboro Southerner,* March 5, 1886; May 7, 1886; June 11, 1891.
694. *Eastern Reflector* (Greenville, North Carolina), November 18, 1898; Robert E. L. Krick, *Staff Officers in Gray: A Biographical Register of the Staff Officers in the Army of Northern Virginia* (Chapel Hill: University of North Carolina Press, 2003), 70.
695. Ruth Smith Williams and Margarete Glenn Griffin, *Tombstone and Census Records of Early Edgecombe County* (Rocky Mount, 1959), 40.
696. John Smith, "The Tarboro Raid":251.
697. Lillian Henderson, comp. *Roster of the Confederate Soldiers of Georgia,* 6:304.
698. *Oswego Palladium-Times,* March 23, 1937.
699. *Oswego Palladium-Times,* June 29, 1940; Mordecai Knapp, 3rd New York Cavalry, Federal Pension Application Records, National Archives.
700. *Daily Reflector*, February 25, 1960

Appendices

701. *Daily Palladium*, March 29, 1866.
702. *Commercial Advertiser and Times*, August 8, 1865.
703. U.S. Department of Veterans' Affairs, Nationwide Gravesite Locator at http://gravelocator.cem.va.gov.
704. *Commercial Advertiser and Times* (Oswego, New York), December 16, 1865.
705. *Annual Report of the Adjutant-General of the State of New York for the Year 1894 Volume III* (Albany: 1895), 1210; *Oswego Commercial Times*, August 8, 1863.
706. Muster Roll, 12th New York Cavalry, Company A, July-August 1863, Record Group 94, National Archives.
707. Muster Roll, 12th New York Cavalry, Company A, July-August 1863, Record Group 94, National Archives; John Byard, "The Bounty Soldiers", *The Valley News,* March 9, 1995; *Oswego Times and Express,* October 17, 1883; *Pensions and increase of pensions for certain soldiers and sailors of the Civil War, etc. February 3, 1911. Serial Set Vol. No. 5843, Session Vol. No. A 61st Congress, 3rd Session S. Rpt. 1066,* 33; John Green, 12th New York Cavalry, Federal Pension Application Records, National Archives.

708. Muster Roll, 12th New York Cavalry, Company A, July-August 1863, Record Group 94, National Archives; pension file card, *Organization Index to Pension Files of Veterans Who Served Between 1861 and 1900,* National Archives.

709 Henry A. Hubbard, 12th New York Cavalry, Compiled Military Service File, Record Group 94, National Archives.

710. Henry Ephraim Mosher, 12th New York Cavalry, Federal Pension Application Records, National Archives.

711. *Annual Report of the Adjutant-General of the State of New York for the Year 1894,* 1316.

712. *Commercial Times,* January 9, 1865; *Annual Report of the Adjutant-General of the State of New York for the Year 1894, Volume III,* 1236.

713. *Oswego Daily Times,* August 26, 1921.

714. William Thompson, 12th New York Cavalry, Federal Pension Application Records, National Archives; *Annual Report of the Adjutant-General of the State of New York for the Year 1894, Volume III,* 1290; *Herald* (New York), Sept. 14, 1863; *Oswego Times and Express,* October 17, 1883.

715. *Commercial Times,* January 9, 1865.

716. *Annual Report of the Adjutant-General of the State of New York for the Year 1894, Volume III,* 1181.

717. *Annual Report of the Adjutant-General of the State of New York for the Year 1894, Volume III,* 1203.

718. *Annual Report of the Adjutant-General of the State of New York for the Year 1894, Volume III,* 1286; U.S. Department of Veterans' Affairs, Nationwide Gravesite Locator at http://gravelocator.cem.va.gov.

719. Chrisfield Johnson, *History of Oswego County, New York* (Philadelphia, 1877), 260; *Annual Report of the Adjutant-General of the State of New York for the Year 1894, Volume III,* 1286; U.S. Department of Veterans' Affairs, Nationwide Gravesite Locator at http://gravelocator.cem.va.gov.

720. Lester Taylor, 12th New York Cavalry, Federal Pension Application Records, National Archives; pension file card, *Organization Index to Pension Files of Veterans Who Served Between 1861 and 1900,* National Archives.

721. *Annual Report of the Adjutant-General of the State of New York for the Year 1894, Volume III,* 1149; Ancestry.com. *Andersonville Prisoners of War* [database on-line].

722. *Annual Report of the Adjutant-General of the State of New York for the Year 1894, Volume III,* 1242; Ancestry.com. *Andersonville Prisoners of War* [database on-line].

723. U.S. Department of Veterans' Affairs, Nationwide Gravesite Locator at http://gravelocator.cem.va.gov; Hiram C. Rude, 12th New York Cavalry, Compiled Military Service File and Federal Pension Application Records, National Archives.

724. July-August 1863 Muster Roll, Company B, 12th New York Cavalry, Record Group 94, National Archives; Stephen Laishley, 12th New York Cavalry, Federal Pension Application Records, National Archives.

725. July-August 1863 Muster Roll, Company B, 12th New York Cavalry, Record Group 94, National Archives; *Oswego Times and Express,* October 17, 1883.

726. July-August 1863 Muster Roll, Company B, 12th New York Cavalry, Record Group 94, National Archives.

Potter's Raid 265

727. July-August 1863 Muster Roll, Company B, 12th New York Cavalry, Record Group 94, National Archives.
728. *Annual Report of the Adjutant-General of the State of New York for the Year 1894, Volume III*, 1037.
729. *Annual Report of the Adjutant-General of the State of New York for the Year 1894, Volume III, 1316.*
730. July-August 1863 Muster Roll, Company F, 12th New York Cavalry, Record Group 94, National Archives; U.S. Department of Veterans' Affairs, Nationwide Gravesite Locator at http://gravelocator.cem.va.gov.
731. *Medical and Surgical History of the Civil War,* 10:626; July-August 1863 Muster Roll, Company F, 12th New York Cavalry, Record Group 94, National Archives; James McKenna, 12th New York Cavalry, Federal Pension Application Records, National Archives.
732. July-August 1863 Muster Roll, Company F, 12th New York Cavalry, Record Group 94, National Archives.
733. *Annual Report of the Adjutant-General of the State of New York for the Year 1894, Volume III*, 1024; U.S. Department of Veterans' Affairs, Nationwide Gravesite Locator at http://gravelocator.cem.va.gov.
734. *Annual Report of the Adjutant-General of the State of New York for the Year 1894, Volume III*, 1081; U.S. Department of Veterans' Affairs, Nationwide Gravesite Locator at http://gravelocator.cem.va.gov.
735. *Annual Report of the Adjutant-General of the State of New York for the Year 1894, Volume III*, 1170; Andersonville Prison Records at http://www.itd.nps.gov/cwss/andDetailp.cfm ; Ancestry.com. *Andersonville Prisoners of War* [database on-line].
736. *Annual Report of the Adjutant-General of the State of New York for the Year 1894, Volume III*, 1153.
737. July-August 1863 Muster Roll, Company F, 12th New York Cavalry, Record Group 94, National Archives; U.S. Department of Veterans' Affairs, Nationwide Gravesite Locator at http://gravelocator.cem.va.gov.
738. *Annual Report of the Adjutant-General of the State of New York for the Year 1894, Volume III*, 1228; National Park Service, Andersonville Prison Records at http://www.itd.nps.gov/cwss.
739. *Annual Report of the Adjutant-General of the State of New York for the Year 1894, Volume III*, 1268.
740. *Annual Report of the Adjutant-General of the State of New York for the Year 1894, Volume III*, 1245.
741. *Annual Report of the Adjutant-General of the State of New York for the Year 1894, Volume III*, 1248; July-August 1863 Muster Roll, Company F, Record Group 94, 12th New York Cavalry, National Archives.
742. *Annual Report of the Adjutant-General of the State of New York for the Year 1894, Volume III*, 1187.
743. July-August 1863 Muster Roll, Company A, 3rd New York Cavalry, Record Group 94, National Archives.
744. July-August 1863 Muster Roll, Company A, 3rd New York Cavalry, Record Group 94, National Archives; Oliver Spoor to Dear Father, August 16, 1863, Oliver Spoor

Papers; *Pensions and Increase of Pensions for Certain Soldiers and Sailors of the Civil War, etc. February 23, 1909. Serial Set Vol. No. 5383, Session Vol. No. B 60th Congress, 2nd Session S. Rpt. 1064,* 54-55.

745. Compiled Military Service File, Peter E. Borst, 3rd New York Cavalry, Record Group 94, National Archives.

746. July-August 1863 Muster Roll, 3rd New York Cavalry, Record Group 94, National Archives; U.S. Department of Veterans' Affairs, Nationwide Gravesite Locator at http://gravelocator.cem.va.gov.

747. July-August 1863 Muster Roll, Company D, 3rd New York Cavalry, Record Group, National Archives, New York State Adjutant General's Office, Civil War Muster Roll Abstracts of New York State Volunteers, United States Sharpshooters, and United States Colored Troops, [ca. 1861-1900], New York State Archives.

748. July-August 1863 Muster Roll, Company E, 3rd New York Cavalry, Record Group 94, National Archives.

Gideon Blackman, 3rd New York Cavalry, Compiled Military Service File, Record Group 94, National Archives.

749. July-August 1863 Muster Roll, 3rd New York Cavalry, Record Group 94, National Archives; New York State Adjutant General's Office, Civil War Muster Roll Abstracts of New York State Volunteers, United States Sharpshooters, and United States Colored Troops, [ca. 1861-1900], New York State Archives.

750. July-August 1863 Muster Roll, 3rd New York Cavalry, Record Group 94, National Archives; *Granting Pensions and Increase of Pensions for Certain Soldiers and Sailors of Civil War, etc. July 26, 1912. Serial Set Vol. No. 6128, Session Vol. No.E 62nd Congress, 2nd Session S. Rpt. 982,* 33.

751. July-August 1863 Muster Roll and Morning Reports, Company G, 3rd New York Cavalry, Record Group 94, National Archives.

752. July-August 1863 Muster Roll, 3rd New York Cavalry, Record Group 94, National Archives; New York State Adjutant General's Office, Civil War Muster Roll Abstracts of New York State Volunteers, United States Sharpshooters, and United States Colored Troops, [ca. 1861-1900], New York State Archives.

753. New York State Adjutant General's Office, Civil War Muster Roll Abstracts of New York State Volunteers, United States Sharpshooters, and United States Colored Troops, [ca. 1861-1900], New York State Archives.

754. July-August 1863 Muster Roll, Company I, 3rd New York Cavalry, Record Group 94, National Archives.

755. July-August 1863 Muster Roll, 3rd New York Cavalry, Record Group 94, National Archives.

756. July-August 1863 Muster Roll, 3rd New York Cavalry, Record Group 94, National Archives.

757. July-August 1863 Muster Roll, 3rd New York Cavalry, Record Group 94, National Archives; *Medical and Surgical History of the Civil War,* 10:560.

758. *Official Records,* ser. 1, 27, pt. 2:971.

759. *Official Records,* ser. 1, 27, pt. 2:970.

760. Janet B. Hewett, ed., *Supplement to the Official Records of the Union and Confederate* Armies, serial vol. 41:693; New York State Adjutant General's Office, Civil War Muster Roll Abstracts of New York State Volunteers, United States Sharpshooters,

and United States Colored Troops, [ca. 1861-1900], New York State Archives; U.S. Department of Veterans' Affairs, National Gravesite Locator at http://gravelocator.cem.va.gov.

761. Thomas Yearney, 23rd New York Cavalry, Service Record, New York State Adjutant General's Department.

762. Joseph Sheriden, 23rd New York Cavalry, Service Record, New York State Adjutant General's Department.

763. Herman Wolf, 23rd New York Cavalry, Compiled Military Service File, Record Group 94, National Archives.

764. David Kaemmerer, 23rd New York Cavalry, Compiled Military Service File, Record Group 94, National Archives.

765. Muster Roll, 1st North Carolina Union Volunteers, July-August 1863, Record Group 94, National Archives, gives his name as Calop Gaylord.

766. Muster Roll, 1st North Carolina Union Volunteers, July-August 1863, Record Group 94, National Archives; Robert Strieback, 1st North Carolina Union Volunteers, Compiled Military Service File, Record Group 94, National Archives; Robert Streeback, 1st North Carolina Union Volunteers, Federal Pension Application Records, National Archives.

767. Phisterer, *New York in the War of the Rebellion* (1912), 2:1268; *Official Records,* ser. 1, 27, pt. 2:973; *Utica Morning Herald and Daily Gazette,* August 5, 1863.

768. New York State Adjutant General's Office, Civil War Muster Roll Abstracts of New York State Volunteers, United States Sharpshooters, and United States Colored Troops, [ca. 1861-1900], New York State Archives; Eleventh Census of the United States, 1880: Pamlico County, North Carolina; Sandra Lee Almasy, *North Carolina Civil War Veterans Census* (1990),17.

769. New York State Adjutant General's Office, Civil War Muster Roll Abstracts of New York State Volunteers, United States Sharpshooters, and United States Colored Troops, [ca. 1861-1900], New York State Archives.

770. *State Journal,* July 29, 1863; July 30, 1863.

771. *Official Records,* ser. 1, 27, pt. 2:964.

772. *Herald* (New York), July 27, 1863.

773. *North Carolina Troops,* 3:90; 15:433-434; Furnifold Powell, 67th North Carolina Infantry, Compiled Military Service File, Record Group 109, National Archives; North Carolina Confederate Pension Application, Furnifold Powell, North Carolina State Archives.

774. *North Carolina Troops,* 3:86.

775. *North Carolina Troops,* 3:87.

776. *North Carolina Troops,* 3:87.

777. *North Carolina Troops,* 3:87.

778. *North Carolina Troops,* 3:88.

779. *North Carolina Troops,* 3:89.

780. Addison P. Whitford, 67th North Carolina Infantry, Compiled Military Service File, Record Group 109, National Archives.

781. J. H. Powers, 67th North Carolina, Compiled Military Service File, Record Group 109, National Archives. A card detailing his parole at Fort Monroe was filed with the Compiled Military Service File of James K. Powell, 8th North Carolina Partisan Rangers. Oddly, the "Roll of Prisoners of War Paroled at Fort Monroe, Va. Augt. 4, 1863",

National Archives, which contains the names of the paroled Potter's Raid enlisted men, lists everyone from Whitford's Battalion as being in the "8th N.C. Batty."

782. *North Carolina Troops,* 3:101.
783. *North Carolina Troops,* 3:98.
784 *North Carolina Troops,* 3:100.
785. *North Carolina Troops,* 3:100.
786. *North Carolina Troops,* 3:101.
787. James H. Satterthwaite, 67th North Carolina Infantry, Compiled Military Service File, Record Group 109, National Archives.
788. *North Carolina Troops,* 1:438.
789. Andrew Dozier, 6th Virginia Infantry, Compiled Military Service File, Record Group 109, National Archives.
790. Bennett P. Jenkins, 7th Confederate Cavalry, Compiled Military Service File, Record Group 109, National Archives.
791. Private Joshua W. Tucker, 7th Confederate Cavalry, Compiled Military Service File, Record Group 109, National Archives.
792. Nathan M. Lawrence, Compiled Military Service File, Record Group 109, National Archives; *Charlotte Observer,* March 12, 1916.
793. Reddick Jones, 12th Battalion, Compiled Military Service File, Record Group 109, North Carolina Cavalry, National Archives; Record of Events, Company Muster Roll, Company B, 12th Battalion, North Carolina Cavalry, dated August 25, 1863, Record Group 109, National Archives.
794. *North Carolina Troops* V: 349.
795. *North Carolina Troops,* 5:253; 15:328.
796. *North Carolina Troops* Vol. 5:255; 15:332.
797. *North Carolina Troops* Vol. 5:254; 15:330.
798. *North Carolina Troops* Vol. 5:255; 15:331.
799. *North Carolina Troops* Vol. 5:258; 15:336.
800. *North Carolina Troops,* 6:202.
801. Thomas W. Chesson, 17th North Carolina, Compiled Military Service File, Record Group 109, National Archives.
802. *North Carolina Troops,* 6:260.
803. *North Carolina Troops,* 6:276; Elisha Jones, 17th North Carolina, Compiled Military Service File, Record Group 109, National Archives.
804. *North Carolina Troops* 4: 408; *Wilmington Journal,* July 30, 1863.
805. Henry G. Jones, 43rd North Carolina Infantry, Compiled Military Service File, Record Group 109, National Archives.
806. *State Journal*, August 5, 1863; W. A Thompson, Co. E, 62nd Georgia Cavalry, Compiled Military Service File, Record Group 109, National Archives.
807. Lillian Henderson, comp. *Roster of the Confederate Soldiers of Georgia,* 6:304.
808. Ezra S. Moody, Capt. Edward Graham's Battery, Compiled Military Service File, Record Group 109, National Archives.
809. Robert J. Turner, Capt. Edward Graham's Battery, Compiled Military Service File, Record Group 109, National Archives.
810. *Western Democrat,* July 28, 1863.
811. Western Democrat , Aug. 11, 1863; *Daily Progress,* July 23, 1863

812. Deborah Virginia Bonner Warren to Dear Daughter, July 21, 1863, Edward Jenner Warren Papers.
813. *Report on the Treatment of Prisoners in the War of the Rebellion by the Rebel Authorities* ...472, 480; John B. Daniel files, Confederate Papers Relating to Citizens or Business Firms, 1861-65, National Archives.
814. Deborah Virginia Bonner Warren to Dear Daughter, July 21, 1863, Edward Jenner Warren Papers.
815. Deborah Virginia Bonner Warren to Dear Daughter, July 21, 1863, Edward Jenner Warren Papers.
816. Deborah Virginia Bonner Warren to Dear Daughter, July 21, 1863, Edward Jenner Warren Papers.
817. This incident was recorded in J. C. Ellington, "Fiftieth Regiment", in Clark, *Histories of the Regiments* Clark, 3:175, and King, *Sketches of Pitt County,* 140.
818. *State Journal*, July 29, 1863.
819. A list of Federal casualties appeared in the *New York Times,* August 26, 1863.
820. Muster Roll, Company B, 3rd New York Cavalry, July-August 1863, Record Group 94, National Archives.
821. New York State Adjutant General's Office, Civil War Muster Roll Abstracts of New York State Volunteers, United States Sharpshooters, and United States Colored Troops, [ca. 1861-1900], New York State Archives.
822. New York State Adjutant General's Office, Civil War Muster Roll Abstracts of New York State Volunteers, United States Sharpshooters, and United States Colored Troops, [ca. 1861-1900], New York State Archives.
823. New York State Adjutant General's Office, Civil War Muster Roll Abstracts of New York State Volunteers, United States Sharpshooters, and United States Colored Troops, [ca. 1861-1900], New York State Archives.
824. Manly Lane, 5th North Carolina Cavalry, Compiled Military Service File, Record Group 109, National Archives.
825. Gabriel Aycock, 7th Confederate Cavalry, Compiled Military Service File, Record Group 109, National Archives.
826. G. W. Bumpass, 7th Confederate Cavalry, Compiled Military Service File, Record Group 109, National Archives. Compiled Military service files of the 7th Confederate Cavalry personnel at the National Archives show that several other men of Company F filed claims for reimbursement for horses that were captured at Kenansville on July 5, 1863.
827. William H. Oliver, 7th Confederate Cavalry, Compiled Military Service File, Record Group 109, National Archives.
828. William K. Parker, 7th Confederate Cavalry, Compiled Military Service File, Record Group 109, National Archives.
829. Alexander Potts, 7th Confederate Cavalry, Compiled Military Service File, Record Group 109, National Archives.
830. William Price, 7th Confederate Cavalry, Compiled Military Service File, Record Group 109, National Archives.
831. Compiled Military Service File, H. G. Worsley, 7th Confederate Cavalry, National Archives.

832. *North Carolina Troops,* 6:293; C. P. Turner, 17th North Carolina, Compiled Military Service File, Record Group 109, National Archives.
833. David Craft, 61st North Carolina Infantry, Compiled Military Service File, Record Group 109, National Archives.
834. *Official Records of the Union and Confederate Navies,* 1, 8:204; *Dictionary of American Biography,* s.v., Lay, John L.
835. *Official Records of the Union and Confederate Navies,* 1, 8:204-205.
836. *Official Records of the Union and Confederate Navies,* 1, 8:204-205; *Philadelphia Inquirer,* November 17, 1862.
837. Porte Crayon, "North Carolina Illustrated", *Harper's New Monthly Magazine,* May 1857, 751; *Official Records of the Union and Confederate Navies,* 1, 8:205.
838. *Official Records of the Union and Confederate Navies,* 1, 8:205; King, *Sketches of Pitt County,* 132; Record of Events, Muster Rolls, September-December, 1862, Company I, 3rd North Carolina Cavalry, Record Group 109, National Archives. In an old roster, George Smith was listed among the burials at New Bern National Cemetery, listed as "killed" on November 9, 1862. The action at Greenville is the only skirmish that has been recorded for that regiment on that date. *Roll of Honor: Names of Soldiers who Died in Defense of the American Union, Interred in the National Cemeteries, Numbers I-XIX.* Vol. 19, 194.
839. King, *Sketches of Pitt County,* 132.
840. *Weekly State Journal,* November 26, 1862.
841. King, *Sketches of Pitt County,* 132.
842. King, *Sketches of Pitt County,* 132-233.
843. *Official Records of the Union and Confederate Navies,* 1, 8:204-205; *North Carolina Standard,* November 19, 1862.
844. *Weekly State Journal,* November 26, 1862; *Greensboro Patriot,* November 20, 1862; King, *Sketches of Pitt County,* 132-3; Eighth Census of the United States, 1860: Pitt County, North Carolina.
845. *Weekly State Journal,* November 26, 1862; King, *Sketches of Pitt County,* 133.
846. *Official Records,* ser. 1, 29, pt. 1:661; *North Carolina Troops* 1:84.
847. *Official Records,* ser. 1. 29, pt. 1:984-985.
848. *Official Records,* ser. 1, 29, pt. 1:984-985; Julius Moore, Company H, 3rd North Carolina Cavalry, Compiled Military Service File, Record Group 109, National Archives.
849. Janet B. Hewett, ed., *Supplement to the Official Records of the Union and Confederate Armies,* serial vol. 48:239-240. The Record of Events spaces in the November-December 1863 muster rolls of those three companies of the 3rd North Carolina Cavalry mention their participation in the skirmish.
850. Janet B. Hewett, ed., *Supplement to the Official Records of the Union and Confederate Armies,* serial vol. 48:240; J. H. Myrover, "Thirteenth Battalion", in Clark, *Histories of the Regiments,* 4:349.
851. Joshua B. Hill, "Forty-first Regiment (Third Cavalry)", in Clark, *Histories of the Regiments,* 2:777; J. H. Myrover, "Thirteenth Battalion", in Clark, *Histories of the Regiments,* 4:349.
852. John L. Baker, William J Hancock, and Loderick W. Jenkins, 3rd North Carolina Cavalry, Compiled Military Service Files, Record Group 109, National Archives; Joshua

B. Hill, "Forty-first Regiment (Third Cavalry)", in Clark, *Histories of the Regiments,* 2:777.
853. *Official Records,* ser. 1, 29, pt. 1:995; Frederick Phisterer, *New York in the War of the Rebellion* (1912), 2:960.
854. *Official Records,* ser. 1, 29, pt. 1:996; NPS, Civil War Soldier Database, Civil War Soldiers and Sailors Program, http://www.civilwar.nps.gov/cwss/soldiers.cfm.
855. Chris E. Fonvielle, Jr., *The Battle of Forks Road* (Wilmington: 2007), 13; 16-17; 41, n.6, n.7.
856. King, *Sketches of Pitt County,* 144.
857. *Fayetteville Observer*, April 21, 1864; *Official Records,* ser. 1, 33:258; King, *Sketches of Pitt County,* 144.
858. *Fayetteville Observer*, April 21, 1864; *Official Records,* ser. 1, 33:258; Carlton J. McKenzie, Charles A. Miller, David M. Stripling, and John W. Taylor, 62nd Georgia Cavalry, Compiled Military Service Files, Record Group 109, National Archives.
859. *North Carolina Times*, February 21, 1865.
860. *North Carolina Times*, February 21; February 24, 1865; Lillian Henderson, *Roster of the Confederate Troops of Georgia,* 6:333-341.
861. *North Carolina Times*, February 21, 1865.
862. *North Carolina Times,* February 24, 1865; *Lillian* Henderson, *Roster of the Confederate Troops of Georgia,* 6:333.
863. New York State Adjutant General's Office, Civil War Muster Roll Abstracts of New York State Volunteers, United States Sharpshooters, and United States Colored Troops, [ca. 1861-1900], New York State Archives.
864. *New York Times,* March 3, 1865; *North Carolina Times,* February 24, 1865.
865. *North Carolina Times,* February 24, 1865.
866. Maj. William Demill, Compiled Military Service Records of Confederate General and Staff Officers, and Non-regimental Enlisted Men, Record Group 109, National Archives.

Potter's Raid Bibliography

Manuscripts

Colorado Historical Society, Denver, Colorado
- W. H. Graves, *A True Narrative of the Incidents Which Happened in the Life of W. H. Graves,* typescript.

East Carolina Manuscript Collection, Special Collections Department, J. Y. Joyner Library, East Carolina University, Greenville, North Carolina
- George Howard Papers, Collection #197, Container #197.1
- William Howard Hooker Collection: Martha Gregory Brown Family Papers, 1862-1865, Collection #472.004,
- F. L. Bond Papers, Collection #296
- Oliver C. Spoor Papers, Collection #3081

National Archives, Washington, D.C.
- Record Group 15, Records of the Department of Veterans Affairs
Federal Pension Application Records
- Record Group 59, General Records of the Department of State
Letters and Applications for US Passports
- Record Group 94: Records of the Adjutant General's Office
Regimental Order Books, July-August 1863, 12th New York Cavalry
Muster rolls of 3rd New York Cavalry; Companies A, B, and F, 12th New York Cavalry, 23rd New York Cavalry, and Company L, 1st North Carolina Union Volunteers, July-August 1863, Regimental Order Book, 1st North Carolina Colored Troops (35th United States Colored Troops), Compiled Military Service Files
- Record Group 109, War Department Collection of Confederate Records Compiled Military Service Files
- Confederate Papers Relating to Citizens or Business Firms
- Record Group 233, Records of the U.S. House of Representatives
- Barred and Disallowed Case Files of the Southern Claims Commission
- Record Group 249, Records of the Commissary General of Prisoners
- "Roll of Prisoners of War Paroled at Fort Monroe, Va. Augt. 4, 1863"

New York State Adjutant General's Office
- New York State Adjutant General's Office, Civil War Muster Roll Abstracts of New York State Volunteers, United States Sharpshooters, and United States Colored Troops, [ca. 1861-1900], New York State Archives.

North Carolina State Archives, Division of Archives and History, Raleigh, North Carolina:
- Zebulon B. Vance, Governors' Papers
- Julia Ward Stickley Papers
- Records of the Quartermaster Department, CSA, Military Collection, Civil War Section

Oswego County Historical Society, Oswego County, New York
- Gleason Wellington Correspondence
- William Davies Correspondence

Personal Collection, Kenneth Jennings Wooster
- Oren T. Wooster Letters

Southern Historical Collection, Wilson Library, University of North Carolina at Chapel Hill:
- Lewis Family Papers, Collection #427
- William A. Holt Papers, Collection #2516
- Edward Jenner Warren Papers, Collection #3692
- Herbert Arthur Cooley Papers, Collection #2431

United States Army Military History Institute, Carlisle Barracks, Pennsylvania
- Alfred Holcomb Correspondence
- Newton Wallace Diary
- William Seagrave Diary

Virginia Historical Society, Richmond, Virginia
- Section 24, Grinnan Family Papers

Official Publications

- *Annual Report of the Adjutant-General of the State of New York for the Year 1894, Volume III.* Albany, New York, 1895.
- *Medical and Surgical History of the Civil War.* Reprint. Wilmington, North Carolina: Broadfoot Publishing Company, 1991.
- *New York State Adjutant General's Office Registers of the 9, 10, 11, 12 Regiments of Cavalry, New York Volunteers, in the War of the Rebellion.* Albany, New York, 1895.
- United States Navy Department. *Official Records of the Union and Confederate Navies in the War of the Rebellion.* 30 volumes. Washington, D.C.: Government Printing Office, 1894-1922.
- *Supplement to the Official Records of the Union and Confederate Armies* 100 vols. (Wilmington, North Carolina: Broadfoot Publishing Company, 1994—)
- United States Surgeon General's Office, *Medical and Surgical History of the Civil War.* Washington, D. C.: U. S. Government Printing Office, 1875-1888.
- United States War Department. *The War of the Rebellion: A Compilation of the Official Records of the Union and Confederate Armies.* 70 volumes in 128 parts. Washington, D.C.: Government Printing Office, 1880-1901.

Newspapers

Auburn Bulletin (Auburn, New York)
Auburn Daily Bulletin (Auburn, New York)
Auburn Morning Dispatch (Auburn, New York)
Baltimore Sun
Brooklyn Daily Eagle
Buffalo Express (Buffalo, New York)
Carolina Watchman (Salisbury, North Carolina)
Christian Recorder (Philadelphia)

Colorado Banner (Boulder, Colorado)
Colorado Daily Chieftain (Pueblo, Colorado)
Commercial Advertiser and Times (Oswego, New York)
Commercial Times (Oswego, New York)
Daily Dispatch (Richmond, Virginia)
Daily Progress (Raleigh, North Carolina)
Dallas Morning News (Dallas, Texas)
Denver Daily Times (Denver, Colorado)
Denver Mirror (Denver, Colorado)
Eastern Reflector (Greenville, North Carolina)
Evening Courier and Republic (Buffalo, New York)
Fayetteville Observer (Fayetteville, North Carolina)
Fort Covington Sun (Fort Covington, New York)
Greensboro Patriot (Greensboro, North Carolina)
Herald (Melbourne, Australia)
Herald (New York)
Idaho Tri-Weekly Statesman, (Boise, Idaho)
Lowville Journal (Lowville, New York)
Macon Telegraph (Macon, Georgia)
Middletown Times-Press (Middletown, New York)
New York Daily Reformer (Watertown, New York)
New York Times
New York Tribune
North Carolina Standard (Raleigh, North Carolina)
North Carolina Times (Beaufort, North Carolina)
North State Whig (Washington, North Carolina)
Oneonta Daily Star (Oneonta, New York)
Oswego Daily Palladium (Oswego, New York)
Oswego Daily Times (Oswego, New York)
Oswego Palladium-Times (Oswego, New York)
Oswego Times and Express (Oswego, New York)
*Petersburg Express (*Petersburg, Virginia)
Philadelphia Inquirer
Plain Dealer (Canton, New York)
Plattsburg Sentinel (Plattsburg, New York)
Raleigh Register (Raleigh, North Carolina)
Republican Advocate (Batavia, New York)
Richmond Daily Dispatch (Richmond, Virginia)
Richmond Sentinel (Richmond, Virginia)
Richmond Whig (Richmond, Virginia)
Ripley Bee (Ripley, Ohio)
Rochester Democrat and Chronicle (Rochester, New York)
Rocky Mountain News (Denver, Colorado)
San Francisco Evening Bulletin (Raleigh, North Carolina)
Spirit of the Age (Raleigh, North Carolina)
State Journal (Raleigh, North Carolina)

Tarboro Southerner (Tarboro, North Carolina)
The Liberator (Boston, Massachusetts)
The National Tribune (Philadelphia)
The New York Spectator
The State (Columbia, South Carolina)
The Times (London, England)
Times and Journal (Oswego, New York)
Union Advance Picket (Washington, North Carolina)
Union and Advertiser (Rochester, New York)
Utica Saturday Globe (Utica, New York)
Utica Morning Herald and Gazette (Utica, New York)
Watertown Daily Times (Watertown, New York)
Weekly Recorder (Fayetteville, New York)
Western Democrat (Charlotte, North Carolina)
Wilmington Journal (Wilmington, North Carolina)
Wilson Ledger (Wilson, North Carolina)
Zanesville Daily Courier (Zanesville, Ohio)

Published Primary Sources

• Carpenter, Kinchen Jahu, *War Diary of Kinchen Jahu Carpenter Company I, Fiftieth North Carolina Regiment War Between the States, 1861-1865*. Rutherfordton, North Carolina, 1955.
• Clark, Walter, "Eighth Battalion. (Nethercutt's Partisan Rangers.)", in Walter Clark, ed., *Histories of the Several Regiments and Battalions from North Carolina in the Great War, 1861-'65,* 5 vols. Goldsboro, North Carolina, 1901. Hereafter cited as Clark, *Histories of the Regiments*.
• Colyer, Vincent, *Brief Report of the Services Rendered by the Freed People to the United States Army, in North Carolina, in the Spring of 1862, after the Battle of New Bern*. New York: Vincent Colyer, 1864.
• Cooper, Alonzo, *In and Out of Rebel Prisons*. Oswego, New York: O. J. Oliphant, 1888.
• Crabtree, Beth G. and Patton, James W., *Journal of a Secesh Lady: The Diary of Catherine Ann Devereaux Edmondston, 1860-1866*. Raleigh, North Carolina: Division of Archives and History, 1979.
• Davis, John Dixon, ed., *A Civil War Diary, January 1, 1863 - May 31, 1864 / by Sergeant Henry S. Lee, Co. B 10 Regt., Arty & Engrs, Kinston, N.C.* Black Mountain: North Carolina, Craggy Mountain Press, 1997.
• Derby, W.P., *Bearing Arms in the Twenty-seventh Massachusetts Regiment of Volunteers Infantry during the Civil War.* Boston, Massachusetts: Wright and Potter Printing Company, 1883.
• Ellington, J. C., "Fiftieth Regiment", in Clark, *Histories of the Regiments*.
• Hill, Joshua B., "Forty-first Regiment (Third Cavalry)", in Clark, *Histories of the Regiments*.
• Howe, W. W., *Kinston, Whitehall, and Goldsboro Expedition December 1862.* New York: W. W. Howe, 1890.

- Johnson, Hugh Buckner, comp., *Records of the Wilson Confederate Hospital.* Wilson, North Carolina, 1954.
- Kennedy, John T., and Parker, W. Fletcher, "Seventy-fifth Regiment (Seventh Cavalry)", in Clark, *Histories of the Regiments.*
- *North Carolina County Court Minutes (Edgecombe County) 1757-1868.* Three rolls, microfilm. Reel 3, 1857-1868. Raleigh, North Carolina: North Carolina Department of Archives and History, 1961.
- Post, Lydia Minturn, ed., *Soldiers' Letters, From Camps, Battle-fields, and Prisons ...* New York: Bunce & Huntington, 1865.
- Ricks, T. E., ed., *Nash County Historical Notes: A Bicentennial Tribute.* Rocky Mount, North Carolina: Nash County Historical Society, 1976.
- Sanders, J. W., "Tenth Regiment (same Companies)" in Clark, *Histories of the Regiments.*
- Smith, John G., "The Tarboro Raid", *Carolina and the Southern Cross,* February 1914.
- Watson, Helen R., "A Bright Future for Stonewall", *The State,* November 1971.
- Wharton, Rufus W., "Sixty-seventh Regiment", in Clark, *Histories of the Regiments.*

Books (References and Secondary Sources)

- Albaugh III, William A., *Confederate Edged Weapons.* Wilmington, North Carolina: Broadfoot Publishing Company, 1993.
- Alexander, E. P., *Iron Horses: American Locomotives 1829-1900.* New York: Dover Publications, 2003.
- Almasy, Sandra L. *North Carolina, 1890, Civil War Veterans Census.* Joliet, Illinois: Kensington Glen Publishing, 1990.
- Barrett, John G., *The Civil War in North Carolina.* Chapel Hill, North Carolina: University of North Carolina Press, 1963.
- Bishir, Catherine W. and Southern, Michael T., *A Guide to the Historic Architecture of Eastern North Carolina.* Chapel Hill, North Carolina: University of North Carolina Press, 1996.
- Bradley, Jr., Stephen E., *North Carolina Confederate Militia Officers Roster as Contained in the Adjutant-General's Officers Roster.* Wilmington, North Carolina: Broadfoot Publishing, 1992.
- Byard, John, "The Bounty Soldiers", *The Valley News* (Fulton, New York), March 9, 1995.
- Coggins, Jack, *Arms and Equipment of the Civil War.* Reprint. Wilmington, North Carolina: Broadfoot Publishing Company, 1990.
- *Confederate Military History, a Library of Confederate States History, Written by Distinguished Men of the South, and Edited by Gen. Clement A. Evans of Georgia.* 12 vols. Atlanta, Georgia: Confederate Publishing Company, 1899.
- Copeland, Elizabeth, ed., *Chronicles of Pitt County.* Greenville, North Carolina: Pitt County Historical Society, 1982.
- Cotter, Michael, ed., with Ohno, Kate and Barnes, Mary Hollis, *The Architectural Heritage of Greenville.* Greenville, North Carolina: Greenville Area Preservation Association, 1988.

- Cummins, Thomas J. and Dunphy, Thomas, *Remarkable Trials of All Countries with the Evidence and Speeches of Counsel, Court Scenes, Incidents, & c. Compiled Military from Original Sources. Vol. II.* New York: S. S. Peloubet & Company, 1882.
- Cunningham, H. H., *Doctors in Gray: the Confederate Medical Service.* Baton Rouge, Louisiana: Louisiana State University Press, 1958.
- *Dictionary of the United States Congress.*
- Duane, J. C., *Manual for Engineer Troops.* New York: D. Van Nostrand, 1862.
- Duncan, John G., *Pitt County Potpourri.* Greenville, North Carolina: East Carolina College Library, 1966.
- Dyer, Frederick H., *A Compendium of the War of the Rebellion Compiled Military and Arranged from the Official Records of the Union and Confederate Armies ...* Des Moines, Iowa: Dyer Publishing Company, 1908.
- Ellis, Edward S., *Low Twelve: "By Their Deeds They Shall Know Them" A Series of Striking and Truthful Incidents Illustrative of the Fidelity of Free Masons to One Another in Times of Stress and Danger.* New York: F. R. Niglutsch, 1907.
- Fleming, Monika S., *Echoes of Edgecombe County, 1860-1940.* Dover, New Hampshire: Arcadia Publishing, 1996.
- Fonvielle Jr., Chris E., *The Battle of Forks Road.* Wilmington, N.C.: 2007.
- Hartung, A. Bruce, "Swordmaker for the Confederacy", *The State,* January 1981.
- Headley, P. C., *Public Men of Today: Being Biographies of the President of the United States ...* Hartford, Connecticut: S. S. Scranton, 1882.
- Heitman, Francis B., *Historical Register and Dictionary of the United States Army From Its Organization, September 29, 1789, to March 2, 1903.* Washington, D. C.: U. S. Government Printing Office, 1903.
- Henderson, Lillian, comp., *Roster of the Confederate Soldiers of Georgia,* 6 vols. Hapeville, Georgia: Longina & Porter, 1959.
- Hill, Michael, ed., *Guide to North Carolina Historical Highway Markers.* Raleigh, North Carolina: Division of Archives and History, 2001.
- Irby, Richard, *Historical Sketch of the Nottoway Grays: Afterwards Company G, Eighteenth Virginia Regiment, Army of Northern Virginia.* Richmond, Virginia: J. W. Fergusson and Son, 1878.
- Johnson, Chrisfield, *History of Oswego County, New York.* Philadelphia: L.H. Everts and Co., 1877.
- King, Henry T., *Sketches of Pitt County.* Raleigh, North Carolina: Edward and Broughton, 1911.
- Krick, Robert E. L., *Staff Officers in Gray: A Biographical Register of the Staff Officers in the Army of Northern Virginia.* Chapel Hill, North Carolina: University of North Carolina Press, 2003.
- Krick, Robert K., *Lee's Colonels: A Biographical Register of the Field Officers of the Army of Northern Virginia.* Dayton, Ohio: Morningside Books, 1992.
- Lichtenstein, Gaston, *Recollections of My Teacher Frank S. Wilkinson By Gaston Lichtenstein. Reprinted from The Daily Southerner, Tarboro', North Carolina.* Richmond, Virginia: Masonic Home Press, 1953.
- Marshall, Jessie Ames, *Private and official correspondence of Gen. Benjamin F. Butler, During the period of the Civil War ... Privately issued.* 5 vols. Norwood, Massachusetts: Plimpton Press, 1917.

- Manarin, Louis and Jordan, Jr., Weymouth T., comps, *North Carolina Troops 1861-1865: A Roster,* 16 volumes to date. Raleigh, North Carolina: North Carolina Office of Archives and History, 1966-.
- William Marvel, *Andersonville: The Last Depot.* Chapel Hill, North Carolina: University of North Carolina Press, 1994.
- Mast, Greg, *State Troops and Volunteers: A Photographic Record of North Carolina's Civil War Soldiers,* Vol. I. Raleigh, North Carolina: Division of Archives and History, 1995.
- Mattson, Richard C., *History and Architecture of Nash County, North Carolina.* Nashville, North Carolina: Nash County Planning Department, 1987.
- McGowan, Faison Wells and McGowan, Pearl Canady, *Flashes of Duplin's History and Government.* Kenansville, North Carolina, 1971.
- Mercer, Gary Carnell, *The Administration of Governor Henry Toole Clark.* Greenville, North Carolina: thesis, East Carolina University, 1965.
- Midgette, Nancy Smith, "Forgotten Hero", Our *State,* May 1999.
- Miller, Francis Trevelyan, *The Photographic History of the Civil War* 10 vols. New York: Review of Reviews Company, 1912.
- *National Cyclopedia of American Biography*
- Navy Department, Office of the Chief of Naval Operations, Naval History Division, *Dictionary of American Naval Fighting Ships.* Washington, D.C.: U.S. Government Printing Office, 1959.
- Norris, David A., "Battle in the Buff", *Civil War Times,* December 1998.
- Norris, David A., "Confederate Gunners Affectionately Called Their Hard-working Little Mountain Howitzers 'Bull Pups'", *America's Civil War,* September 1995.
- Norris, David A., "The Gallant but Ill-fated 12th New York Cavalry Paid a Steep Price for its Fidelity to the Union", *America's Civil War,* January 1997.
- Norris, David A., "The Men of the Stalwart Petersburg Artillery Served from the Beginning of the War to the End", America's *Civil War,* March 1995.
- Phisterer, Frederick, *New York in the War of the Rebellion.* Albany, New York: Weed and Parson, 1890.
- Phisterer, Frederick, *New York in the War of the Rebellion* 5 vols. Albany, New York: J. B. Lyon and Company, 1912.
- Pierrepont, Alice V. D., *Reuben Vaughan Kidd: Soldier of the Confederacy.* Petersburg, Virginia: privately published, 1947.
- "Porte Crayon", "North Carolina Illustrated", *Harper's New Monthly Magazine,* May 1857.
- Powell, William H., *List of the Officers of the Army of the United States from 1779 to 1900.* New York: L. R. Hamersly & Co, 1900.
- Powell, William S., *The North Carolina Gazetteer.* Chapel Hill, North Carolina: University of North Carolina Press, 1968.
- *Quinquaennial Catalogue of the Officers and Graduates of Harvard University 1636 - 1915 Cambridge, Massachusetts, Harvard University Press in the Two Hundred and Seventy-Ninth Year of the College 1915.* Cambridge, Massachusetts: Harvard University Press, 1915.
- *Rocky Mount Mills: A Case History of Industrial Development 1818-1943.* (Rocky Mount, North Carolina: Rocky Mount Mills, 1943.

- Sandbeck, Peter B., *The Architectural History of New Bern and Craven County*. New Bern, North Carolina: Tryon Palace Commission, 1988.
- Sikes, Leon H., "The Swords of Kenansville", *Footnotes*, #58, November 1995.
- Snyder, Charles McCool, *Oswego County, New York in the Civil War*. Oswego, New York: Oswego County Historical Society and the Oswego County Civil War Committee, 1962.
- Stick, David, *Outer Banks of North Carolina*. Chapel Hill, North Carolina: University of North Carolina Press, 1958.
- Taylor, Roland, ed., *Mabrey Bass's Tarboro: from 1950 to 1990: Including Twenty-two Articles of Historical interest by Dr. Spencer P. Bass*. Fuquay-Varina, North Carolina: Research Triangle Publishing, 1997.
- Tenney, William Jewett, *The Military and Naval History of the Rebellion in the United States: With Biographical Sketches*. New York: D. Appleton and Company, 1866.
- Thorne, Barbara M. Howard, ed., *The Heritage of Craven County, North Carolina, Volume I*. New Bern, North Carolina: Eastern North Carolina Genealogical Society, 1984.
- Viverette, Eugene, "The Skirmish at Daniel's Schoolhouse", *The Connector*, Fall, 1998.
- Warner, Ezra J., *Generals in Blue: Lives of the Union Commanders*. Baton Rouge, Louisiana: Louisiana State University Press, 1964.
- Warner, Ezra J., *Generals in Gray*. Baton Rouge, Louisiana: University of Louisiana Press, 1959.
- Webb, Jo, "Troops Raided Tarboro, 1863 Recollections of Raid Given by Local Resident", *Lines and Pathways of Edgecombe* May 1997.
- Williams, Ruth Smith and Griffin, Margarete Glenn, *Tombstone and Census Records of Early Edgecombe County*. Rocky Mount, North Carolina, 1959.

Index

Abbott, Cpl. Johnson...201
Acapulco, Mexico...190
Adams, Lt. William K. ...229
Adkinson, Pvt. William...215
African-American sailors...254
African-Americans as guide for Potter...70, 82, 125, 141
African-Americans, escape with Potter...30, 81, 139, 140, 141, 142, 143, 144, 161
Alabama Units:
• Montgomery True Blues...9, 120, 121, 123, 126, 127, 135, 150, 198, 199, 203, 251, 262
• 3rd Alabama Infantry...120
Albany, N.Y. ...24, 190, 235, 249, 263
Albemarle Sound...7, 184, 239
Albemarle, CSS...98, 131, 182, 185, 186, 197, 225
Albert, Bugler John...35
Albritton, B.G. ...227
Alcohol...97
Allis, Lt. James...24, 54, 70, 153, 240
Allison (Union steamer)...154
Ambulances, Union Army...55, 142, 195
Ambushes, during Potter's Raid...66, 95, 104, 119, 122, 123, 126, 137, 142, 147, 149

Anderson, Joseph Reid...76
Andersonville National Cemetery...199, 206, 208
Andersonville Prison...81, 178, 193, 194, 197, 206, 207, 208, 209, 210, 211
Andrews, Capt. W.G. ...120
Annapolis National Cemetery...206
Annapolis, Md. ...206, 208, 209, 212, 213
Arizona...200
Atkinson, Virginia Streeter (Mrs. Peyton Atkinson)...8, 64, 65, 66, 76, 169, 233, 242, 243, 244, 258
Aunt Mae...81
Aycock, Pvt. Gabriel...223, 269
Baden, Germany...97
Baker, Dr. Julius M. ...93
Baker, Pvt. John F. ...35, 222
Baker, Surgeon Joseph...118
Ball's Bluff, Battle of...24
Baltimore Sun...162
Baltimore, Md. ...94, 180, 217
Bank, at Tarboro...100
Banta, Jr., Lt. William...93, 94
Barlow, Lucy...103, 109
Barnes, Pvt. John H. ...211
Barrett, Capt. Lycurgus...9, 132, 133, 135, 145, 150

Barrington, Capt. Stephen G. ...216
Barton, Brig. Gen. Seth...200
Barton, Capt. T.S. ...200
Barton, Clara...199
Bass, Mabry...108, 246
Battle, Jas. S. ...82
Battle, Joel...78, 79
Battle, Kemp P. ...82
Battle, William S. ...78, 83, 199, 221
Beaufort, N.C. (Town of)...14
Beaufort County, N.C. ...15, 97, 192, 214
Beckstein, Pvt. Louis...208
Beecher, Col. James C. ...27
Bell & Blackman...33
Bell, Mr. ...33
Belle Isle, Va., prison...177, 206, 209
Bermuda Hundred, Va. ...210
Big Bethel, Battle of...77, 94, 95
Big Sandy, Battle of...193
Black Jack Church...58, 230
Black Jack Church, skirmish March 26, 1864...230
Black market, selling Confederate money on,...76
Blackman, Pvt. Gideon F. ...75, 192, 210, 261, 266
Blakely, Capt. Theodore...228
Blockade...ii, 5, 7
Blount, Tom...221

Blount's Creek, skirmish...20
Blount's Mill...231
Blow, Dr. William...64, 135, 136, 226, 227, 242
Boat howitzers...225, 227
Bombshell, Union steamer...49, 154, 239
Bond, F.L. ...88, 251
Bonds, stolen in Potter's Raid...80
Boon's Mill...183, 184, 185
Boonville, N.Y. ...24
Borst, Pvt. Peter E. ...210, 265
Bowden, Pvt. B. B. ...216
Boyd's Ferry (Tar River)...94, 227
Bragg, Lt. Gen. Braxton...33
Brandy...66, 82, 100, 172
Breede, Sgt. Henry G. ...207
Bridges, Tar River...60, 89, 93, 115, 117, 241
Brooklyn, N.Y. ...134, 213
Brown, Capt. George...175, 221
Brown, Capt. Harvey W. ...226
Brown, Jesse...170
Brown, Pvt. William "Bill", a.k.a. Daniel Mulligan...43, 107, 197
Bruce, Lt. Thomas T. ...208
Buckshot...50, 104, 177
Budlong, Lt. Walter F. ...133, 212
Buffalo Lithia Springs...200
Buffaloes (Union sympathizers)...82

Bumpass, Pvt. G.W. ...223, 269
Bunting, Pvt. Thomas B. ...218
Burke, Lt. William H. ...148
Burnette, Cpl. Josiah...207
Burney Place, N.C. ...142, 143, 144, 145, 147, 161, 201, 221
Burnside, Maj. Gen. Ambrose...13, 14, 16, 18, 19, 24, 27
Butler, Maj. Gen, Benjamin F. ...163, 164
Butler, Pvt. Manuel...27
Calvary Episcopal Church, Tarboro...171
Camp Baker, near Greenville, N.C. ...226
Camp Palmer, near New Bern...44
Camp Washington, Staten Island...40
Camp, Lt. David...229
Canister...107, 112, 127, 133, 151, 152
Carbines...73, 91, 120, 150, 151, 154
Cardner, Lt. Edson D. ...163
Carpenter, Pvt. Kinchen Jahu...155, 167, 201, 257
Carteret County, N.C. ...179
Case shot...105, 111, 151, 152
Cedar Grove Cemetery...199
Cemeteries...180, 190, 191, 196, 198, 199, 204, 206, 207, 208, 210, 212, 217, 218, 230, 260, 270
Chambers, Lt.-col. John G. ...35

Chancellorsville, Battle of...71, 218
"Chapel" (Four Corners)...58, 59, 62, 215
Chapman, Russell...100
Charleston, S.C. ...ii, 3, 5, 13, 20, 66, 177, 202, 205
Charleston, S.C., prison...209
Chasseur, USS...225, 226
Cherry Hospital...198
Chesson, Eleanor...103
Chesson, John B. ...103
Chesson, Maggie...103, 109
Chesson, Pvt. Thomas W. ...113, 219
Chimborazo Hospital...71, 218
Chowan River...183
Church Street, Tarboro, picture...86
Church, Capt. Cyrus...41, 42, 52, 56, 105, 106, 204
Church, Capt. Simeon...41, 104, 194, 207
Cincinnati, Ohio...24, 211
City Point, Va. ...177, 178, 224
Claiborne, Col. William C. ...8, 9, 118, 120, 121, 122, 126, 127, 129, 133, 135, 136, 146, 167, 168, 213
Claiborne, Maj. Thomas...118, 119, 120, 121, 122, 150, 152, 154
Clark Place (plantation)...8, 64
Clark, Henry T. ...2, 47, 92, 141, 170, 171
Clark, Lt. John D. ...24, 54, 96, 112, 213
Clark's Mill...111

Clarke, Pvt. Patrick...209
Clarkson, Maj. Floyd...52, 53, 70, 91, 93, 95, 96, 97, 103, 104, 105, 106, 107, 109, 110, 113, 115, 116, 119, 120, 141, 156, 160, 161, 162, 189, 194, 213
Cobb, James...227
Cobb, Sheriff Joseph...100
Cody, William F. "Buffalo Bill"...193
Coffee...56, 96, 160
Cogdell, Capt. Daniel A. ...216
Cohen, Michael, describes Confederate gunboats, joins Potter...97
Cohen, Michael, wanted by police...198
Cole, Maj. George W. ...53, 54, 70, 93, 110, 111, 112, 113, 115, 116, 117, 124, 125, 127, 133, 141, 142, 144, 151, 153, 156, 159, 188, 190, 191, 193
Cole, Sen. Cornelius...190
Coleman, Capt. Thaddeus...61
Colonel Hill...93, 94, 95, 161
Colorado State Prison...193
Colt revolvers...50, 105, 106
Columbia, S.C., prison...177
Columbus, Ohio...212
Colyer, Vincent...14
Comfort, N.C. ...29, 35
Commissary officers and personnel Comsy...64
Commissary supplies...32, 63, 64, 88, 97
Concord Lodge No. 58, Tarboro...200

Confederate Hospital, Wilson, N.C. ...72, 83
Confederate Navy...88, 97, 98, 197
Confederate units
• 7th Confederate Cavalry...7, 8, 9, 12, 30, 34, 37, 92, 117, 118, 119, 132, 133, 135, 136, 141, 143, 150, 154, 165, 167, 180, 187, 198, 199, 203, 214, 217, 223
Contentnea Bridge...59
Contentnea Creek...119, 128, 133, 134, 135, 139, 167, 168
Contrabands...27, 28, 35, 139, 141, 142, 143, 144, 152, 156, 161, 162, 222
Conwell, Dr. Russell H. ...197
Cooley, Sgt. Herbert A. ...55, 67, 104, 115, 117, 120, 121, 122, 123, 126, 127, 147, 148, 149, 150, 151, 155, 156, 159
Cooper, Adjutant General Samuel...132, 170
Cooper, Lt. Alonzo...41, 177, 194, 195
Corey, B.A. ...227
Corkry, Pvt. Timothy...210
Corl, Pvt. David...109, 195, 204
Cormack, Pvt. William...210
Cotton gins...82, 196
County Bridge (Rocky Mount)...68
County Bridge, Rocky Mount, fire extinguished...81
County Home Road...58
Couriers...83, 89, 90, 103, 132, 155

Court martial...164, 167, 193
Coward's Bridge...118, 119
Cox, Col. William Ruffin...82
Craft, Pvt. David...224
Craven County, N.C. ...11, 48, 57, 147
Cromack, Cpl. William...42, 45, 110, 177, 178, 196, 206
Culpepper, Pvt. James M. ...218
Cummings, Capt. Emory...26, 120, 212
Curry, Mr. ...164
Cushing, Lt. William B. ...225
Custer, George A. ...51
Cutlasses...10, 31, 227
Dail, M.E. ...130
Dail, T.T. ...130
Dancy, Capt. John S. ...90
Dancy, Joseph...227
Dancy, Mrs. ...99
Daniel, John B. ...221
Daniel, John Henry...90, 200
Daniel, Meniza...200
Daniel's Schoolhouse...i, 90, 95, 102, 103, 106, 107, 108, 109, 194
Daniel's Schoolhouse, skirmish...103, 105, 107, 110, 113, 115, 116, 123, 133, 161, 165, 174, 175, 176, 177, 178, 192, 193, 194, 195, 196, 198, 200, 201, 204, 205, 206, 207, 208, 214, 220
Daniel's Schoolhouse, demolished...107
Danielhurst...90
Danielhurst, picture...102

Dannison (Dennison), Pvt. John...206
Danville, Ill. ...210
Davies, Mary...196
Davies, Pvt. William, admires 3rd New York Cavalry...25
Davis, President Jefferson...35, 120, 132
Delhi, N.Y. ...54, 190, 200
Demill, Maj. William, papers scattered during Potter's Raid...63, 64, 231
DeMille, Cecil B. ...64
Dennis...144
Dennison Hospital...212
Denver, CO...193
Department of North Carolina (Confederate)...5, 6
Department of North Carolina (Union)...13, 14
Department of Virginia and North Carolina (Union)...163, 185
Dermoulin, Pvt. Charles...208
Dern, Lt. George F. ...211
Deserter(s)...7, 12, 14, 41, 197, 206, 207, 222
Destrall, Pvt. Dennis...215
Devlin, Pvt. James...208
Dickenson Avenue, Greenville, N.C. ...60
District of North Carolina (Union)...6, 7, 185
District of the Cape Fear (Confederate)...5, 6, 7, 121
Dixon, Mr. ...130
Dixon, Sgt. Josiah...136, 137
Dobbin, Pvt. John H. ...229

Donaldson, Pvt. Andrew J. ...215
Dortch, Sen. William T. ...169
Dosier, Mr., slave of...144, 222
Dowd, Col. Henry A. ...77, 78
Dozier, Pvt. Andrew...74, 178, 216
Drake, Mrs. ...126, 127
Dudley, Pvt. William H. ...215
Dunham, Pvt. Pembroke J. ...81, 211
Duplin County Courthouse...29, 32
Duplin County Courthouse, picture...30
Duplin County Jail...30
Duplin County, N.C. ...ii, 29, 33, 100, 101
Dupree Ford (Dupree Crossing)...122
Dupree, James...119
Dupree, Sgt. William T. ...71, 218
Dupree, Thomas Byrd...121
Dutchess County, N.Y. ...192
Dykes, Benjamin...199
Eager, Pvt. Henry H. ...81, 211
East Carolina University...i, 201
Eastern Reflector...200
Ebbs, Capt. John...93, 156
Edgecombe County Court...97, 171
Edgecombe County, N.C. ...1, 67, 71, 78, 89, 90, 100, 108, 117, 121, 125, 126, 133, 140, 144, 145, 170, 216, 218, 219

Edgerton, Capt. James B. ...8, 90, 95, 103, 104, 220
Edison, Thomas...189
Edmondston, Catherine Anne Devereaux...131
Edward's Ferry...185
Edwards, Capt. D.W. ...136, 216
Edwards' Bridge...133, 135, 136, 150, 167
Edwards' Bridge, picture...133
Ellington, Lt. J.C. ...142, 153
Ellis, Capt. William L.A. ...8, 104, 220
Ellis, John W. ...1, 6
Elmira Prison, N.Y. ...50, 181, 210, 215
Elmira, N.Y. ...24
England...ii, 7, 30, 40, 64, 97, 162, 189, 212
Ephraim, escaped slave...140
Ericsson, John...190
Escort, Union steamer...20, 21, 231
Estvan, Bela...31
.58 caliber ammunition...104
Fairfield, N.C. ...25
Falkland, N.C. ...i, 8, 60, 64, 65, 66, 119, 123, 124, 125, 126, 141, 144, 213
Farquahar, Lt. Francis U. ...51
Ferral, Pvt. Francis B. ...229
Fieldsboro, N.C. ...125
Flag-of-truce steamers...173
Flags, from units in Potter's Raid...199
Flinn, Capt. John W. ...43, 208

Florence, S.C., prison...206, 208
Flusser, Lieutenant-commander Charles W. ...182, 183, 185, 186
"Flying Battery", 3rd New York Cavalry...24, 54, 70
Fonvielle, Jr., Dr. Chris E. ...229
Forbes, Alfred...64, 227
Forbes, James...227
Foreman, William...66, 100
Forrest Farm...132
Fort Anderson, Union post near New Bern,...49, 56, 148, 149, 231
Fort Branch, N.C. ...8, 9, 10, 89, 90, 110, 111, 116, 170, 198
Fort Cobb, Indian Territory...200
Fort Covington, N.Y. ...42, 43, 197
Fort Delaware...231
Fort Fisher, N.C....5, 15, 64, 121, 229
Fort Harrison, Va. ...187
Fort Laramie, Wyoming Territory...25
Fort Leavenworth, Kan. ...193
Fort Macon, N.C. ...14, 16
Fort McHenry, Md. ...180, 217
Fort Norfolk, Va. ...180, 215, 217
Fort Totten, New Bern, N.C. ...52, 56
Fort Union, N.M. ...191
Fortress Monroe, VA. ...178
Foster commands 18th Army Corps; ...19, 27

Foster General Hospital...158, 212
Foster, Maj. Gen. John Gray...ii, 2, 13, 165, 214
Foster's Mill, skirmish...184
Four Corners ("The Chapel")...58, 59, 215
Fowler, Henry...221
Frayser's Farm, Battle of...72, 219
Fredericksburg, Battle of...18, 19
Fremont, Col. Sewall L. ...36, 69, 71, 85, 170
Froelich, Louis...31, 32, 36, 37
Fulton, N.Y. ...42, 109, 196, 204
Funeral for soldiers killed at Daniel's Schoolhouse...109
GAR (Grand Army of the Republic)...189
Garfield, James A. ...54
Garnett, Philip...118
Garrard, Maj. Jeptha...188
Garysburg, N.C. ...184
Gasper, Capt. J. Ward...41
Gaston House...163, 164
Gaylord, Pvt. Caleb...213
Georgia Units:
• Macon Light Artillery...184
• 8th Georgia Cavalry...199, 230
• 62nd Georgia Cavalry...7, 8, 9, 64, 90, 110, 113, 6, 132, 134, 152, 154, 165, 167, 187, 198, 199, 200, 201, 203, 220, 230
German-born soldiers...10, 213
Germany...97, 213
Gettysburg, Battle of...3, 71, 72, 88, 171, 201

Goldsboro Expedition, December 1862...18, 19, 51, 53, 183
Goldsboro, Battle of...26
Goldsboro, N.C. ...3, 12, 14, 18, 19, 23, 26, 48, 51, 53, 84, 89, 116, 117, 118, 131, 144, 169, 175, 183, 198, 220
Gordon, Maj. Adam...172
Gouraud, Capt. George...51, 189, 211
Governor Morehead...94, 61
Graham, Capt. Edward...10, 112, 187, 220
Graham, George W. ...19, 26, 53, 192, 228, 230
Grant, Gen. Ulysses S. ...194
Granville Street, Tarboro...93
Grapeshot...6, 112
Graton, Louis...200
Graves, Cpl. William H. ...39, 88, 96, 121, 134
Graves, Maj. Charles C. ...228
Graves, Richard...149
Gray, Capt. Patrick...8, 230
Gray, Surgeon J.W. ...151, 211
Green Wreath (plantation, Pitt County, N.C.)...66, 100
Green, Bob...227
Green, Charles...227
Green, Pvt. John...205
Greene, George...57, 59, 66, 221
Greenville and Raleigh Plank Road...60
Greenville and Wilson Plank Road...125

Greenville, N.C. …i, ii, 7, 8, 9, 12, 21, 48, 57, 58, 59, 60, 62, 63, 64, 65, 66, 69, 76, 87, 89, 90, 94, 116, 117, 118, 119, 125, 132, 135, 144, 200, 201, 215, 221, 225, 226, 227, 228, 230, 231
Greenville, N.C., fortifications…21, 60, 61
Greenville, N.C., Union Navy raid; …225
Greenville, population 1860…60
Greenwood, Capt. …225
Grieg, Lt. Sherman…35
Griffin, Col. Joel R. …7, 199
Griffin, Cpl. J. J. …218
Grimes, Brig. Gen. Bryan…8, 81
Grimes, Charlotte Emily Bryan…81
Grimes, William…8
Grimes' Farm…8
Grimsley, W.P., house, pictured;…128
Grimsley's Church…127, 129, 131, 132, 133
Grison, Pvt. John…205
Grove Camp, near New Bern, N.C. …28
Gum Swamp, skirmish…21
Haddocks' Crossroads, N.C., Union cavalry raids…228, 229, 230
Hahn, A. W. …26, 54
Hahn, Mr. …229
Halifax County, N.C. …48, 131, 185
Hall, Capt. Newton…63, 211
Hall, Capt. Rowland M. …25, 53, 63, 73, 75, 150, 151, 160, 191, 210

Hall, Pvt. Hamilton H. …73
Halleck, General-in-chief Henry W., suggests Foster attack railroads…21
Hallsville, N.C. …29, 34
Hamblin, Florence…192
Hamblin, Lavinia…192
Hamblin, Sgt. Abram H. …107, 192, 214
Hamilton Road (or Plymouth Road)…90, 93, 95, 96, 111
Hamilton, N.C. …8, 9, 17, 18, 89
Hardtack…79
Harlem Oil…56
Harman, Pvt. Henry A. …106
Harper, J.J. …83, 221
Harris, Private John, enlists in 3rd New York Cavalry during a raid…25
Harris, Sen. Ira…191
Hart, Spencer…82
Harvey, escaped slave…140, 144
Hats, lost by Potter's men (caps)…126
Hatton, Mr. …221
Heath, Pvt. A. L. …215
Heckman, Brig. Gen. Charles A. …28, 29, 35
Hendricks Creek…91
Henry, Cpl. Addison G. …209
Herald (Melbourne, Australia)…162
Herald (New York)…27, 59, 65, 91, 162, 173, 176, 206
Hertford County, N.C. …183
High Shoals Iron Company…80

High, Sheriff W. H. …131
Hill, Lt. Gen. Daniel Harvey…5, 20, 94
Hill, Mr. …131
Hill, Pvt. William H. …215
Hilma (home of Henry T. Clark)…92
Himes, James M. …196
Hinson, Sheriff John W. …100
Hiscock, L.H. …190, 191
Hodges, Joel or Josiah…227
Hoell, Ed…227
Hoffman, Lt.-col. Southard…180
Hoke, Brig. Gen. Robert F. …178, 186
Holcombe, Pvt. Alfred…76
Holt, Pvt. A.C. …231
Holtzscheiter, Julius…97
Honey Hill, Battle of…189
Hookerton, Lt. Hubbard killed near in 1865; …177
Hookerton, N.C. …i, 134, 136, 205, 213
Hookerton, skirmish…134
Horn(e), Cpl. Jacob H. …229
Horn, Capt. John W. …230
Horn, Private…163
Horne Family Cemetery…230
Horne, Hosea Louis…229, 230
Horses, captured in Potter's Raid "John Horse"…81
Horses, losses during raid…29, 30, 33, 35, 37, 45, 66, 80, 82, 83, 93, 100, 104, 109, 110, 119, 124, 129, 130, 136, 144, 145, 151, 156, 160

"Hospital Defenders"...83, 85
Hospitals, at Greenville, Tarboro, Wilson, Goldsboro, New Bern...4, 61, 72, 83, 88, 93, 117, 118, 131, 158, 198, 205, 208, 210, 211, 212, 214, 220, 231
Hotels...4, 43, 71, 88, 101, 141, 163, 190
Houstain, Maj. John R. ...175, 176
Howard, Judge George...101, 166
Howard, Jr., George...2
Hubbard, Lt. Henry A. ...108, 109, 174, 176, 177, 205
Hunter, Maj. Gen. David...20
Hyde County, N.C. ...25, 192
Hyman, Col. Joseph H. ...82
In and Out of Rebel Prisons...195
Inflation, wartime...80
Ireland...10, 49, 112, 207, 209, 212
Ithaca, N.Y. ...200
Jackson, Bugler James H. ...64
Jackson, Maj. George...34
Jackson, N.C. ...184
Jackson, Sgt. William...27
Jacksonville, Fla. ...205
Jacobs, Jr., Maj. Ferris, promoted to major...25, 29, 53, 54, 70, 190, 200
Jane (slave of George Howard, Jr.)...4, 101, 141
Jenkins, Lt. Bennett P. ...92, 117, 180, 217

Jocknick, Capt. Gustavus...25, 211
"John Horse"...81
John Myers & Son...94
Johnson, President Andrew...168
Johnson's Island, prison...179, 180, 216, 217, 218
Johnson's Mills, N.C. ...142, 147
Jones County, N.C. ...11, 28, 35
Jones, Pvt. Elisha C. ...117, 219
Jones, Pvt. Henry G. ...117, 220
Jones, Pvt. James...207
Jones, Pvt. Reddick...74, 217
Jordan and Williford...80
Jourdan, Col. James...29, 49, 50, 56, 203
Joy, Lt. Henry S. ...142
Kaemmerer, Pvt. David...213
Kahlbaum, Pvt. Adolphus...209
Kautz, Brig. Gen. August V. ...187, 188
Kelly, Isaac...33
Kelly, Pvt. Hubert...208
Kenansville Armory...31, 32
Kenansville, N.C. ...7, 23, 29, 30, 31, 32, 33, 34, 36, 37, 48, 54, 62, 101, 121, 223
Kenansville-Warsaw Raid...154, 222
Kennedy, Maj. John T. ...7, 90, 103, 113, 155, 167, 198
King, Coffield...82
King, Dr. ...140

King, Henry...59, 65, 119, 123, 125, 143, 226, 227
Kinney, Pvt. David...211
Kinston, N.C. ...7, 9, 10, 12, 18, 21, 36, 61, 89, 116, 129, 131, 132, 135, 140, 142, 143, 144, 152, 155, 156, 165, 168, 169, 172, 175, 203
Kitten Creek...120
Knapp, Cpl. Mordecai...76, 201
Knapp, Henry J. ...74
Knight, James...3, 4
Kromer, Lt. Charles C. ...148, 149
Laetsch, Pvt. John...223
Laishly, Sgt. Stephen...104
Lamb, Lt-col. John Calhoun...106
Lane, Capt. William K. ...30
Lane, Pvt. Manly...223
Lawrence, Capt. J. J. ...9
Lawrence, Dr. Joe...109
Lawrence, Lt. Nathan M. ...117, 180, 217
Laws, Cpl. Abial W. ...207
Lay, 2nd Asst. Engineer John L. ...225
Lee, General Robert E. ...ii, 132
Lee, Lt. Edgar J. ...120
Lee, Rear Admiral S. P. ...20, 183
Lee, Sgt. Henry S. ...136
Lehmann, Col. Theodore F. ...184
Lenoir County, N.C. ...35
"Lennox"...120
Lewis, Elfrida C. ...190
Lewis, Elizabeth Herritage Bryan...199
Lewis, Kenelm...81, 83, 140, 144, 169, 171, 172, 199

Lewis, L.C. ...103
Lewis, Lt.-col. George W. ...190
Lewis, Martha Elizabeth Hoskins Foreman...100
Lewis, Martha Foreman...140
Leyden, Capt. Maurice
Leyden, picture...63
Libby Prison, Richmond, Va., ...109, 176, 205, 206; picture...174
Lincoln, Abraham...25, 53; reviews 3rd New York Cavalry...24
Lincoln, Pvt. Riley...208
Lipkin, Pvt. William...205
Liquor...41, 80, 97
Little Contentnea Creek...135, 139, 167, 216
Little Creek (Martin County, N.C.)...18
"Little Dennis"...144
Locomotives...76
Longstreet, Maj. Gen. James...6, 20, 74, 216
Looting...63, 226
Louisiana, USS...15
Love, James...33
Lower New Bern Road...58
Lynch, Commodore William F. ...84; picture...84
Macon County, Ga. ...8, 177, 184
Macon, Ga., prison...176
Magnolia, N.C. ...29, 32, 34
Mail...3, 4, 29, 32, 33, 72, 173
Malvern Hill, Battle of...77
Mann, Lt. Barnabas N. ...19

Marble Cemetery, New York City...190
Marietta National Cemetery...210
Marietta, Ga. ...210
Marlboro, N.C. ...125
Martin County, N.C. ...8, 18, 89, 184
Martin, Brig. Gen. James G. ...6, 167, 203
Martin, Col. William Francis...90
Martin, Pvt. Collins...206
Masonic Lodges...29, 100, 191, 200
Masons...64, 79, 180, 200
Massachusetts units:
• 17th Massachusetts Infantry...19
• 23rd Massachusetts Infantry...28, 35
• 25th Massachusetts Infantry...28, 49, 50, 203
• 27th Massachusetts infantry...49, 76, 203
Massett, Bugler Joseph F. ...211
Matix, E.F. ...33
Matthews, Lt. William D. ...119
McCarthy, Mr. ...33
McCue, Pvt. John...209
McDonald, Gunner Edwin A. ...225
McGinn, Patrick...198
McIntyre, Pvt. Andrew J. ...72, 74, 80, 82, 124, 165, 219
McKenna, Pvt. Francis...231
McKenna, Sgt. James...116, 208
McKenzie, Lt. Carlton J. ...230
McKenzie, Pvt. William Newton...110, 201, 220

McLane, Lt. John B. ...226
McNary, Lt.-col. William H. ...49
Mead, Pvt. Charles N.D. ...74, 126, 152
Mecklenburg County, Va. ...200
Menan, Mr. ...99
Meredith, Brig. Gen. Sullivan Amory...180
Merry, Pvt. George W. ...25
Miami, USS...186
Militia...2, 10, 33, 53, 66, 83, 84, 96, 112, 120, 123, 124, 126, 131, 132, 139, 149, 165, 170, 187, 198, 215
Miller, Pvt. Charles A. ...230
Miller, Pvt. William W. ...214
Miller, Samuel...196
Miller, Sgt. John P. ...204
Mills, grist...78, 97, 197
Mitchell, Pvt. James...222
Mitchell, Pvt. Truman...206
Mix, Col. Simon Hoosick...24
Mix, Lt.-col. John H. ...16, 25
Monroe, James...190
Montgomery, Alabama...9, 120, 121, 126, 127, 135, 150, 198, 199
Moody, Sgt. Ezra S. ...117, 220
Moore, Capt. Julius W. ...228
Moore, Maj. Roger...228
Moore, Pvt. Jefferson...222
Mora, N.M. ...191
Morris County, N.J. ...16
Morton & Zaery...33

Mosher, Lt. Henry Ephraim...109, 174, 176, 177, 205
Mountain howitzers...54, 55, 69, 70, 89, 96, 104, 111, 112, 118, 119, 120, 121, 133, 143, 150, 151, 152, 153, 154
"Mud March"...2, 13, 17, 18
Mules...4, 33, 35, 55, 56, 61, 80, 81, 82, 83, 93, 99, 110, 124, 130, 139, 143, 144, 161, 172, 225, 227, 228
Mulford, Maj. John E. ...177, 178
Mulligan, Daniel...42, 43, 107, 197
Mulway, Pvt. Narcisse...108, 109, 196, 208
Muskets...83, 97, 105, 107, 112, 115, 126, 131, 185
Myers, Lt. Jasper...51, 111, 112, 113
Myers, Mr. ...144
Myrover, Lt. James H. ...228, 229
Mystic (Union steamer)...231
Nash County, N.C. ...78, 81
NC Highway 111...32
NC Highway 43...65, 149
NC Road 1102...125
NC Road 1753...142
NC Road 1917...142
Nethercutt, Maj. John H. ...10, 11, 34, 132, 203
Neuse River...ii, 2, 4, 7, 18, 19, 49, 55, 56, 75, 84, 89, 135, 148, 149, 150, 168
Neuse, CSS...18, 19, 98

New Bern...ii, 2, 4, 5, 7, 8, 10, 11, 14, 15, 16, 18, 19, 20, 21, 23, 24, 25, 27, 28, 29, 30, 33, 35, 36, 39, 41, 42, 44, 45, 46, 48, 49, 50, 51, 52, 56, 57, 58, 74, 78, 81, 89, 97, 98, 109, 115, 116, 127, 129, 132, 135, 139, 141, 142, 143, 145, 146, 148, 149, 151, 154, 155, 158, 161, 162, 163, 164, 165, 167, 173, 175, 179, 180, 181, 183, 184, 185, 186, 197, 199, 205, 207, 210, 211, 212, 214, 216, 217, 218, 230, 231
New Bern, Battle of...15, 16
New Era...54
New Hamburgh, N.Y. ...192
New Jersey units:
• 9th New Jersey Infantry...19, 28, 35
New Orleans, La. ...200
New York (Union steamer)...178
New York Times...ii, 62, 179, 205, 223
New York Units:
• Angel's Battery...49
• Mix's Cavalry Battalion...26
• 1st New York Marine Artillery...15, 225
• 3rd New York Artillery...16, 24, 49, 55, 96, 107, 112, 123, 134, 187, 192, 199, 203, 213
• 3rd New York Cavalry...16, 23, 24, 25, 26, 27, 28, 35, 39, 45, 51, 53, 54, 55, 58, 59, 61, 62, 63, 67, 70, 72, 74, 76, 77, 89, 93, 94, 100, 101, 104, 117, 119, 120, 121, 122,

123, 126, 136, 141, 148, 149, 150, 151, 154, 156, 159, 160, 163, 164, 187, 188, 190, 191, 192, 201, 203, 209, 210, 222
• 12th New York Cavalry...24, 25, 39, 40, 41, 43, 44, 45, 46, 52, 53, 58, 63, 65, 89, 93, 95, 96, 104, 105, 108, 109, 110, 116, 134, 162, 174, 176, 177, 178, 184, 191, 193, 194, 195, 196, 199, 201, 203, 204, 228, 229, 230, 231
• 23rd New York Cavalry...24, 25, 35, 53, 94, 120, 136, 160, 196, 203, 212, 222, 228
• 24th New York Independent Battery...19
• 81st New York Infantry...28, 206
• 98th New York Infantry...151, 212
• 158th New York Infantry...49, 50, 203
Newspaper advertisements...55
Newton, Col. Walter...122, 123, 139, 141
Newton, W.B.F. ...119, 123
Nicholl, Capt. Sylvester D. ...15
Nichols, Capt. P. ...74, 180, 218
Nichols' Company...74, 218
Norfleet, John...100
Norfleet, Robert...82
Norfleet, William...4
Norfolk, Va. ...20, 178, 180, 192, 215, 217
Norman, Capt. Thomas J. ...90

North Atlantic Blockading Squadron...20
North Carolina General Assembly...100, 199
North Carolina Science Museum...198
North Carolina Units: (Confederate)
Artillery:
- Bunting's Battery...9, 153, 204
- Cape Fear Light Artillery...10
- Cummings' Battery...10, 64, 204
- Dickson's Battery (2nd Company G, 3rd North Carolina Artillery)...9, 204
- Saunders' Battalion...203
- Southerland's Battery...32, 153, 154, 204
- Wilmington Horse Artillery...9, 152, 204, 229
- 1st North Carolina Artillery...3, 10, 11, 15, 84, 136, 204
- 2nd North Carolina Artillery...10, 64, 152, 204
- 3rd North Carolina Artillery...9, 117, 180, 204, 216
- 13th Battalion, North Carolina Artillery...228

Cavalry:
- 1st North Carolina Cavalry...136
- 3rd North Carolina Cavalry...15, 226, 228, 229, 230
- 5th North Carolina Cavalry...175, 223
- 16th Battalion, North Carolina Cavalry...198

Infantry:
- Whitford's Battalion (1st North Carolina Local Defense Troops)...11, 50, 59, 135, 136, 137, 144, 154, 181, 199, 203, 215, 216, 222, 228
- Nethercutt's Battalion...203
- 2nd North Carolina Infantry...82
- 8th North Carolina Infantry...117, 180, 217
- 12th Battalion, North Carolina Infantry...74
- 13th Battalion, North Carolina Infantry...74, 180, 204, 218
- 13th North Carolina Infantry...71, 218
- 15th North Carolina Infantry...77
- 17th North Carolina Infantry...9, 10, 90, 110, 111, 112, 116, 117, 123, 167, 187, 204, 219, 224
- 18th North Carolina Infantry...72, 219
- 24th North Carolina Infantry...184
- 42nd North Carolina Infantry...10, 132, 135, 136
- 43rd North Carolina Infantry...117, 220
- 44th North Carolina Infantry...94
- 50th North Carolina Infantry...10, 61, 132, 142, 145, 153, 155, 167, 199, 201, 204, 221
- 55th North Carolina Infantry...15
- 56th North Carolina Infantry...21, 171
- 61st North Carolina Infantry...34, 224
- 66th North Carolina Infantry...74, 218
- 67th North Carolina Infantry (formerly Whitford's Battalion)...59, 199, 215

Militia:
- 17th North Carolina Militia...123
- 39th North Carolina Militia...33

North Carolina Units (Union)
- 1st North Carolina Union Volunteers...16, 24, 26, 27, 134, 143, 192, 203, 213, 214, 225, 228, 229, 230
- 1st North Carolina Colored Troops...22, 27, 30, 53, 70, 141, 222

North State (Union steamer)...225
Northampton County, N.C. ...184
Northeast Cape Fear River...29
Northen, Lt. B. Arnold...231
O. Henry (William Sidney Porter)...61
Oats...44, 56, 159
Ohio units:
- 6th Independent Ohio Cavalry...24

Oliver, Pvt. William H. ...223
Onslow County, N.C. ...121
Oregon (*Colonel Hill*)...94

Oregon Inlet…94
Oswego County, N.Y.
 …41, 42, 201
Oswego, N.Y. …39, 41,
 42, 45, 177, 194, 196,
 204, 205
Otter Creek…114, 119,
 120, 121, 122, 123, 124,
 126, 127, 129, 133, 141,
 143, 149, 160, 167, 219
Otter Creek Church
 Road…125
Owen, Rev. Thomas…103
Palamountain,
 Elizabeth…97
Palamountain, Isaac B.
 …97, 118
Palmer, Brig. Gen. Innis N.
 …163
Palmer, George…133, 205
Palmer, Surgeon William
 H. …55, 149
Pamlico County, N.C.
 …192, 214
Pamlico River…14, 15, 20,
 161
Parker, Lt. William F. …37
Parker, Pvt. William K.
 …223
Parker, W.W. …80, 172
Parole…59, 62, 74, 178,
 179, 180, 199, 205, 206,
 208, 209, 210, 211, 214,
 215, 216, 217, 218, 219,
 220, 221, 223, 224
Parole camp…212
Partisan rangers…10, 11,
 132, 203
Patrick, Edward…130
Patrick, John M. …130
Paul, Pvt. Thomas
 John…212
Pay, soldiers'…28, 41, 76,
 80, 161
Paymasters…41, 62, 193,
 225

Peck, Brig. Gen. John J.
 …185, 229
Pedrick, Captain…20
Pender, Maj. Gen. William
 Dorsey…88, 171
Pennsylvania units:
 • 58th Pennsylvania
  Infantry…228
 • 103rd Pennsylvania
  Infantry…184
Pension(s)…42, 109, 192,
 197, 205, 206, 207, 208,
 210, 212, 213
Pentland, Pvt.
 George…209
Petersburg Artillery…9,
 10, 90, 110, 112, 117,
 187, 188, 194, 203, 220
Petersburg Express…7,
 131, 162, 176
Petersburg, Va. …10, 71,
 131, 132, 163, 170, 175,
 176, 185, 187, 188, 198,
 219
Petition, for release of
 Potter's Raid
 captives…180
Pettigrew, Brig. Gen.
 James Johnston…20
Petway, R.S. …82
*Philadelphia
 Inquirer*…229
Phillips, J.A.D. …129
Phillips, Mary Jane…132
Picket, USS…15
Pigott, Emeline…179
Piney Neck Road…147,
 149
Pioneers…27, 28, 36, 53,
 58, 77, 155, 203
Pippin, Mr. …169, 173
Pistols…29, 31, 50, 67, 71,
 73, 91, 93, 105, 106, 108,
 118, 151, 177, 190, 226
Pitchkettle Landing…147

Pitt County, N.C. …i, 8,
 12, 58, 59, 60, 118, 125,
 126, 132, 136, 139, 142,
 147, 185, 192, 219, 222,
 227, 228, 230
Pitt, Capt. Franklin G.
 …133
Pittsylvania County, Va.
 …8
Plymouth Road (or
 Hamilton Road)…110,
 111, 187
Plymouth, Battle of…4,
 10, 178, 193, 194
Plymouth, N.C. …4, 7, 10,
 14, 16, 18, 21, 26, 90,
 134, 177, 183, 184, 186,
 197, 206, 207, 208, 209,
 213, 225, 239
Pocahontas Mine, CO
 …193
Point Lookout Prison, Md.
 …50, 181, 215, 231
Pollock Street Jail, New
 Bern…179
Pollocksville, N.C. …27,
 29, 35
Pontoon bridge…10, 148,
 154, 155, 156, 170, 176,
 184
Pool, Lt. James H. …4
Pool, Lt.-col. Stephen D.
 …4, 12, 15, 167
Pope, William E. …80
Port Royal, Union
 steamer…49, 154, 156
Porter, William Sidney (O.
 Henry)…61
Post office, at
 Greenville…82
Potter, Asst. Surgeon,
 Albert…55, 116, 208
Potter, at Green Wreath
 Plantation…66
Potter, Brig. Gen. Edward
 E. …i, ii, 2, 8, 15, 16, 18,

19, 26, 46, 51, 53, 54, 55, 58, 59, 60, 61, 64, 65, 66, 67, 70, 84, 88, 89, 92, 97, 98, 110, 115, 116, 117, 118, 119, 121, 122, 124, 125, 129, 131, 132, 133, 134, 135, 136, 139, 140, 141, 145, 146, 148, 149, 150, 154, 161, 162, 163, 169, 170, 171, 179, 189, 203, 225
Potter, Pvt. Newet S. ...216
Potter's Raid, casualties...204
Potts, Mr. ...221
Potts, Pvt. Alexander...223
Powell, Mrs. ...82
Powell, Pvt. Furnifold...50, 181, 215
Powers, Cpl. John H. ...216
Price, Pvt. William I. ...216
Princeville, site of skirmish...111
Prisoners, captured on Potter's Raid...204
Proctor, Celia...82
Proctor, Frederick...82
Provost marshal...50, 129, 163, 220
Quartermaster supplies...64, 88, 97
Quinn, Cpl. Michael...20
Railroad bridge, Rocky Mount, N.C. ...75, 78, 171, 176
Railroad bridge, temporary, at Rocky Mount...170
Railroad tracks, destruction of...22, 32, 51, 70, 76, 77
Rainbow Banks...89
Rainey, Pvt. Theophilus...10

Raleigh and Gaston Railroad Guard...74, 218
Raleigh National Cemetery...196, 204, 208, 212
Raleigh, N.C. ...1, 30, 33, 34, 36, 60, 74, 81, 124, 129, 131, 143, 165, 168, 196, 198, 199
Randolph County, N.C. ...90, 219
Raney, escaped slave...140
Ransom, Brig. Gen. Matthew...132, 170, 184, 185
Rhode Island units...29, 55, 208
Rations...52, 55, 56, 154, 159, 192
Red Banks Church...228, 229, 230
Relief funds, for Confederate families...57
Renshaw, Lt. R.T. ...225
Reservoir Hill, Petersburg...188
Respress (Respess), Isaiah...163, 164
Revolvers...20, 35, 41, 45, 50, 73, 105, 106, 118, 176, 222, 227
Rhode Island units:
• 5th Rhode Island Artillery...55, 208
Richardson, Cpl. William...226
Richmond Dispatch...32, 131
Ridgeway, N.C. ...198
Riley, Pvt. John...207
Rivenbark, Mr. ...33
River Bend, CO ...193
River Road (Neuse River)...147, 149, 150

River Road (Tar River)...65, 121, 221
Roals, Mr. ...33
Roanoke Island, Battle of...10, 16
Roanoke River...2, 3, 8, 9, 14, 17, 48, 89, 98, 131, 185
Robertson, Brig. Gen. Beverly...9
Rochester, New York...23, 24
Rocky Mount Mills...68, 71, 78, 79, 81, 161, 197, 199
Rocky Mount Station...71, 72, 210
Rocky Mount, N.C. ...i, ii, 3, 4, 12, 47, 48, 68, 69, 70, 71, 72, 74, 75, 76, 77, 78, 79, 80, 81, 82, 83, 84, 85, 88, 89, 101, 115, 116, 117, 124, 131, 132, 140, 141, 144, 160, 161, 166, 169, 170, 171, 172, 175, 176, 178, 184, 190, 191, 192, 199, 201, 211, 217, 218, 219, 221
Rodgers, John...99
Rogers, John...144
Rogers, Pvt. Thomas...209
Rose, Mr. ...172
Rosita, CO ...193
Rote, Saddler Charles...209
Rude, Lizzie...109
Rude, Pvt. Hiram...109
Rumors of Potter's Raid...2, 3, 129, 130, 131
Rutherfordton, N.C. ...201
6-pounder guns...15, 111, 120, 121, 153
S.R. Spaulding (Union steamer)...178

Sabers...31, 37, 41, 59, 91, 106, 122, 195, 229
Saloons...60, 65, 193
San Francisco Evening Bulletin...35, 162
Sanders, Lt. John W. ...168
Sandusky, Ohio...179, 180, 216, 217, 218
Sandy Foundation, N.C. ...35
Satchwell, Surgeon Solomon S. ...83, 84, 85
Satterthwaite, Cpl. James A. ...216
Saunders, Maj. William...9, 132
Savannah, Ga. ...210
Scuffleton Bridge...134, 135, 136, 139, 142, 165
Scuffleton, N.C. ...i, 119, 134, 135, 136, 141, 147, 148, 150, 167, 173
Seddon, Secretary of War James...4, 169
Selby, B. ...81
Sharpe, Lt. Van Buren...121, 133
Shaw, Pvt. James R. ...151, 211
Shawsheen, USS...177
Sheriden, Pvt. Joseph...212
Sherman, Lt. Gen. William T. ...130
Shiloh (head of navigation on Tar River)...87
Shirley, Pvt. Henry...216
Shotgun(s)...50, 60, 107, 248
Shurley, Mrs. ...99
Silver...63, 64, 65, 66
Slade, Lt. William...230
Slaves, escape from Stonewall...81, 140

Slover House (Union headquarters), New Bern...19
Smith, Lt. John G. ...7, 12, 95, 103, 155, 200
Smith, Pvt. Charles...209
Smith, Pvt. John L. ...210
Snead's Ferry, N.C. ...121
Snell, Pvt. Asa W. ...113, 219
Snow Hill Road...125, 127
South Carolina units:
• 5th South Carolina Cavalry...34
Spalding County, Ga. ...8
Spanish-American War...198
Sparta Township...126
Sparta, N.C. (Old Sparta)...57, 65, 69, 70, 71, 88, 89, 103, 110, 115, 116, 117, 118, 119, 124, 132, 133, 160; bridges...60, 93; Potter's men camp there...67
Spear, Col. Samuel P. ...183
Spencer, Capt. W. H. ...97
Spies...7, 11, 12, 14, 34, 179
Spinola, Brig. Gen. Francis Barretto...20, 50
Spoor, Pvt. Oliver...149, 151, 209
Spring Bank, N.C. ...84
St. Andrew Street, Tarboro N.C., picture...91
St. John's Episcopal Church...142
St. Vrain, Ceran...191
Stanton, Secretary of War Edward,...164
Stantonsburg and Falkland Road...66
Stanwix Hall...190

State Hospital for the Colored Insane, Goldsboro...198
State Journal (Raleigh)...99, 101, 129, 130, 144, 165, 172, 214
Stearns, Capt. Alonzo...120
Stephens, Pvt. Melvin F. ...96, 104, 195
Stewart, Lt. Thomas J. ...117, 180, 216
Stocks, William...227
Stonewall (plantation near Rocky Mount)...81, 140, 171, 199
Stowe, Harriet Beecher...27
"Streeback", Nancy...213
Street's Ferry Road...147, 149
Street's Ferry, N.C. ...ii, 126, 148, 149, 150, 151, 152, 153, 154, 155, 165, 167, 169, 172, 183, 184, 201, 209, 211, 212, 213, 214
Street's Ferry, skirmish...147, 150
Strieback, Cpl. Robert...134
Stripling, Pvt. David M. ...230
Stuart, Maj. Gen. J. E. B. ...9
Sugg, Dr. Aquilla, house, pictured...128
Swain Place...119
Sweetwater Creek...184
Swift Creek...11, 49, 50, 66, 132, 215
Swift Creek Village, N.C. ...48, 49, 50, 56, 57, 67, 76, 118. 142, 147, 148, 149, 153, 181, 203, 221

Syracuse, N.Y. ...24, 190
3-inch rifle...111, 120, 121
12-pounder guns...55, 120, 153, 225
Tar River...2, 7, 8 48, 60, 64, 70, 71, 78, 81, 87, 88, 89, 94, 95, 98, 111, 116, 161, 169, 170, 171, 176, 199, 225, 226, 227, 230
Tar River Bridge...65, 73, 92, 113, 114, 115, 118, 171
Tar River Road...65, 121, 221
Tarboro Branch Railroad...18, 72, 73, 84, 87
Tarboro Female Academy...88
Tarboro gunboat...98, 161, 197
Tarboro hospital (Way Hospital No. 7)...88
Tarboro Male Academy...88
Tarboro Southerner...9, 88
Tarboro, Confederate cap factory...88
Tarboro, N.C. ...i, ii, 1, 2, 3, 4, 7, 9, 12, 13, 14, 17, 18, 21, 47, 48, 60, 61, 62, 69, 70, 71, 72, 73, 74, 78, 81, 82, 83, 84, 86, 87, 88, 89, 90, 91, 92, 93, 94, 95, 96, 97, 98, 99, 100, 101, 103, 105, 106, 107, 108, 109, 110, 111, 112, 113, 114, 116, 117, 118, 119, 124, 126, 127, 131, 132, 134, 140, 141, 144, 145, 149, 155, 161, 166, 167, 169, 170, 171, 175, 187, 194, 196, 197, 198, 200, 204, 205, 206, 207, 208, 209, 210, 212, 213, 214, 215, 216, 217, 218, 219, 220, 221, 222, 225
Tarboro, steamboat landing...93, 95
Tarborough (locomotive)...76
Taylor, Pvt. Edgar...153, 212
Taylor, Pvt. John W. ...230
Taylor, Pvt. Lester...207
Taylor, Pvt. Myron...206
Taylor, Pvt. Roswell...206
Telegraph...3, 12, 32, 33, 35, 36, 69, 71, 77, 83, 85, 89, 131, 162, 168, 170, 193
Telegraph operators, absent from post...84, 168
Texas...8, 196, 197
The Battle of Forks Road...229
Thompson, Amanda...206
Thompson, Capt. William A. ...8, 42, 104, 110, 220
Thompson, Pvt. William (1st)...42, 109, 195, 205
Thompson, Pvt. William (2nd)...42, 109, 206
Thorburn, Col. Charles Edmonston...35
Thorn, Cpl. Thomas...216
Tillery, John...80
Times (London)...162
Tobacco...65, 144, 164, 172
Toisnot Creek...83, 84
Tool, Bettie...99
Tools, for wrecking railroad tracks...22, 76, 77
Toothbrushes...80
Tories (Union sympathizers), aid Union forces...7, 130, 166, 167
Town Common (Greenville)...226
Town Common (Tarboro)...88
Town Creek...67, 89
Towns, Lt.-col. Randolph...7
Tracy, Pvt. John...207
Trade Street, Tarboro...93, 95
Train wreck between Tarboro and Rocky Mount...3
Train, Charles R. ...164
Tredegar Iron Works...76
Trenton, N.C. ...28, 29, 35, 46, 52
Tucker, Capt. R. S. ...15
Tucker, Pvt. Joshua W. ...117, 217
Turner, Cullen P. ...224
Turner, Lt. William S. ...231
Turner, Pvt. Robert J. ...117, 220
Tyson, Allen...227
Tyson's Creek, ambush on night of July 19, 1863...63
U-iron...76
Union Navy (U.S. Navy), enlists black sailors...227
Union Navy...i, 5, 14, 17, 20, 48, 95, 139, 197
United States Military Academy...6
United States units:
• 1st U.S. Colored Cavalry...188
• 2nd U.S. Colored Cavalry...188, 190
• 2nd U.S. Dragoons...25, 190
• 10th U.S. Cavalry...193
• 35th U.S. Colored Troops...235

Upper New Bern
  Road...58
US Highway 258...125
US Highway 264...60, 125
US Highway 64...90, 108
Van Alen, Col. James H.
  ...24
Vance, Gov. Zebulon
  Baird...4, 33, 64, 66,
  169, 170
Vicksburg, Miss. ...ii, 3,
  21, 108, 166, 201
Villa, Pancho...198
Vine, Charles...119
Vinson, Lt. Daniel...231
Virginia units:
• Petersburg Artillery...9,
  10, 90, 110, 112, 117,
  187, 188, 194, 203, 220
• 6th Virginia Infantry...74,
  178, 216
Virginia (Merrimac), CSS
  ...10
Vought, Lt.-col. P. J. ...52
Wake County, N.C. ...33,
  131, 213
Wakeman, Cpl. Chester F.
  ...73, 81, 101, 117, 118,
  124, 126, 127, 129
Wallace, Pvt. Newton...49
Walstonburg, N.C. ...125
War Department, U.S.
  ...14, 40
War with Mexico...6, 25
Warren, Deborah Virginia
  Bonner...83
Warren, Edward
  Jenner...83
Warsaw, N.C. ...ii, 22, 23,
  25, 32, 33, 34, 35, 36, 47,
  48, 51, 70, 77, 82, 101,
  163, 222
Washington Academy...15
Washington County, N.C.
  ...103

Washington, Col. James A.
  ...10
Washington, George...149
Washington, N.C. ...4, 5,
  6, 7, 8, 10, 14, 15, 16, 17,
  18, 20, 50, 51, 54, 59, 60,
  61, 63, 64, 90, 93, 94,
  115, 149, 163, 166, 186,
  225, 226, 227, 228, 229,
  231
Washington, N.C. Battle,
  September 6, 1862...15
Watches...33, 63, 64, 66,
  99, 100
Watson, Robert A. ...69,
  74
Wayne County, N.C. ...7,
  8, 131, 198
Weather...3, 45
Weldon, N.C. ...131, 184
Wellington, Sgt.
  Gleason...41, 45, 52, 53,
  56, 63, 89, 105, 110, 133,
  193, 194
West, Capt. R.R. ...228,
  230
Whiskey...65, 99
White, Capt. Charles A.
  ...59, 215, 222
White, Pvt. George A.,
  captures locomotive in
  Rocky Mount...73
Whitehall, Battle of...18
Whitford, Maj. John N.
  ...10, 11, 152, 167, 169,
  180, 199, 215
Whitford, Pvt. Addison P.
  ...215
Whiting, Maj. Gen.
  William Henry Chase...5
Wild, Brig. Gen. Edward
  A. ...27, 53, 139
Williams &
  Palamountain...97
Williams Branch...120

Williams, Asst. Paymaster
  William W. ...225
Williams, Caroline...125
Williams, Pvt. Joseph E.
  ...30
Williams, Reddin...97
Williamston, N.C. ...8, 184
Wilmington & Weldon
  Railroad...ii, 3, 6, 12, 15,
  18, 22, 23, 28, 29, 32, 36,
  46, 47, 48, 69, 71, 72, 78,
  82, 83, 87, 88, 131, 132,
  161, 166, 170, 171, 183,
  185, 224
Wilmington Journal...64,
  166
Wilmington, N.C. ...ii, 5,
  6, 7, 15, 16, 19, 31, 32,
  35, 64, 69, 71, 72, 85, 98,
  121, 132, 168, 170, 183,
  229, 230
Wilson Road...1, 91, 92
Wilson Street
  (Tarboro)...91
Wilson, Capt. Henry W.
  ...27, 36, 58, 77
Wilson, Maj. Gen. James
  H. ...199
Wilson, N.C. ...60, 61, 72,
  83, 84, 85, 124, 166
Wilson, N.C. Hospital
  (General Hospital No.
  2)...72, 83
Wilson, Pvt. David...208
Wilson, Sgt. Henry...206
Wilson-Tarboro Road...84
Winchell, Pvt.
  Phillman...210
Winslow's Stables,
  Tarboro, location of
  Confederate Army
  commissary...93
Winton, N.C. ...183
Wise, Capt. William B.
  ...111

Wolf, Pvt. Harman...212
Wood, Pvt. James H.
   ...218
Wooster, Pvt. Oren T. ...65, 124
World War I...192, 198
Worsley, Pvt. H.G. ...224
Xenia, Ohio...24
Yankee Hall, N.C. ...227
Yearney, Pvt. Thomas...212
Zeke's Island...64

About the Author...

Freelance writer and artist David A. Norris was born in Charlotte. He has a BFA degree in art from East Carolina University, and lived in Greenville for a number of years after graduation. David has written over two hundred magazine and encyclopedia articles. His work has appeared in *Our State, American Heritage, CNN.com, America's Civil War, History Magazine, Civil War Times, American History,* the *North Carolina Historical Review, Family Chronicle, Internet Genealogy, South Carolina Magazine, True West, Mental Floss,* and *Learning Through History.* In addition, he has contributed articles to the *Encyclopedia of the American Civil War,* the *Encyclopedia of New Jersey,* the *Encyclopedia of Appalachia,* the *Encyclopedia of North Carolina History,* and the upcoming *Mississippi Encyclopedia.*

Although the Civil War is a favorite subject, he has also written on topics ranging from the Roman Army to the celluloid collar and the derby hat. David is currently the president of the Cape Fear Civil War Round Table in Wilmington. He now lives in Wilmington with his wife Carol.

www.ingramcontent.com/pod-product-compliance
Lightning Source LLC
Chambersburg PA
CBHW071655160426
43195CB00012B/1475